THE COMPLETE INDIAN REGIONAL COOKBOOK

THE COMPLETE INDIAN
REGIONAL COOKBOOK

300 classic recipes from the great regions of India,
shown in over 1500 vibrant photographs

MRIDULA BALJEKAR

LORENZ BOOKS

This edition is published by Lorenz Books, an imprint of Anness Publishing Ltd, Blaby Road, Wigston, Leicestershire LE18 4SE

info@anness.com

www.lorenzbooks.com; www.annesspublishing.com

If you like the images in this book and would like to investigate using them for publishing, promotions or advertising, please visit our website www.practicalpictures.com for more information.

Publisher: Joanna Lorenz
Executive Editor: Joanne Rippin
Project Editors: Lucy Doncaster and Melanie Hibbert
Designer: Lucy Doncaster
Photography: Jon Whitaker
Food Stylists: Joy Skipper and Aya Nishimura
Prop Stylists: Penny Markham and Liz Hippisley
Production Controller: Wendy Lawson

© Anness Publishing Ltd 2013

Previously published as two separate volumes, *Vegetarian Cooking of India* and *The Food and Cooking of India*

PUBLISHER'S NOTE
Although the advice and information in this book are believed to be accurate and true at the time of going to press, neither the authors nor the publisher can accept any legal responsibility or liability for any errors or omissions that may have been made, nor for any inaccuracies, nor for any loss, harm or injury that comes about from following instructions or advice in this book.

NOTES
• Bracketed terms are intended for American readers.
• For all recipes, quantities are given in both metric and imperial measures and, where appropriate, in standard cups and spoons. Follow one set of measures, but not a mixture, because they are not interchangeable.
• Standard spoon and cup measures are level. 1 tsp = 5ml, 1 tbsp = 15ml, 1 cup = 250ml/8fl oz.
• Australian standard tablespoons are 20ml. Australian readers should use 3 tsp in place of 1 tbsp for measuring small quantities of gelatine, flour, salt, etc.
• American pints are 16fl oz/2 cups. American readers should use 20fl oz/2.5 cups in place of 1 pint when measuring liquids.
• Electric oven temperatures in this book are for conventional ovens. When using a fan oven, the temperature will probably need to be reduced by about 10–20°C/20–40°F. Since ovens vary, you should check with your manufacturer's instruction book for guidance.
• The nutritional analysis given for each recipe is calculated per portion (i.e. serving or item), unless otherwise stated. If the recipe gives a range, such as Serves 4–6, then the nutritional analysis will be for the smaller portion size, i.e. 6 servings. Measurements for sodium do not include salt added to taste.
• Medium (US large) eggs are used unless otherwise stated.

CONTENTS

Introduction

Indian dishes are possibly among the most popular in the world. Brightly coloured vegetables in richly flavoured sauces; tender meat, poultry and fish; nutty-flavoured beans and lentils; and of course, an incredible array of spices epitomize an exciting cuisine that warms the body and soothes the spirit. Besides offering fabulous flavours, Indian cooking can be extremely healthy, with the emphasis being firmly on freshness. Some commonly used ingredients are even believed to have medicinal properties.

The vast and vibrant land of India conjures up images of mystery, magic and romance. It is a land steeped in heritage and history, one that has witnessed great empires rise and crumble.

Exotic spices have been grown in India for centuries, and the country has long been known as the spice bowl of the world. The use of premium-quality spices in this sun-drenched, monsoon-fed land was an established way of life long before the traders arrived, and it is the carefully prepared blends of these ingredients that provide the mouthwatering tastes, flavours and aromas of the many dishes eaten throughout the country.

FOREIGN INFLUENCES

Among those lured to the country by the valuable spices were Arab, English, Dutch, Portuguese and Spanish traders. These foreign travellers introduced cooking styles that are still practised today. The north continues to be dominated by Mughal cuisine, while the east pays tribute to tribal and Anglo-Indian styles. In the south, Syrian Jews and French traders passed on their cooking techniques, and western India came under the influence of the Portuguese and the Persians (Parsis). The result is a rich, colourful and multi-dimensional cuisine with a repertoire of recipes that is unmatched anywhere else in the world.

LOCAL INGREDIENTS

Spectacular scenery, fascinating ancient customs and glorious foods all continue to draw foreigners to India. Just like the breathtakingly beautiful scenery, culinary traditions have also been influenced by geographical and climatic conditions. With vast distances to be travelled and no means of transporting fresh produce efficiently, cooks have had to make the best of the many and varied ingredients available to them locally.

Rice or breads form the staple diet in India. Meat and fish are served in small quantities, and their use depends upon where in the country the cooks live and what religion they practise. These dishes tend to be surrounded by inviting accompaniments, such as pickles, chutneys and salads, which are flavoured with fresh herbs and chillies, yogurt or lime juice. Many of the ingredients used in everyday recipes are known for their curative and preventative powers. For example, there is strong evidence that garlic and fresh root ginger, two of the most essential components in curries, contain properties that can help to combat heart diseases and stomach ulcers respectively.

The beauty of Indian cooking is in its variety. Different areas and traditions have developed their own regional specialities,

Below *Fresh root ginger, with its fresh and pungent flavour, is just one of the ingredients commonly used in Indian cooking .*

Left *Fresh, local produce such as herbs and vegetables are often sold in open air markets and bought on a daily basis.*

Above *Clay-oven-baked tandoori dishes originate from the north of India but their mild flavours are enjoyed worldwide.*

Above *The typical vegetarian Indian meal, called a thali, from Kerala in southern India, is made up of a variety of small dishes.*

Above *Many curries are served in the pan in which they are cooked, accompanied by naan to soak up the delicious juices.*

and recipes have been handed down through the generations. Although many Indian dishes are fiery with chillies, there are others that are mellow. Many of the most familiar regional dishes we enjoy come from northern India. These include koftas, mild kormas and tandoori recipes. Balti cuisine, which is Kashmiri cooking from the area that is now north Pakistan, is beautifully aromatic but does not use chillies excessively, so it is not too hot. The most fiery spice blends, such as those used in the famous vindaloo, come from western India.

Coconuts are a favourite ingredient in eastern and southern India, and are used for making both sweet and savoury dishes, including deliciously creamy sauces. From western India there are recipes that use dairy products including yogurt and buttermilk, and the meals are typically accompanied by all kinds of unusual and tangy pickles. As southern Indian cuisine is predominantly vegetarian, owing to the dominance of Jainism and Hinduism in the region, there is no shortage of delectable meat-free recipes to choose from, which utilize nuts, beans, peas and lentils, making hearty and nutritious meals that appeal to vegetarians and meat-eaters alike.

Right *With its many and varied side dishes, an Indian meal is perfect for sharing with friends and family.*

HOW THIS BOOK WORKS

The book is divided into regional sections that represent the best of the different cuisines of India, from soups and appetizers to fish and shellfish, as well as meat, poultry and vegetable dishes. It also includes a variety of accompaniments, salads, chutneys and relishes, as well as breads, desserts and drinks – in fact everything you need to create the perfect meal, whether it be a simple supper or a more elaborate dinner party.

Many recipes are quick and easy, whereas others call for more varied spices and flavourings, including some lesser-known ingredients, such as mango powder (amchur) and compressed tamarind. Most of these are available from supermarkets, and health-food and Asian stores.

Featuring classic recipes from all around India, this book will whet your appetite and equip you with the skills to create a magnificent repertoire of Indian classics.

A land of contrasts

India is an incredibly varied country, both geographically and climatically, from the mighty snow-clad Himalayas in the extreme north to the wonderfully fertile flatlands of the Indus and Ganges rivers, and the dry and sandy wastes of the deserts of Rajasthan. In rural areas the daily diet is governed by what grows locally, but in cities and towns, where people from all parts of India converge, there is a greater range of ingredients and the food there reflects both the diversity of the population and the wealth of choice.

Wherever you look in India there is evidence of the local culinary traditions, from the smoking *tandoors* on the streets of the cities to the fish markets along the coast.

RUGGED NORTH
The states of Himachal Pradesh, Jammu, Kashmir, the Punjab and Uttar Pradesh make up northern India. The highest mountain range in the world, the Himalayas stretch majestically from the rugged north-west to the river Brahmaputra in the east. The valleys of the Himalayas are famous for growing exquisite basmati rice and sugar cane.

The magnificent mountains stand in stunning contrast to lush green valleys dotted with lakes, where the mighty river Indus flows. Recipes based on lamb or succulent, firm-fleshed river fish of various kinds are favourites in this part of northern India. Trees are laden with sweet, juicy plums, peaches, rich red cherries, almonds and walnuts, and these feature regularly in many mouthwatering sweet and savoury dishes of the northern regions.

Right *A vibrant array of fruit and vegetables at a market stall in southern India.*

TROPICAL SOUTH
The areas of southern India conjure up visions of coconut palm trees, golden beaches and lush tropical scenery. The states of Andhra Pradesh, Tamil Nadu, Karnataka and Kerala make up south India. Each of these is rich in history and has its own culinary traditions and styles that draw on the local heritage.

Here in the south, the Deccan plateau is kept fertile by two major rivers. In the state of Karnataka the landscape is varied, with sandy beaches, rugged mountains, winding rivers and acres of flourishing green coffee plantations. The state of Andhra Pradesh is called the 'granary of the south' because of the variety of its abundant crops of rice. It is also noted for its chilli crop – this includes the famed pungent red chillies of Guntur.

Kerala is the smallest state in India, and it is a land of exuberant beauty. There are monsoon-fed rivers, beguiling backwaters and beautiful lagoons. Sandy beaches shimmer with golden sunshine filtering through the palm tree fronds. Fish, shellfish and coconuts are available in abundance, and these ingredients feature in many of the local favourite recipes. Kerala's most prized treasure is its fabulous spice plantations. Indeed, the state is often referred to as the 'spice bowl of India'.

LANDSCAPES OF THE EAST
The east Indian states of Bengal, Bihar, Jharkhand and Orissa provide some of the most stunning contrasts in the entire sub-continent. Here, as well as the Ganges plains, you will find the eastern stretch of the Himalayas, which includes Darjeeling with its rolling tea plantations, together with Sikkim and Bhutan with lakes and rivers full of fish.

West Bengal is rich in natural resources such as jute, tea, coal and iron, and has a diverse cultural heritage. Rice crops flourish

Left *Boats moored on the tranquil palm-fringed backwaters in Kerala, southern India.*

Above *Fish and shellfish is readily available in the eastern state of Orissa, a coastal city situated on the shores of the Bay of Bengal.*
Above right *The east-Indian district of Darjeeling is famed for its lush tea plantations, which cascade down the slopes of the Himalayas.*

in eastern India, with approximately 30 per cent of the country's total output being produced in this region. Fish is abundantly available in the Bay of Bengal, and is put to fabulous use in the local dishes.

HILLY NORTH-EAST
The north-east of India comprises seven states – Assam, Arunachal Pradesh, Meghalaya, Manipur, Tripura, Nagaland and Mizoram – each of which has distinct cultures and traditions. Rice, tea and turmeric are the main food crops here and the region is also renowned for its silk. The hill states have a unique style of food, with many meat dishes, although fruits and vegetables are grown and eaten fresh, or dried for use in winter.

FERTILE HEARTLAND
Central India (Madhya Pradesh) is known as 'the heart of India'. It offers beautiful hill ranges overlooking the Ganges plain, and has fertile black volcanic soil. There is an abundance of wildlife in the dense forests. There is no definitive cuisine in this area, but it borrows from neighbouring states such as Gujarat, Rajasthan and Bihar.

Right *India extends from the tropical south to the magnificent mountains of the north.*

WESTERN SEABOARD
The states of Rajasthan, Maharashtra, Gujarat and Goa form western India. The breathtaking variety of landscapes in this region include tidal mudflats, steep ravines, beautiful beaches and coastal lowlands where coconut palms and paddy fields create an incredible panorama. Wheat, cotton, bananas, sorghum and millet, together with rice, are grown extensively inland, while fish and shellfish are the main products in the coastal region. Coconut milk, coconut oil and groundnut oil are produced and used in everyday cooking. The princely state of Rajasthan, an arid land near the borders of Pakistan, gave rise to a sumptuous royal cuisine. Gujarat and Maharashtra are mainly vegetarian, while Goa has a unique style of cuisine – a blend of East and West.

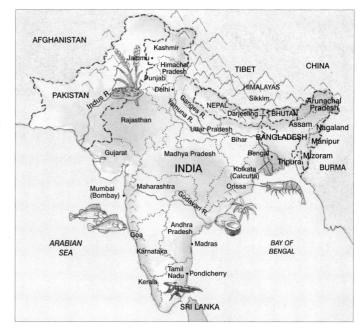

History, religion and festivals

India is a vast country, with a total population of around 1.5 billion. The huge variations in terms of climate, geography and customs have had a powerful influence on the cuisine, but history and the influence of the many different religions practised across the land have also played their part in the development of cultural and culinary traditions and the shaping of eating habits. Together, these elements have helped the country's cuisine to emerge as one of the most colourful and exotic in the world.

From Persia and Portugal to China and Britain, India has lured both traders and invaders from all over the world for many centuries, and these have inevitably had a marked and lasting impact on the country.

THE ROLE OF IMMIGRANTS

The Khyber Pass, in the north of the country, has provided an access point for immigrants and invaders throughout the centuries, enabling each to introduce their particular styles of cooking and play their part in shaping Indian cuisine. The mighty Mughals from Persia are perhaps the most famous of these to make their presence felt in India, entering the country via the Khyber Pass during the 16th century. They went on to rule India for many years and this stability ensured that their elaborate and sophisticated cuisine would become very popular, not only in India, but also outside it.

The western side of India came under the influence of the ancient Persians who fled their country to avoid religious persecution. They landed in the province of Gujarat and became known as the 'Parsis'. Their contribution to Indian cooking has been

Above *The stunning Taj Mahal mausoleum was built by Mughal Emperor Shah Jahan in memory of his favourite wife.*

invaluable, as they applied their finely honed meat-cooking skills to the traditional vegetarian cuisine of Gujarat and produced rich and uniquely flavoured dishes.

Adventurous Portuguese traders came to India in search of spices and other precious items such as silk during the late 15th century, and established themselves as traders on the west coast. Indeed, such was the permanence of their presence that they ruled Goa for 400 years. During that time, they made significant contributions to the food culture of the region. The influences and tastes they left behind are reflected in the colourful and exotic cuisine of this area, including in the famous vindaloo curry.

The eastern belt of India offers a dramatically different range of food from that of the rest of the country. The native cuisine is Bengali, which presents a diverse array of dishes, many of them based on fish and rice, with unique flavours. The influence of

Tibetan cooking is still strong in this region, as well as Anglo-Indian cuisine, which serves as a reminder of the time when the British lived in the area during the early days of the Raj, when Calcutta was the capital city.

Southern India offers an inimitable range of food but with very clear regional variations. The beautiful palm-fringed Malabar coast in the south lured foreign powers for centuries, starting with the early Arabians, then the Romans, Chinese, Portuguese and English. These immigrants later spread right across India, and were actively (and profitably) involved in the flourishing spice trade. In the state of Kerala there are still some Jewish-influenced dishes such as spiced fish, brought by the Jews who came to India from Syria.

Above *Silk as well as spices have drawn traders from all over the world to India for centuries.*

Right *A Hindu woman carries bananas during the Chhath festival celebrations in Kolkata, India. This is one of the most important celebrations in the north-east Indian states of Uttar Pradesh and Bihar.*

RELIGIOUS INFLUENCES

India is a land of many religions: Hindu, Muslim, Christian, Sikh, Jain and Buddhist. The impact of these on Indian food has been profound. Hindus and Muslims predominate overall, and they have certain restrictions: for example, Hindus do not eat beef, as the cow is considered to have been the companion of Lord Krishna, which made it sacred. The holy Koran prohibits Muslims from eating pork or consuming alcohol. The Sikh community's holy scripture, Adi Granth, prohibits them from consuming beef and alcohol.

In the Hindu religion, each of the gods and goddesses is worshipped as the patron of a particular profession. For example, a farmer would worship the Sun God and the God of Rain. Each god is believed to have his particular favourite dish, which the farmer would make as an offering so that the god blesses him with a fruitful harvest.

The Sikh, Jain and Buddhist religions have been carved out of Hinduism and, therefore, have some customs in common with Hinduism, although they also display many distinctive features of their own.

FESTIVAL FOOD

The sheer number of different religious affiliations in India has given rise to a huge variety of special foods for both family events, such as weddings, births and deaths, and national celebrations.

Festivals are very important and there are 13 major ones in the country every year. Each of these belongs to a different religion, and each has its own distinct style of food, with religious traditions dictating what is to be cooked. However, it is not just the religious aspect that determines celebratory cuisine: secular festivals associated with the season and the crops that are growing or have been harvested are also important, and are marked with bountiful feasts.

Muslims observe a month-long fast during Ramadan, after which comes the festival of Eid al-Fitr. The celebration table for this major event in India includes such delicacies as pilaus, biryanis, all kinds of kebabs and speciality breads.

Diwali, referred to internationally as the Festival of Lights, is a major religious celebration, which is marked by Hindus, Jains and Sikhs throughout India, and indeed anywhere else in the world where adherents of these faiths live. During the Diwali festival, sweets and fruit are distributed among family and friends in order to celebrate the victory of good over evil and light over darkness. Fireworks are set off to light up the night sky during this joyful celebration.

Left *Young women carry oil lamps on the eve of Diwali, the Hindu Festival of Lights. Hindus around the world light lamps during Diwali to symbolize the victory of good over evil.*

Regional cooking

Through the centuries, each state of India has developed its own unique signature dishes and distinct style of cooking. From the clay-oven-baked tandooris of the north to the coconut-fuelled dishes of the south, cooking styles and recipes are heavily influenced by the diversity of climate and geography, which determines the choice of ingredients available. Nevertheless, there are similarities nationwide, such as the almost universal use of cardamom pods, cumin, coriander (cilantro), ginger and chillies.

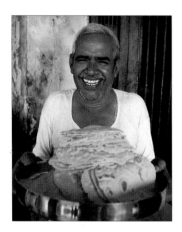

Above *A baker in Mumbai proudly shows off a tray piled high with freshly prepared naan.*

In every region of India, food plays an intrinsic role in the lives of the inhabitants, not only for nourishment, but also as an expression of people's identity and religion.

RURAL CUISINE

In more remote parts of the country, where transport and communication are not as efficient as they are in urban areas, people rely heavily on locally grown produce. In general, lentils, peas and fresh vegetables are very important to an Indian family. These are cooked and served on a daily basis with small helpings of meat, poultry or fish. Chapatis or other bread products provide dietary fibre, while rice is essential for the required daily amount of carbohydrates, giving plenty of energy for an outdoor life based on farming or fishing.

CITY LIFE

The main cities of India are set far apart – Delhi in the north, Kolkata (formerly Calcutta) in the far east, Chennai (Madras) on the south-eastern seaboard and Mumbai

(formerly Bombay) on the west coast. These busy centres with their thronging populations developed their own cuisines, with local delicacies such as *Alur Chop*, the tasty little meat and potato patties created in Kolkata and now found on every street corner. Cities such as Jaipur and Udaipur in Rajasthan boast game recipes, which originated in royal kitchens. The kings and princes would return from hunting laden with game, which their chefs turned into deliciously rich dishes such as Stuffed Quails (*Batair Mussallam*).

The chapati is the most commonly eaten bread throughout the country. It is made from whole-wheat flour and water, and accompanies most meals. In more affluent families, breads such as parathas, naans and puris are more popular.

TRADITIONS OF THE NORTH

In the remote mountainous areas all along the north and the north-east borders of India, cooking is restricted to what grows naturally in the area and what the farmers can produce and preserve themselves. The staples in the far north consist mainly of rice, millet, maize and potatoes. These are eaten with vegetables for a balanced diet. In some northern areas people cook or smoke locally reared meat over wood fires. Tea plantations are everywhere, and the distinctive taste of Assam tea from this area is world famous.

Away from the remote border regions the food of northern India is more diverse. Staples include wheat, rice and roti. In rural areas, people grind their own wheat, using traditional hand utensils and techniques to make flour, which is mixed with water and salt and baked on a cast iron griddle.

In the capital city of Delhi there are spicy tandoori delicacies alongside an exquisite, rich Mughal cuisine, with its silky smooth sauces, fragrant biryanis and pilaus. The city of Lucknow in Uttar Pradesh, in the provinces bordering remote Nepal, has developed its

own style of cuisine, known as *Awadhi*, that is a reminder of the luxury of the bygone times of maharajahs and princes.

Kashmir, the beautiful northernmost state, has yet another unique cuisine based on locally grown fruits and nuts, which are added during cooking to produce a variety of sumptuous meat and poultry dishes. Kashmiri cuisine is prized for its unusual richness and varied textures and flavours, and dishes such as kormas, pasandas and biryanis are now firmly established as some of the most popular foods of the north.

Another legendary tradition is the Kashmiri banquet known as *wazawaan*. The banquet is named after chefs known as *wazas*, who are famous for using aromatic spices such as aniseed, cinnamon and cardamom.

The technique of blending and cooking with spices has developed in different ways throughout India. In the state of the Punjab, for example, spices are used to marinate meat, fish and vegetables for its renowned tandoori cooking, which gives the food a unique character and flavour.

Below *Traditional techniques for grinding grain can still be observed in rural India.*

EASTERN FLAVOURS

In rural east India people have developed their own culinary styles using locally grown fresh ginger, turmeric, mustard and sweet peppers. Dairy products, fresh mangoes and coconuts are available in abundance, and there are numerous varieties of fish from the rivers and the sea. Bengali cuisine uses an extensive range of spices, including the wonderfully fragrant panchforon, a spice blend that consists of five types of seeds: black mustard, cumin, nigella (kalonji), fennel and fenugreek. Again, rice is the staple on which all dishes are based. All of the recipes of this area are characterized by the distinctive, pungent flavour of mustard oil, which is the only type of oil used.

One of the most fascinating features of Bengal is Mog cuisine. This style of cooking is named after a Buddhist tribe whose origins are found in the hilly parts of Bangladesh, in the far north-east. The Mog cooks were skilled in creating a range of dishes based on the principles of 'East Meets West', and these were favourites among the British living in the state of Assam, and have persisted beyond independence, in 1947.

THE DIVERSE WEST

Western India, especially the state of Gujarat, is well known for its dairy produce, which plays an important part in the mainly vegetarian daily diet. The generous Gujarati *thali* (large platter) meals are famous throughout the country. Rajasthan, to the

Below A Kashmiri cook pounds mutton to make haleem *for a banquet or* wazawaan.

Above *Herbs and spices are abundantly available at vibrant street markets.*

north of Gujarat, is home to many vegetarians, and the food there has a unique richness and flavour due to the copious amount of pure butterfat ghee used.

The west is home to a vast patchwork of paddy fields, and their raised borders and swaying coconut palm trees makes a memorable sight. Along the coastline there is plenty of fish and shellfish, and this, combined with rice, forms the basis of the daily diet of the coastal population. Root vegetables, lentils and groundnut oil are also produced and used in everyday cooking, and mangoes, coconuts and cashew nuts grow in profusion and feature in any number of recipes.

Maharashtra, a large province along the shores of the Arabian Sea, has its own distinct cuisine, except in the capital city of Mumbai (Bombay), which is a kaleidoscope of food cultures because of its mixed population, both Indian and foreign.

Farther down to the south of Mumbai is the tiny state of Goa, where the food tradition was shaped by a rich tapestry of historical influences, a blend of East and West, owing to its colonization by the Portuguese five centuries ago. Goa is particularly renowned for its range of fish and shellfish dishes, such as *Jhinga Caldeen*, a delicious mixture of prawns (shrimp), spices and creamed coconut. The flesh of coconuts and vinegar made of coconut sap give Goan cuisine its distinctive flavour, and coconut *feni*, a very potent liquor made from the sap of the coconut palm tree, is the most popular drink in Goa.

THE HOT SOUTH

The southern Indian economy thrives on spices and rice, as well as coconut and its by-products. South India is one of the leading exporters of prime quality spices and the international trade in them has enjoyed phenomenal growth in recent years. This is also the land of tea and coffee plantations, as well as the golden harvest of rice. A huge industry has grown up based around coconut – as well as cooking with the flesh and milk, coconut oil is used all over southern India; the outer shell is cleaned and polished to make bowls, and other parts of the plant are used to make such essentials as roofs and pillars for rural huts. In more far-flung country areas, the outer hairy coir is used as a cooking fuel.

In the south-east, the state of Andhra Pradesh has developed its own distinctive cuisine that is based on meat rather than vegetables, as a result of the strong Muslim influence. Mughal cuisine thrives in the city of Hyderabad, where the last Mughal emperor made his home. It is a way of cooking that uses many rich ingredients such as cream, meat, spices, fruit and nuts to make sumptuous dishes for special occasions.

Chilli peppers grow abundantly in the south, so the food tends to be quite fiery. On the other hand, the cuisine of Kerala evolved around the abundance of salty seafood and soothing coconut, and is rather similar to the classic dishes of Goa farther up the coast.

Types of dish

The structure of an Indian meal is different to the traditions of western style dining, where food is divided into appetizers, main courses and desserts. In India all the dishes are served at the same time and diners help themselves in any order, while desserts are usually only served on special occasions.

In recent times Indian meals have been broken down into courses, particularly outside India, to conform with other countries' eating habits. For this reason, almost all Indian restaurants now divide their menus into appetizers and main courses, and the same practice is also being followed in some homes when entertaining.

SOUPS AND SNACKS

People do not generally associate soups with Indian cuisine, but there are a number of traditional soup recipes. History has it that soups were first served in India in the fourteenth century, having been brought from ancient Persia to north India by the Mughals. The Hindi name for soups, *shorba*, literally means 'broth', and indeed many do consist of a range of vegetables in a highly flavoured stock. Rich *shorbas*, which may have been thickened by puréeing the ingredients, were an integral part of most Mughal banquets and remain popular today, especially during the bitterly cold winter months in the northern and eastern regions. Traditionally, they were served during a meal rather than before it, and this practice continues in some private homes. North

Below *Simple soups, such as this tomato and coriander recipe from southern India, are often served in cups to accompany a meal.*

Above *These Bengali deep-fried spiced potato cakes are often enjoyed at afternoon tea but can also be served as an appetizer.*

Indian soups tend to be rich and the spicing is subtle, whereas in southern India they are often lighter and spicier, and may include the ubiquitous coconut milk.

Within the huge diversity of Indian cuisine there exists a large range of dishes that can be enjoyed both as appetizers and snacks, from world-famous favourites such as onion bhajiyas to less well-known delicacies such as lotus root kebabs. While these are generally eaten in the afternoon with tea in India, they are equally delicious served with drinks before a meal or as a first course.

Snacks are a big part of the Indian way of life. There are street vendors in every city, town and village, selling enticing treats that are enjoyed in cinemas, at sports events and even walking down the road. Snacks are often eaten with one of the many different types of Indian chutney, as their diverse flavours, colours and textures both contrast with and complement the food.

FISH AND SEAFOOD

Although the majority of the Indian population is vegetarian, fish and seafood are very popular with the rest of the nation. Even among the vegetarians, there are

some who eat fish and seafood, as these are considered to be gifts of the sea and therefore exempt from the rule of not taking another life for one's own pleasure.

Almost two-thirds of the country is surrounded by sea. Fish found on the shores are firm-textured and ideal for curries. In western India, Mumbai (formerly Bombay) is on the banks of the Arabian Sea and the most famous export here is Bombay Duck, a fish similar to mackerel that is dried in the sun before cooking. Unfortunately, some countries have banned the import of Bombay Duck, so smoked mackerel or kippers are used as the closest substitute.

In Goa, fish and seafood from the Arabian sea are abundant. A beautiful silver-skinned fish known as pomfret is the most popular, and tandoori pomfret is a delicacy. In the West, sea bass, mullet and monkfish lend themselves well to this style of cooking. Huge prawns, mussels, lobster and crab, caught every morning and brought to the local markets, are also cooked in sauces, often with coconut milk, chillies and coconut palm vinegar. Crab in roasted coconut sauce, prawn rissoles, mackerel in coconut milk and mussels in spicy garlic and

Below *Mackerel is a popular fish in the south of India, and this dish, flavoured with tamarind and coconut, comes from Chennai.*

tamarind sauce from south India are just some of the imaginative and flavourful fish dishes from this region.

Kerala in the southern tip of the country has a similar cuisine to Goa, with extensive use of coconut milk and chillies, but using tamarind juice as the souring agent.

Far from any coast, north and north east India relies on fish from its beautiful rivers and lakes, and the cooking styles here are different from the rest of the country. North Indian fish and shellfish curries are either tomato-based, or cooked in cream and nut pastes. In other dishes fish is cooked in mustard oil with aromatic spices such as 'panch phoron' to which a mixture of five whole spices added. Fish in spicy mustard sauce is a fragrantly spiced dish from Bengal, while fish in tangy tomato sauce is cooked almost daily in Assam.

MEAT AND POULTRY

Poultry, game and mutton are the basis of many dishes in different regions of India, especially in the north. Chicken is still the most popular meat in the country, and tandoori chicken and chicken tikka are often the favourite dishes. Chicken that is cooked in rich and luxurious sauces such as korma and pasanda have their origins in the Royal kitchens, while different types of chicken biryanis are cooked all over India. Duck, guinea fowl and quail are also used, most notably in the Royal kitchens of India where there is a tradition of hunting, especially in the princely state of Rajasthan in western India. Over the years the royal chefs have developed a repertoire of exquisite game dishes, which have delighted the palates of many generations. As game birds tend to be on the drier side, these are often marinated first with tenderizing ingredients such as vinegar, lime juice or yogurt. They are then cooked in deliciously-spiced sauces.

Mutton is popular throughout India, and goat's meat is also used in many regions. The climate in the Himalayan region is ideal for rearing sheep, and this is the only area where fresh lamb is readily available. Raw papaya paste is often used to tenderize mutton, which is much tougher than lamb and needs long slow cooking. The enzyme in papaya, known as papin, makes the meat delectable and melt-in-the-mouth, yogurt or red wine vinegar has a similar effect.

Above *The most popular Indian lamb dish around the world is probably the piquant Dhansak, a recipe that originated in Gujarat.*

Beef is not consumed by the Hindus as the cow is seen as a holy animal. However, it is eaten by the Muslim and Christian communities. In the hilly terrain of north east India, dishes such as beef stew with green chillies, and in north India noodle soup with minced (ground) beef are popular dishes.

Pork is not eaten by Muslims, again for religious reasons, but like beef, pork is sold without restriction in Goa, and eaten by the Christian community. Pork vindaloo is Goa's most famous export, and smoked pork with bamboo shoots from Nagaland in north east India is another delectable dish.

VEGETARIAN DISHES

Because of the large number of vegetarian communities throughout the Indian population, there is a strong tradition of meat-free cooking that goes back for centuries, and cooks have perfected the art of creating a vast array of tempting, sustaining and nutritious dishes. Indeed, the dishes are so numerous, delicious, and economical, that it is quite common for meat-eaters to base their meals around vegetarian food and consume only a small amount of meat.

There is a huge range of fresh vegetables available in Indian street markets and stores, from leafy greens, tomatoes, aubergines (eggplants) and crunchy (bell) peppers to starchy staples such as root vegetables, squashes and plantains. Spicing also depends on geographical location, with some regions favouring subtle flavours and others preferring intensely hot food.

Protein, essential for well-being and particularly important in a vegetarian diet, is often supplied in the form of lentils, beans

Below *This dish from the Punjab, based on chickpeas, is a perfectly balanced nutritious main vegetarian dish.*

Above *In this recipe paneer and potatoes make a fragrant vegetarian dish.*

and peas, which are used on a daily basis. Gram flour (besan) is also packed with protein, and appears in many guises. High in calories and full of protein, nuts and seeds are added whole to curries and fried dishes for texture and flavour, or ground and used to make thick, rich sauces.

Dairy products feature strongly on the vegetarian menu. The Indian cheese, paneer, is packed with as much protein as meat or poultry, and is widely used. Eggs are similarly important, and provide a delicious and economical alternative to meat. Home-made yogurt is an integral part of a vegetarian meal. As well as being cooked in dishes and used for making creamy sauces, it can also make a dressing for salads and forms the basis for raitas.

RICE DISHES

Initially, in India, rice production was mainly confined to monsoon-fed areas or delta areas, where conditions were best suited to its growing requirements. Today, however, with modern farming methods, rice can be grown all over India.

Rice is considered sacred in India and is required for every religious ritual. A symbol of wealth, it is thrown at a newly-wed couple in much the same way that confetti is strewn in the west, wishing them great riches in their married life. In addition, before a new bride enters her husband's home, a bowl of rice is placed at the door. The bride has to gently kick it so that the grains are scattered on the floor, symbolizing the good fortune she is bringing to her new house.

Half the population of India eats rice on a daily basis, usually simply served boiled and accompanied by curries of various types. Pilaus and biryanis are generally cooked only for celebrations and other special occasions. Long grain rice, of which there are several varieties, is the usual choice for serving with curries and for making savoury dishes. Among long grain types, basmati is universally popular. Short grain rice is used to make desserts, or ground to create rice flour.

SIDE DISHES

Indian cuisine is famous for its colourful side dishes and no meal is complete without at least two vegetable accompaniments. Choosing side dishes requires care and attention, as they must complement rather than compete with the flavours of the main dish. Rich and complex main courses are best served with the simplest sides, while a rich side dish is usually served with a plainer meat or fish recipe. Following this basic principle will help you to maintain the overall balance of flavours.

Potatoes are a useful carbohydrate that carry other flavours well, and appear in numerous dishes. Beans, peas and lentils are also popular, not least because they are filling and nutritious. Other, less sustaining vegetables such as okra, courgettes

HOW TO COOK RICE

Weigh the rice and then wash it in cold water until the water runs clear. Soak the rice in cold water for 20–30 minutes, then leave it to drain in a sieve (strainer). Next, transfer the rice to a large, heavy pan with a tight-fitting lid. The slender grains expand considerably once cooked, so to allow for this, use a pan that will be two-thirds full when the rice is cooked. Measure the water accurately, following the recipe guidelines, and once the lid is on, set the timer, and never lift the lid. Finally, when the rice is cooked, switch off the heat and let the pan sit undisturbed for 15–20 minutes. After this time, simply fork through the rice and serve.

(zucchini), cauliflower and carrots, and even some fruits, are generally used to make simple side dishes, especially in the east and north-east of the country. Elsewhere, the addition of cream, nuts or coconut milk result in more complex flavours and, when several of these richer side dishes are served together, with rice or bread, they make a complete meal.

In addition to cooked vegetable and fruit dishes, Indian cuisine has a wide repertoire of cold accompaniments, including fresh and zesty salads that cleanse the palate, cool and creamy yogurt dressings and raitas, and of course chutneys. Raitas, made with yogurt, usually include chopped raw vegetables such as cucumber, but can also contain more unusual additions such as bananas, the sweetness of which balances the spice of other dishes.

BREADS

Northern India, where the climate is cooler, is ideal for wheat production, and people who live in this area thrive on a daily diet of numerous kinds of bread with their curries. These are generally made from the same three ingredients: ground grains, salt and water. Unleavened flat breads, ranging from simple, fat-free chapatis to rich, layered parathas (similar to flaky pastry), are made daily at home. Leavened breads such as naan, of which there are numerous varieties, are generally commercially made now, although they are still cooked on *tandoors* in some remote villages.

In India, especially in rural areas, people grind their own wheat to make flour, and bake their bread on a cast-iron griddle called a *tawa*. The wheat flour, known as atta, is very fine and is made by grinding the entire wheat kernel, which is packed with essential nutrients, including a high proportion of roughage. In addition to wheat flour, breads are also made from rice flour, maize flour, gram (besan) flour, ground barley, and even semolina; all of these also contain nutrients and, in the case of gram flour, vitally important protein.

The most common breads, chapatis, are simply dry-roasted, and are ideal with more complex dishes and for everyday eating. They do not keep particularly well as they tend to dry out, and are best made and consumed on the same day. Other flat

Above *Chapatis are a universally loved Indian bread, eaten daily throughout the regions.*

breads are brushed with a small amount of oil or ghee during cooking to add moisture as well as flavour. Some types, such as ginger and cumin puffed bread, are deep-fried, creating a luxurious and tasty treat that is perfect with a simple curry. Naan, with its soft texture and slightly sour taste from the yogurt in the dough, is best cooked on a *tandoor*, which imparts a smoky flavour and cooks the bread very quickly, ensuring the desired soft finish. Naan can accompany practically any dish but is also fabulous on its own or topped with chutneys and raitas.

A wide range of spices, herbs and leafy vegetables such as spinach or spring greens (collards) can be added to the basic doughs, creating infinite variations on a theme, although the flavour of the flour used

Below *Sweet lassi is popular in central India where it is flavoured with rose water.*

in the simpler breads is delicious without any embellishment. Cumin, ginger and fenugreek are among the favoured spices, depending where in the country you are. Flaky breads have a soft texture that lends itself to rich, spicy stuffings made from satisfying ingredients such as potatoes or eggs, creating all-in-one meals or light snacks that are perfect when on the go.

DRINKS, DESSERTS AND SWEETMEATS

Although both drinks and desserts are integral parts of any cuisine, they rarely feature prominently as part of a meal in India. Plain water is the most commonly consumed drink, and desserts were, and still are to a large extent, reserved for special occasions. On a day-to-day basis, people usually opt for a piece of fresh fruit, or some chilled, sweetened yogurt.

For those whose religion permits its consumption, alcohol is generally drunk before dinner. However, drinking wine with food has become popular in recent years, and India produces several types that complement spicy dishes.

Away from mealtimes, Indians consume vast quantities of tea and coffee, often flavoured with spices such as cardamom, served with a lot of milk and often sugar too.

Chilled thirst-quenchers made from fruits such as lime or mango, as well as the plethora of different lassis made throughout the country, provide relief in the heat, and often contain salt for hydration.

Cool, refreshing palate-cleansers such as saffron-scented strained yogurt or the world-renowned classic, kulfi, are appropriate after a spicy meal in a hot climate, while richer warm desserts such as cardamom-scented coconut dumplings or coconut-filled wheat pancakes are ideal after a lighter, less heavily spiced meal.

India loves its sweetmeats, which tend to be rather heavy and very sugary, so are often more suitable as a snack with tea and coffee than for a dessert. Each region has its traditional speciality. East India, and particularly Bengal, for instance, is famed for its dazzling range of milk-based sweets, including milk balls in cardamom-scented syrup. In western India sweetmeats come in the form of dry balls (*laddus*), which can be made of sesame seeds, rice or skinless mung beans. Indian 'fudges' also appear in many guises, and can be made from coconut, sesame seeds or even lentils.

Below *These sweet coconut dumplings, flavoured with cardamom, are served for breakfast in Assam.*

Planning and serving an Indian meal

Traditionally, Indian dishes are not strictly categorized into appetizers and main courses. Several dishes are cooked and served at the same time and the diners simply help themselves. People generally have second helpings of everything that is on offer. It is customary to start the meal with bread and the curries, followed by rice with the same dishes. In recent years, however, it has become more common in the restaurants to follow a more Western pattern and divide the dishes into courses.

When planning an Indian feast, you should be aiming to provides guests with a main dish, an accompaniment and a staple, which could be rice or bread. Chutneys, salads and raitas can also be served if you like, to add a tangy taste.

PLANNING THE MENU

When deciding which foods to serve, consider the main dish. Is it going to be highly spiced, as with a vindaloo or a bhuna? Or will it have subtle flavours, as does a korma or a pasanda? A little careful planning will ensure that the flavours of the dishes complement, rather than counteract, each other. Choose the side dish according to the strength of the main one. A lightly spiced side dish is more enjoyable when the main dish is spicier. This does not apply in reverse, however, and a side dish with complex spice blends is not the ideal accompaniment to a mild main dish.

Dishes with a drier consistency are generally accompanied by a vegetable curry or a lentil dish. Biryanis and pilaus are traditionally presented with a simple raita, but they can also be served with a vegetable curry.

Above *In India, dishes are served at the same time so diners can mix and match combinations of main dish, accompaniment and staple.*

HOW TO SERVE

An Indian meal is traditionally not served as separate courses, i.e. with an appetizer, followed by a main dish and one or two side dishes. Although the meal will usually consist of several dishes, all complement each other and are brought to the table at the same time, with diners helping themselves to each in any order.

For entertaining and more lavish occasions, you can add other dishes, such as a range of main dishes, several accompaniments and more than one type of staple. One or two dry meat dishes, such as a kebab or tandoori chicken, in addition to some chutneys, pickles, raitas and poppadums, with a dessert to follow, can turn an ordinary family meal into dinner-party fare.

In the classic style, the food is served in many parts of India in a *thali* (a large platter), which is made of stainless steel. Rice and

bread are placed on the *thali* and small steel bowls are used to serve curries. Pickles, chutneys and raitas are also served in separate small bowls. You can recreate this at home, either by using a round tray, or by buying a *thali* from an Asian store – they are not expensive.

Above *A thali is a neat way of presenting the many dishes that make up an Indian meal.*

INDIAN DESSERTS

In India, a meal will usually end with fresh fruit, which can be served with real flair, and is often combined with other ingredients to create imaginative and exciting flavours. Choose one or two exotic fruits, such as papaya, pomegranate or star fruit (carambola), and combine them with everyday fruits in a salad. Serve with Greek (US strained plain) yogurt flavoured with rose water and a little ground cardamom. *Kulfi* is also a popular choice as it provides a soothing, cooling contrast to the spicy food that has come before. Indian sweets (candies) are quite heavy and are served as a snack with tea and coffee.

DRINKS

Until recent years alcoholic drinks did not accompany an Indian meal. This is because most Indians prefer to drink before dinner and have only water with the meal. This practice is changing fast, however, and beer, lager and wine are all being served with a meal. India now produces good-quality wines which complement spicy food, and the lager industry is booming, with brands such as Kingfisher and Cobra available worldwide.

FREEZING CURRIES

In today's busy world, it is not always possible to serve a meal while it is still sizzling in the pan. If you are entertaining, you may prefer to cook the curry in advance, or you may like to cook a larger quantity than you will need and freeze some for another meal; you may even have leftovers.

COOKING FOR A PARTY

It is a good idea to cook the curry dishes a day ahead of the party, storing them in the refrigerator until you are ready to reheat them. Accompanying dhal dishes can also be prepared 24 hours in advance, although the seasonings should not be added until just before serving. You can prepare vegetables in advance, but do not cook them more than a few hours ahead. Likewise, you can prepare ingredients for raitas a day ahead, but do not assemble them until a few hours before they are needed; the yogurt for raitas should always be fresh. Pickles and chutneys will benefit from advance preparation, but follow individual recipes for timing guides, as some will deteriorate more quickly than others. The bread dough for rotis can be made the day before. The rotis can be made 2 hours before you plan to serve them. Spread them with butter and wrap in foil to keep warm, then set them aside; reheat in the oven before serving.

Spicy food is ideal for freezing as the flavours seem to improve when the food is thawed and reheated. Most of the spices used in Indian cooking have natural preservative qualities, as does the acid in the souring agents. However, you should bear in mind the following factors if cooking specifically for the freezer:
• Leave the food slightly underdone.
• Cool the food rapidly. The best way to do this is to pour it into a large tray (a roasting pan is ideal) and leave it in a cool place.
• Once the food has cooled completely, spoon it into plastic containers, then label and chill it in the refrigerator for a couple of hours, before transferring it to the freezer. The food will keep in the freezer for 6–8 months, depending on the star rating of your freezer.

• Food that you did not plan to freeze, such as leftovers, should not be kept in the freezer for longer than 2–3 months, again, depending on the efficiency of your freezer.
• Meat and poultry curries freeze very successfully, as do curries made from vegetables, lentils and pulses. Fish curries can be frozen, but they are generally less successful as changes in the water balance may damage the more delicate texture of cooked fish.

THAWING AND REHEATING

It is important to thaw frozen food thoroughly and slowly. Leave it in the refrigerator for 18–24 hours before reheating. After reheating, always make sure the food is piping hot before serving. These steps are crucial in order to ensure that any potentially harmful bacteria are destroyed. If you have a temperature probe, check that the reheated food is at least 85°C/185°F all the way through before serving.

A certain amount of water separation is to be expected as frozen food thaws out. The dish will return to its normal consistency when it is reheated, as the water will be reabsorbed by the meat or vegetables.

Thawed food can be reheated in the microwave or in a covered casserole on the stove top. If you are using a microwave, cover the food with microwaveable clear film (plastic wrap). Stir the food from time to time to ensure the heat passes all the way through. You may need to add a small amount of water when reheating, to ensure that the dish does not dry out.

Above *Sweet and soothing,* Kulfi *is the ideal dessert to serve at the end of a spicy meal.*

Above Kingfisher *beer is just one of the many brands of lager that is popular in India.*

Tools and equipment

The use of appropriate equipment and specialist techniques helps to produce the range of flavours, colours and textures that are characteristic of each type of dish in India. Most of the cooking is done in various types of heavy cast iron, steel or copper cooking pans, which help to distribute the heat evenly and enable spices to be pre-fried without sticking to the bottom of the pan. Tight-fitting lids allow the food to cook without losing any of the natural moisture, resulting in intense flavours.

The types of cooking utensils employed vary across India. In the coastal regions of the south, terracotta cooking pans are preferred. These are generally unglazed, making aeration easier, and this means that the food does not need immediate refrigeration in spite of the extreme heat of the weather. In the north, the emphasis is more on pans that have a very good seal so that the flavour of the food is concentrated inside – a method of cooking known as dum.

TANDOOR

Leavened breads such as naans are cooked in a *tandoor*, a barrel-shaped clay oven. This is believed to have found its way into India from Egypt, where it is known as a *tanoor*. History has it that the practice of using it to make naan began during the construction of the pyramids. Because of the demand for food, especially bread, for the workers, the Egyptians used the same kind of stones that were being used to construct the pyramids to make a grinding stone for wheat, which was mixed with water to make bread, and baked in the *tanoor*. Thus baking was born, and today it is an everyday event.

Bread is not the only food that can be cooked in the *tandoor*, however, as it can be used to create a huge range of succulent

meat and fish dishes, such as tandoori chicken and chicken tikka, which have established themselves as firm favourites all over the world.

HANDI

This cooking utensil is used to make many dum dishes. It is traditionally a copper pan with a neck that is narrower than the base, rather like a bigger version of a *degchi*. Decorated ovenproof *handis* made from terracotta are commonly available in Asian stores, and have become a favourite in the modern kitchen.

KADHAI/KARAHI

Fried puffed breads (*puri* and *luchi*) are deep-fried in a round-bottomed pan, similar to a wok, known as a *kadhai* or *karahi*. It is also used for making bhuna (stir-fried) dishes all over north India and the north-west frontier (now in Pakistan), including *bhuna gosht* (stir-fried goat or lamb), *kadhai murgh* (stir-fried chicken) and *kadhai paneer* (stir-fried Indian cheese).

Probably one of the oldest cooking utensils in India, the *kadhai* is still a common sight in every domestic and restaurant kitchen and can be seen in most street-side eateries in north India and Pakistan.

Above *A patila has a tight-fitting lid.*

PATILA

A heavy steel pan with a lid, known as a *patila*, is used for making stocks, kormas and bhuna dishes. Kormas need to be made in a heavy cooking pan with a tight-fitting lid as very little liquid is used during the cooking process in order to encourage the meat or poultry to cook in their own delicious juices. 'Korma', which means 'braising', is a cooking technique rather than a recipe.

LAGAN

In Lucknow, northern India, a shallow copper receptacle known as a *lagan* is used for cooking large cuts of meat such as lamb shanks or chops and whole chickens. The *lagan* has a slightly rounded bottom and a heavy, tight-fitting lid, which also makes it ideal for dum dishes, especially in this part of northern India, where the traditional method of using both direct and indirect heat is used. The temperature for dum cooking needs to be quite gentle, so when the prepared food is first heated, the temperature is turned down very low, and indirect heat is created by placing live charcoal on the lid (*seeni*), surrounding the pan with heat. This method can be replicated by cooking the dish in a low oven, as long as the pan is sealed well.

Above *A handi is usually made of copper.*

Above *A kadhai is used for deep-frying.*

DEGCHI

Pilau and biryani dishes require a specially shaped pan called a *degchi*, which is capable of generating steam from within. The food is cooked entirely in the steam, which produces succulent meat or poultry and slender, dry grains of rice. The *degchi* is traditionally made of either brass or copper, and is pear-shaped, with a narrow neck to help keep all the steam inside, so the food can 'breathe' as it cooks. This cooking technique is known as dum. A sticky dough made of flour is used all around the neck of the pan in order to hold the lid in place and to ensure that no steam can escape.

It is possible to cook biryanis and other dum dishes successfully in a standard heavy steel or copper cooking pan. To ensure a tight seal, cover the top of the food with well-moistened baking parchment, followed by a damp dish towel and a double layer of foil.

TADKA PAN

A small, heavy pan shaped like a miniature wok, a tadka pan is used to heat a little oil. A choice of whole spices are then thrown into the pan, where they release their amazing aroma. Everything is then folded into the cooked dish to add a final layer of flavour. This technique is known as tadka, and means 'seasoning'. A steel ladle that can be held over a flame on a gas stove, or a small pan, make ideal substitutes.

TAPELI

Used for cooking rice, a *tapeli* is a useful pan made of heavy stainless steel or copper. It is shaped like a normal pan, but has a tight-fitting lid that is ideal for cooking rice by the absorption method.

THE SPICE BOX

A *masala dani*, or spice box, is the pride and joy of any Indian housewife. The box is traditionally handed down within a family from mother to daughter or sometimes even grandmother to granddaughter. Spice boxes are available in all manner of shapes, colours and sizes. The most common type contains small steel, cup-like containers which are neatly arranged inside a large box with a lid. The small containers are used for storing the whole spices that are added to everyday dishes. Popular spices include mustard, cumin and nigella seeds, dried red chillies, black

Above *A traditional* masala dani.

peppercorns, and many more. These spices are generally used to flavour pulses and vegetables.

TAWA

Chapati is cooked on a cast iron griddle known as a *tawa*, which is also used for cooking the majority of the unleavened flat breads. You can also use a griddle pan.

ELECTRIC GRINDERS

It is worth buying a coffee grinder to keep solely for spice grinding if you make a lot of Indian food, as the aroma and flavour of freshly ground spices is unmatchable. Coffee grinders can also be used to crush small quantities of dry ingredients, such as nuts.

A food processor is worth its weight in gold for today's busy cooks. It can be used to chop and slice onions in an instant, as well as creating ginger and garlic purées and spice pastes, all of which are essential ingredients in Indian cooking.

MORTAR AND PESTLE

Perfect for grinding small amounts of ingredients to a very precise coarseness, these are invaluable in the Indian kitchen.

CHAPATI ROLLING BOARD

This round wooden board on short stubby legs is used to mould breads into shape. A standard bread board can be used instead.

CHAPATI SPOON

The square, flat-headed chapati spoon is used for turning breads on a chapati griddle. A fish slice (metal spatula) can also be used.

SLOTTED SPOON

Stirring cooked rice with a slotted spoon will make it soft and fluffy. It is also useful for lifting food out of oils and liquids.

Above *A degchi* is perfect for dum cooking.

Above *A tawa* is used for making chapatis.

Above *Use a mortar and pestle to grind spices.*

Cooking techniques

Several methods are used to create the many types of Indian dish. Dum cooking, for instance, involves braising the ingredients in a tightly sealed pan, which traps the steam and produces succulent and well-flavoured food. Tandoori cooking, on the other hand, relies on the kebabs or breads being cooked extremely quickly at a very high temperature, lending the ingredients a uniquely smoky flavour. Other techniques call for spices to be fried in different ways and added to the food at a strategic point in the cooking time.

Although they may sound complex, the cooking techniques that are primarily used in Indian cooking are actually very easy to carry out. Simply follow the methods and timings given and practise often. Even if something doesn't work the first time, the dish will in all probability still taste good and it will give you a target to work towards the next time you use the technique.

BAGHAR/TADKA

This method is used to flavour cooking fat with whole and/or ground spices, and sometimes with onion, garlic and ginger. This oil is then folded into the finished dish to intensify its flavour. If a combination of whole and ground spices is used, the whole ones are first fried for 10–15 seconds before the heat is turned off and the ground spices are mixed in.

This technique is used primarily in vegetable and lentil dishes and, to a lesser extent, with salads, meat and fish recipes. The combination of spices varies from region to region, as does the cooking

medium. Ghee is used to add a richer flavour, but vegetable or mustard oil is also commonly used.

In India, a specially made miniature tadka pan, shaped like a wok, is used for frying spices. These are usually made of cast iron or heavy aluminium and steel. In a Western kitchen, a small pan can be used. A steel ladle is also traditionally used to transfer the sizzling spices and oil from the pan to the dish, where the ladle is immersed for a few seconds until the spices stop sizzling.

BHUNA/BHOONA

This technique involves frying spices over a high temperature with a small amount of water added at regular intervals to stop them burning and sticking to the bottom of the pan too much. The spices will, however, stick very slightly to the sides and bottom, and they need scraping down and stirring into the rest of the mixture. It is this scraping, stirring and mixing of the spices without letting them burn that creates the unique bhuna flavour.

Above *It is important to scrape down the spices during bhuna cooking.*

Bhuna dishes tend to be drier than others, with little or no sauce, and they are normally served with bread or plain boiled basmati rice, especially if they are accompanied by a simple lentil dish. After the spices are fried, the remaining ingredients are added to the pan and allowed to sweat. Salt is added halfway through the cooking process to enable the food to release its natural juices, keeping the dish moist. Small quantities of water are added at intervals during the cooking time, before the heat is increased, and the food is stir-fried to add an all-important finishing touch.

Heavy cooking utensils are ideal for this method because they distribute heat evenly, allowing the food to cook to perfection. A cast iron wok is ideal as it means that very little oil is required.

Left *Frying whole and ground spices in sizzling oil and then folding everything into a finished dish (tadka) adds great depth of flavour.*

Above *To ensure a tight seal when using dum, cover the food with a damp dish towel, then a lid.*

Above *Nut pastes are often added to kormas, giving them extra flavour and a creamy finish.*

MAKING A NUT PASTE

1 Put the nuts in a heatproof bowl and pour over enough boiling water to cover. Leave the nuts to soak for about 20 minutes, to soften them before they are ground to a paste.

2 Pound the nuts to a paste using either use a mortar and pestle, which will give you greater control over the texture of the paste, or in a food processor or blender, with a little of the soaking water added.

DUM

This method is a more relaxed form of creating Indian recipes. After the initial cooking process, the food is put into a heavy pan with a tight-fitting lid and left to cook for a precise amount of time. The pan must be sealed completely so that no steam can escape. Traditionally, the pan would be sealed with a dough made from flour and water and the cooking would be done over charcoal, with more coal placed on top of the lid to provide heat from all sides. In a modern kitchen, however, it is easier to seal the pan with moist baking parchment, covered with a damp dish towel and topped with a double layer of foil or the pan lid.

KORMA

This term is commonly misunderstood as being the name of a dish, when in fact it refers to a simple braising technique. There are different types of kormas, depending on which part of the country they originated in. Northern kormas tend to be rich and creamy with subtle flavours and smooth, velvety sauces. Nut pastes, often made with cashew nuts and almonds, are used, as well as cream and saffron. Kormas from south India are enriched with coconut milk or cream and can be quite fiery.

Right *Most kormas, except Do-piaza, contain double (heavy) cream and/or some nut paste, which makes them rich and luscious.*

The richer version of korma involves marinating prime cuts of meat or chicken in a spice-laced yogurt mixture, before braising it very slowly in ghee and its own juices, without the addition of any stock or water.

To get best results, pans should be as heavy as possible and have tight-fitting lids. The size of the pan is also very important: if the pan is too big the food will dry out quickly, and if it is too small it will produce too much juice. It should just be big enough to hold the meat comfortably. The oven temperature should be correct and that the food must be cooked for the stated amount of time.

TESTING THE TEMPERATURE OF OIL USING BREAD

If you don't have a thermometer, you can gauge the temperature of oil using bread instead.

1 Heat the oil over a medium-high heat until the surface starts to shimmer. Drop a cube of bread into the hot oil.

2 When the bread rises to the surface after a few seconds and then browns after about 1 minute, the temperature is correct.

TALANA

This is a method of deep-frying that produces an exciting range of mouthwatering snacks, such as the Indian version of tempura, comprising chunks of meat, fish or vegetables coated in a gram flour batter and quickly fried. In India, a *karahi*, which is shaped like a wok, is generally used for talana. It is made of heavy cast iron and, because of its shape, a small quantity of oil can be used, eliminating the need to strain any excess oil or drain the food on kitchen paper.

A few simple rules will ensure crispy deep-fried food. Firstly, it is essential to use a light cooking oil, such as sunflower oil. Secondly, the oil needs to be at the right temperature, usually about 180°C/350°F on a thermometer.

KEBAB

Brought to India by Turkish travellers, kebab has become one of the popular techniques used for Indian cooking. The meat can be minced (ground) and rolled into balls or formed around skewers into sausage shapes, cut into cubes, or flattened and cut into strips. The meat is often marinated in a fragrant, yogurt-based mixture or, if it is minced, laced with herbs and spices.

Most of the kebabs in India are cooked in the *tandoor*, the Indian clay oven, but they are ideal for a barbecue as the hot coals impart the crucial smoky flavour. They can also be grilled (broiled) in the oven, although the taste won't be quite the same.

TANDOORI COOKING

This is an age-old technique, which is believed to have been introduced to India by ancient Persians. The key to the method lies in the use of a *tandoor*, a barrel-shaped clay oven that is capable of grilling (broiling), roasting and baking simultaneously.

Charcoal is used to fuel the *tandoor* and the food is cooked on a spit. The combination of clay and charcoal produces a fierce heat that seals the outer surface of the meat instantly, so that the inside remains moist and succulent during cooking. In a domestic kitchen, a grill (broiler) or a barbecue can

Above *Deep-frying (talana) is a common sight on Indian streets, where experienced vendors cook a wide range of delectable snacks.*

TIPS FOR COOKING ON A BARBECUE

- When setting and lighting a barbecue, you are aiming to create a very hot area in the centre, and cooler areas around the edge. Pile the charcoal or other fuel in the middle, light it and wait until it has a layer of white ash, then spread two-thirds of the fuel out to the sides, keeping a deeper, and hotter, area in the middle.
- Seal meat by placing it over the hottest part in the centre, then move it to the side to finish cooking more slowly and to prevent the outside burning while the inside remains raw. Baste the food regularly as it cooks.
- Cut open one piece of meat to check that it is thoroughly cooked through. Red meat doesn't need to be completely cooked, and you may prefer some pinkness.
- Use long-handled implements to turn the food and stoke the fire, so you don't risk burning yourself.

Above *Cooking kebabs and other marinated meat on a barbecue is a good way of recreating an authentic tandoori flavour at home.*

Above *Cubes of marinated meat are divine when chargrilled in the fiery belly of a* tandoor.

also produce delicious tandoori-style food. An oven that is fitted with a rotisserie is preferable to a grill, but an outdoor barbecue will give the best results.

The two key points to remember in order to produce perfect tandoori dishes are the correct preparation of the food and the temperature of the oven. The food needs to be marinated in an acidic mixture for several hours. There are usually two stages of marination: firstly, lemon juice, salt, fresh ginger and garlic purée are rubbed into the meat, so that the acid from the lemon juice can break down the muscle fibres and enable the meat to absorb flavours. Secondly, it is combined with yogurt and spices and left for a few more hours. The meat is then placed on long, thick iron skewers and these are inserted into the clay oven horizontally, where the food is cooked within a matter of minutes. In a domestic oven the cooking temperature needs to be set at its highest, and it is important to stick to the cooking times given to prevent the food from drying out. Basting the meat or fish regularly with any remaining marinade keeps it moist and tender.

A *tandoor* is also traditionally used for cooking naans, which should always be shaped by hand and never rolled. They are then placed on a small cushion and slapped on the side of the *tandoor*, where they cook almost instantaneously, producing a gorgeous fluffy texture that melts in the mouth. Again, it is possible to bake naan in a very hot domestic oven, but the flavour will not be quite the same.

Above *Naans are slapped on the sides of a* tandoor, *where the intense heat means they cook in seconds, making them soft and fluffy.*

TIKKA PASTE

Makes about 450ml/15fl oz/2 cups
25g/1oz coriander seeds
15g/½oz cumin seeds
25g/1oz garlic purée
25g/1oz ginger purée
15ml/1 tbsp garam masala
10ml/2 tsp Kashmiri chilli powder
5ml/1 tsp ground turmeric
5ml/1 tsp dried fenugreek leaves
  (kasuri methi)
5ml/1 tsp salt
150ml/¼ pint/⅔ cup wine vinegar
150ml/¼ pint/⅔ cup vegetable oil

1 Grind the coriander and cumin seeds to a fine powder using a spice mill, an electric coffee grinder or a mortar and pestle.

2 Spoon the ground spice mixture into a large bowl and add the remaining spices, fenugreek leaves and salt, stirring well.

3 Mix the spice powder with the wine vinegar and add 30ml/2 tbsp water to form a thin paste.

4 Heat the vegetable oil in a large pan, wok or *karahi*, and stir-fry the paste for 10 minutes, until all the water has been absorbed. When the oil rises to the surface, the paste is cooked.

5 Allow to cool before spooning into airtight jars. The paste will keep in the refrigerator for up to two weeks.

Fish and shellfish

Almost two-thirds of India is surrounded by sea and the fish found in these waters, such as mackerel, sardine, tuna and monkfish, form the basis of an amazing range of recipes. Among the shellfish, prawns (shrimp) are the most popular, and mussels, crabs and lobsters are cooked in spicy coconut broth all along the southern coastal regions. Inland, the rivers and waterways teem with more than 400 species of freshwater fish, including tilapia and the much-prized rainbow trout.

Most coastal communities depend on saltwater fish and shellfish for protein in their daily diet. Elsewhere, freshwater fish is used more as a supplement than a staple. Fish market stall-holders traditionally bought their fish direct from the fishing boats and, before the days of refrigeration, all fish had to be cooked on the same day it was bought. This still applies in many rural areas and has trained the local taste buds to expect extremely fresh ocean produce.

Above *Fishing is an important part of life in coastal India, especially in the Bay of Bengal.*

COD AND HADDOCK
These white fish break down into succulent flakes when they are cooked, meaning they are not suitable for use in curries as they simply disintegrate. However, they are ideal for dishes containing little liquid, and are often coated with a spicy paste and fried. As cod stocks are low, haddock is the more environmentally friendly choice.

RAINBOW TROUT
A revelation among often-bland freshwater fish, rainbow and brown trout are found in the clear, icy waters of the Himalayas, where angling tours are increasingly popular.

Rainbow trout do not have scales and are easy to de-bone, so are quick to prepare. The delicious, slightly nutty-tasting pink flesh needs little embellishment, and is best treated simply so the natural flavour shines through. In northern India they are usually coated with a marinade and baked.

TILAPIA
Found in warm reservoirs in southern India, tilapia are fast-growing fish that feature heavily on local menus. They have firm white flesh and are perfect for use in curries as the fish itself does not have a strong flavour, making it an ideal carrier for spices. They are also a good source of cheap protein.

MONKFISH
With succulent white flesh and a delicious taste that is quite similar to lobster, monkfish can be used as an alternative to tilapia to make spectacular curries and baked dishes.

MACKEREL
These beautiful, nutritious oily fish are found in the warm waters of the Indian Ocean, especially along the Maharashtra and Gujarat coasts. Best eaten as fresh as possible, they are usually marinated in a spicy paste and simply cooked on a barbecue or pan-fried, although they are also wonderful in spicy stews such as Mackerel Cooked in Coconut Milk.

SARDINES
Like mackerel, these oily fish have a strong flavour that can withstand the intensity of pungent spices. Sardines are slightly smaller than mackerel, but are generally prepared and cooked in much the same way, being coated in a spice paste and grilled (broiled) or fried.

Above *Tilapia are a good source of protein.*

Above *Sardines are flavoursome and nutritious.*

Above *Crabs are often used in coconut curries.*

Above *Scallops are both delicious and beautiful.*

TUNA

This valuable fish thrives in the warm waters of the Indian Ocean, which is home to more than 20 per cent of the world's tuna stocks. There are three main types: yellowfin tuna, bigeye tuna and albacore, and all are intensively fished, predominately for export in canned form. The rich, meaty flesh is perhaps best appreciated when simply grilled on a barbecue and lightly seasoned, but it is also used in curries and stews.

PRAWNS AND SHRIMP

All sizes of prawns (shrimp) are caught and eaten along the coasts of India, from succulent king prawns (jumbo shrimp) and tiger types to tiny shrimp. They are ideal for use in many delectable dishes, from rissoles and curries to pilaus and spicy mixed seafood broths, among many others. They require a little preparation before use (see box), but cook very quickly and are extremely versatile.

CRABS

These pretty crustaceans abound in the warm waters of India and there are many different species, including the mighty coconut crab, which is the largest living arthropod in the world. They are especially popular in the coastal south and west of the country, and their sweet, nutty flesh makes the perfect partner to spicy coconut sauces and broths. Whole crabs are often available pre-prepared or you can use crab claws.

MUSSELS

The mussel farming industry in India is growing fast, and they are increasingly appearing on menus. Requiring only minimal cooking, these delectable bivalves are ideal in stews and broths or fragrant sauces made from garlic and turmeric.

To prepare, check over the mussels and discard any that have broken shells or fail to shut when tapped. Scrub the shells in clean water, scrape off any barnacles and remove the straggly 'beard' that may protrude from the shell. Cook according to the recipe, and discard any that fail to open when cooked.

SCALLOPS

These beautiful, succulent bivalves are a common sight along the coasts of India and appear in many local dishes, such as marinated pan-fried scallops and as part of mixed seafood soups. Although they are more expensive, try to buy hand-dived scallops as others are usually gathered by dredgers, which damage the ocean floor.

To prepare, ensure that the shells are tightly shut and discard any that are not. Holding the scallop flat, insert a sturdy knife in the hinge and give it a twist to open the shell slightly, so you can insert a knife. Run the knife over the flat side of the shell to release the scallop, then carefully open the shell fully and remove it. Pull off the black frill, then use the flesh and juices as required.

SQUID

Primarily eaten in coastal areas, especially in Kerala, squid are usually deep-fried or used in curries and coconut broths with other seafood. They should be either cooked slowly or very quickly, or they can become tough and chewy. They require preparation (see box), or alternatively you can buy pre-prepared frozen squid, also called calamari.

PREPARING PRAWNS (SHRIMP)

1 Cut off the heads, then run your thumb under the shell to separate it from the body. Some recipes may require you to leave the tail on, which helps the prawn retain its shape.

2 To devein the prawn, locate the black vein that runs along the back, insert the tip of a sharp knife under it and push it up. Pull out the vein using the knife. Alternatively you can slice either side of the vein to cut it out.

PREPARING SQUID

1 Pull the head away from the body of the squid, then cut off and reserve the tentacles, and peel off the membrane with your fingers.

2 Pull out the quill from inside the squid, then stuff or slice into rings, as required.

Meat

Meat is an important ingredient in many parts of India, especially in the mountainous areas where it is hard to grow vegetables and there is no coastline so access to fish and shellfish is limited. As a result, there is a huge number of meat dishes on offer, from succulent mountain lamb to fragrant pork dishes and tender beef stews. The preparation and cooking of the different cuts is very important, and most meat is tenderized and/or marinated before being cooked in a particular way.

The consumption of meat varies from region to region, often depending on the dominant faith. In general, the choice of meats tends to be related to religious restrictions. Hindus and Buddhists are often vegetarian and even if they do eat meat, they do not eat beef. Muslims eschew pork, while Jainists are very strict vegetarians. Christians tend to be meat-eaters, although Catholics are not allowed meat on many religious days.

The availability of alternative ingredients also plays a role in determining the level of meat consumed. In areas where very little grows, meat and a staple such as rice form the basis of the diet. In areas where there is a wealth of vegetables, and fish and shellfish, these make up a larger proportion of the diet.

Preparing meat correctly is important in Indian cooking. Certain dishes are made from boneless meat for which a stock, known as *yakhni*, is made from the bones and added to the seared flesh. In general, however, most meat is trimmed of fat and cut into pieces, but kept on the bone for flavour, and marinated in an acidic mixture before being cooked.

BEEF

Cows and water buffalo are common in India, and their meat and dairy is transformed into all manner of dishes. Meat tends to be trimmed, diced and stewed, or minced (ground) and mixed with other flavourings to make dishes such as kebabs. However, because over 80 per cent of the population are Hindus, who hold the cow sacred, beef is not as common as mutton or goat.

PORK

Packed with flavour, pork is used in many parts of India, and especially in Goa, where the signature dish is Pork in Garlic and Vinegar, a fusion dish that was introduced by Portuguese traders. It is also found in fragrant Chinese-inspired dishes.

Cubed leg steaks and shoulder meat are normally used for slow-cooked dishes, while minced pork is shaped into meat patties. Home-smoked pork adds flavour to stews, while spicy dishes of pig's liver are served with rice. As with all offal (innards) it is very important that the liver is extremely fresh.

Above *Livestock such as pigs wander the streets in small rural villages.*

MUTTON AND LAMB

By far and away the most common meat, mutton features in dishes all over the country. In the West, however, lamb is more often the meat of choice. Hardy sheep can survive in even the most arid conditions and travel well, so it is no surprise that they can be found both on the slopes of the Himalayas and grazing on Gangetic plains.

Many cuts of meat are used, from leg chops and whole legs of lamb to bitesize chunks of meat. All are usually tenderized by being marinated in an acidic mixture, often containing yogurt and/or lemon or tamarind juice or vinegar, before being slow-cooked with a range of spices and flavourings to produce mouthwatering curries and stews, or skewered and grilled (broiled) in a *tandoor* as kebabs. Minced lamb is also used in pilaus and to make meat patties, and as fillings for samosas and keema naan.

Goat is consumed in some parts of India, especially in highland areas, and is usually slow-cooked as it can be tough and stringy.

Left *Hardy and versatile, sheep and goats provide meat and milk in the most arid locations.*

Poultry

Chicken and other forms of poultry are extremely popular in Indian cooking, even though the meat is expensive, and there is a thriving commercial industry to keep up with the demand. Chickens and ducks are also bred by many rural families and are kept in makeshift coops on smallholdings, and even in some highly urbanized areas. All over the country, vendors wend their way through the traffic on bicycles and motorbikes laden with live birds, on their way to the many open-air markets.

Above *Bicycles are commonly used to transport live birds to market.*

DUCK

The rearing of ducks in India is largely confined to rural communities, where they are fed on scraps and forage for insects and worms outside. The meat is used in much the same way as chicken, being rubbed with spices and grilled, or simmered in a spicy sauce. It is always cooked through, with no traces of pink remaining.

GUINEA FOWL AND QUAIL

Small birds such as guinea fowl and quail are most commonly eaten in western India, especially in Rajasthan, where hunting was commonplace and a wide range of game dishes was created by skilled Mughal chefs to satisfy the appetites of the emperors. Today, they are usually reserved for special occasions as they are quite fiddly to prepare.

EGGS

A key source of protein, eggs appear in many guises in India: scrambled with spices, hard-boiled and served with pilau, or simply used as a binding ingredient.

Used in a huge number of curries and other dishes, poultry is the first choice for most meat-eating Indians, although it is also the most expensive, so for poorer families its consumption may be restricted to special occasions such as weddings.

CHICKEN

Often sold as whole birds and then jointed at home, chicken is also available in most cities and large towns pre-prepared. Chicken breast fillets are commonly used, especially for dishes that require meat to be skewered and grilled (broiled), although other cuts, such as thighs, drumsticks and wings are also enjoyed with gusto in a wide range of slow-cooked dishes, where they impart a greater depth of flavour. It is never cooked with the skin on even when grilled or roasted because the skin would prevent the flavours of a marinade or rub from permeating the flesh. Any visible fat is usually removed from the meat, making it a lean and healthy choice.

Marinades play an important part in Indian cooking, and chicken is often steeped in a mixture of spices, salt and an acidic ingredient such as lemon or tamarind juice and/or yogurt, as this helps tenderize the meat. Some marinades are quite stiff pastes, while others are looser and more liquid, and are added to the pan to create a delicious sauce. Having been left to absorb the flavours for anything from 30 minutes to 12 hours, the flesh is generally then grilled on skewers on a barbecue or in a *tandoor*, or slow-cooked with the addition of liquid to make a curry or braised dish. Double (heavy) cream and thickening pastes made from nuts are stirred into most korma dishes, while in the southern states, such as Goa, coconut milk or cream is often added, lending the finished dish a rich and voluptuous note.

Above *Dishes made from game, such as quail, originated in western India.*

Vegetables

With such a large percentage of the population being vegetarian, and with such a wealth of produce on offer, it is little surprise that Indian cooking specializes in truly stunning vegetable dishes. From deep-fried snacks through to curries, the recipes make wonderful use of everything from cauliflower, potatoes and peas to more exotic and unusual varieties, such as okra, bottle gourds and aubergines (eggplants). When it comes to Indian cooking, vegetables are simply indispensable.

Most of the vegetables used in Indian cooking are commonplace and widely available, while others, such as bottle gourds, may be a little harder to track down. Asian and African stores and markets are often a good place to look.

AUBERGINES (EGGPLANTS)

Available in different varieties, the shiny deep purple aubergine is the most widely grown and commonly used type in Indian cooking. Aubergines have a strong flavour and some have a slightly bitter taste. To prepare, simply cut in half lengthways and then slice into rounds or cut into cubes, as required. The cut flesh may be sprinkled with salt to extract the bitter juices, if you like, then rinsed well and patted dry with kitchen paper before use. The spongy flesh readily absorbs other flavours, making them ideal for curries.

Below *Vibrant street markets all over India sell a wide range of fresh vegetables.*

Above *Glossy purple aubergines (eggplants) are ideal carriers for a range of spices.*

BOTTLE GOURDS

The long, knobbly, green bottle gourd has a strong, bitter taste. It is known to have properties that purify the blood. To prepare, peel off the ridged skin, scrape away and discard the seeds and chop the flesh.

PREPARING BUTTERNUT SQUASH

1 Cut off the top and bottom of the butternut squash. Cut the vegetable in half widthways, just above the bulbous bottom part. Stand each half upright on a board and carefully cut down to remove the skin.

2 Cut each piece in half lengthways. Scoop out the seeds using the knife or a spoon, then cube the flesh, or cut it into strips, as required.

BUTTERNUT SQUASH

With soft, vibrant flesh and a sweet flavour this vegetable is a brilliant partner for spices. Packed with carbohydrates and vitamins, including vitamin C, it can be used to add substance and colour to curries and other baked dishes. Encased in a tough skin, it does not require refrigeration (ideal in the heat of India) and also travels very well, which is perhaps why it is so popular.

YAM

Packed with starch, this humble vegetable is an invaluable part of the local diet in India, providing a welcome alternative to rice as a staple carbohydrate. Although it does not have a strong flavour, the firm flesh can be cubed and cooked with a range of spices, whereupon it will soften and absorb all the wonderful flavours.

To prepare, simply peel the tough skin using a vegetable peeler and slice into rounds or cut into cubes, as required. If frying, it is best to first soak the prepared yam in cold water for 30 minutes to start softening it.

POTATOES

Like yams, potatoes are a very good source of carbohydrate, and are also infinitely versatile. They appear in many curries all over the country, especially vegetarian ones, providing flavour as well as substance. They can be peeled if you prefer, but for optimum nutrition and flavour, simply scrub the skins to remove all traces of soil and cut into cubes or slice into rounds.

PLANTAINS

Related to bananas, these starchy fruits are usually used in savoury dishes, such as Plantain Curry, or dusted with spices, fried and served as an accompaniment. Their earthy flavour is the perfect foil for a plethora of spices, and they are most popular in eastern India. They are very easy to prepare: simply peel and slice or cube.

CARROTS

Crunchy, sweet and packed with nutrients, carrots appear in all manner of curries and stewed vegetable dishes. Like other root vegetables, they keep well in heat and are easy to transport as they do not bruise and spoil easily, unlike many other vegetables. If they are tender young carrots they may not need peeling, and if small enough can be left whole, with the green top removed. Older specimens will usually require peeling before being chopped or sliced.

PARSNIPS

Although not grown in India, parsnips make a wonderful addition to vegetable curries, where they impart their sweet flavour and add substance. They can also be fried and then blended with other flavourings to make sweet and spicy patties, which are shallow-fried in hot oil and served with chutney as an appetizer. Prepare in the same way as carrots.

CAULIFLOWERS

Usually braised with a range of spices and other vegetables, tender, creamy cauliflower is a popular ingredient in most regions of India. It can also be dipped in spicy batter and deep-fried to make a tasty appetizer, or separated into tiny florets and used in chutneys and preserves, including the famous British condiment piccalilli, which arguably originated in east India. Cauliflower florets are often blanched before being added towards the end of the cooking time.

Above *Similar in appearance to bananas, plantains are used in savoury dishes.*

Above *The tough outer skin of yams protects them during transportation.*

Above *The humble cauliflower can be transformed into any number of exciting dishes.*

PREPARING GREENS (COLLARDS)

1 Separate the greens into individual leaves, and thoroughly wash these in a colander under cold running water to remove all traces of dirt.

2 If the leaves have a tough, woody core, remove with a knife. Tender leaves will not require this.

3 Roll up the leaves into a sausage shape and slice across this to finely shred the greens.

BEANS

These are among the most popular vegetables in India, and they are sold almost everywhere at colourful street markets. Both French (green) beans and runner (green) beans are used in spicy stir-fries, cooked with lentils, or lightly steamed and seasoned with whole spices to make salads. They can also appear in chutneys and relishes, adding substance as well as flavour.

Above *The growing and harvesting of vegetables such as onions provides a major source of employment for many in rural India.*

To prepare them, remove the tops and tails and, if they have them, the strings that run along either side of the bean. If they are tough and woody French beans, cut them into thin strips using a knife or a special implement that can be found in most cookshops. Beans are often blanched before being added at the end of cooking.

PEAS

Vibrant and sweet, fresh green peas are added to a number of Indian dishes, such as potato cakes, curries and side dishes, to add colour, texture and taste. Frozen ones are just as good as the fresh type, if not better, and require only a quick rinse under cold water in a sieve before being used in the same way as fresh ones, making them the perfect stand-by ingredient.

SPINACH

Available all year round, this leafy green vegetable has a mild, delicate flavour. The leaves vary in size and only the large thick ones need to be trimmed of their stalks. Spinach is a favourite vegetable in Indian cuisine, and it is cooked in many ways, with meat, other vegetables, and with beans, peas and lentils.

GREENS (COLLARDS)

Both mustard and spring greens are grown and used in parts of India where conditions permit the growing of vegetables. They are used in much the same way as spinach, and require only minimal preparation and cooking.

Above *French (green) beans are very versatile and require little preparation.*

Above *The vibrant colour and sweet flavour of peas makes them a favourite ingredient.*

Above *Okra, or ladies' fingers, are one of the most commonly used vegetables in India.*

Above *Colourful (bell) peppers make a crunchy and tasty addition to many dishes.*

REMOVING THE SKINS FROM TOMATOES

1 Score the skins of the tomatoes with a sharp knife.

2 Place the tomatoes in a small heatproof bowl and pour over enough boiling water to cover. Leave for about 5 minutes, until the skins look loose around the tomatoes.

3 Lift out the tomatoes with a slotted spoon, leave until cool enough to handle, then peel off the skins.

DICING ONIONS

1 Using a sharp knife, make a shallow slit down the side of the onion. Peel off the skin, using your fingers.

2 Cut the onion in half, from top to bottom. Slice through the onion at regular intervals at right angles to the root end. Leaving the root on will hold the onion together and make it easier to dice.

3 Cut across the slices you have made to dice the onions.

OKRA
Also known as ladies' fingers, okra are one of the most popular and ubiquitous vegetables. These small, green, five-sided pods are indigenous to India. They have a distinctive flavour and a sticky, pulpy texture when they are cooked. To prepare, simply trim off the ends, rinse in a colander and use as directed in the method.

ONIONS
A versatile vegetable belonging to the allium family, onions have a pungent flavour and aroma and are one of the key ingredients, along with garlic and ginger, used in almost every Indian dish. They are grown all over the country, except in arid areas, where they are bought in.

Globe onions are the most commonly used variety for Indian cooking, although smaller, sweeter shallots are also used in some dishes that call for onions to be left whole, such as *Do-piaza*. Spring onions (scallions) are often added to some dishes towards the end of the cooking time, or to raitas, to add colour and for their mild taste.

CORN
Although it originated in South America, corn is now grown worldwide, and is produced extensively in north India. It has a sweet, juicy flavour, which is at its best just after picking. Baby corn can be eaten whole, in curries, or dipped in a spicy batter and deep-fried to make Baby Corn Fritters.

TOMATOES
An essential ingredient in a huge range of Indian dishes, tomatoes grow well in the heat of India and are a common sight at most markets. Adding acidity as well as colour and flavour, they are used to make sauces for curries, chutneys and relishes. Peeled and deseeded salad tomatoes are often adequate for most recipes, but they do need to be really ripe and flavoursome. Use canned tomatoes in sauces and curries for their rich colour and intense flavour, and as an alternative to salad varieties when these are not at their best.

PEPPERS
Large, crunchy, hollow pods belonging to the capsicum family, (bell) peppers are available in a variety of colours. Red peppers are the sweetest, orange and yellow ones are mild and quite sweet, while green ones have a stronger, more peppery flavour. They are used in a wide variety of dishes, adding both colour and flavour.

To prepare, cut the peppers in half lengthways, then remove the stem, core and all the bitter white membrane using your fingers or a knife. Slice or dice the remaining fruit as required.

Fruit, nuts and seeds

Indians love fruit and, as well as eating fresh varieties raw as a snack or for dessert at the end of a meal, they will also cook them in savoury dishes. Fruit is often preserved by being sun-dried or converted into spicy chutneys, and these invaluable ingredients are cherished in the months when the fresh type is not available. Nuts and seeds – especially cashew nuts, almonds and sesame seeds – are often used as a thickening agent in curries, or are scattered on top of dishes to add an extra layer of flavour and texture.

Most of the fruit that is indigenous to India is now widely available in supermarkets and Asian stores. Choose ripe, unblemished specimens, as these will taste best. Nuts and seeds should be bought fresh and used quickly, as they can become rancid.

MANGOES

These fruits grow in India throughout the summer months, and ripe ones are used in sweet dishes. Unripe green mangoes, sold in the springtime, are used to make pickles and chutneys, and are added to curries as a souring agent. The unripe fruit is also sun-dried and ground into a powder called amchur, which has a sour taste and is sprinkled over dishes as a garnish.

PAPAYAS

Also known as pawpaw, these pear-shaped fruits are native to tropical America, and were not introduced to Asia until the 17th century. When ripe, the skin turns yellow and the pulp is a vibrant orange-pink. The edible black seeds taste peppery when dried. Peel off the skin and eat the creamy flesh raw. The unripe green fruit is used to tenderize meat.

Above *Ripe papayas can be eaten raw, while unripe fruits are used to tenderize meat.*

Above *Ruby-red pomegranate seeds can be eaten whole or pressed to extract their juice.*

PINEAPPLES

These distinctive-looking fruits have sweet, golden and exceedingly juicy flesh. Unlike most other fruits, pineapples do not ripen after picking, although leaving a slightly unripe fruit at room temperature will help to reduce its acidity. Pineapples are cultivated in India, mainly in the south, and are generally cooked with spices to make palate-cleansing side dishes.

BANANAS

The soft and creamy flesh of bananas is high in starch, and is an excellent source of energy. Indians use several varieties of banana in vegetarian curries, including plantains, green bananas, and the sweet red-skinned variety.

POMEGRANATES

The seeds of these beautiful fruits can be extracted by cutting fresh pomegranates into quarters and then picking out the seeds. Discard the bitter white membrane. As doing this is quite time-consuming, for convenience they can be bought in jars from Asian food stores. Pomegranate seeds impart a delicious tangy flavour.

LEMONS AND LIMES

These citrus fruits are indigenous to India, although limes, which in India are confusingly called lemons, are the most commonly available of the two. Both fruits are used as souring agents and are added to curries at the end of the cooking process.

Left *Roadside stalls sell ripe yellow and red bananas as well as unripe green fruits.*

GINGER AND LIME DRINK

Serves 4
50g/2oz fresh root ginger, grated
600ml/1 pint/2½ cups water
50g/2oz/¼ cup caster (superfine) sugar
5ml/1 tsp salt, or to taste
juice of 2 limes
crushed ice and slices of lime, to serve

1 Squeeze the juice out of the grated
ginger, either with your fingers over a bowl,
by placing in a piece of muslin (cheesecloth)
and catching the juices, or by pressing it
through a sieve with the back of a spoon.

2 In a large jug, stir together the water, sugar,
salt and lime juice, until the sugar and salt
have dissolved. Add 10ml/2 tsp of the ginger
juice and mix thoroughly

3 Taste and add a further 5ml/1 tsp ginger
juice, if liked (remember that the flavour will
be diluted by the crushed ice).

4 Fill four tall glasses with crushed ice and
pour over the prepared drink. Garnish each
with a slice of lime and serve immediately as
a refreshing drink to accompany a spicy meal.

Per portion Energy 56kcal/239kJ; Protein 0g; Carbohydrate 14g, of which sugars 14g; Fat 0g, of which saturates 0g; Cholesterol 0mg; Calcium 0mg; Fibre 0.0g; Sodium 493mg.

COCONUT

Used in both sweet and savoury Indian
dishes, fresh coconut is available from
Indian food stores and supermarkets.
Desiccated (dry unsweetened shredded)
coconut, as well as coconut cream and
creamed coconut, which are made from
the grated flesh, will all make acceptable
substitutes in most recipes if the fresh type
is out of season. Coconut milk is used in
Indian curries to thicken and enrich sauces.
In Western supermarkets, it is sold in cans
and in powdered form, as a convenient
alternative to the fresh fruit; the powdered
milk has to be blended with hot water before
use. Coconut milk can be made at home
from desiccated coconut. Coconut cream is
used to add fragrance and aroma to dishes,
while creamed coconut adds richness.

ALMONDS

These nuts are often soaked and pulped,
then used for making rich sauces,
especially kormas and pasandas. They
grow in abundance in Kashmir in the north,
where a superb chutney is made from
ground blanched almonds and spices.
Flaked (sliced) almonds are often toasted
and used as an attractive garnish,
especially for pilaus, and add a contrasting
crunchy texture to the finished dish.

CASHEW NUTS

These full-flavoured nuts are an important
ingredient in Indian cooking. In the north
they are soaked and ground to a purée to
make thick, rich sauces. In Goa, a powerful
liquor called *kaju feni* is made from the sap
of the cashew plant.

PISTACHIO NUTS

These vibrant green nuts are used mainly
in desserts and sweets. Raw or toasted
pistachio nuts make attractive garnishes
for pilaus and biryanis. *Pista burfi*, a
fudge-like sweetmeat, is very popular.

WALNUTS

These are commonly used whole or
chopped in sweetmeats, salads and
raitas in India.

SESAME SEEDS

These small, flat pear-shaped seeds are
usually white, but can be cream, brown,
red or black. When roasted or dry-fried
they take on a slightly nutty taste, and
when ground and made into a paste they
act as a thickening agent in curries.

Above *Many different coconut products can be
used in Indian cooking, but fresh is best.*

Above *Both whole blanched almonds and
flaked almonds are used in recipes.*

Above *White sesame seeds can be made into
a paste that is added to curries to thicken them.*

Beans, peas and lentils

Playing an important role in regional cooking, pulses are an excellent source of protein and fibre, which is especially crucial for the many vegetarians in India. Some types are eaten whole, some are puréed and made into soups or dhals, and others are combined with vegetables or meat to make all manner of delectable and healthy dishes. It is important to follow the instructions regarding their preparation carefully, as some can be toxic if they are not treated properly.

Beans and chickpeas should be soaked before cooking, but if you are in a rush then you can use canned varieties. Lentils do not need to be soaked before use. Red and green split lentils have a soft consistency when cooked, while whole ones hold their shape. Do not add salt until the end of the cooking time when using lentils, apart from red split ones, as it will make them tough.

CHICKPEAS

These round, beige-coloured pulses have a strong, nutty flavour when cooked. As well as being used for curries, they are added to Indian snacks and are also ground into gram flour, which is used in many dishes, such as pakoras and bhajiyas.

Above *Tender and creamy, black-eyed beans (peas) appear in many Indian dishes.*

Above *Highly nutritious, cheap and versatile, lentils are a staple ingredient.*

PREPARING AND COOKING PULSES

It is very important to carefully follow preparation instructions when using beans and pulses.

1 Wash the beans or peas under cold running water, then place in a bowl of fresh cold water and leave to soak overnight. Drain and rinse again.

2 Put in a large pan and cover with cold water. Bring to the boil and cook on high for 10–15 minutes. Reduce the heat and simmer until tender. Lift out and drain, then use as required.

BLACK-EYED BEANS (PEAS)

These are small and cream-coloured, with a black spot or 'eye'. When cooked, black-eyed beans have a creamy texture and a mild, smoky flavour.

FLAGEOLET (SMALL CANNELLINI) BEANS

These white or pale green oval beans have a very mild, refreshing flavour and add substance to many vegetarian dishes.

HARICOT (NAVY) BEANS

Ideal for Indian cooking because they retain their shape well and absorb flavours easily, these small, white oval beans contain more soluble fibre than any other type of pulse, making them a healthy addition to the daily diet in India.

KIDNEY BEANS

These red-brown kidney-shaped beans have a distinctive flavour and hold their shape when cooked. They belong to the same family as the pinto bean. It is important to soak and cook all beans before use, but especially kidney beans, as they are highly toxic if not prepared properly.

MUNG BEANS

These small, round green beans have a sweet flavour and creamy texture when cooked. When sprouted, mung beans produce beansprouts. Split, hulled mung beans are called yellow split lentils, and their Indian name is mung or moong dhal.

CHANNA DHAL

This round, yellow split lentil is also called yellow split gram or skinless split chickpeas.

GREEN LENTILS

Also known as continental lentils, these have a strong flavour and retain their shape well.

MASOOR DHAL

These red split lentils can be used in dishes instead of tuvar dhal.

TOOR OR TUVAR DHAL

Dull orange split peas with an earthy flavour, toor or tuvar dhal are often called pigeon peas and are available plain and in an oily variety.

URID DHAL

This lentil is available split, either with the blackish hull retained or removed.

Dairy products, ghee and oils

Used on a daily basis, these ingredients are the cornerstone of the Indian diet, except in regions where veganism is practised. Milk, yogurt and cheese appear in a huge range of dishes, adding much-needed protein and flavour, as well as being consumed on their own as drinks or snacks. Yogurt is especially important in marinades, as the acidity helps tenderize meat. Butter (often in the form of ghee) or oil appear in almost every recipe, for frying off spices and flavourings, browning meat or deep-frying delectable snacks.

Used in drinks or cooked in both savoury and sweet dishes, milk is important in Indians' diet. Natural (plain) yogurt accompanies most Indian meals, and drinks based on yogurt, such as lassis, are also very popular. Paneer, the only Indian cheese, is a key ingredient in many specialities, such as Indian Cheese with Fenugreek and Spinach.

Sunflower oil is the most popular cooking medium because of its neutral flavour, but in some regions cooks favour groundnut or mustard oil. Rich, nutty-tasting ghee was the traditional medium of cooking until recent years.

MILK AND BUTTERMILK

The volume of milk produced in India is one of the highest in the world and the dairy industry is big business. In addition to milk from cows, more than half of the milk comes from buffalo, and is sold in liquid form, as a stable, creamy yogurt and as cheese. Buttermilk, the by-product of the butter-making process, is also drunk and used in cooking.

YOGURT

In India, yogurt is known as curd, and is very thick and rich as it is made with buffalo's rather than cow's milk. It can be added to sauces to give a creamy texture, although it is most often used as a souring agent, particularly in the dairy-dominated north.

Yogurt will curdle quickly when heated, especially if it does not have a high enough fat content, so it is best to use a full-fat (whole) version, such as Greek (US strained plain) yogurt. Other types of full-fat yogurt can be strained through muslin (cheesecloth) to remove water and make them more stable.

CREAM

Double (heavy) cream is added to some curries, such kormas, where it adds depth of flavour and a silky texture to the dish.

PANEER

This traditional north Indian cheese is made from rich dairy milk. Paneer is white in colour and smooth-textured. It is usually available from large supermarkets, but tofu and beancurd are adequate substitutes.

GHEE

The main fat used in Indian cooking until recent years, ghee is still widely used, although people are increasingly using vegetable oil, as it is healthier. There are two types: the traditional one, made from pure butterfat; and a more recent kind, which is made from vegetable fat. Butterfat ghee is rich with a golden colour and nutty taste. It is made by separating the milk solids and eliminating the moisture from unsalted butter. The result is a golden liquid, which is strained and stored in an airtight tin or jar in the refrigerator for up to six months. The kind made from vegetable fat has less flavour but is healthier. Unsalted butter, mixed with 15ml/1 tbsp oil, can be used as a substitute.

Below Buffalo are a common sight in India, and their milk is used to make a range of products.

Above Traditional butterfat ghee has a delicious nutty flavour.

COOKING OILS

Corn oil and sunflower oil are most popular types of oil in India. Sesame oil and groundnut oil are also used, and in the south, where coconuts are abundant, coconut oil is most popular. Pungent mustard oil is used in everyday cooking in Kashmir, Bengal and in the north-eastern states. When it reaches a high temperature it loses its astringent taste and aroma.

Rice

A staple grain that is grown nearly everywhere, rice is served with almost every meal in most parts of India, so it is no surprise that the Indians have created a variety of distinctive ways of cooking it. Plain boiled rice, cooked by the absorption method, is an everyday accompaniment to curries and other wet dishes. For special occasions and entertaining, it is often combined with other ingredients to make delectable pilaus and biryanis. Basmati rice is the grain of choice in most regions.

There is no definitive way to cook plain rice, but whatever the recipe, the aim is to produce dry, separate-grained rice that is cooked through yet still retains some bite. The secret is the amount of water added: the rice must be able to absorb it all, so it must be added in the correct ratio.

BASMATI RICE
Known as the 'prince of rices', basmati is the recommended rice for Indian curries – not only because it is easy to cook and produces an excellent finished result, but because it has a cooling effect.

Basmati is a slender, long grain, milled rice grown in northern India, the Punjab, parts of Pakistan and in the foothills of the Himalayas. Its name means 'fragrant', and it has a distinctive and appealing aroma. After harvesting it is aged for a year, which gives it its characteristic flavour and a light, fluffy texture. Basmati can be used in almost any savoury dish, particularly curries or pilaus, and is the essential ingredient in biryanis. White and brown basmati rices are widely available from supermarkets and Indian food stores.

Above *White basmati rice is grown in the north, and is the most common type of rice in India.*

PATNA RICE
This rice takes its name from Patna in Bihar, eastern India. At one time, most of the long grain rice sold in Europe came from here, and the term was used to mean any long grain rice, whatever its origin. The custom still persists in parts of the United States, but elsewhere patna describes this specific variety of rice. It is used in the same way as other long grain rices.

Above *Rice flour has a very fine texture and is used for making dumplings and pancakes.*

OTHER RICE PRODUCTS
Rice can be used to make other ingredients, such as rice flour, which is used for making sweets (candies), dumplings, pancakes and other foods requiring a batter. The grains may also be flattened to make flaked rice, which is used for delicious snacks; or placed in very hot sand to make puffed rice, which is used for creating various snacks and sweets.

PLAIN BOILED RICE

Always wash rice in several changes of water until the water runs clear, and soak it for 15–20 minutes before cooking, then drain.

Serves 4
275g/10oz/1⅓ cups basmati rice
15ml/1 tsp butter
2.5ml/½ tsp salt

1 Wash the rice in several changes of water until the water runs clear. Soak it in fresh water for 20 minutes. Drain well.

2 In a medium-sized pan, bring 550ml/18fl oz/2½ cups water to the boil and add the butter, salt and the drained rice. Bring it to the boil and let it boil steadily for 1 minute.

3 Reduce the heat to low and cover the pan tightly. Cook for 8–9 minutes, then switch off the heat source. Leave the pan to stand undisturbed for 10–12 minutes.

4 Fluff up the rice with a fork and serve with a main course or vegetable side dishes.

Per Portion Energy 256kcal/1071kJ; Protein 5.1g; Carbohydrate 54.9g, of which sugars 0g; Fat 1.4g, of which saturates 0.7g; Cholesterol 3mg; Calcium 13mg; Fibre 0g; Sodium 255mg.

Bread

An integral part of many meals, Indian breads are served alongside or instead of rice as a staple carbohydrate to balance out the other dishes. Most traditional Indian breads are unleavened (made without any raising agent) and recipes tend to use wholemeal (whole-wheat) flour, known as chapati flour or atta. They are all delicious hot from the oven, but generally do not keep very well so should be made and eaten on the same day. They are also cheap and readily available to buy.

Throughout India, breads vary from region to region, depending on local ingredients and customs. Some breads are cooked dry on a hot griddle, while some are fried with a little oil, and others are deep-fried to make small savoury puffs.

NAAN

Probably the most well-known Indian bread outside India is naan, from the north of the country. Naan is made with plain (all-purpose) flour, yogurt and yeast; some contemporary recipes favour the use of a raising agent such as bicarbonate of soda (baking soda) or self-raising (self-rising) flour as a leaven in place of yeast. The yogurt is important for the fermentation of the dough, and some naan are made entirely using a yogurt fermentation. This gives the bread its puffy texture and soft crust.

The flavour comes partly from the soured yogurt and partly from the *tandoor*, in which the bread is traditionally cooked. The dough is flattened against the hot walls of the oven and the pull of gravity produces the teardrop shape. As the dough scorches and puffs up, it produces a bread that is soft yet crisp.

CHAPATIS

The favourite bread of central and southern India, the chapati is a thin, flat, unleavened bread usually made from ground wholemeal (whole-wheat) flour. Chapatis are cooked on a hot *tava*, a concave-shaped Indian griddle. They have a light texture and fairly bland flavour, which makes them an ideal accompaniment for curry dishes. Spices can be added to the flour to give more flavour.

ROTIS

There are many variations of chapatis, including rotis and dana rotis. These are unleavened breads, made using chapati flour to which ghee, oil, celery seeds and/or fresh coriander are added. They are rolled out thinly and cooked like chapatis.

POORIS

Another popular variation on the chapati is the poori, which is a small, deep-fried puffy bread made from chapati flour. Pooris are best eaten sizzling hot and are traditionally served for breakfast. They can be plain or flavoured with spices, such as cumin, turmeric and chilli powder.

Above *Freshly cooked naan is an essential part of the daily diet in north India.*

PARATHAS

A paratha is similar to a chapati except that it contains ghee, which gives the bread a richer flavour and flakier texture. Parathas are much thicker than chapatis and are shallow-fried. Plain ones are often eaten for lunch, and they go well with most vegetable dishes. They can be stuffed with various fillings, the most popular being spiced potato, and served as a snack.

POPPADUMS

Now widely available outside of India, poppadums are large, thin, crisp discs, which can be bought ready-cooked or ready-to-cook. In India they are served with vegetarian meals. They are sold in markets and by street vendors, and are available plain or flavoured with spices or seasoned with ground red or black pepper. The dough is generally made from dried beans, but can also be made from potatoes or sago.

Above *Rotis are a type of chapati enriched with the addition of ghee.*

Above *Crunchy poppadums are the ideal accompaniment to chutneys and relishes.*

Herbs, spices and other flavourings

The key to Indian cooking lies in the various combinations and treatments of the panoply of spices and flavourings that are indigenous to the region. Some types are used principally for the taste they impart, while other ones, known as aromatics, are used mainly for their aroma. One individual spice can completely alter the taste of a dish and a combination of several spices will also affect its colour and texture, so it is little wonder that there is such a huge number of possible variations in Indian cuisine.

The key to getting the most from herbs, spices and flavourings is to buy the freshest ones you can, which means it is often better to buy smaller quantities more frequently. This is especially true of spices, which go stale and lose their piquancy fairly quickly.

HERBS
Fresh and dried herbs add colour, flavour, aroma and texture to a dish. Because herbs require only a minimal amount of cooking, they retain a marvellous intensity of flavour and fragrance.

Chillies
It is surprising that chillies, without which Indian food is difficult to imagine, were not known in India until the 16th century when the Portuguese introduced them to the southern region. South Indians consume the most fresh chillies, while the state of Andhra Pradesh in central India produces the largest quantity. Removing the seeds will decrease the potency of fresh chillies (see box), or you can reduce the quantity used. Dried red chillies and chilli powder are popular all over India. A little goes a long way with these products, so be sure to measure quantities carefully.

Below *Used whole or chopped, fresh chillies add colour and heat to Indian dishes.*

Fenugreek
This fresh herb has very small leaves and is sold in fragrant bunches at the many street markets. It is used to flavour meat and vegetarian dishes. The stalks should be discarded as they will impart bitterness to a dish if used. Fenugreek seeds are flat, extremely pungent and slightly bitter.

Fresh coriander (cilantro)
The leaves of this fragrant and pretty plant are used to garnish almost every savoury dish throughout the country, and the stems and leaves are also chopped and added during cooking to impart freshness and their unique flavour.

Bay leaves
Glossy green bay leaves can be used fresh or dried to add flavour to stocks and slow-cooked curries.

Curry leaves
These pungent leaves (kariveppilai) are ubiquitous in the dishes from the south of country, especially in Tamil Nadu. They are available fresh or dried, although the fresh version has a much stronger flavour and is generally the preferred form.

Below *Fresh fenugreek has small leaves but a big flavour. Discard the bitter stalks before use.*

PREPARING FRESH CHILLIES

To produce a milder flavour, you can reduce the amount of chilli used in a dish, and remove the seeds and membrane, as this is where the most potent heat lies. Wear gloves to do this if you have sensitive skin.

1 Cut the chillies in half lengthways. Remove the membranes and seeds.

2 Cut the chilli flesh lengthways into long, thin strips.

3 If required, cut the strips of chilli crossways into tiny dice.

Below *Curry leaves are found in almost every dish in the south of India.*

SPICES

The quantities of spices specified in recipes are measured to achieve a balance of flavours, so it is important that you follow them. Having tried a dish, however, you may prefer to change the quantities according to taste.

Asafoetida

This spice has a powerful aroma and is often used when cooking pulses, as it is a digestive aid. It is usually fried in hot oil, which mellows its strong smell and changes its flavour from bitter to onion-like.

Cardamom, cinnamon and cloves

These three sweetish spices have been an integral part of Indian cooking since ancient times, and they appear over and over again in any number of dishes. They are also used

Above *Whole spices are widely available at markets, and are ground at home.*

in the north to make an infusion that raises the body temperature, which is ideal in the cold winter climate.

Cardamom is native to India, where it is considered to be the most prized spice after saffron. The pods can be used whole or the husks can be removed to release the seeds, which have a slightly pungent, aromatic taste. Southern Indians use ground cardamom in sweetmeats and desserts, while northerners are passionate about its heady aroma in many chicken dishes, pilaus and biryanis.

Cinnamon is usually used in its bark form, rather than ground, and cloves are also normally left whole, so you may choose to remove them prior to serving, although this is not strictly necessary.

GARAM MASALA

Makes about 90g/3oz
15g/½oz brown cardamom seeds
15g/½oz whole green cardamom pods
15g/½oz cinnamon sticks
10 cloves
7g/¼oz black peppercorns
1 whole nutmeg, lightly crushed
1 mace blade

1 Preheat a small, heavy frying pan over a low–medium heat and add all of the spices. Dry roast them for 30–40 seconds, when they will release their aroma. Immediately remove the pan from the heat.

2 Transfer the spices to a plate to stop them roasting further. Let them cool completely, then grind in a coffee grinder or with a mortar and pestle until fine.

3 Store in an airtight container away from direct light. It will keep well for 3–4 months.

WHOLE SPICES OR GROUND?

Whole spices have a much longer shelf life than ground ones, and can be prepared in small quantities as and when required, so they are generally preferable. However, ground spices, stored correctly, will also produce good flavours and aromas for a limited time; once the spices have been ground the essential oils in them start to dry up quite rapidly. To prevent this happening, store ground spices in airtight containers away from direct light. Home-ground whole spices will also keep well for several weeks if they are stored in this way. You can enhance the flavours of slightly stale spices by heating them gently in a pan before using them.

Above *Yellow and black mustard seeds, along with mustard oil, are widely used in Indian food.*

Above *Nutmeg and mace are from the same plant and feature in north Indian cuisine.*

DRY-ROASTING SPICES

Dry spices, ground or whole, should be gently sizzled over a very low heat so that they do not burn, as this would make the dish bitter. It is crucial not to rush this process as the raw smell of the spices must be eliminated in order to achieve a fragrant, well-rounded flavour.

Aniseed

These liquorice-flavoured seeds are used in many fried and deep-fried Indian dishes as an aid to digestion.

Coriander and cumin

These two spices appear in almost every savoury dish in India. Dried coriander seeds are pale and round, and have a sweet, mellow flavour, while white cumin seeds are oval, ridged and greenish-brown in colour. They have a strong aroma and flavour and can be used whole or ground. Ready-ground cumin powder is available, but it should be bought in small quantities as it loses its flavour rapidly. Black cumin seeds are dark and aromatic and are one of the ingredients used to make garam masala.

Fennel seeds

These are similar in appearance to cumin seeds, have a sweet taste and are used to flavour curries. Fennel seeds can also be chewed as a mouth-freshener after a meal.

Mustard seeds

These are another essential ingredient in Indian cooking, especially in vegetarian dishes. In the south, jet-black mustard seeds adorn yogurt as a dressing for all kinds of salads. On the other hand, the creamy-yellow variety is used to make curries as well as the majority of pickles.

Onion seeds

Black, triangular shaped and aromatic, onion seeds (kalonji) are used in pickles and to flavour vegetable curries and lentil dishes, as well as on top of Peshwari naan.

Nigella

This spice has a sharp, tingling taste and is mainly used to add flavour to vegetable dishes. They are often referred to as onion seeds as they are similar in appearance.

Nutmeg and mace

The nutmeg plant is unique as it produces two spices in one: nutmeg and mace. These are both highly aromatic and are used extensively in northern Indian cuisine. Ground mace, along with cardamom, gives a distinctive flavour to poultry dishes.

Saffron

This is used in both sweet and savoury dishes, and is known to have medicinal values such as curing skin and stomach disorders. The stigmas of the saffron crocus flower are hand picked and sun-dried, and they are so light that it takes about 500,000 dried stigmas to make 450g (1lb) of saffron. A few strands soaked in milk or water add an exotic taste and appearance to any dish.

Star anise

The fruit of the Chinese evergreen magnolia tree, star anise is an eight-pointed liquorice-flavoured pod that adds a warm and pungent note to curries all over India.

Turmeric

The rich golden hue of turmeric has a bitter taste that disappears when it is blended with other ingredients. It is highly antiseptic, with exceptional preserving qualities. Fish is often sprinkled with turmeric and salt if it cannot be cooked on the same day as it is bought. It stains, so be careful when using it!

OTHER FLAVOURINGS

Often termed 'wet spices', the main trio of flavourings in Indian cooking undoubtedly consists of ginger, onion and garlic, which appear in almost every dish. Salt is also key and plays a vital role in developing and blending flavours. The addition of sweet and sour notes lends an extra dimension to many curries, and these are usually imparted by the judicious use of palm sugar (jaggery), dry mango powder and tamarind.

Garlic, ginger and onion

These three aromatics are often the key elements in Indian food. Garlic and ginger are standard ingredients in most curries, and they are generally pulped, crushed or chopped. In the north, the trio are often used as an all-in-one paste, or onions are boiled and puréed before being cooked with ginger, garlic and dry spices. Browned onion purée, used in conjunction with the other two ingredients, creates a distinctive flavour.

Above *The most commonly used ingredients in Indian cooking are onion, garlic and ginger.*

PULPING GARLIC

Fresh garlic is used so often in Indian cooking that you may find it more practical to prepare garlic in bulk and store it until needed.

Separate the garlic bulb into cloves and peel off the papery skin. Process the whole cloves in a food processor until smooth. Freeze the garlic pulp in ice-cube trays used specially for the purpose. Put 5ml/1 tsp in each compartment, freeze, remove from the tray and store in the freezer in a sealed freezerproof bag. Alternatively, store the pulp in an airtight container in the refrigerator for 3–4 weeks.

Salt
This essential ingredient is always added at the beginning of or during the cooking process rather than at the end, except in lentil dishes, where the addition of salt too early would cause the lentils (except red split ones) to become tough. Although the quantity of salt used in Indian cooking may seem excessive at times, it is treated almost as a spice and is vital for balancing the other flavours in a dish. In dry spiced vegetable dishes salt is added at the very beginning, which helps to release the juices from the vegetables and create the necessary liquid for cooking.

Palm sugar (jaggery)
Available as blocks of solidified sugar or in paste form, this distinctive sugar is used as a sweetener in savoury dishes and desserts. It is made from the concentrated juice that is extracted either from sugarcane or palm trees, with that made from the date palm being the most highly prized as it has a better flavour. Soft dark brown sugar can be used as an adequate substitute.

Dry mango powder
Mangoes are indigenous to India, and they have many uses in Indian cooking. The fruit is used in curries at different stages of ripeness, but the unripe fruit is also sun-dried and ground into a dry powder called amchur. The powder has a sour taste, and is sprinkled over dishes as a garnish; it is not used in cooking.

Tamarind
Dried black tamarind pods are sour in taste and very sticky. Tamarind can be bought in paste form, but lemon juice can be used as a substitute.

PREPARING COMPRESSED TAMARIND

Most Asian food stores and supermarkets sell compressed tamarind in a solid block, and in this form it looks rather like a packet of dried dates.

1 To prepare compressed tamarind, tear off a piece that is roughly equivalent to 15ml/1 tbsp. Put the tamarind in a jug (pitcher) and add 150ml/ ¼ pint/⅔ cup warm water. Leave to soak for 10 minutes.

2 Swirl the tamarind around with your fingers so that the pulp is released from the seeds. Using a nylon sieve, strain the juice into a bowl.

3 Discard the contents of the sieve, and use the liquid as required.

4 Store any leftover tamarind juice in the refrigerator for up to 2 weeks, for use in another recipe.

Above Palm sugar (jaggery) has a molasses-like flavour and is available in block or paste form.

FRYING ONIONS

- It is important to fry onions for the correct time and at the right temperature when making a curry. They should usually be fried over a gentle heat and allowed to become soft and translucent before adding other ingredients. Browned onions are used mainly for garnishing and in a few curries.
- Do not to be tempted to add more oil than stated in the recipe, even if the oil seems to disappear. This is caused by the moisture content released by the onion when it starts cooking, and once this moisture has evaporated the oil will be visible again. When this happens it is time to add the spices.
- For best results, stir the onion and spices regularly so that they cook evenly. Once the dry spices are added, a little water is often sprinkled over in order to stop the spices sticking. If the recipe calls for tomatoes, these add moisture, but you may still need to add water, depending on the technique used.

Accompaniments

There is a vast range of salads, chutneys and raitas on offer in India, and they vary tremendously from one region to another, depending on what ingredients are available locally. Chutneys are used as a way of preserving ingredients for the months when fresh produce is not available, but they have the added benefit of being extremely tasty. Usually served alongside main dishes, all these tempting accompaniments are eaten in small quantities to add zest, as well as being used as flavoursome garnishes and dips.

An Indian meal would not be complete without several small bowls of assorted accompaniments, which enable diners to mix and match and create different flavour sensations with every mouthful. Often served at the start of the meal with poppadums in Indian restaurants in the West, they should also accompany the main dishes and be almost like additional seasonings.

RAITAS
Originating in northern India, raita always consists of a yogurt base to which grated or finely chopped vegetables are added. In southern India, *pachadi* is flavoured with whole spices such as mustard and cumin seeds, curry leaves and chillies, which are added to a small quantity of hot oil and incorporated into the yogurt mixture. In northern India the spicing is different, comprising a fiery combination of crushed black pepper, roasted cumin seeds and chilli powder. In the state of Maharashtra in western India the flavourings are different again, and *koshimbir* generally contains lemon juice, fresh green chillies, chopped onion and coriander (cilantro) leaves. Raita is also occasionally made with fruit, such as banana, in place of the cucumber.

SALADS
Served hot or cold, as an accompaniment or as the star of the show, Indian salads are an important element of many meals. Often consisting of simple mixtures of vegetables such as carrots, they add a lightness and crunch to contrast with the softer textures of rice and curries. More robust versions made with beans, peas and lentils are also popular, and these are usually liberally doused with a spicy dressing and served as a main course.

GARNISHES
Fresh coriander (cilantro) is the most commonly used garnish in Indian cooking, and its bright green leaves and fresh flavour provide a visual and taste sensation. Parsley and mint are also sometimes used. Finely chopped fried onions give a crispy topping to rice dishes, while wedges of lemon or lime are served with many fish dishes, to be squeezed over by the diner. Slivers of raw chilli add a vibrant, fiery note to spicy dishes, and this can be offset by a spoonful

Below *Salads and raitas can be made from many different ingredients, depending on what is available locally and what is in season.*

Above *A great way of preserving ingredients, chutney makes a delicious accompaniment.*

of raita or plain yogurt. Toasted slivers of coconut or nuts such as flaked (sliced) almonds can be scattered over both sweet and savoury dishes, including the much-loved rice puddings.

PRESERVES
A ubiquitous element of an Indian meal, chutneys, or *chatnis*, originally evolved during the British Raj in the days before refrigeration, as a means of preserving fresh foods that were slightly past their best. Cooked with vinegar and sugar, the fruit and vegetable mixtures are then flavoured with a huge range of spices to create myriad different variations. Pickles were created for similar reasons, although in this instance only seasonal produce in peak condition is used. In the summer, seasonal fruits and vegetables are also dried in the sun and made into leathers for use during the colder months.

Chutney
There are two categories of chutney: fresh and cooked. In India, fresh chutneys are made in small quantities and consumed there and then, as they do not keep well. Made daily, the ingredients, such as

LIME PICKLE

Makes about 900g/2lb/4 cups
10–12 limes
15ml/1 tbsp salt
120ml/4fl oz/½ cup malt vinegar
250ml/8fl oz/1 cup vegetable oil
5ml/1 tsp asafoetida
10–12 garlic cloves, crushed
2.5cm/1in piece of fresh root ginger,
  grated or minced (ground)
10–12 curry leaves
30ml/2 tbsp black mustard seeds,
  finely ground
15ml/1 tbsp cumin seeds, finely ground
10ml/2 tsp fenugreek seeds, finely ground
10ml/2 tsp ground turmeric
10ml/2 tsp chilli powder
10 green chillies, halved
20ml/4 tsp salt
20ml/4 tsp sugar

1 Wash the limes and dry them thoroughly with a cloth. Trim them, then cut them into quarters. Sprinkle the quarters with the salt and put them in a colander, placed over a bowl. Set aside for 2 hours, then transfer them to another bowl and add the vinegar. Stir until any remaining salt is dissolved and drain in the colander again.

2 Heat the oil in a pan over a medium heat and add the asafoetida, followed by the garlic, ginger and curry leaves. Allow them to brown in the pan slightly.

3 Add the ground seeds, turmeric and chilli powder, and stir-fry for 1 minute, then add the chillies, salt and sugar. Stir-fry for 1 minute more, then add the limes. Remove the pan from the heat and allow to cool completely.

4 Store the lime pickle in sterilized, airtight jars. To enjoy it at its best, leave the pickle in the jar for 4–5 weeks to mature before eating. The pickle will keep for about 10–12 months.

Per portion Energy 120kcal/492kJ; Protein 0.1g; Carbohydrate 0.3g, of which sugars 0.2g; Fat 13.1g, of which saturates 1.6g; Cholesterol 0mg; Calcium 9mg; Fibre 0.1g; Sodium 436mg.

---

peanuts, cashew nuts, dried peas, fresh herbs, chillies, ginger and garlic, are ground in a traditional grinding stone, which produces a fine texture and blends the flavours. A mortar and pestle can also be used.

Cooked chutneys are made from seasonal fruits and vegetables such as raw and ripe mangoes, pineapples, plums and tomatoes. In addition to the traditional method of cooking the ingredients with vinegar and sugar, there is another type of cooked chutney which is made by dry-roasting certain types of lentils and dried peas and mixing these with selected spices.

Pickles

Comprising small chunks of fruits and vegetables cooked in oil with spices such as asafoetida, chilli powder, turmeric and an ample amount of salt, pickles are usually prepared in the summer, when the ingredients are at their best. Ones made with mangoes and limes are very common, although they can be made with a huge range of produce – from carrots, onions and tomatoes to rose petals, jackfruit and Indian gooseberries. The flavour of the condiments is affected by the choice of spices as well as the type of oil used, with mustard oil being the preference in the north and sesame oil more often used in the south. Meat and fish are also pickled in brine with in some regions.

ROASTED TOMATO CHUTNEY

Serves 4
350g/12oz ripe tomatoes
15ml/1 tbsp sunflower or light olive oil
1 onion, chopped
2 large cloves of garlic, chopped
2 green chillies, chopped
  deseeded if preferred)
1 fresh red chilli, chopped
  (deseeded if preferred)
10ml/2 tsp ground cumin
5ml/1 tsp salt
15ml/1 tbsp sugar, or to taste
15ml/1 tbsp roughly chopped fresh
  coriander (cilantro)

1 Preheat the grill (broiler) to high and line the grill pan with foil.

2 Make a slit on each tomato with a sharp knife, then place under the grill until the skin is blistered and peeling.

3 Remove from under the grill and allow to cool. Peel away the skins using your fingers and roughly chop the tomatoes.

4 Heat the oil in a heavy pan over a medium heat and fry the onion and garlic, stirring constantly, for 3–4 minutes. Add the chillies and cumin and cook for 30–40 seconds.

5 Purée the tomatoes, the onion mixture, salt, sugar and coriander in a blender.

6 Transfer to a serving dish and serve.

Per portion Energy 80kcal/337kJ; Protein 2g; Carbohydrate 10g, of which sugars 9g; Fat 4g, of which saturates 1g; Cholesterol 0mg; Calcium 35mg; Fibre 1.5g; Sodium 504mg.

North India

Drawing on a wealth of locally grown produce as well as a long heritage of immigration and external influences, north Indian cuisine features a dazzling array of hearty yet healthy dishes. From satisfying noodle soups and crispy corn fritters to marinated fish, succulent meat dishes and refreshing iced *Kulfi*, these distinctive recipes showcase the very best of Indian cooking, melding fresh ingredients with centuries of culinary skills.

North India

The Himalayas dominate the states of north India, from Kashmir in the north west to Uttar Pradesh in the south east of the region. All of the 14 highest peaks in the world can be found here, including Mount Everest, and with precipitous slopes and changeable weather it is no wonder that the food in the northern region is very different from that of the hot, ocean-bathed south. Main dishes often use lamb, goat, chicken, or delicate river fish such as rainbow trout, and there is an abundance of fruit and vegetables.

JAMMU AND KASHMIR

In this stunning, northernmost region of India, the brightly dressed women tend floating gardens full of vegetables and fruit that flourish around the lakes in the pleasant warmth of summer. In the autumn, trees are laden with plums, peaches, cherries, almonds and walnuts, and these are dried and stored for the bitterly cold winter months. The rivers and lakes offer their own bounty, including lotus roots and snow trout, both of which are local delicacies. Arguably the most important ingredient grown in Kashmir is saffron – the crocus flower from which it is produced grows in large quantities in the cool northern fields.

The rich supply of good quality ingredients leads to all sorts of splendid traditions, including that of the Kashmiri banquet. These enormous feasts consist of many courses, most of them containing meat, each served on large platters that are shared among the entire community. The dishes are skilfully prepared by chefs known as *wazwans*, who carefully blend generous amounts of spices such as aniseed, cinnamon and cardamom to produce

Above *Oxen are used on the terraced Himalayan rice paddies in Himachal Pradesh.*

delectable treats, including *Rogan Josh*, *Tabakmaaz* (spiced lamb chops) and several variety of meatballs.

Kashmiri chefs have a unique tradition of shaping ground spices into discs, from which small amounts can be broken off and added to dishes as required. The spicing is different in Hindu and Muslim cooking, with Hindus favouring asafoetida, fenugreek, ginger and fennel and Muslims favouring onion and garlic. Both groups, however, use Kashmiri chillies, which lend an intense colour without being overly pungent.

HIMACHAL PRADESH

Just south of Kashmir, Himachal Pradesh, 'the mountain state', is a stunning mosaic of dense forests, snow-clad peaks and lush,

Left *Many crops, including (bell) peppers, grow in the mountain state of Himachal Pradesh.*

green valleys. Spiky pines and verdant, broad-leafed trees cling to the lower slopes of the precipitous mountains, while gently meandering rivers and serene lakes create a beautiful panorama.

Agriculture is the main source of income in Himachal Pradesh and wheat, maize, barley and rice are grown in abundance where the terrain flattens out below the Himalayan foothills. Trout fishing is a major sport in the state, and both rainbow and brown trout are available in the rivers and lakes of Kullu valley.

The food in this state is not dissimilar to that found in other parts of north India. Meat features strongly on most menus, and spices such as cardamom, cloves, chillies and cinnamon are used liberally to add

Above *The Kashmiri lakes at the foot of the Himalayas abound with freshwater fish.*

Above *Wheat is harvested and ground to make flour for bread in Himachal Pradesh.*

flavour and character to the dishes. A typical meal in many households will often, as elsewhere in north India, consist of *dal-chawal-subzi-roti*, a lentil broth served with rice, a vegetable curry and bread.

THE PUNJAB

Situated at the foot of the Himalayas, the Punjab is home to Delhi, which was the heart of the Mughal empire and remains one of the most important cities in India. The name 'Punjab' is derived from two Persian words *Panj* and *Aab*, the former meaning 'five' and the latter 'water' or 'river'; the state is rich in natural resources as well as in superb architecture. Primarily an agrarian state, agriculture is the focal point of the economy. The main crops are wheat and maize, and the state is popularly known as the 'granary of the nation'.

As elsewhere in northern India, the region has long been influenced by invaders, pilgrims and traders from north of the mountains, who made their way across the Himalayas centuries ago, aiming to subdue and rule the native people and to make use of their agricultural land. They brought some of their own traditions of farming and cooking with them. The most succesful of the invaders were the Mughal lords, who rode through the Khyber Pass in 1526 and

imposed their rule on almost the whole of India for 200 years. Their legacy is the popular tradition of Mughal cuisine, with its silky sauces and the fragrance of saffron, as well as many monuments and tombs.

The Punjab is also famous for its tandoori cooking. The *tandoor* is a barrel-shaped clay oven that it is believed to have originated in Egypt. Charcoal is used to fuel the *tandoor* and the food is usually cooked on a spit as a kebab. The combination of clay and charcoal produces a fierce heat – usually around 400°C/750°F – which seals the outer surface of the marinated meat or poultry instantly, locking in flavour and keeping the inside moist and succulent. The temperature is then lowered for the remainder of the cooking time, and the result is meltingly tender and flavoursome kebabs. Naans are also cooked in the tandoor, and these breads make the ideal accompaniment to any number of kebabs and spicy meat curries.

As elsewhere in the north, Mughlai food features prominently on the menus, especially in Delhi, which is often called the gastronomic heart of India as it is such an eclectic mixture of cultures and cuisines. Among the many dishes on offer are kormas, pasandas, pulaos and biryanis and, of course, kebabs cooked in the tandoor. Mughal-influenced rich *shorbas* (soups) and *Kulfi*, the popular Indian iced dessert, are also of Mughal origin.

UTTAR PRADESH

Lying in close proximity to Nepal, Uttar Pradesh is home to the oldest city in the world, Benares (or Varanasi), through which flows the Ganges, India's holy river. The land is very fertile and the state is India's largest producer of oil seeds and food grains, including wheat, barley, maize and sugarcane, as well as some of the best basmati rice in the country. As such it is an important area in economic terms, and agriculture is the primary source of income for the region.

Over the centuries the state has been influenced by many religions, such as Hinduism, Islam, Jainism and Buddism, and these have all had an impact on the cuisine. Today, the diet of the local population is rich and varied, with lamb and chicken being the most popular meats for those who are permitted to eat it, usually accompanied by rice or bread and a large pot of locally grown vegetables, including mustard greens, corn, spinach and tomatoes, and split peas or lentils.

Dairy products, such as milk, ghee, paneer (Indian cheese) and yogurt supply much of the protein in the diet, which is especially important for the vegetarians, and these also feature in the many delicious desserts on offer.

Noodle soup with minced meat and vegetables

From the Himalayan region of northern India, where meat features strongly on most menus, this hearty soup, *Thukpa*, makes an all-in-one meal that is perfect for keeping out the cold on chilly winter days. Serve as a main dish with hot, crusty bread, or in smaller portions as a tasty first course.

SERVES 4

30ml/2 tbsp sunflower oil
1 large onion, finely chopped
500g/1¼lb/2 cups lean minced (ground)
   pork, beef or chicken
5cm/2in piece fresh root ginger, grated
4 cloves garlic, finely chopped
2–3 green chillies, finely chopped
   (deseeded if preferred)
2 vegetable stock (bouillon) cubes
115g/4oz/¾ cup carrots, diced
115g/4oz/¾ cup green beans, cut into
   1cm/½in pieces
salt and pepper, to taste
15ml/1 tbsp chopped coriander (cilantro)
300g/11oz/2½ cups egg noodles, to serve
15ml/1 tbsp olive oil
1 fresh red chilli, deseeded and cut into
   julienne strips, to garnish

1 Heat the sunflower oil in a wok over a medium heat and add the onion. Fry for about 8–9 minutes or until the onion turns golden brown, stirring regularly.

2 Add the pork, ginger, garlic and chillies. Increase the heat to high and cook for 10–12 minutes, stirring often.

3 Pour in 2 litres/3½ pints/8 cups warm water and add the stock cubes. Bring to the boil and stir until the cubes are dissolved. Add the carrots and cook for 5 minutes.

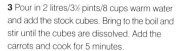

4 Add the green beans and salt to taste. Cook for 5–6 minutes longer, then sprinkle in the chopped coriander and stir. Remove the wok from the heat.

5 Cook the noodles according to the packet instructions, then drain and rinse in cold water.

6 Season the noodles with salt and pepper and add the oil to prevent them sticking. Place the noodles in serving bowls, ladle over the soup and garnish with chilli strips.

COOK'S TIP

In the Himalayas, yak meat is widely used but minced (ground) pork, beef or chicken is more common elsewhere.

Per portion Energy 614kcal/2579kJ; Protein 38.4g; Carbohydrate 64.8g, of which sugars 9.7g; Fat 24.2g, of which saturates 7.7g; Cholesterol 92.5mg; Calcium 75.5mg; Fibre 4.85g; Sodium 362.5mg.

Baby corn fritters

Corn is grown extensively in the state of the Punjab and is used in many different ways in local cooking. Made from whole baby corn, these fritters, *Makki Ke Pakore*, can accompany a wide selection of dishes. With their bite of Indian spices and chillies, they also make a mouthwatering snack to serve with afternoon drinks.

SERVES 8
175g/6oz/1½ cups gram flour (besan)
pinch of bicarbonate of soda (baking soda)
5ml/1 tsp salt, or to taste
5ml/1 tsp crushed dried red chillies
5ml/1 tsp nigella seeds
2.5ml/½ tsp fennel seeds
2.5ml/½ tsp cumin seeds
2.5ml/½ tsp ground turmeric
5ml/1 tsp ground cumin
sunflower oil, for deep-frying
225g/8oz/1⅓ cups whole baby corn
chutney, to serve (optional)

1 In a bowl, mix all the dry ingredients together and gradually add 200ml/7fl oz/ ¾ cup water to form a thick paste of a consistency that will stick to the corn.

2 Heat the oil over a medium heat in a wok or other suitable pan for deep-frying. When the surface of the oil takes on a faint shimmer of rising smoke, dip each baby corn into the batter and shake off any excess mixture.

3 Fry the corn fritters in a single layer, without overcrowding them in the pan, for about 7–8 minutes, until they are crisp and golden brown. Lift them out of the pan using a slotted spoon and drain the corn fritters on kitchen paper.

4 Serve the fritters immediately with mango or other chutney if you wish, although they also taste delicious enough to be eaten on their own. They taste especially good when served with a glass of cold beer or chilled white wine.

VARIATION
You could use many different ingredients to make these fritters, including wedges of (bell) pepper, strips of courgette (zucchini), grated onion mixed with the batter, chunks of banana or plantain, or even slices of paneer or halloumi.

Per portion Energy 222kcal/928kJ; Protein 6g; Carbohydrate 22.3g, of which sugars 1.1g; Fat 12.9g, of which saturates 1.6g; Cholesterol 0mg; Calcium 29mg; Fibre 3.2g; Sodium 431mg.

Bread fritters

Sold by street vendors everywhere in north India, these little bread fritters, *Double Roti Ke Pakore*, are an ideal way to liven up stale bread and are absolutely irresistible eaten hot, straight from the pan. Store-bought sauces are used in this recipe to make a quick and easy snack or appetizer, but you can vary the fillings.

MAKES 12

45ml/3 tbsp chilli sauce
5ml/1 tsp mint sauce
15ml/1 tbsp mango chutney, mashed to
   a pulp
6 large slices of slightly stale white bread,
   crusts removed
115g/4oz/1 cup gram flour (besan)
2 fresh green chillies, finely chopped
   (deseeded if preferred)
30ml/2 tbsp fresh coriander (cilantro)
   leaves, chopped
5ml/1 tsp fennel seeds
7.5ml/1½ tsp garam masala
2.5ml/½ tsp ground turmeric
3.75ml/¾ tsp salt, or to taste
sunflower oil, for deep-frying

1 Mix together the chilli sauce, mint sauce and mango chutney in a small bowl.

2 Divide the mixture between three of the slices of bread. Top each slice with the remaining bread to make three sandwiches. Cut each sandwich into four triangles or squares.

3 Mix the remaining ingredients, except the oil, in a large bowl and gradually add 175ml/6fl oz/¾ cup cold water.

4 Stir until you have a thick batter of coating consistency.

5 Heat the oil in a wok or other suitable pan for deep-frying over medium heat. Test that the temperature is right by dropping a tiny (size of a lemon pip) amount of the batter into the oil. If it floats quickly to the surface without browning, then the temperature is just right.

6 Dip one triangle into the batter, using your fingers or two forks. Make sure it is well coated with batter all over, including the edges.

7 Carefully lower the triangle into the hot oil and fry for 3–4 minutes, until crisp and well browned. Lift out using a slotted spoon and drain on kitchen paper.

8 Repeat the dipping and frying with the remaining triangles. Serve immediately.

Per portion Energy 341kcal/1441kJ; Protein 12g; Carbohydrate 53g, of which sugars 9g; Fat 11g, of which saturates 1g; Cholesterol 0mg; Calcium 141mg; Fibre 6.4g; Sodium 1061mg.

Pear and cucumber salad

This is a delicious and unusual salad from across the north Indian border in Nepal. The Nepalese use nothing but salt, lemon juice and pepper to make *Naspati Aur Kheera Ke Salat,* but this version of the recipe includes several other ingredients to create a refreshing accompaniment.

SERVES 4

7.5ml/1½ tsp cumin seeds
3 firm William or Bartlett pears
15ml/1 tbsp lime juice
½ large cucumber
15ml/1 tbsp mayonnaise
30ml/2 tbsp Greek (US strained plain) yogurt
5ml/1 tsp wholegrain mustard
2.5ml/½ tsp salt
5ml/1 tsp sugar
2.5ml/½ tsp chilli powder

1 Preheat a small, heavy pan over a medium heat. Add the cumin seeds and stir for about 1 minute, until they are a shade darker and they release their aroma. Transfer the seeds to a plate and allow to cool.

2 Peel and core the pears, then cut them into bitesize pieces. Put them into a mixing bowl and sprinkle over the lime juice.

3 Halve the cucumber lengthways and scoop out the seeds and pulp.

4 Chop the cucumber into pieces the same size as the pears and mix them together. Crush the roasted cumin seeds with a mortar and pestle or using the back of a wooden spoon.

5 Beat the mayonnaise and yogurt together in a bowl and stir in the mustard, salt, sugar, half the chilli powder and half the crushed cumin seeds.

6 Add the yogurt mixture to the pear and cucumber pieces and mix well. Transfer to a serving dish and sprinkle the remaining chilli powder and crushed cumin on top. Serve immediately.

Per portion Energy 110kcal/459kJ; Protein 2g; Carbohydrate 18g, of which sugars 17g; Fat 4g, of which saturates 1g; Cholesterol 4mg; Calcium 50mg; Fibre 0.3g; Sodium 335mg.

Crushed parsnips in spiced mustard oil

Parsnip is not an Indian ingredient, but the sweet flesh of this root vegetable provides an exciting contrast in flavour when seasoned the north Indian way with pungent mustard oil, and can be used to create delicious variations on classic dishes, including this favourite, *Parsnip Bharta*.

SERVES 4

675g/1½lb parsnips, peeled and cut into
  even dice
salt and ground black pepper
30ml/2 tbsp mustard oil
2.5ml/½ tsp black or brown
  mustard seeds
30ml/2 tbsp finely chopped red onion
1 fresh green chilli, finely chopped
  (deseeded if preferred)
30ml/2 tbsp fresh coriander (cilantro)
  leaves, finely chopped
Plain Boiled Rice and a lentil or paneer
  dish, to serve

1 Put the parsnips into a pan and pour in enough water to cover them. Add a pinch of salt and boil for 7–8 minutes, until tender but firm. Drain in a colander.

2 Heat the oil in a wok or a non-stick frying pan over a high heat, until smoking. Add the mustard seeds and immediately add the parsnips and the remaining ingredients. Stir-fry for 3 minutes. Remove from the heat.

3 Lightly mash a few pieces of parsnip with the back of the spoon. Stir everything well, then serve with Plain Boiled Rice, accompanied by a lentil or paneer dish.

VARIATION

If you can't get mustard oil, use vegetable oil and add a dash of English mustard.

COOK'S TIP

Make sure that you heat the oil until it is smoking, because it is at this point that mustard oil mellows and transforms into a deliciously nutty ingredient.

Per portion Energy 182kcal/760kJ; Protein 3g; Carbohydrate 22g, of which sugars 10g; Fat 10g, of which saturates 1g; Cholesterol 0mg; Calcium 78mg; Fibre 7.5g; Sodium 116mg.

Lotus root kebabs

In the Hindu religion, the beautiful lotus flower is synonymous with spiritual awakening. In this Kashmiri recipe, *Nadhru Kababs*, exotic lotus flower roots are lightly mashed and blended with potatoes to create kebabs that are as enticing as they are delectable.

MAKES 12

400g/14oz canned lotus roots, drained
   and rinsed well
350g/12oz boiled potatoes
30ml/2 tbsp sunflower oil or light olive oil
1 small onion, finely chopped
1cm/½in piece of fresh root ginger, grated
1 fresh green chilli, finely chopped
   (deseeded if preferred)
1 fresh red chilli, finely chopped
   (deseeded if preferred)
2.5ml/½ tsp fennel seeds
5ml/1 tsp garam masala
7.5ml/¾ tsp salt, or to taste
30ml/2 tbsp fresh coriander (cilantro)
   leaves, chopped, plus sprigs, to garnish
1 egg, beaten
75g/3oz white poppy seeds
vegetable oil, for shallow-frying
Almond Chutney, to serve

3 Add the fried mixture to the lotus root and potato mixture and stir in the fennel seeds, garam masala, salt and chopped coriander. Mix well, then chill for 35–40 minutes.

4 Divide into 12 equal parts and make flat cakes 1cm/½in thick. Dip each cake in the beaten egg, then roll in the poppy seeds.

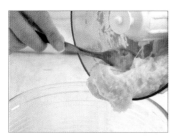

1 Blend the lotus roots and potatoes in a food processor; the potatoes should be smooth, but the lotus roots should still have a rough texture. Transfer the mixture to a bowl.

2 Heat the oil over a medium heat and fry the onion, ginger, and green and red chillies for 3–4 minutes, until the onion is soft.

5 Heat the oil in a frying pan over a medium heat and fry the kebabs for 2 minutes on each side. Garnish with coriander and serve with Almond Chutney.

Per portion Energy 118kcal/491kJ; Protein 2.4g; Carbohydrate 5.5g, of which sugars 1g; Fat 9.8g, of which saturates 1.3g; Cholesterol 16mg; Calcium 63mg; Fibre 1.3g; Sodium 32mg.

Stuffed sweet peppers

Sweet (bell) peppers are grown extensively in the hilly terrain of Kashmir and Shimla, and in India they are known as *pahadi mirch*, meaning 'mountain chillies'. In this recipe, B*harwan Shimla Mirch*, the peppers are stuffed with a mixture of crushed boiled potatoes, cashew nuts and spices. Green (bell) peppers are used, but for a more colourful dish, you can also use red and yellow ones, which will vary the taste.

SERVES 4–6

275g/10oz potatoes
75ml/5 tbsp sunflower oil or light olive oil
2.5ml/½ tsp black mustard seeds
2.5ml/½ tsp cumin seeds
1 large onion, finely chopped
1 fresh green chilli, finely chopped
   (deseeded if preferred)
2.5ml/½ tsp ground turmeric
2.5ml/½ tsp chilli powder
5ml/1 tsp garam masala
50g/2oz/½ cup raw cashew nuts, chopped
5ml/1 tsp salt, or to taste
30ml/2 tbsp fresh coriander (cilantro)
   leaves, finely chopped
15ml/1 tbsp lemon juice
4 medium-sized green (bell) peppers
Roasted Tomato Chutney, to serve

1 Boil the potatoes in their skins (this is important as the potatoes, when mashed, should not be mushy), in a large pan of salted boiling water for 10–12 minutes, or until cooked and soft.

2 Leave the potatoes to cool, then peel. Crush them lightly with a fork or potato masher so that some larger pieces remain.

3 Heat 45ml/3 tbsp of the oil in a frying pan over a medium heat and, when it is quite hot but not smoking, throw in the mustard seeds, followed by the cumin seeds. Let the seeds pop for 10–15 seconds.

4 Add the onion and green chilli. Fry, stirring regularly, for 5–6 minutes, until the onion is soft.

5 Add the turmeric, chilli powder, garam masala and cashew nuts to the pan, cook for 1 minute, then remove from the heat.

6 Add this mixture to the mashed potato, and stir in the salt, chopped coriander and lemon juice. Mix thoroughly and set aside. Preheat the oven to 190°C/375°F/Gas 5.

7 Wash the peppers and slice off the tops. Using a small knife, carefully remove the white pith and the seeds.

VARIATION
You can use the potato filling to stuff other vegetables, such as courgettes (zucchini), marrows (large zucchini) and even tomatoes.

8 Fill the peppers with the potato mixture, pressing the filling down into the cavity. Smooth the surface with the back of a spoon.

9 Heat the remaining 30ml/2 tbsp oil in a pan over a medium heat and add the peppers. Using tongs, turn to coat with oil.

10 Stand the peppers in an ovenproof dish or roasting pan and bake for 25–30 minutes, turning and basting them occasionally. Serve with Roasted Tomato Chutney.

Per portion Energy 224kcal/933kJ; Protein 4.6g; Carbohydrate 20.2g, of which sugars 10.1g; Fat 14.5g, of which saturates 2.2g; Cholesterol 0mg; Calcium 29mg; Fibre 3.1g; Sodium 36mg.

Stuffed baked marrow

This elegant dish, *Lazeez Ghia Mussallam*, is from Lucknow in north India. It involves hollowing out a marrow (large zucchini) and stuffing it with a filling made of paneer, the ubiquitous Indian cheese; the filling is deliciously spiced with onion, fresh root ginger, chilli and fresh coriander (cilantro). When buying marrows, look for ones with skins that are an even green colour with no hint of brown or yellow.

SERVES 4–6

a good pinch of saffron threads, pounded
30ml/2 tbsp hot milk
1 medium marrow (large zucchini)
5ml/1 tsp salt
60ml/4 tbsp sunflower oil or light olive oil
1 large onion, roughly chopped
10ml/2 tsp ginger purée
10ml/2 tsp garlic purée
115g/4oz/½ cup full-fat (whole) natural
  (plain) yogurt
50g/2oz/½ cup roasted cashew nuts
115g/4oz paneer (Indian cheese), grated
2 fresh green chillies, finely chopped
15ml/1 tbsp fresh coriander (cilantro) leaves
  and stalks, finely chopped
30ml/2 tbsp fresh mint leaves, finely
  chopped, or 5ml/1 tsp dried mint
2.5–5ml/½–1 tsp chilli powder
5ml/1 tsp ground coriander
2.5ml/½ tsp garam masala
30ml/2 tbsp tomato purée (paste)
2.5ml/½ tsp sugar
2.5ml/½ tsp salt, or to taste
Indian bread, to serve

1 Put the pounded saffron and the hot milk in a small bowl and set aside.

2 Slice off both ends of the marrow and, using an apple corer or a medium-sized knife with a narrow blade, scoop out the seeds. Do this with a rotating movement. Use a long-handled spoon to scrape out any remaining seeds.

3 Peel the marrow, then prick it all over with a fork and rub in the salt. Place in a colander in the sink and leave to drain.

4 Preheat the oven to 190°C/375°F/Gas 5. Heat half the oil in a large frying pan, add the onion and fry over a medium heat for 4–5 minutes. Add the ginger and garlic and fry for a further 2–3 minutes.

5 Remove the onion, ginger and garlic with a slotted spoon, leaving behind the oil, and put into a blender with the yogurt, saffron-infused milk and the saffron, and the cashew nuts. Blend to form a coarse paste.

6 Transfer half the yogurt paste to a mixing bowl and add the cheese, half the chillies, half the fresh coriander and half the mint. Season to taste and mix thoroughly.

7 Wipe the marrow with kitchen paper and stuff it with the cheese mixture, leaving a 1cm/½in gap at both ends.

8 Add the remaining oil to the pan and heat over a high heat. Add the marrow and brown it on all sides. Transfer to a roasting pan.

9 In the frying pan, cook the chilli powder, coriander and garam masala for 30 seconds, then add the tomato purée and sugar.

10 Cook for 1–2 minutes, then stir in the reserved yogurt paste, the remaining chillies and coriander, the mint, 120ml/4fl oz/½ cup lukewarm water and the salt.

11 Pour the mixture over the marrow and spread it down the sides. Cover the roasting pan with a piece of foil and bake in the centre of the oven for 20–25 minutes.

12 Remove from the oven and allow to rest for 10 minutes. Transfer to a serving dish. Mix the spice paste with the cooking juices and spread it all over the marrow, then carve the marrow into thick slices. Serve with any Indian bread.

Per portion Energy 241kcal/998kJ; Protein 5g; Carbohydrate 10g, of which sugars 8g; Fat 21g, of which saturates 6g; Cholesterol 13mg; Calcium 92mg; Fibre 1.7g; Sodium 236mg.

Potatoes in aromatic yogurt sauce

In Indian cooking, the humble potato is given gourmet status in many different dishes, and *Dum Aloo Kashmiri* is one of the most delicious. Here, whole potatoes are fried before being simmered in a yogurt sauce. The people of Kashmir cook these potatoes in mustard oil, which needs to be heated until smoking hot to reduce its pungency and give the dish a superbly nutty, mellow flavour.

4 Place the pan back over a low heat. Add the chilli powder, followed by 30ml/2 tbsp water. Cook for 1 minute, then add the remaining spices. Cook for a further minute.

5 Add the browned potatoes, salt and yogurt. Cover the pan tightly and reduce the heat to low. Cook for 5–6 minutes, until the sauce thickens and coats the potatoes. Serve with naan or chapatis.

SERVES 4

60ml/4 tbsp mustard oil
700g/1½lb small potatoes, boiled and peeled
2.5–5ml/½–1 tsp chilli powder
2 brown cardamom pods, bruised
4 green cardamom pods, bruised
2.5ml/½ tsp ground ginger
5ml/1 tsp ground coriander
5ml/1 tsp ground fennel
5ml/1 tsp salt, or to taste
150g/5oz/⅔ cup full-fat (whole) natural (plain) yogurt, whisked
naan or chapatis, to serve

1 In a medium-sized pan, heat the oil until smoking, add half the potatoes and fry until they are well browned.

2 Remove from the heat and drain on kitchen paper. Repeat with the remaining potatoes.

3 When they are cool enough to handle, prick the potatoes all over to allow the flavours to penetrate.

Per portion Energy 261kcal/1092kJ; Protein 5.8g; Carbohydrate 33.2g, of which sugars 5.1g; Fat 12.7g, of which saturates 1.8g; Cholesterol 1mg; Calcium 93mg; Fibre 1.8g; Sodium 53mg.

Turnips in cream sauce

This recipe comes from Himachal Pradesh, where, until recently, the only two vegetables used in the local cuisine were potatoes and turnips. The latter play the starring role in this dish, which consists of fried turnips cooked with an array of flavourings and spices and some cream. If you can find them, use small turnips for this recipe, they have a sweeter flavour and work well here.

SERVES 4

675g/1½lb turnips
60ml/4 tbsp sunflower oil or light olive oil
4 green cardamom pods, bruised
1 large onion, finely sliced
10ml/2 tsp ginger purée
10ml/2 tsp garlic purée
1–2 fresh green chillies, finely chopped
  (deseeded if preferred)
10ml/2 tsp ground coriander
2.5ml/½ tsp ground turmeric
2.5ml/½ tsp chilli powder
2.5ml/½ tsp salt
150ml/¼ pint/⅔ cup double (heavy) cream
2.5ml/½ tsp garam masala
Indian bread, to serve

5 Add the ginger, garlic and chillies, and continue to cook for a further 2–3 minutes or until the onion is just beginning to brown. Add the coriander, turmeric and chilli powder and cook, still stirring, for about 1 minute

6 Add the fried turnips and 200ml/7fl oz/ scant 1 cup lukewarm water. Add salt, bring it to the boil, reduce the heat, cover and simmer for 12–15 minutes. Add the cream and cook, uncovered, until thickened. Stir in the garam masala and serve.

1 Peel the turnips and and cut them into bitesize pieces.

2 Heat the sunflower or olive oil in a frying pan over a medium heat.

3 Add the turnip pieces in batches and brown them in the oil. Remove with a slotted spoon, drain on kitchen paper, and set aside.

4 Add the cardamom pods to the remaining oil in the pan and heat, stirring, to allow them to puff up. Add the onion and fry, stirring continuously, for 5–6 minutes, until it is soft but not brown.

Per portion Energy 384kcal/1587kJ; Protein 3g; Carbohydrate 14g, of which sugars 12g; Fat 36g, of which saturates 14g; Cholesterol 51mg; Calcium 127mg; Fibre 5.1g; Sodium 71mg.

Smoked aubergine with ginger

The delicious smoky flavour of aubergine (eggplant) is matched with a few well-chosen whole spices and chillies to create this Punjabi dish, *Baingan Bharta*. Traditionally, the aubergine was cooked on the smouldering ashes of a *tandoor* to enhance the smoky flavour.

SERVES 4

2 large aubergines (eggplants), about
    675g/1½lb
45ml/3 tbsp sunflower oil or light olive oil
2.5ml/½ tsp fennel seeds
1 onion, finely chopped
2.5cm/1in piece of fresh root ginger,
    peeled and finely grated
2–3 large cloves garlic, peeled
    and crushed
2 fresh green chillies, finely chopped
    (deseeded if preferred)
2.5ml/½ tsp ground turmeric
2 fresh tomatoes, skinned and chopped
5ml/1 tsp salt, or to taste
30ml/2 tbsp fresh coriander (cilantro)
    leaves, finely chopped, plus extra sprigs,
    to garnish

4 Cut the aubergines in half. Scrape the flesh into a bowl and mash with a fork.

5 Heat the oil over a medium heat. Add the fennel. Cook for 30 seconds, until browned.

1 Preheat the grill (broiler) to high. Make two lengthways slits on the surface of each aubergine, without cutting through.

2 Rub a little oil on the skins. Place the aubergines on a grill pan and grill (broil) about 15cm/6in below the heat source.

3 Cook for 15–20 minutes, turning them over frequently, until the aubergines are tender and the skin is slightly charred. Remove from the heat and let them cool.

6 Add the onion, ginger, garlic and chillies. Fry for 5–6 minutes, until the onion is soft but not brown, stirring often. Stir in the turmeric.

7 Reserve some of the tomato and add the remainder to the onions. Cook for 4 minutes, stirring, then add the mashed aubergine and salt. Continue to cook for 2–3 minutes.

8 Reserve a few of the coriander leaves and stir the remainder into the aubergine mixture. Serve garnished with the reserved tomatoes and coriander.

Per portion Energy 142kcal/588kJ; Protein 2g; Carbohydrate 7g, of which sugars 6g; Fat 12g, of which saturates 2g;
Cholesterol 0mg; Calcium 32mg; Fibre 3.6g; Sodium 499mg.

Corn on the cob poached in coconut milk

Fresh corn on the cob is used in India to make this northern Indian recipe, *Nariyal-Makki Masala*, but this version of the classic dish uses frozen corn, so it can be made all year round. It is very quick and easy, and makes an ideal light snack or appetizer or can be served as an accompaniment.

SERVES 4

4 fresh or frozen corn on the cob, green skins and any fibres removed if fresh
150ml/5fl oz/½ cup coconut milk
2 dried red chillies, chopped
5ml/1 tsp salt, or to taste
30ml/2 tbsp sunflower oil or light olive oil
2.5ml/½ tsp black mustard seeds
2.5ml/½ tsp cumin seeds
2 fresh green chillies (deseeded if preferred), finely chopped
25ml/1 tbsp fresh coriander (cilantro) leaves, finely chopped
22.5ml/1½ tbsp lemon juice

1 Carefully slice the corn on the cob into 2cm/1in thick rounds using a large sharp knife (*see* Cook's Tip if using frozen corn). You will need to apply quite a bit of pressure to cut through, so take care.

2 Put the rounds into a large pan and add the coconut milk, chillies and salt.

3 Add 90ml/3fl oz water and bring to a slow simmer, then cover and cook for 10 minutes, stirring half way through.

4 Meanwhile, heat the oil in a small pan over a medium heat. When it is hot, but not smoking, add the mustard seeds, followed immediately by the cumin seeds. Let the seeds crackle and pop for 5–10 seconds, then pour them over the corn with the oil.

5 Stir to combine, then add the chopped green chillies, chopped coriander and lemon juice.

6 Stir gently to combine thoroughly, then cook, uncovered, for 3–4 minutes, until all the liquid evaporates and the coconut sauce coats the corn.

7 Remove from the heat, transfer to a serving dish and serve immediately.

COOK'S TIP
Thaw frozen corn on the cob slightly in the microwave to make it easier to slice it into rounds. Check the microwave manufacturer's instructions for times.

VARIATION
You can use frozen corn kernels, but you will need to reduce the cooking time in step 3 to 3 minutes, or the corn will be mushy.

Per portion Energy 164kcal/689kJ; Protein 4.2g; Carbohydrate 20.1g, of which sugars 4g; Fat 8g, of which saturates 1.1g; Cholesterol 0mg; Calcium 19mg; Fibre 2g; Sodium 44mg.

Royal corn curry

Corn is extremely popular in northern India, where the cornfields of Punjab make a wonderful sight as the crops sway in the breeze. In India, fresh corn kernels would be used for this dish, *Shahi Bhutta*, but frozen or canned kernels save time and work equally well when the fresh cobs are not in season.

3 Fry for 8–9 minutes, until the onion is lightly browned, stirring frequently to encourage even cooking.

4 Add the turmeric and ground ingredients. Cook for 1 minute, then add the corn, milk and salt. Simmer for 8–10 minutes, until thickened, stirring occasionally.

5 Stir in the tomatoes and garam masala, and transfer to a serving dish. Serve with bread and/or Saffron-scented Pilau Rice.

SERVES 4

15ml/1 tbsp white poppy seeds
15ml/1 tbsp desiccated (dry unsweetened shredded) coconut
5ml/1 tsp coriander seeds
60ml/4 tbsp sunflower oil or light olive oil
60ml/4 green cardamom pods, bruised
1 large onion, finely chopped
10ml/2 tsp ginger purée
2 fresh green chillies, finely chopped (deseeded if preferred)
2.5ml/½ tsp ground turmeric
450g/1lb/2½ cups frozen corn, thawed and drained, or canned corn, drained and rinsed
225ml/8fl oz/scant 1 cup full-fat (whole) milk
5ml/1 tsp salt, or to taste
110g/4oz tomatoes, skinned and chopped
2.5ml/½ tsp garam masala
bread and/or Saffron-scented Pilau Rice, to serve

1 Grind the poppy seeds, desiccated coconut and coriander seeds in a coffee grinder until fine, then set aside.

2 Heat the oil in a large pan over a low heat and fry the cardamom pods gently for 25–30 seconds, until they puff up, then increase the heat to medium and add the onion, ginger and chillies.

Per portion Energy 368kcal/1539kJ; Protein 7.7g; Carbohydrate 43.6g, of which sugars 21.6g; Fat 19.4g, of which saturates 5.2g; Cholesterol 8mg; Calcium 128mg; Fibre 4.4g; Sodium 343mg.

Vegetable korma

Korma-style cooking was originally used only for meat and poultry dishes, but it proved so popular that vegetarian and fish recipes were created later. Hard to resist, this colourful vegetarian dish, *Subziyon Ka Korma*, is a combination of vegetables coated in almond sauce, spiced with coriander.

SERVES 4

115g/4oz fine green beans, cut into
  5cm/2in pieces
375g/13oz cauliflower, divided into
  1cm/½in florets
115g/4oz carrots, cut into batons
375g/13oz potatoes, boiled in their
  jackets and cooled
50g/2oz blanched almonds, soaked in 150ml/
  5fl oz/⅔ cup boiling water for 20 minutes
60ml/4 tbsp sunflower oil or light olive oil
2 medium onions, finely chopped
2 green chillies, deseeded
10ml/2 tsp ginger purée
15ml/1 tbsp ground coriander
1.25ml/¼ tsp ground turmeric
2.5ml/½ tsp chilli powder
5ml/1 tsp salt, or to taste
2.5ml/½ tsp sugar
120ml/4fl oz/½ cup double (heavy) cream
Plain Boiled Rice, to serve

4 Heat the oil in a heavy pan over a medium heat and add the onions, green chillies and ginger purée. Fry, stirring, for 10–12 minutes until a light brown colour. Add the coriander, turmeric and chilli powder to the onion mixture. Reduce the heat to low and fry for 1 minute.

5 Add the vegetables, salt and sugar. Pour in 150ml/5fl oz/⅔ cup warm water, stir once and then bring to the boil.

6 Reduce the heat to low, add the cream and cook for 2–3 minutes, then serve immediately with some Plain Boiled Rice.

1 Blanch all of the vegetables separately: the beans for 3 minutes, the cauliflower for 3 minutes and the carrots for 5 minutes.

2 Plunge them immediately into cold water to stop the cooking. Cut the cooked potatoes into 2.5cm/1in cubes.

3 Purée the blanched almonds in a blender or food processor with the water in which they were soaked, and set aside.

Per portion Energy 381kcal/1577kJ; Protein 5.1g; Carbohydrate 20.9g, of which sugars 9.9g; Fat 31.4g, of which saturates 19.3g; Cholesterol 78mg; Calcium 95mg; Fibre 3.9g; Sodium 108mg.

Spiced chickpeas with cumin and coriander

The people of Punjab have mastered the art of cooking chickpeas and combining them with a fragrant mixture of spices. This dish, *Chole*, is a true delight and, served garnished with tomato, raw onion, green chilli and mint, makes a sumptuous, balanced and healthy meal.

SERVES 4
60ml/4 tbsp sunflower oil or light olive oil
10ml/2 tsp ginger purée
10ml/2 tsp garlic purée
1 large onion, finely sliced
5ml/1 tsp ground cumin
5ml/1 tsp ground coriander
2.5ml/½ tsp ground turmeric
5ml/1 tsp chilli powder
125g/4oz canned chopped tomatoes,
    with their juice
400g/14oz/3 cups canned chickpeas,
    drained and rinsed
175g/6oz boiled potatoes, cut into
    2.5cm/1in cubes
5ml/1 tsp salt or to taste
5ml/1 tsp sun-dried mango powder
    (amchur), or 22.5ml/1½ tbsp lemon juice
2.5ml/½ tsp garam masala
15ml/1 tbsp fresh coriander (cilantro)
    leaves, finely chopped
15ml/1 tbsp fresh mint leaves, chopped
Deep-fried Leavened Bread or any other
    bread, to serve

To garnish:
1 small tomato, seeded and cut into
    julienne strips
1 small onion, coarsely chopped
1 fresh green chilli, deseeded and cut into
    julienne strips
sprigs of fresh mint

1 Heat the oil over a low heat in a heavy pan and add the ginger and garlic; stir-fry for 30 seconds.

COOK'S TIP
Dried mango powder, or amchur, is made from ground dried unripe mangoes and is used in Indian cooking as a souring agent. It is much sourer than other acidity regulators, such as lemon juice, so far less is required.

2 Add the sliced onion, increase the heat to medium and fry for 6–7 minutes or until the onion is soft and beginning to colour.

3 Add the cumin, coriander, turmeric and chilli powder and stir-fry for 1 minute, then add the tomatoes. Cook for 3–4 minutes or until the oil begins to separate from the spiced tomato mixture.

4 Add the chickpeas, potatoes, salt and 150ml/5fl oz/½ cup warm water. Bring it to the boil and reduce the heat to low. Cover and simmer for 10–12 minutes.

5 Blend the sun-dried mango powder with a little water and add to the chickpeas, or add the lemon juice.

6 Stir in the garam masala, chopped coriander and mint leaves and remove the pan from the heat.

7 Transfer to a serving dish and garnish with the ingredients listed. Serve immediately with Deep-fried Leavened Bread or any other bread.

VARIATION
You could use dried chickpeas instead of canned ones, if preferred. Simply rinse, then soak in cold water overnight. Drain, then simmer in a pan of water for 1–2 hours, until tender, then use in the same way as canned ones.

Per portion Energy 300kcal/1256kJ; Protein 10.1g; Carbohydrate 33.7g, of which sugars 7.5g; Fat 15g, of which saturates 1.8g; Cholesterol 0mg; Calcium 82mg; Fibre 6.2g; Sodium 232mg.

Chickpeas in a spice-laced yogurt sauce

The people of the Himalayan state of Himachal Pradesh are predominantly meat-eaters, but they also have some delicious vegetarian dishes, and *Channa Madra* is one of the most popular. Chickpeas are simmered in yogurt infused with cardamom and cloves, producing a beautifully fragrant sauce.

3 Add the cinnamon, green and brown cardamom, cloves, black pepper, cumin, turmeric and ginger. Stir-fry for 30 seconds.

4 Add the yogurt, increase the heat slightly and cook, stirring regularly, for 4–5 minutes.

5 Add the chickpeas, salt and sugar. Cover the pan and reduce the heat to low. Simmer for 10–12 minutes, then stir in the garam masala and remove from the heat.

6 Transfer to a serving dish, garnish with mint and serve with chapatis or *Phulkas*.

SERVES 4

300g/10oz/1¼ cups full-fat (whole) natural (plain) yogurt
10ml/2 tsp gram flour (besan)
50g/2oz/4 tbsp ghee
1.25ml/¼ tsp Asafoetida
2.5cm/1in piece cinnamon stick
4 green cardamom pods, bruised
2 brown cardamom pods, bruised
4 cloves
2.5ml/½ tsp black pepper, crushed
5ml/1 tsp ground cumin
2.5ml/½ tsp ground turmeric
15ml/1 tsp ginger purée
600g/1¼lb/4 cups canned chickpeas, drained and rinsed
5ml/1 tsp salt, or to taste
3.75ml/¾ tsp sugar
2.5ml/½ tsp garam masala
sprigs of fresh mint, to garnish
chapatis or *Phulkas*, to serve

1 Whisk the yogurt and gram flour together in a bowl, then set aside.

2 Melt the ghee over a low heat and add the Asafoetida.

VARIATION
This recipe uses ghee, but sunflower oil or light olive oil would work too.

Per portion Energy 367kcal/1540kJ; Protein 15.9g; Carbohydrate 34.3g, of which sugars 7.5g; Fat 19.6g, of which saturates 7.7g; Cholesterol 8mg; Calcium 225mg; Fibre 6.2g; Sodium 392mg.

Lentils with spiced butter

North India's most famous lentil dish, *Dhal Makhani*, is made with black lentils, known as urid dhal. They are available in Indian stores and some large supermarkets. No north Indian wedding banquet or special occasion meal is complete without this fragrant and satisfying dish.

SERVES 4

175g/6oz/¾ cup whole black lentils
   (urid dhal)
10ml/2 tsp garlic purée
10ml/2 tsp ginger purée
2.5–5ml/½–1 tsp chilli powder
2–3 whole fresh green chillies
50g/2oz/⅓ cup canned red kidney beans,
   drained and rinsed
30ml/2 tbsp tomato purée (paste)
150g/5oz tomatoes, skinned and chopped
5ml/1 tsp salt, or to taste
2.5ml/½ tsp sugar
50g/2oz/4 tbsp butter
150ml/5fl oz/⅔ cup double (heavy) cream
fine julienne strips of fresh root ginger and
   fresh tomato, to garnish
naan or *Phulkas*, to serve

4 Add the kidney beans, tomato purée, fresh tomatoes, salt and sugar. Stir to combine thoroughly, then cover the pan and simmer for 5–6 minutes.

5 Add the butter and cream, then simmer gently for a further 5 minutes. Serve, garnished with strips of ginger and tomato, accompanied by naan or *Phulkas*.

VARIATION
If you cannot get urid dhal, try split Bengal gram (channa dhal) instead.

---

1 Wash the lentils in several changes of water and soak them for 3–4 hours, or overnight. Drain well and put them into a heavy pan with 600ml/1 pint/2½ cups water.

2 Bring to the boil. Add the garlic, ginger, chilli powder and chillies. Reduce the heat to low, cover and simmer for 30 minutes.

3 Mash about a quarter of the lentils with the back of a spoon in the pan.

Per portion Energy 420kcal/1750kJ; Protein 13g; Carbohydrate 27.9g, of which sugars 4.9g; Fat 31.4g, of which saturates 18.1g; Cholesterol 78mg; Calcium 71mg; Fibre 5.5g; Sodium 184mg.

The five jewels

The word *punj* means 'five' and *ab* is 'river', so Punjab – where this delicious vegetarian dish originates – literally translates as 'five rivers'. To mirror this, a combination of five different varieties of lentil are used in this classic recipe, *Dhal Punj Rattani*.

SERVES 4

25g/1oz/⅛ cup whole brown lentils
   (sabut masoor dhal)
25g/1oz/⅛ cup pigeon peas
   (toor or tuvar dhal)
25g/1oz/⅛ cup red split lentils (masoor dhal)
25g/1oz/⅛ cup yellow split gram
   (channa dhal)
25g/1oz/⅛ cup yellow split lentils
   (mung or moong dhal)
45ml/3 tbsp sunflower or light olive oil
5ml/1 tsp cumin seeds
5ml/1 tsp fennel seeds
1 small onion, finely chopped
2.5ml/½ tsp ground turmeric
2.5–5ml/½–1 tsp chilli powder
10ml/2 tsp ground cumin
15ml/1 tbsp ghee or unsalted butter
2–3 dried red chillies
2.5ml/½ tsp garam masala
2 tomatoes, chopped
45ml/3 tbsp whole-milk natural
   (plain) yogurt
5ml/1 tsp salt, or to taste
30ml/2 tbsp roughly chopped fresh
   coriander (cilantro)
Plain Boiled Rice, to serve

1 Put all the lentils in a sieve and rinse under cold running water. Transfer to a bowl, pour over plenty of cold water and leave to soak for 1 hour.

2 Heat the oil in a heavy pan over a medium heat and add the cumin and fennel seeds. Let them crackle for a few seconds, then add the onion. Fry, stirring frequently, until the onion begins to brown. Stir in the turmeric, chilli powder and cumin.

3 Drain the lentils and add them to the pan. Reduce the heat to low and stir-fry for 3–4 minutes. Pour in 900ml/1½ pints/ 3¾ cups boiling water, stir and bring to the boil. Cover with a lid and cook gently for 20–25 minutes.

4 Meanwhile, melt the ghee or butter in a small pan over a medium heat. Add the chillies and cook until blackened in places, then remove from the pan and set aside.

5 Add the garam masala, tomatoes and yogurt to the pan the chillies were in, and cook until the oil separates from the rest of the ingredients.

6 Stir the salt into the lentils and mash about a quarter of them with the back of a spoon to thicken the mixture. Pour the tomato mixture over the cooked lentils, add the coriander and stir.

7 Transfer to a warmed serving dish, garnish with the blackened chillies and serve with Plain Boiled Rice.

Per portion Energy 252kcal/1052kJ; Protein 9g; Carbohydrate 20g, of which sugars 3g; Fat 17g, of which saturates 4g; Cholesterol 12mg; Calcium 92mg; Fibre 2.2g; Sodium 523mg.

Peppers with Indian cheese

Paneer (Indian cheese) has a bland taste, but it absorbs other flavours well and adds protein as well as texture to a dish. In this north Indian recipe, *Shimla Mirch Aur Paneer Ka Salan*, it is combined with the warmth of roasted cumin and sweet red pepper.

SERVES 4

1 large green (bell) pepper
1 large red pepper
7.5ml/1½ tsp cumin seeds
30ml/2 tbsp sunflower oil or light olive oil
3–4 large cloves of garlic, crushed
2.5ml/½ tsp chilli powder
2.5ml/½ tsp salt, or to taste
225g/8oz paneer (Indian cheese), cut into
  2.5cm/1in cubes
30ml/2 tbsp chives, snipped
Indian bread or Plain Boiled Rice, and a
  vegetable curry, to serve

1 Preheat the grill (broiler) to high. Place the peppers on a grill pan and position it 15cm/6in below the heat source. Grill (broil) the peppers for 8–10 minutes, until the skin is charred, turning them over frequently. Put them in a plastic bag until cool.

2 Pull off the skin, deseed the the peppers and remove the pith. Cut the flesh into 2.5cm/1in strips. Reserve any juices.

3 Meanwhile, dry-roast the cumin seeds in a small, heavy pan over a medium heat for 1 minute, until they are a shade darker and release their aroma.

4 Leave the cumin to cool, then crush in a mortar and pestle or with the back of a wooden spoon.

5 Heat the oil over a low heat and fry the garlic for 2 minutes, until it is just beginning to brown. Add the chilli powder, salt and paneer. Stir gently and cook for 2–3 minutes.

6 Add the crushed cumin and the prepared peppers along with any reserved juice. Stir until the peppers are heated through, then stir in the chives. Serve with any bread or Plain Boiled Rice and a vegetable curry.

Per portion Energy 259kcal/1067kJ; Protein 3g; Carbohydrate 5g, of which sugars 4g; Fat 26g, of which saturates 12g;
Cholesterol 36mg; Calcium 58mg; Fibre 1.9g; Sodium 368mg.

Indian cheese with spinach

Paneer (Indian cheese) contains the same amount of protein as meat, making it ideal for a vegetarian diet. The cheese is cut into cubes and sautéed until browned, before it is simmered in the sauce.

SERVES 4

225g/8oz paneer (Indian cheese)
60ml/4 tbsp sunflower oil or olive oil
1 large onion, roughly chopped
25g/1oz fresh root ginger, roughly chopped
4 large garlic cloves, roughly chopped
15ml/1 tbsp dried fenugreek leaves
1–2 fresh red chillies, chopped,
   (deseeded if preferred)
5ml/1 tsp ground cumin
5ml/1 tsp ground coriander
2.5ml/½ tsp chilli powder
2.5ml/½ tsp ground turmeric
150g/5oz canned chopped tomatoes
   with their juice
15ml/1 tbsp tomato purée
275g/10oz/2½ cups fresh spinach, chopped
2.5ml/½ tsp salt, or to taste
45ml/3 tbsp double (heavy) cream
2.5ml/½ tsp garam masala
warm naan, to serve

1 Slice the paneer lengthways into five slices, then cut each slice into 1cm/½in cubes. In a non-stick frying pan, heat 15ml/1 tbsp of the oil over a medium heat and sauté the cubes of paneer until they are browned. Remember to take care as paneer tends to splutter in hot fat. Drain the cheese cubes on kitchen paper and allow to cool slightly.

2 Process the onion, ginger, garlic, fenugreek and chopped red chillies in a food processor or blender until they are very finely chopped and well blended.

3 Heat the remaining oil in a medium pan. Add the puréed ingredients and cook over a medium heat, stirring, for 5–6 minutes, or until the ingredients begin to stick slightly to the bottom of the pan.

4 Reduce the heat to low and add the cumin, coriander, chilli powder and turmeric. Simmer for 30 seconds, then add the tomatoes, and cook over a medium heat, stirring regularly, until the tomatoes are pulpy and the sauce has thickened.

5 Add 30–45ml/2–3 tbsp water and continue to cook for a further 2 minutes. Carefully stir in the tomato purée and the sautéed paneer cubes.

6 Add the spinach and salt. Stir continuously until the leaves have wilted. Reduce the heat to low and cook for 3–4 minutes.

7 Add the cream and garam masala and cook for 2–3 minutes, then remove from the heat. Serve with warm naan.

Per portion Energy 296kcal/1227kJ; Protein 13g; Carbohydrate 15.6g, of which sugars 9.8g; Fat 21.4g, of which saturates 6.4g; Cholesterol 22mg; Calcium 211mg; Fibre 3.3g; Sodium 333mg.

Fillets of fish coated in green spice paste

A delicious paste of fresh coriander (cilantro), tamarind juice, root ginger and chilli is used to marinate the chunks of white fish in this recipe, *Hara Masale Ki Machchi*, creating a refreshing taste. Any white fish may be used – even flaky fish – as it is coated with gram flour before frying, which helps it retain its shape.

2 Process the shallots, ginger, chillies, coriander, tamarind or lemon juice and salt in a food processor or blender. If you are using a blender, add 30–45ml/2–3 tbsp water to prevent the blade from sticking.

3 Add the blended ingredients to the fish and, using a metal spoon, mix gently, but thoroughly. Set aside for about 30 minutes.

4 Add the sifted gram flour to the bowl with 30–45ml/2–3 tbsp water, if necessary, and mix thoroughly until the fish is coated with the paste. You can add a little more water if the paste is not wet enough, to ensure the fish pieces are coated thoroughly.

5 Heat the oil in a wok or other suitable pan for deep-frying over a medium to high heat, then fry the fish in batches for 2½ minutes on each side until they are golden brown.

SERVES 4

675g/1½lb fillet of white fish
2 shallots, roughly chopped
25g/1oz/2 tbsp fresh root ginger, chopped
2–4 green chillies, roughly chopped
15g/½oz/¼ cup fresh coriander (cilantro)
  leaves and stalks, roughly chopped
30ml/1 tbsp tamarind juice or 30ml/2 tbsp
  lemon juice
5ml/1 tsp salt, or to taste
75g/3oz/⅔ cup gram flour (besan), sifted
vegetable oil, for deep-frying
vegetable or lentil dish and Plain Boiled
  Rice, to serve

1 Wash the fish and pat dry with kitchen paper. Cut into 5cm/2in pieces and put them in a large mixing bowl.

6 Drain the deep-fried fish on kitchen paper and serve with any vegetable or lentil dish, accompanied by Plain Boiled Rice.

Per portion Energy 356.8kcal/1490kJ; Protein 35g; Carbohydrate 13.6g, of which sugars 1.6g; Fat 18.3g, of which saturates 2.2g; Cholesterol 80.5mg; Calcium 55.8mg; Fibre 2.6g; Sodium 116.2mg.

Rainbow trout in lemon and mustard marinade

This recipe, *Kullu Trout*, showcases the delectable rainbow trout, which is found in abundance in the rivers of Himachal Pradesh. Whole fish are marinated in a mixture of mustard oil, chilli, lemon juice and rind before being baked. Serve them with basmati rice, and spoon the spicy hot sauce over the top of the fish.

SERVES 4

4 rainbow trout, about 250g/9oz each,
   scaled and gutted

For the marinade:
60ml/4 tbsp mustard oil
5ml/1 tsp salt, or to taste
5ml/1 tsp fennel seeds
2.5ml/½ tsp crushed dried chilli
grated rind and juice of 1 lemon
2.5ml/½ tsp ground turmeric

For the sauce:
30ml/2 tbsp mustard oil
2.5ml/½ tsp mustard seeds
1 medium onion, finely chopped
2.5ml/½ tsp crushed dried chilli
45ml/3 tbsp chopped fresh coriander
   (cilantro) leaves
Plain Boiled Rice, to serve

1 Lay the fish on a flat surface and make three diagonal slits on each side. Put them in a shallow dish.

2 Mix the marinade ingredients together and pour over the fish. Gently rub in the marinade, working it well into the slits. Cover the dish with clear film (plastic wrap) and place in the refrigerator for 1 hour.

3 Preheat the oven to 180°C/350°F/Gas 4. Line a roasting pan with foil and brush it generously with oil. Lay the fish in the roasting pan and cook in the centre of the oven for 20 minutes.

4 For the sauce, heat the oil in a pan over a medium heat. When it is smoking, remove the pan from the heat and add the mustard seeds, then the onion. Fry the mixture for about 5 minutes, stirring often, until the onion is translucent. Do not allow it to brown. Add the crushed dried chilli and cook for 1 minute.

5 Pour in 120ml/4fl oz/½ cup warm water and cook for 2–3 minutes. Transfer the fish to a serving plate.

6 Add the fish juices to the onion mixture, then stir in the chopped coriander and cook for 1 minute. Spoon the sauce over the fish and serve with Plain Boiled Rice.

Per portion Energy 368.8kcal/1542kJ; Protein 40.7g; Carbohydrate 9.1g, of which sugars 5.9g; Fat 19.2g, of which saturates 3g; Cholesterol 160mg; Calcium 114.5mg; Fibre 2g; Sodium 153mg.

Fish in creamy almond sauce

Making a curry with an almond purée is a classic style of cooking that was passed down from the Mughals centuries ago. It is thought that this recipe, *Machchi Badami*, was created for the Mughal Emperor Shah Jahan, who was noted for his love of good food.

SERVES 4

675g/1½lb firm white fish fillets, such as
  tilapia, sole, monkfish or turbot, skinned
  and bones removed
30ml/2 tbsp lemon juice
5ml/1 tsp salt, or to taste
large pinch of saffron, pounded
30ml/2 tbsp hot milk
75g/3oz/¾ cup blanched almonds
25g/1oz unsalted (sweet) butter
30ml/2 tbsp sunflower or light olive oil
4 green cardamom pods, bruised
2 cloves
1 bay leaf
1 large onion, finely chopped
2 cloves garlic, crushed, or 10ml/2 tsp
  garlic purée
2.5cm/1in fresh root ginger, grated,
  or 10ml/2 tsp ginger purée
2.5–5ml/½–1 tsp chilli powder
120ml/4fl oz/½ cup single (light) cream
fine strips of red and green chillies,
  to garnish
Pilau Rice with Raisins, to serve

1 Cut the fish into 5cm/2in pieces. Sprinkle with lemon juice and salt and place in a dish. Cover with clear film (plastic wrap) and chill in the refrigerator for 20 minutes.

2 Crumble the saffron into a bowl and pour over the hot milk.

3 Put the almonds in another bowl and pour over 150ml/¼ pint/⅔ cup boiling water. Leave both to soak for 15–20 minutes.

4 Heat the butter and oil in a heavy frying pan over a low heat until the butter has melted and starts to sizzle.

5 Add the cardamom, cloves and bay leaf to the pan. Cook for about a minute, until the cardamom pods puff up.

6 Add the onion to the pan and increase the heat to medium. Fry until soft but not brown, stirring. Add the garlic and ginger and continue to fry for about a minute.

7 Stir in the chilli powder, then pour in 200ml/7fl oz/scant 1 cup hot water. Stir, then add the fish in a single layer. Reduce the heat to low and cook for 2–3 minutes.

8 Meanwhile, drain the soaked almonds and put them in an electric blender or food processor with the cream. Blend to a smooth purée.

9 Pour the almond purée over the fish, mix gently, and simmer for 3–4 minutes.

10 Remove from the heat and transfer to a warmed serving dish. Garnish with fine strips of red and green chillies, and serve with Pilau Rice with Raisins.

Per portion Energy 546kcal/2275kJ; Protein 37g; Carbohydrate 8g, of which sugars 5g; Fat 41g, of which saturates 16g; Cholesterol 138mg; Calcium 118mg; Fibre 2.3g; Sodium 612mg.

Prawns in chilli-tomato sauce

This easy curry, *Kadhai Jhinga*, has a spicy kick. The sauce is prepared first to allow all the flavours to develop and intermingle, then the prawns are added for the last few minutes.

SERVES 4

60ml/4 tbsp sunflower or light olive oil

5ml/1 tsp fennel seeds

2.5cm/1in piece fresh ginger, cut into
  julienne strips

1 large onion, finely chopped

1 green chilli, chopped (deseeded if
  preferred)

2 garlic cloves, crushed, or 10ml/2 tsp
  garlic purée

5ml/1 tsp ground cumin

7.5ml/1½ tsp ground coriander

2.5ml/½ tsp ground turmeric

2.5–5ml½–1 tsp chilli powder

200g/7oz canned chopped tomatoes

500g/1¼lb peeled raw tiger prawns (jumbo
  shrimp), tail-on and deveined

5ml/1 tsp salt, or to taste

5ml/1 tsp dried fenugreek leaves

2.5ml/½ tsp garam masala

30ml/2 tbsp chopped fresh coriander
  (cilantro)

warm Indian bread and a green salad,
  to serve

1 Heat the oil in a wok or large, heavy frying pan over a medium heat and add the fennel seeds followed by the ginger. Stir-fry for 30 seconds, then add the finely chopped onion and the green chilli. Fry for 3–4 minutes, until the onion is lightly browned, stirring frequently.

2 Add the garlic and fry for a few more seconds. Stir in the cumin, coriander, turmeric and chilli powder.

3 Stir-fry the onion and spice mixture for about 30 seconds, then add the chopped tomatoes to the pan.

4 Stir-fry for about 4–5 minutes or until oil appears on the surface of the spice paste. Add 30ml/2 tbsp water and continue to stir-fry for a further 4–5 minutes until oil floats on the surface again.

5 Add the prawns, salt and fenugreek. Stir-fry for 1 minute, then add 175ml/6fl oz/ ¾ cup hot water. Increase the heat slightly and stir-fry for 3–4 minutes or until the prawns are pink and just cooked through.

6 Stir in the garam masala and chopped coriander. Remove from the heat and serve with warm Indian bread and a green salad.

Per portion Energy 243kcal/1011kJ; Protein 23g; Carbohydrate 2g, of which sugars 2g; Fat 16g, of which saturates 2g; Cholesterol 244mg; Calcium 132mg; Fibre 0.4g; Sodium 759mg

Chicken with stir-fried onions and shallots

This richly spiced, very hot chicken dish, *Murgh Do-piaza*, makes a delectable main course for a light summer dinner, and is delicious when accompanied by basmati rice and fresh vegetable side dishes. The onions are sautéed with the spices and tomatoes, which adds a rich depth of flavour, and then the shallots are browned whole and added right at the end of the cooking time so they retain their shape.

SERVES 4

675g/1½lb skinned chicken thigh or
  breast fillets
juice of ½ a lemon
5ml/1 tsp salt
60ml/4 tbsp sunflower oil or light
  olive oil
2 medium onions, finely chopped
15ml/1 tbsp ginger purée
15ml/1 tbsp garlic purée
7.5ml/1½ tsp ground coriander
5ml/1 tsp ground cumin
5ml/1 tsp ground turmeric
2.5–5ml/½–1 tsp chilli powder
225g/8oz canned chopped tomatoes,
  with their juice
15ml/1 tbsp ghee, or 5ml/1 tsp unsalted
  butter plus 10ml/2 tsp sunflower oil
8–10 small whole shallots
2.5–5ml/½–1 tsp garam masala
15ml/1 tbsp chopped fresh mint or
  5ml/1 tsp dried mint
4–5 whole green chillies
30ml/2 tbsp chopped fresh coriander
  (cilantro) leaves
Plain Boiled Rice, naan and a vegetable
  side dish, such as Mustard Greens with
  Ginger, Chilli and Garlic, to serve

1 Cut the skinned chicken thigh or breast fillets into 5cm/2in pieces and place in a mixing bowl. Add the lemon juice and salt and mix thoroughly.

2 Cover the bowl with clear film (plastic wrap) and set aside in a refrigerator for around 30 minutes, to tenderize the chicken meat.

3 Heat the oil in a medium-sized pan, preferably non-stick. Add the chopped onions, ginger and garlic and fry over a medium heat for 7–8 minutes, until the mixture begins to brown.

4 Add the ground coriander, cumin, turmeric and the chilli powder to the pan and cook gently for about 1 minute.

5 Add the chopped tomatoes. Cook, stirring regularly, until the tomatoes reach a paste-like consistency and the oil rises to the surface.

6 Increase the heat to high and add the chicken pieces. Cook, stirring constantly, for 4–5 minutes or until the chicken becomes white and opaque.

7 Pour in 250ml/8fl oz/1 cup warm water, bring it to the boil, then reduce the heat to low. Cover the pan with a lid and cook for 15–20 minutes, stirring the mixture occasionally to ensure an even flavour.

8 In a separate pan, heat the ghee or butter and oil over a medium heat. Add the shallots and stir-fry until they are lightly browned, then stir in the garam masala.

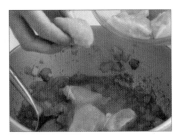

9 Add this to the chicken. Stir over medium heat until the sauce has thickened.

10 Add the mint, chillies and coriander. Stir them in and cook for 1–2 minutes longer. Serve with naan and a vegetable side dish. A light cold beer makes a refreshing accompaniment.

Per portion Energy 401kcal/1678kJ; Protein 42.6g; Carbohydrate 18.2g, of which sugars 10.6g; Fat 18.3g, of which saturates 3.3g; Cholesterol 75mg; Calcium 99mg; Fibre 3.7g; Sodium 143mg.

Chicken in a mint and coriander sauce

Pahadi Murgh is a typical dish of Himachal Pradesh, which is surrounded by lush green fields and valleys. The chicken is marinated in a thick aromatic paste made from fresh herbs and chillies.

SERVES 4

4 green chillies, roughly chopped
   (deseeded if preferred)
25g/1oz fresh coriander (cilantro)
15g/½oz fresh mint
2.5cm/1in fresh root ginger, grated,
   or 10ml/2 tsp ginger purée
2 cloves garlic, crushed, or 10 ml/2 tsp
   garlic purée
juice of 1 lime
5ml/1 tsp salt, or to taste
675g/1½lb chicken thighs, skinned
45ml/3 tbsp mustard oil
5ml/1 tsp fennel seeds
5ml/1 tsp cumin seeds
2.5ml/½ tsp garam masala
warm Indian bread, to serve

1 Put the green chillies, the coriander and the mint in a food processor or blender, add 45ml/3 tbsp cold water and pulse in bursts to form a fairly smooth paste.

2 Transfer the paste to a large mixing bowl. Add the ginger, garlic, lime juice and salt to the paste and stir to combine.

3 Add the chicken thighs, turning to coat in the marinade. Cover the bowl with clear film (plastic wrap) and place in the refrigerator for about 30 minutes.

4 Heat the oil in a large, shallow pan with a lid over a high heat until smoking hot. Turn down the heat to low and add the fennel and cumin seeds, followed by the pieces of marinated chicken.

5 Cook the chicken, turning frequently for 4–5 minutes, until the flesh is opaque. Add any marinade left in the bowl to the pan, stir, cover the pan with a lid and simmer for 30 minutes.

6 Remove the lid from the pan and continue cooking until the sauce is very thick and clings to the pieces of chicken. Stir in the garam masala and serve the chicken with warm Indian bread.

COOK'S TIP

You can use chicken breast fillets instead of thighs, if you wish, but cook them, uncovered, for 10–15 minutes only in step 5.

Per portion Energy 274kcal/1145kJ; Protein 33g; Carbohydrate 1g, of which sugars 00g; Fat 22g, of which saturates 3g; Cholesterol 158mg; Calcium 53mg; Fibre 0.1g; Sodium 633mg.

Chicken tikka

Murgh Tikka is probably one of the best-known Indian dishes. The secret lies in marinating the meat, first briefly in lemon juice and salt, then in a richly spiced yogurt mixture, preferably overnight.

SERVES 4

675g/1½lb skinless chicken breasts,
   cut into 5cm/2in cubes
30ml/2 tbsp lemon juice
5ml/1 tsp salt, or to taste
150ml/¼ pint/⅔ cup Greek (US strained
   plain) yogurt
10ml/2 tsp gram flour (besan) or cornflour
   (cornstarch)
30ml/2 tbsp double (heavy) cream
50g/2oz/½ cup finely grated mild Cheddar
2 cloves garlic, crushed, or 10ml/2 tsp
   garlic purée
2.5cm/1in fresh root ginger, grated,
   or 10ml/2 tsp ginger purée
2.5ml/½ tsp ground turmeric
5ml/1 tsp garam masala
5ml/1 tsp ground cumin
2.5ml/½ tsp chilli powder
10ml/2 tsp clear honey
45ml/3 tbsp sunflower or light olive oil
50g/2oz/¼ cup butter, melted
warm Indian bread, lettuce leaves, sliced
   red onions and wedges of lemon, to serve

1 Put the cubed chicken breasts in a mixing bowl, sprinkle with lemon juice and salt and stir until the chicken is coated. Cover with clear film (plastic wrap) and set aside in the refrigerator for 30–40 minutes.

2 Meanwhile, blend the yogurt, gram flour and cream together in another bowl. Add all the remaining ingredients, except the butter. Mix well.

3 Add the chicken and stir until coated. Cover with clear film and leave to marinate in the refrigerator for at least 2 hours or overnight, if possible.

4 Allow the chicken to come to room temperature. Thread onto eight oiled metal or soaked bamboo skewers (*see* Cook's Tip), leaving a slight gap between each piece and reserving any remaining marinade. Preheat a grill (broiler) to high.

5 Turn the skewers over and brush any remaining marinade over the chicken. Grill (broil) for about 2 minutes, then brush with half the melted butter. Cook for a further 2–3 minutes or until slightly charred.

6 Turn the skewers over and brush them with the remaining butter. Cook for a further 2–3 minutes or until cooked through.

7 Remove the chicken from the skewers. Serve with warm Indian bread and a salad of lettuce and onion, and lemon wedges.

> **COOK'S TIP**
> If using bamboo skewers, soak them in cold water for 30 minutes before threading on the chicken; this will help stop them burning under the grill (broiler).

Per portion Energy 537kcal/2239kJ; Protein 47g; Carbohydrate 7g, of which sugars 5g; Fat 36g, of which saturates 16g; Cholesterol 173mg; Calcium 175mg; Fibre 0.3g; Sodium 793mg.

Chicken in a rich buttercream sauce

One of the most popular dishes in India, *Murgh Makhani*, or 'butter chicken', is an ingenious invention from creative Indian chefs who were seeking a way to reheat tandoori chicken without drying it out. You can use any leftover tandoori chicken, cooked on the bone, or you can make it with freshly cooked chicken, as here.

SERVES 4

For the chicken tikka:
675g/1½lb skinless chicken breast fillets, cut into 5cm/2in cubes
30ml/2 tbsp lemon juice
5ml/1 tsp salt, or to taste
115g/4oz/½ cup Greek (US strained plain) yogurt
15ml/1 tbsp garlic purée
15ml/1 tbsp ginger purée
2.5ml/½ tsp ground turmeric
5ml/1 tsp garam masala
2.5ml/½ tsp chilli powder
10ml/2 tsp gram flour (besan) or cornflour (cornstarch)
5ml/1 tsp sugar
45ml/3 tbsp sunflower oil or light olive oil
50g/2oz/4 tbsp butter, melted

For the sauce:
150g/5oz/10 tbsp unsalted butter
5cm/2in cinnamon stick, broken up
3 cardamom pods, bruised
4 cloves
2 green chillies, roughly chopped
15ml/1 tbsp garlic purée
15ml/1 tbsp ginger purée
400g/14oz canned chopped tomatoes
30ml/2 tbsp tomato purée
10ml/2 tsp sugar
10ml/2 tsp salt
5–10ml/1–2 tsp chilli powder
200ml/7fl oz/¾ cup warm water
10ml/2 tsp dried fenugreek leaves
150ml/5fl oz/½ cup double (heavy) cream
Indian bread or Plain Boiled Rice, to serve

COOK'S TIPS
To get ahead, you can make the sauce in advance and store it in the refrigerator overnight, covered with the clear film (plastic wrap), while the chicken marinates. Then simply reheat when ready to use it.

1 Put the chicken in a mixing bowl. Rub in the lemon juice and salt. Cover with clear film (plastic wrap) and set aside in the refrigerator for 30 minutes.

2 Whisk the yogurt and stir in the remaining tikka ingredients, except the butter. Add to the chicken, then stir until the chicken is evenly coated. Cover with clear film and refrigerate for 2–3 hours or overnight. Bring to room temperature before cooking.

3 Preheat the grill (broiler) to high and lightly brush the skewers with oil. If using bamboo skewers, soak them in water for 30 minutes first to prevent them burning.

4 Thread the chicken pieces on to skewers, reserving the remaining marinade, and place on the grill pan. Cook 7.5cm/3in below the heat source for 5 minutes.

5 Meanwhile, mix the leftover marinade with melted butter. Remove the chicken from the grill and brush with this mixture.

6 Continue to cook for 3–4 minutes, until the chicken is slightly charred. Turn the skewers over and baste the meat with the remaining spiced butter. Cook for 2–3 minutes longer or until charred on the other side. Remove the skewers from the heat and wrap them in foil to keep them hot.

7 To make the sauce, melt half the butter in a pan. Add the whole spices, then the garlic and ginger purées. Cook for 2–3 minutes. Add the remaining ingredients except the cream. Cover and simmer for 20 minutes.

8 Remove from the heat and allow to cool slightly, then purée the ingredients until smooth using a hand blender or by pushing the sauce through a sieve.

9 Return the pan to the heat and then add the remaining butter and the cream. Let the mixture come to a slow simmer, then add the cooked chicken pieces. Simmer for 5–6 minutes, remove from the heat and serve with Indian bread or Plain Boiled Rice.

Per portion Energy 793kcal/3293kJ; Protein 45.8g; Carbohydrate 14.2g, of which sugars 9g; Fat 64.4g, of which saturates 37.1g; Cholesterol 227mg; Calcium 102mg; Fibre 1.2g; Sodium 1491mg.

Chicken with saffron yogurt and cashews

Created for the Empress Mumtaz Mahal, in whose memory the world famous Taj Mahal was built, this rich and elegant dish, *Murgh Mumtaz Mahal*, is typical of Mughal cuisine and makes an aromatic and impressive dish for entertaining. The sauce is based on a silky smooth nut purée, coloured and flavoured with a generous amount of golden saffron and sweetened with fragrant rose water.

SERVES 4

675g/1½lb chicken breasts, skinned and
   cut into 2.5cm/1in cubes
30ml/2 tbsp lemon juice
5ml/1 tsp salt, or to taste
large pinch of saffron, pounded
30ml/2 tbsp hot milk
50g/2oz/¼ cup cashew nuts
60ml/4 tbsp sunflower or light olive oil
15g/½oz fresh root ginger, cut into fine strips
2.5cm/1in piece cinnamon stick, split in half
8 green cardamom pods, bruised
4 cloves
1 large onion, finely sliced
2 cloves garlic, crushed, or 10ml/2 tsp
   garlic purée
2.5ml/½ tsp ground cardamom
2.5ml/½ tsp ground cumin
5ml/1 tsp ground coriander
2.5ml/½ tsp chilli powder
120ml/4fl oz/½ cup natural (plain) yogurt
15ml/1 tbsp rose water
15ml/1 tbsp toasted flaked (sliced)
   almonds, to garnish
Indian bread or Plain Boiled Rice, to serve

1 Put the chicken in a bowl and sprinkle with the lemon juice and salt. Stir, cover and leave to marinate for 30 minutes.

2 Soak the saffron in the milk in a bowl. Put the cashew nuts in a separate bowl and pour over 150ml/¼ pint/⅔ cup boiling water. Leave both to soak for 20 minutes.

3 Heat the oil in a large, heavy pan over a low heat and fry the ginger for 30 seconds, then add the cinnamon, cardamom pods and cloves.

4 Cook for 1 minute, then add the chicken pieces to the pan. Increase the heat to high and stir-fry for 4–5 minutes, until the chicken turns opaque.

5 Remove the chicken and spices with a slotted spoon, leaving behind any oil in the pan. Set aside.

6 Add the onion and garlic to the pan and fry over a medium heat for 6–7 minutes, until the onion is soft. Add the ground cardamom, cumin, coriander and chilli powder and cook, stirring, for 2 minutes.

7 Return the chicken and spices to the pan and pour in 175ml/6fl oz/¾ cup hot water. Bring to the boil, cover and reduce the heat to low. Simmer for 15 minutes.

8 Meanwhile, purée the cashews along with the water in which they were soaked, in a blender or food processor.

9 Add the cashew purée to the pan with the soaked saffron and the yogurt. Stir, then cover and simmer for a further 15 minutes.

10 Remove the lid and cook uncovered for a few minutes to thicken the sauce. Stir in the rose water and remove from the heat. Garnish with toasted almonds and serve with Indian bread or Plain Boiled Rice.

Per portion Energy 448kcal/1871kJ; Protein 46g; Carbohydrate 11g, of which sugars 7g; Fat 25g, of which saturates 4g; Cholesterol 122mg; Calcium 116mg; Fibre 1.4g; Sodium 630mg.

Tandoori chicken

The Punjab is the home of tandoori chicken, *Tandoori Murgh*, one of the most popular dishes in India. Traditionally cooked in a *tandoor* – a bell-shaped clay oven fired by charcoal or wood, which reaches a very high temperature – the chicken is crispy on the outside, yet wonderfully moist within.

SERVES 4

4 chicken joints, skinned
30ml/2 tbsp lemon juice
2.5ml/½ tsp salt
25g/1oz/¼ cup cashew nuts
120ml/4fl oz/½ cup double (heavy) cream
120ml/4fl oz/½ cup Greek (US strained plain) yogurt
1 small onion, roughly chopped
10ml/2 tsp gram flour (besan)
2 garlic cloves, crushed, or 10ml/2 tsp garlic purée
2.5cm/1in fresh root ginger or 10ml/2 tsp ginger purée
2.5–5ml/½–1 tsp chilli powder
2.5ml/½ tsp ground turmeric
5ml/1 tsp garam masala
45ml/3 tbsp sunflower or light olive oil
50g/2oz/¼ cup butter, melted
fresh coriander (cilantro) leaves, to garnish
wedges of lemon, to serve

1 Lightly score the chicken joints all over with a sharp knife.

2 Rub in the lemon juice and salt. Cover with clear film (plastic wrap) and set aside in the refrigerator for 30–40 minutes.

3 Put the cashew nuts in a heatproof bowl and pour over enough boiling water to cover. Leave to soak for 20 minutes.

4 Drain the cashews and put in a blender or food processor with the cream, yogurt, onion and gram flour, and blend to a smooth purée. Pour into a bowl and stir in the remaining ingredients, except the butter.

5 Add the chicken to the marinade, turn to coat all over, cover with clear film and chill for 6 hours or overnight.

COOK'S TIP

This dish is the perfect recipe for a summer barbecue. Make sure that the chicken is completely cooked through before serving.

6 Let the chicken come to room temperature before you start cooking. Preheat the grill (broiler) to high, and line a grill (broiling) pan with a piece of foil. Lightly brush the foil with oil.

7 Lift the chicken out of the marinade and place on the foil, reserving the marinade. Place the grill pan 13cm/5in below the heat source and cook for 10 minutes.

8 Baste the chicken with half the remaining marinade and cook for a further 5 minutes. Brush with half the melted butter and cook until lightly charred in places.

9 Turn the chicken over and cook for 10 minutes. Baste with the remaining marinade and continue to cook for a further 5 minutes. Brush with the remaining butter and cook until lightly charred and cooked through.

10 Lift the chicken on to a serving dish, garnish with coriander and serve with lemon wedges to squeeze over.

Per portion Energy 599kcal/2486kJ; Protein 38g; Carbohydrate 7g, of which sugars 3g; Fat 47g, of which saturates 21g; Cholesterol 204mg; Calcium 84mg; Fibre 0.7g; Sodium 471mg.

Royal-style marinated leg of lamb

Typical of regal cuisine from the time of the 13th-century Mongolian warrior Ghenghis Khan, this recipe, *Nawabi Raan*, is a joy to make – once the meat is marinated, you are free to get on with making the fragrant sauce while it roasts in the oven. The yogurt used in the marinade must be thick.

SERVES 4–6

3kg/6¾lb/10oz leg of lamb
120ml/4fl oz/½ cup red wine vinegar
6.25ml/1¼ tsp salt, or to taste

For the marinade:
50g/2oz/½ cup blanched almonds
pinch of saffron threads, pounded
1 large onion, roughly chopped
5cm/2in piece of fresh root ginger, chopped
4–5 garlic cloves, roughly chopped
75g/3oz/⅓ cup Greek (US strained plain)
   yogurt or thick natural (plain) yogurt
5ml/1 tsp chilli powder
5ml/1 tsp ground cumin
25g/1oz/2 tbsp butter, melted

For the sauce:
15ml/1 tbsp unsalted butter
2.5ml/½ tsp ground cardamom
1.25ml/¼ tsp freshly grated nutmeg
2.5ml/½ tsp ground black pepper
15ml/1 tbsp gram flour (besan)
30ml/2 tbsp brandy
105ml/3½fl oz/7 tbsp double (heavy) cream

For the garnish:
15ml/1 tbsp toasted flaked (sliced) almonds
1 medium red onion, cut into rings
onion rings, sprigs of fresh mint and
   wedges of lime, to garnish

1 Remove any excess fat from the meat. Using a sharp knife, make small, deep incisions on both sides to allow the flavours to penetrate. Rub the vinegar and salt into the meat. Cover with clear film (plastic wrap) and set aside for 1 hour.

2 Place all the marinade ingredients, except the butter, in a food processor, blending until smooth. Pour the marinade over the meat and rub all over the surface, working it well in. Cover with clear film and chill for 6–8 hours or overnight. Bring the meat to room temperature 2 hours before cooking.

3 Preheat the oven to 180°C/350°F/Gas 4. Put the marinated leg of lamb in a deep roasting pan. Scrape off remaining marinade from the dish and spread it over the meat. Pour in enough water to cover up to three-quarters of the meat's depth.

4 Cover the roasting pan with foil and cook in the centre of the oven for 1 hour. Turn the joint over and cook for another hour.

5 Remove the foil and baste the meat with the pan juices. Return the pan to the oven and cook for 6–7 minutes, then baste with the melted butter. Cook for a further 6–8 minutes and remove from oven.

6 Transfer the meat to a serving dish. Allow to stand for 20–30 minutes, then strain the juices and reserve.

7 To make the sauce, melt the butter over a low heat. Add the cardamom, nutmeg and black pepper. Stir once, then pour in the strained juices. Blend the gram flour with a little water to make a pouring consistency. Pour this into the pan and reduce the sauce to the desired thickness. Add the brandy and cream, cook for 3–4 minutes and remove from the heat.

8 Spoon some sauce over the meat and sprinkle toasted almonds over the top. Serve the remaining sauce separately. Garnish the meat with onion rings, sprigs of mint and lime wedges, then serve.

Per portion Energy 661kcal/2746kJ; Protein 56.5g; Carbohydrate 4.1g, of which sugars 1.1g; Fat 46.5g, of which saturates 22g; Cholesterol 242mg; Calcium 66mg; Fibre 0.9g; Sodium 185mg.

Lamb in rich chilli-tomato sauce

One of the most popular lamb dishes in the Kashmir region of India, this sumptuous dish, *Rogan Josh*, makes wonderful festive fare. It has a rich, red colour, achieved by using Kashmiri chilli powder, which is hot but not too pungent. A vegetable dish made with cauliflower would make a fabulous accompaniment.

SERVES 4

675g/1½lb boned leg of lamb, cut into 2.5cm/1in cubes and trimmed of any visible fat
30ml/2 tbsp red wine vinegar
5ml/1 tsp salt, or to taste
50g/2oz/4 tbsp ghee or unsalted butter
30ml/2 tbsp sunflower oil or light olive oil
2.5cm/1in piece of cinnamon stick
2 brown cardamom pods, bruised
5 cloves
1 large onion, finely chopped
10ml/2 tsp ginger purée
10ml/2 tsp garlic purée
7.5ml/1½ tsp ground coriander
10ml/2 tsp ground cumin
5ml/1 tsp ground turmeric
2.5–7.5ml/½–1½ tsp Kashmiri chilli powder (or *see* Variation)
400g/14oz canned chopped tomatoes with their juice
2.5ml/½ tsp ground cardamom
2.5ml/½ tsp ground nutmeg
30ml/2 tbsp roughly chopped fresh coriander (cilantro)
Plain Boiled Rice or warm Indian bread, and Cauliflower and Green Peas in Mustard Oil, to serve

1 Put the meat in a non-metallic bowl and add the vinegar and salt. Rub them well into the meat, cover and set aside for 1 hour.

2 Reserve 15ml/1 tbsp ghee or butter, then heat the remainder with the oil in a large, heavy pan over a low heat. Add the cinnamon, cardamom and cloves, and let them sizzle for about 1 minute.

3 Add the onion to the pan, increase the heat slightly, and cook for 5–6 minutes, until it has softened. Add the ginger and garlic purées and continue to cook, stirring frequently, until the mixture is tinged a light brown colour.

4 Add the ground coriander, cumin and turmeric and the chilli powder and cook for about 1 minute, then add half of the tomatoes. Cook over a medium heat until the tomato juice has evaporated, then add the remaining tomatoes. Continue to cook until the mixture resembles a thick paste and the oil separates out.

5 Add the meat, increase the heat to high, and cook until the lamb changes colour. Add 150ml/5fl oz/⅔ cup warm water and bring the mixture to the boil. Reduce the heat to low, cover with a lid and simmer for 45–50 minutes, stirring occasionally.

6 In a small pan, melt the reserved 15ml/1 tbsp ghee or butter over a low heat and gently fry the cardamom and nutmeg for 25–30 seconds. Pour the spiced butter over the meat and stir in half the chopped coriander. Remove the pan from the heat and garnish with the remaining coriander.

7 Serve with Plain Boiled Rice or warm Indian bread, and a vegetable side dish, such as Cauliflower and Green Peas in Mustard Oil.

> ## VARIATION
> If you can't find Kashmiri chilli powder, add beetroot (beet) juice to standard chilli powder.

Per portion Energy 557kcal/2334kJ; Protein 54.2g; Carbohydrate 20.4g, of which sugars 18.7g; Fat 29.5g, of which saturates 13.5g; Cholesterol 190mg; Calcium 139mg; Fibre 4.6g; Sodium 277mg.

Slow-cooked lamb with turnips

This delectable dish, *Shab Deg*, contains both cubes of tender lamb and minced (ground) lamb combined with spices and made into meatballs. Together with baby turnips and a large amount of ghee, these were traditionally cooked through the night (*shab*) in a sealed pan known as a *deg*. This is a simplified version of the traditional dish, without the ghee, which cooks in less than 3 hours.

SERVES 4

50g/2oz/¼ cup blanched almonds
450g/1lb lean minced (ground) lamb
1 slice day-old white bread, crusts removed
  and torn into small pieces
30ml/2 tbsp double (heavy) cream
25g/1oz/¼ cup grated mild Cheddar
5ml/1 tsp garam masala
30ml/2 tbsp finely chopped mint
30ml/2 tbsp chopped fresh coriander (cilantro)
2 fresh green chillies, chopped
2.5cm/1in fresh root ginger, grated, or
  10ml/2 tsp ginger purée
2 cloves garlic, crushed, or 10ml/2 tsp
  garlic purée
5ml/1 tsp salt, or to taste
60ml/4 tbsp sunflower or light olive oil
450g/1lb baby turnips, peeled
1 large onion, roughly chopped
2.5cm/1in piece of cinnamon stick
6 green cardamom pods, bruised
5 cloves
450g/1lb boned leg of lamb, cut into
  2.5cm/1in cubes
2.5–5ml/½–1 tsp chilli powder
2.5ml/½ tsp ground turmeric
10ml/2 tsp ground cumin
150ml/¼ pint/⅔ cup whole-milk natural
  (plain) yogurt
Indian bread or Plain Boiled Rice, to serve

1 Put the almonds in a heatproof bowl and pour over enough boiling water to cover. Leave to soak for 20 minutes.

2 Meanwhile, put the lamb, bread, cream, cheddar, garam masala, mint, coriander and green chillies into a food processor.

VARIATION
Larger turnips, cut into 4cm/1½in chunks, may be used instead of the whole baby turnips, if preferred.

---

3 Add half the ginger and half the garlic, and add salt to taste. Blend until the mixture is well mixed and fairly smooth. Transfer to a bowl, cover and chill for 30 minutes.

4 Shape the meat mixture into 16 small meatballs with dampened hands, which will help prevent the meatballs from sticking to your hands.

5 Heat 15ml/1 tbsp of the oil in a heavy frying pan over a medium heat and fry the meatballs, turning them frequently, until they are browned all over. Remove the meatballs from the pan with a slotted spoon and set aside.

6 Fry the turnips in the fat and juices left in the pan, turning them until lightly browned. Lift out with a slotted spoon and set aside.

7 Add 15ml/1 tbsp more oil to the pan and fry the onion for about 5 minutes, until softened. Transfer to a blender.

8 Lift the almonds out of the soaking water with a slotted spoon and add to the blender. Measure the soaking water and add enough boiling water to make up 250ml/8fl oz/1 cup fluid. Pour the liquid into the blender and blend with the onion to a smooth purée.

9 Add the remaining 30ml/2 tbsp oil to a large, heavy pan over a low heat, then add the cinnamon, cardamom and cloves. Let them sizzle gently for a few seconds then add the remaining ginger and garlic.

10 Fry for 30 seconds, then add the cubed lamb, chilli powder, turmeric and cumin. Increase the heat to medium-high and fry for 6–7 minutes, stirring frequently until the meat is browned.

11 Reduce the heat to low and add the yogurt, turnips, meatballs and the nut purée. Mix gently and cover the pan with a piece of foil. Press the foil all around the edges of the pan to seal it completely and place the pan lid on top of the foil.

12 Cook on a very low heat for 1½ hours, giving the pan a gentle shake occasionally. If you prefer, place the pan in the oven and cook at 160°C/325°F/Gas 3 for the same amount of time.

13 Remove from the heat and serve with Indian bread or Plain Boiled Rice.

Per portion Energy 725kcal/3016kJ; Protein55g; Carbohydrate 19g, of which sugars 12g; Fat 49g, of which saturates 15g; Cholesterol 187mg; Calcium 294mg; Fibre 4.7g; Sodium 802mg.

Pork dumplings

This recipe comes from Tibet, just across the Indian border. *Momos* are delicious pork parcels that are steamed and served with tomato chutney. Street vendors often sell these snacks from ramshackle stalls in the mountainous regions of north and north-east India.

MAKES ABOUT 16

For the dough:

175g/6oz plain/½ cups plain (all-purpose) flour, plus 30–45ml/1–2 tbsp for dusting
15ml/1 tbsp sunflower oil
75–120ml/2½–4fl oz/5 tbsp–½ cup cold water

For the filling:

250g/9oz minced (ground) pork
1 small onion, roughly chopped
15g/½oz fresh root ginger, roughly chopped
1–2 green chillies, chopped (deseeded if preferred)
2.5ml/½ tsp salt
Roasted Tomato Chutney, to serve

1 Sift the flour into a large mixing bowl, then sprinkle over the oil and stir it into the flour with a fork.

2 Make a hollow in the middle. Pour in the smaller quantity of water and bring together using your fingers until a dough is formed, adding more of the water if it is necessary.

3 Turn out the dough onto a lightly floured surface and knead for about 10 minutes until it is soft and pliable.

4 Transfer the dough to a clean, lightly oiled bowl, cover with clear film (plastic wrap) and set aside for 30 minutes.

5 Meanwhile, put all the ingredients for the filling into a food processor and blend until the mixture is fairly smooth.

6 Divide the dough into two and re-wrap one piece of dough to keep it moist. Roll out the other piece to a 25cm/10in round, then, using a 5cm/2in plain cutter, stamp out small circles.

7 Place a heaped teaspoon of the pork mixture in the middle of one circle. Dampen the edges with water, cover with another circle and seal the edges by pressing them together. Repeat with the remaining piece of dough and the filling mixture.

8 Place the dumplings on a piece of oiled greaseproof paper in a steamer (take care not to completely block the steam vents or the steam won't be able to circulate). Steam over a pan of boiling water for 10 minutes, or until the filling is thoroughly cooked. Serve with Roasted Tomato Chutney.

Per portion Energy 67kcal/282kJ; Protein 4g; Carbohydrate 9g, of which sugars 0g; Fat 2g, of which saturates 0g; Cholesterol 10mg; Calcium 18mg; Fibre 04g; Sodium 73mg.

Pilau rice with aromatic spices and fruit

This north Indian pilau rice recipe, *Kashmiri Pulao*, is quite different from any other made around the country. It is cooked in milk instead of water, and is further enriched with the addition of cream. The rice is then given an exotic appearance by folding in locally grown fruits such as apricots, cherries and plums. It makes an exquisite and very satisfying vegetarian main dish that is perfect for a dinner party.

SERVES 4

225g/8oz/generous 1 cup basmati rice
a good pinch of saffron threads, pounded
30ml/2 tbsp hot milk
25g/1oz glacé cherries
50g/2oz/¼ cup unsalted butter
30ml/2 tbsp sunflower oil or light
   olive oil
4 green cardamom pods, bruised
4 cloves
5cm/2in piece cinnamon stick, halved
5ml/1 tsp Royal cumin (shahi zeera)
5ml/1 tsp salt, or to taste
450ml/¾ pint/scant 2 cups lukewarm milk
50ml/2fl oz/¼ cup single (light) cream
25g/1oz/¼ cup walnut pieces
25g/1oz/¼ cup blanched and
   slivered almonds
25g/1oz/⅙ cup dried ready-to-eat
   apricots, sliced
25g/1oz/⅙ cup dried ready-to-eat
   plums, sliced

4 Heat half the butter and half the oil in a heavy pan over a low heat and add the cardamom, cloves, cinnamon and Royal cumin. Stir-fry gently for 25–30 seconds, then add the drained rice.

5 Stir and fry for 2–3 minutes, until the rice grains are coated with the butter/oil mixture.

6 Stir in the salt and pour in the milk. Increase the heat to medium and bring the mixture to the boil.

10 Add the walnut pieces and fry for about 2 minutes, or until lightly browned. Drain on kitchen paper. Fry the almonds until lightly browned, then drain on kitchen paper.

11 Rinse the cherries and cut them in half. Add the apricots, plums and cherries to the pan and cook for 3–4 minutes, until softened.

12 Pile the fruits over the cooked rice and add the nuts. Mix well and serve.

1 Wash the rice in several changes of water by tossing and turning the grains gently in a sieve (strainer) until the water runs clear. Soak in a bowl of cold water for 30 minutes, then leave to drain in the sieve.

2 Place the pounded saffron in a small bowl, pour over the hot milk and set aside.

3 Put the cherries in a separate bowl of lightly salted water and leave to soak for 10 minutes.

7 Add the steeped saffron along with the milk it was soaked in and stir well. Add the cream, reduce the heat to very low, cover the pan tightly and cook for 10 minutes.

8 Switch off the heat and let the pan stand undisturbed for a further 10 minutes.

9 Meanwhile, heat the remaining butter and oil together in a frying pan over a low heat.

Per portion Energy 551kcal/2310kJ; Protein 62g; Carbohydrate 23g, of which sugars 9g; Fat 24g, of which saturates 4g; Cholesterol 205mg; Calcium 22mg; Fibre 0.9g; Sodium 1699mg.

Saffron-scented pilau rice

Pilau rice, sometimes studded with dried fruits such as apricots and raisins and often with nuts such as almonds, is a delicacy enjoyed in the hilly terrain of northern India. *Kesar Pulao* is a basic recipe for spicy saffron-scented rice, which provides a fragrant accompaniment to so many main dishes.

SERVES 4

225g/8oz/1 cup basmati rice
a good pinch of saffron threads, pounded
30ml/2 tbsp hot milk
25g/1oz/4 tbsp ghee or unsalted butter
4 green cardamom pods, bruised
2.5cm/1in piece of cinnamon stick
4 cloves
2 star anise
2.5ml/½ tsp salt
22.5ml/1½ tbsp rose water
45ml/3 tbsp blanched almonds
chapatis or *Phulkas*, to serve

1 Wash the rice in several changes of water until the water runs clear, then soak for 20–30 minutes.

2 Soak the saffron in the milk for 10 minutes.

COOK'S TIP
Pounding the saffron helps release maximum flavour and colour.

3 Melt the ghee or butter over a low heat, then add the cardamom, cinnamon, cloves and star anise. Sizzle for 30 seconds.

4 Drain the rice and add to the spiced butter. Add the salt and stir to mix well, then pour in 450ml/16fl oz/2 cups hot water and bring to the boil. Let it boil for 1–2 minutes, then reduce the heat to low, cover the pan and cook for 7–8 minutes.

5 Remove the pan from the heat, then sprinkle the saffron-infused milk and the rose water over the top.

---

6 Cover the pan again and let it stand for 10 minutes, without removing the lid.

7 Meanwhile, heat a heavy frying pan over a medium heat. When hot, add the almonds and toast, stirring often, for 2–3 minutes, until golden. Take care not to let the almonds burn.

8 Fluff up the rice with a fork, transfer it to a serving dish and garnish with the almonds. Serve with chapatis or *Phulkas*.

VARIATION
Add stir-fried cubes of paneer (Indian cheese) and garden peas, or rinsed canned chickpeas tossed with garlic and root ginger purée.

Per portion Energy 262kcal/1090kJ; Protein 4.4g; Carbohydrate 45.3g, of which sugars 0.4g; Fat 6.7g, of which saturates 3g; Cholesterol 0mg; Calcium 20mg; Fibre 0g; Sodium 4mg.

Griddle-roasted wholemeal flat breads

Flat breads are a great accompaniment to vegetarian dishes. They can be served with chutneys and pickles or as part of a main meal. *Chapatis* are dry-roasted on an iron griddle (*tawa*). The dough can also be used to make *Phulkas*, which puff up like balloons under the grill and are delicious spread with melted butter.

MAKES 16

400g/14oz/3½ cups chapati flour (atta)
  or fine wholemeal (whole-wheat) flour,
  plus a little extra for dusting
5ml/1 tsp salt
250ml/9fl oz/1 cup water

1 Mix the flour and salt together in a mixing bowl. Gradually add the water.

2 Continue to mix with your fingers until a dough is formed.

3 Transfer the dough to a lightly floured surface and knead it for 4–5 minutes.

4 When all the excess moisture has been absorbed by the flour, wrap the dough in clear film (plastic wrap) and let it rest for 30 minutes. Alternatively, make the dough in a food processor, using a dough hook and following manufacturer's instructions.

5 Divide the dough into two equal parts and pinch or cut eight equal portions from each. Form the portions into balls and flatten them into neat, round cakes.

6 Dust the cakes lightly in the flour and roll each one out to a 15cm/6in circle. Keep the rest of the cakes covered with a damp dish towel while you work.

7 To make *chapatis*: preheat a heavy cast iron griddle over a medium/high heat. Place a dough circle on it, cook for about 30 seconds, then turn it over using a thin metal spatula.

8 Cook until bubbles begin to appear on the surface and turn it over again. Press the edges down gently with a clean dish towel to encourage the *chapati* to puff up (they will not always puff up, but this does not affect the taste).

9 Cook until the underneath begins to brown, then remove from the heat and keep them hot by wrapping them in foil lined with kitchen paper while you make the remaining breads in the same way.

10 For *phulkas*: preheat a grill (broiler) to high, and also preheat a heavy griddle as above. Place a dough circle on the griddle over a medium/high heat.

11 Cook for 35–40 seconds, then immediately place the pan under the grill, with the uncooked side of the bread facing up, about 13cm/5in below the heat source.

12 Let the *phulka* puff up until brown spots appear on the surface. Watch it carefully as this happens quite quickly. Remove and place the *phulka* on a piece of foil lined with kitchen paper. Repeat with the remaining dough.

VARIATION
You could add dried herbs, such as dried fenugreek leaves (kasuri methi), to the mixture if you like.

Per portion Energy 78kcal/330kJ; Protein 3.2g; Carbohydrate 16g, of which sugars 0.5g; Fat 0.6g, of which saturates 0.1g; Cholesterol 0mg; Calcium 10mg; Fibre 2.3g; Sodium 124mg.

Deep-fried leavened bread

Bhature served with a local dish of spiced chickpeas is a Punjabi speciality. The dough for the bread is enriched with yogurt and egg, and contains a little baking powder for leavening, which results in a soft and luscious bread that is ideal served with any type of curry.

MAKES 8

350g/12oz/3 cups plain (all-purpose) flour,
  plus extra for dusting
2.5ml/½ tsp salt
2.5ml/½ tsp sugar
5ml/1 tsp baking powder
150g/5oz/generous ½ cup natural
  (plain) yogurt
1 egg
30–45ml/2–3 tbsp warm water
sunflower oil, for deep-frying

1 Sift the flour, salt, sugar and baking powder into a large bowl and mix well.

2 Beat the yogurt and egg together and add to the flour along with the warm water. Mix until a dough has formed.

3 Transfer the dough to a flat surface. Knead it for 4–5 minutes, until soft and pliable. Alternatively, use a food processor, following manufacturer's instructions.

4 Place the dough in a plastic food bag and leave to rest in a warm place for 2–3 hours, until doubled in size.

5 Divide the dough into eight equal parts and form each one into a ball, then flatten to a smooth, round cake. Dust in flour and roll out to circles about 13cm/5in across.

6 Heat the oil in a wok or other suitable pan for deep-frying over a medium heat. Check that the temperature is right by dropping a little of the dough into the oil. If it floats to the surface immediately without turning brown, then the temperature is just right.

7 Place a dough cake in the hot oil and fry for about 1 minute. When it puffs up, turn it over and fry the other side for 1 minute more or until browned. Drain on kitchen paper.

Per portion Energy 244kcal/1027kJ; Protein 5.9g; Carbohydrate 35.7g, of which sugars 2.4g; Fat 9.7g, of which saturates 1.2g; Cholesterol 24mg; Calcium 101mg; Fibre 1.4g; Sodium 149mg.

Punjabi cornmeal bread

This tasty bread, *Makki Ki Roti*, is the mainstay of cooking in the Punjab and is used as an accompaniment for mopping up the juices at most meals. It is traditionally made using fine cornmeal, which has a distinctive flavour and is widely available from Indian grocers and health food stores.

MAKES 8
175g/6oz/1½ cups cornmeal (cornstarch)
90g/3½oz/¾ cup plain (all-purpose) flour
2.5ml/½ tsp salt
butter and Mustard Greens with Ginger,
  Chilli and Garlic, to serve

> ### VARIATION
> You can substitute the cornmeal with polenta. It is advisable to avoid quick-cook varieties, which lack the flavour of slow-cook versions.

1 Mix the cornmeal, flour and salt together in a large mixing bowl. Gradually add about 250–300ml/ 8–10fl oz/1–1¼ cups warm water to the dry ingredients and blend them together until a moist but firm dough forms.

2 Turn out the dough onto a lightly floured surface and knead it for about 10 minutes, until the dough is soft and pliable.

3 Cover the dough with a damp cloth and let it rest for 30 minutes. Meanwhile, preheat a cast-iron griddle or frying pan over a medium heat.

4 Divide the dough into eight balls. Rotate each ball gently between your palms, then flatten into a round cake 13cm/5in in diameter, patting and stretching gently with your fingertips. You may find it easier to place the cakes between layers of clear film (plastic wrap) before shaping.

5 Gently lift a cake and place it on the preheated griddle. Cook for 1 minute, then turn it over with a thin spatula. When the bread has set, cook both sides until brown patches appear, flipping it to check every few seconds. Remove from the griddle and cook the rest in the same way.

6 Spread butter on one side of the breads (as much or as little as you like) and serve with Mustard Greens with Ginger, Chilli and Garlic for an authentically Punjabi meal.

Per portion Energy 119kcal/500kJ; Protein 3.1g; Carbohydrate 24.7g, of which sugars 0.2g; Fat 0.9g, of which saturates 0g; Cholesterol 0mg; Calcium 17mg; Fibre 0.8g; Sodium 123mg.

Tandoori leavened bread

Naan breads are found all over the country and are one of the main types of bread served at most meals in India. Naan can be varied by adding your own toppings such as seeds, herbs and chillies. They are the perfect accompaniment for Indian curries and other liquid dishes, and also make a filling snack.

MAKES 8

500g/1¼lb/4½ cups self-raising
  (self-rising) flour
5ml/1 tsp baking powder
5ml/1 tsp salt
10ml/2 tsp sugar
50g/2oz/4 tbsp softened butter
250ml/8fl oz/1 cup warm milk
melted butter, to glaze

1 Sift the flour into a large mixing bowl and add the baking powder, salt and sugar.

2 Mix well, then rub in the butter. Add the milk and mix until a dough is formed.

VARIATION

Before cooking the naan, brush with a little beaten egg and sprinkle on flavourings such as cumin seeds, nigella seeds, poppy seeds, chopped garlic, chopped green chillies or fresh coriander (cilantro).

3 Transfer the dough to a lightly floured pastry board and knead for 10 minutes, until soft and pliable.

4 Shape the dough into a ball, cover with a damp cloth and leave to rest for 30 minutes.

5 Preheat the grill (broiler) to high and heat for 8–10 minutes, then line a grill (broiling) pan with a piece of foil and brush it with a little dab of oil.

6 Divide the dough into eight equal-sized portions, then form into cakes.

7 Roll each cake into a circle 13cm/5in in diameter, then gently pull the lower end to form it into the traditional teardrop shape.

8 Roll again, maintaining the teardrop shape, into a 23cm/9in naan.

9 Place a naan in the prepared grill pan and cook it 13cm/5in below the heat source for about 1½ minutes until it puffs up. Keep an eye on it as it can burn easily when it puffs up if it gets too close to the element in the oven.

10 Turn it over and grill for a further minute or until brown patches appear.

11 Place the cooked naan on a clean dish towel and brush the surface with a little melted butter. Wrap it in the towel to keep it hot while you finish cooking the other naans.

12 Serve warm with any meat, poultry or vegetable curry dish.

Per portion Energy 630kcal/2666kJ; Protein 18.7g; Carbohydrate 117g, of which sugars 2.95g; Fat 13g, of which saturates 2.2g; Cholesterol 127mg; Calcium 246mg; Fibre 4.6g; Sodium 712mg.

Spiced potato-filled flaky bread

This type of bread, known as paratha, is traditionally a rich, unleavened bread that can be plain or stuffed. This version, *Aloo Paratha*, is stuffed with spiced potatoes, and olive oil is used instead of ghee. The wholesome taste of the flour used more than makes up for the absence of ghee or butter.

MAKES 8

450g/1lb/4 cups wholemeal (whole-wheat) bread flour, plus extra for dusting
2.5ml/½ tsp salt, or to taste
30ml/2 tbsp sunflower oil or light olive oil
290ml/9fl oz/scant 1⅔ cups warm water
sunflower oil or olive oil, for shallow-frying

For the filling:
15ml/1 tbsp sunflower oil or light olive oil
2.5ml/½ tsp black or brown mustard seeds
2 shallots, finely chopped
10ml/2 tsp fresh root ginger purée
1 fresh green chilli, finely chopped (deseeded if preferred)
30ml/2 tbsp fresh coriander (cilantro) leaves, finely chopped
2.5ml/½ tsp salt, or to taste
225g/8oz potatoes, boiled in their jackets then peeled and mashed

1 Put the flour and salt in a bowl and work in the oil with your fingertips. Gradually add the water and mix until a soft dough is formed.

2 Transfer the dough to a floured surface and knead for 3–4 minutes or until all traces of stickiness disappear. Alternatively, put all the ingredients into a food processor with a dough hook and run the machine for about 5 minutes, until the dough feels soft and there is no stickiness.

3 Cover the dough with a damp dish towel and set aside for 30 minutes.

4 Meanwhile, prepare the filling. Heat the oil over a medium heat and add the mustard seeds. As soon as they start popping, add the shallots, ginger and chilli.

5 Stir-fry for 2–3 minutes, then stir in the chopped coriander and salt and remove from the heat. Transfer to a large bowl.

6 Add the mashed potato to this mixture and mix well. Divide the dough into two equal parts and make four portions out of each. Shape each portion into a ball and flatten it into a smooth cake.

7 Form the cake into a saucer shape by gently stretching, and moisten the edges with cold water. Place a portion of the filling in each, bring up the sides of the dough and seal the edges by pressing them together. Press the ball to form a flat cake.

8 Preheat a cast iron griddle or other heavy frying pan over a medium heat. Dust each of the flat cakes with the flour and, with gentle pressure, roll out to a 15cm/6in disc.

9 Place one disc on the hot griddle and cook for 1 minute, then turn it over and cook the other side for 1 minute. Spread 5ml/1 tsp oil on the cooked side, turn it over and spread oil on the other side. Flip it over again and cook the side that was oiled first for 2–3 minutes, until brown patches appear.

10 Turn it over and cook the other side for a further 2–3 minutes, until brown patches appear. Place the paratha on a piece of foil lined with kitchen paper. Cover while you cook the remaining parathas.

Per portion Energy 286kcal/1207kJ; Protein 9g; Carbohydrate 46g, of which sugars 2g; Fat 9g, of which saturates 1g; Cholesterol 0mg; Calcium 30mg; Fibre 5.1g; Sodium 252mg.

Deep-fried stuffed bread

In north India, breads like *puri* and *bhatoora*, which are deep-fried in oil, are very popular. *Babru* are similar to the *dhal puri* (fried breads stuffed with lentils) eaten in the northern territory. Traditionally, black gram dhal is used for the stuffing, but here yellow split gram (channa dhal), also known as Bengal gram, is used as it is more readily available. You will need to soak the channa dhal for at least 3 hours.

MAKES 12

For the filling:

75g/3oz/½ cup yellow split gram (channa dhal)
15ml/1 tbsp sunflower or light olive oil
1cm/½ in fresh root ginger, grated, or 5ml/1 tsp ginger purée
1 green chilli, finely chopped and deseeded
salt, to taste
15ml/1 tbsp finely chopped fresh coriander (cilantro)

For the bread:

350g/12oz/3 cups plain (all-purpose) flour, plus extra for dusting
2.5ml/½ tsp baking powder
2.5ml/½ tsp salt, or to taste
25g/1oz butter or ghee
oil, for deep-frying

1 For the filling, rinse the channa dhal under cold running water. Put in a bowl, cover with cold water and soak for 3–4 hours.

2 Drain the channa dhal and rinse again in a sieve. Put in a pan with 300ml/½ pint/1¼ cups cold water and bring to the boil. Skim off any foam that rises to the top, reduce the heat to low and cook, uncovered, for 12–15 minutes, until the lentils absorb most of the water and just a spoonful or two of liquid remains.

3 Cool for a few minutes, then grind to a thick, dry paste in a food processor.

4 Heat the oil over a low heat in the rinsed-out and dried pan. Add the ginger and green chilli and fry for 1 minute, then turn off the heat. Add the ground channa dhal, salt and coriander. Mix well and set aside.

5 To make the bread, put the flour, baking powder and salt into a bowl and mix well. Rub in the butter or ghee. Make a hollow in the middle and pour in 175ml/6fl oz/¾ cup warm water. Stir, gradually working in the flour from the sides, to make a soft dough.

6 Knead the dough on a lightly floured surface for 10 minutes, until smooth. Wrap in clear film (plastic wrap) and set aside for 20–30 minutes.

7 Divide the dough into 12 equal pieces and shape each piece into a ball. Using a rolling pin, roll each ball into a round.

8 Form a cup shape from each round by making a depression in the centre, then pressing and stretching around the edges.

9 Place 30ml/2 tsp of the spiced channa dhal in the centre and moisten the edges with water. Gather the edges together, pressing them to seal, then flatten slightly between your hands.

10 Gently roll out the ball to a round approximately 13cm/5in in diameter. Cover with a clean dish towel to prevent the *babru* from drying out. Repeat with the remaining dough balls and filling.

11 Heat the oil in a deep, heavy pan or frying pan over a medium heat. Fry each bread until well browned on both sides.

12 Lift out using a slotted spoon and drain on kitchen paper. Serve immediately on its own or with dishes such as Chicken in a Mint and Coriander Sauce.

Per portion Energy 192kcal/808kJ; Protein 4g; Carbohydrate 26g, of which sugars 1g; Fat 8g, of which saturates 2g; Cholesterol 4mg; Calcium 46mg; Fibre 1.3g; Sodium 118mg.

Mustard greens with ginger, chilli and garlic

This delicious Punjabi side dish, *Sarson Ka Saag*, uses mustard greens that are first blanched with spinach and puréed, then mixed with fresh root ginger, garlic and green chillies, and served with chilled butter. You could substitute other greens, such as spring (collard) greens or shredded cabbage.

SERVES 4

450g/1lb fresh mustard greens, chopped
250g/9oz fresh spinach leaves, chopped
5cm/2in piece of fresh root ginger,
  finely chopped or grated
4–5 large garlic cloves, finely chopped
2–3 fresh green chillies, deseeded
  and chopped
5ml/1 tsp salt, or to taste
5ml/1 tsp soft dark brown sugar
5ml/1 tbsp fine cornmeal or polenta

For the spiced butter:
10ml/2 tsp ghee or unsalted butter
2.5cm/1in piece of fresh root ginger,
  cut into strips
2 red chillies, deseeded and cut into strips
2.5ml/½ tsp chilli powder
40g/1½oz unsalted butter, chilled and cut
  into cubes
Punjabi Cornmeal Bread, to serve

1 Bring 300ml/½ pint/1¼ cups water to the boil in a heavy pan. Add the mustard greens, spinach, ginger, garlic and green chillies. Bring back to the boil, reduce the heat, cover, and cook for 25–30 minutes.

2 Remove the pan from the heat and leave the mixture to cool slightly before transferring it to a blender or food processer and puréeing it with all the cooking liquid.

3 Transfer the puréed greens back into the pan and place over a medium heat. When they begin to bubble, add the salt, sugar and cornmeal or polenta. Stir and cook over a low heat for 15–20 minutes, or until the excess moisture evaporates.

4 For the sauce, heat the ghee or butter in a small pan over a medium heat and add the ginger and red chillies. Cook for about 1 minute, then stir in the chilli powder and pour the spiced butter over the greens.

5 Transfer to a serving dish and top with the cubes of chilled butter. The sharp flavours of the dish are accentuated when accompanied by Punjabi Cornmeal Bread.

VARIATION

You can also use spring greens (collards) and add a dash of prepared English (hot) mustard for an authentic Punjabi flavour.

Per portion Energy 138.5kcal/573.2kJ; Protein 4.9g; Carbohydrate 9.5g, of which sugars 7.8g; Fat 9.1g, of which saturates 5.5g; Cholesterol 23mg; Calcium 173mg; Fibre 4.1g; Sodium 172.5mg.

Almond chutney

Almonds are very popular throughout northern India, where beautiful almond blossoms appear in the orchards of Kashmir at the onset of spring. In Indian cooking, fresh chutneys such as this tasty almond one, *Badam Ki Chutney*, are made by simply grinding all the ingredients to a smooth purée.

SERVES 4–5

50g/2oz/½ cup blanched almonds
1 fresh green chilli, roughly chopped
  (deseeded if preferred)
1 small clove garlic
1cm/½in piece of fresh root ginger,
  roughly chopped
15g/½oz fresh coriander (cilantro)
30ml/2 tbsp fresh mint leaves
2.5ml/½ tsp salt
5ml/1 tsp sugar
15ml/1 tbsp lemon juice

1 Soak the almonds in 175ml/6fl oz/¾ cup boiling water for 15 minutes.

2 Transfer to a blender, with the water in which they were soaked. Add the remaining ingredients and blend until smooth.

3 Transfer to a serving bowl and chill. Serve with fried and grilled (broiled) snacks or use as a dip with poppadums.

Per portion Energy 79kcal/330kJ; Protein 3.1g; Carbohydrate 3.4g, of which sugars 1.3g; Fat 6.1g, of which saturates 0.5g; Cholesterol 0mg; Calcium 61mg; Fibre 0.7g; Sodium 201mg.

Indian iced dessert

Although described as an Indian ice cream, the ever-popular *Kulfi* has a much denser texture than standard ice cream. Various nuts and fruits and even chocolate can be added to the basic mixture. In this quick recipe, an almond-based ice is topped with passion fruit for a refreshing flavour.

SERVES 4

50g/2oz/½ cup blanched almonds
400g/14oz can of evaporated milk
300ml/½ pint/1¼ cups double (heavy) cream
115g/4oz/½ cup caster (superfine) sugar
2.5ml/½ tsp ground cardamom
the pulp and seeds of 2 passion fruits,
  to serve

1 Put the blanched almonds in a heatproof bowl and pour over 120ml/4fl oz/½ cup of boiling water. Set aside and leave to soak for 20 minutes.

2 Put the evaporated milk, cream and sugar into a large, heavy pan and place over a low heat. Heat gently, stirring, until the sugar has dissolved.

3 Remove from the heat and set aside until cold. Keep an eye on the mixture, and stir from time to time to prevent a skin forming.

4 Purée the almonds in a food processor or blender with the soaking water. Add to the milk mixture with the cardamom.

5 Stir the mixture well, then transfer to a jug (pitcher), then pour into *kulfi* moulds or small freezer-safe containers. Freeze for at least 5–6 hours. If you do not have individual containers, use one large freezer-proof container.

6 Remove from the freezer 10–15 minutes before serving. Up-end small containers on to serving plates. For larger portions, turn out on to a board and cut the block into the desired portions. Serve with toasted flaked almonds or the pulp and seeds of two passion fruits.

> **VARIATION**
> Serve with 15ml/1 tbsp toasted flaked (sliced) almonds instead of passion fruit, if you wish.

Per portion Energy 260kcal/1082kJ; Protein 10.9g; Carbohydrate 18.3g, of which sugars 18.1g; Fat 16.2g, of which saturates 7.8g; Cholesterol 40mg; Calcium 344mg; Fibre 0.6g; Sodium 171mg.

Ground rice in saffron-scented milk

Phirni is a luxurious dessert in which a little ground rice is cooked in milk flavoured with saffron and spices until it is reduced to the consistency of evaporated milk. In Kashmir, where it originates, the dessert is served in earthenware bowls, but stemmed glasses or glazed ramekins work just as well.

SERVES 4–5
a pinch of saffron threads, pounded
15ml/1 tbsp hot milk
300ml/10fl oz/1¼ cups full-fat (whole) milk
50g/2oz/⅓ cup ground rice
400ml/14fl oz/1½ cups canned
  evaporated milk
50g/2oz/¼ cup granulated (white) sugar
25g/1oz/¼ cup blanched, flaked
  (sliced) almonds
25g/1oz/¼ cup pistachio nuts
5ml/1 tsp ground cardamom
15ml/1 tbsp rose water
2–3 dried ready-to-eat apricots, sliced,
  to garnish

1 Soak the saffron threads in the hot milk for 10 minutes, then set aside.

2 Brush the surface of a heavy pan with a little oil, then pour in the milk.

3 Sprinkle the ground rice evenly over the milk and place the pan over a medium heat. Bring it to the boil, stirring frequently.

4 Add the evaporated milk, sugar and almonds. Reserve a few pistachio nuts, then add the remainder to the milk.

5 Continue to cook over a low heat, stirring frequently, until the mixture thickens and resembles the consistency of cooked custard, coating the back of the spoon.

6 Stir in the ground cardamom and rose water and remove from the heat. Transfer to stemmed glasses or ramekins.

7 Crush the reserved pistachio nuts and sprinkle over the top with the sliced apricots. Chill for 2 hours before serving.

Per portion portion Energy 262kcal/1096kJ; Protein 11.1g; Carbohydrate 30.2g, of which sugars 22g; Fat 11.3g, of which saturates 3.9g; Cholesterol 22mg; Calcium 308mg; Fibre 0.7g; Sodium 127mg.

Royal-style bread pudding

This dish, *Shahi Tukde*, originates from royal cuisine; the word *shahi* meaning 'royal' and *tukde* meaning 'pieces'. Like many milk-based desserts, it is traditionally enriched with *khoya*, which is made by simmering full-fat milk until it is almost solid. As this is so time-consuming, Indian cheese has been used instead.

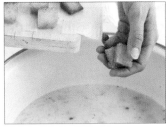

2 Heat 2.5cm/1in oil into a deep frying pan over a medium heat. When the oil is hot, fry the cubes of bread until they are well browned, turning them often, so that they colour evenly. Drain on kitchen paper.

3 Put the milk, cream, sugar, raisins and saffron in a non-stick pan and bring to simmering point, stirring occasionally, until the sugar has dissolved.

4 Add the fried bread and cook until the bread has absorbed all the milk. Stir in the ground cardamom.

5 Spoon the mixture on to a serving plate and sprinkle over the crumbled paneer, followed by the pistachio nuts. Serve at room temperature.

SERVES 4

4 large slices of day-old white bread
sunflower or light olive oil, for deep-frying
200ml/7fl oz/scant 1 cup full-fat (whole) milk
100ml/3½fl oz/scant 1 cup single (light) cream
90g/3½ oz/scant ½ cup caster (superfine) sugar
30ml/2 tbsp raisins
115g/4oz/½ cup paneer (Indian cheese),
  crumbled
pinch of saffron, pounded
2.5ml/½ tsp ground cardamom
15ml/1 tbsp toasted pistachio nuts,
  roughly chopped, to serve

1 Trim the crusts from the bread and cut the bread into 2.5cm/1in cubes.

VARIATION
If you can't get paneer (Indian cheese), try ricotta cheese instead.

Per portion Energy 473kcal/1979kJ; Protein 7g; Carbohydrate 49g, of which sugars 32g; Fat 29g, of which saturates 14g; Cholesterol 48mg; Calcium 156mg; Fibre 0.7g; Sodium 314mg.

Vermicelli dessert with dates and pistachios

This popular dessert, *Sheer Khurma*, is a contribution from the Muslim community in India. The vermicelli is first sautéed in ghee, then cooked in thickened milk with a hint of spices. Chunks of dates and pistachio nuts are then added, which create a beautiful pattern and add sweetness and flavour.

SERVES 6
30ml/2 tbsp ghee or unsalted butter
25g/1oz dried vermicelli
50g/2oz/½ cup dried ready-to-eat dates,
   coarsely chopped
25g/1oz/¼ cup pistachio nuts
600ml/1 pint/2½ cups full-fat
   (whole) milk
50g/2oz/¼ cup sugar, or to taste
2.5ml/½ tsp ground cinnamon
2.5ml/½ tsp ground nutmeg
25g/1oz/¼ cup chopped pistachio nuts and
   2.5ml/½ tsp cinnamon, to garnish

1 Melt the ghee or butter in a heavy, non-stick pan over a low heat, then add the vermicelli. Cook for 3 minutes, then add the dates and pistachio nuts.

2 Stir-fry for 2–3 minutes or until the vermicelli is golden brown. Add the milk and sugar to the pan and bring it to the boil.

3 Reduce the heat to low and simmer gently for 20 minutes, stirring regularly to prevent sticking.

4 Stir in the spices, then remove from the heat. Garnish with chopped pistachio nuts and cinnamon and serve hot or cold.

Per portion Energy 231kcal/964kJ; Protein 5g; Carbohydrate 23g, of which sugars 19g; Fat 14g, of which saturates 7g; Cholesterol 28mg; Calcium 136mg; Fibre 0.7g; Sodium 89mg.

Savoury yogurt drink

Lassi is made with different flavourings and it is a very welcome drink during the oppressive heat of the summer months. This version, *Namkeen Lassi*, is flavoured with black pepper and mint and is ideal as an appetizer or just as a refreshing drink, served in tall glasses lined with crushed ice.

MAKES 1.2 LITRES/2 PINTS/5 CUPS

2.5ml/½ tsp black peppercorns
2.5ml/½ tsp cumin seeds
450g/1lb/2 cups natural (plain) yogurt
10–12 fresh mint leaves
5ml/1 tsp salt, or to taste
10ml/2 tsp caster (superfine) sugar
crushed ice, to serve

COOK'S TIP
Use whole-milk yogurt, which resembles the home-made Indian version in terms of taste and texture.

1 Preheat a small, heavy pan over a medium heat and dry-roast the peppercorns and cumin seeds for about 1 minute, until they release their aroma.

2 Crush the peppercorns and cumin with a mortar and pestle. Alternatively, place them in a plastic bag and crush with a rolling pin.

3 Put the yogurt, mint, salt, sugar and the spices into a blender and add 300ml/½ pint/1¼ cups water. You could also use a bowl and stick blender. Blend until smooth.

4 Add 300ml/½ pint/1¼ cups more water and blend well. Put the crushed ice in tall glasses, pour the lassi over and serve.

Per portion Energy 396kcal/1670kJ; Protein 26g; Carbohydrate 46g, of which sugars 26g; Fat 14g, of which saturates 8g; Cholesterol 50mg; Calcium 925mg; Fibre 0.0g; Sodium 4293mg.

Spice-infused Kashmiri tea

Tea made with spices is enjoyed all over India, and the regional difference lies in the variation of the spices. During the freezing winters in this Himalayan region of Kasmir, *Qahwa* is brewed throughout the day to help keep inhabitants warm, as well as for its rehydrating and fortifying effects.

SERVES 2

450ml/16fl oz/2 cups water
1cm/½in piece of cinnamon stick
2 green cardamom pods, bruised
2 cloves
a small pinch (about 8 threads) of
  saffron, pounded
15ml/3 tsp leaf tea or 2 tea bags
milk and sugar, to taste (optional)

1 Bring the water to the boil in a pan and add all the spices. Simmer for 5 minutes.

COOK'S TIP
Spices such as cinnamon, cloves and cardamom are known to raise body temperature.

2 Rinse out a teapot with boiling water and put in the leaf tea or tea bags. Pour over the spiced water along with all the whole spices.

3 Brew the tea for 5 minutes, until the liquid is dark and strong, then strain the tea into individual cups. Add milk and sugar if you like, but it is also delicious without milk.

Per portion 15kcal/66kJ; Protein 1g; Carbohydrate 1.8g, of which sugars 0g; Fat 0.7g, of which saturates 0.1g; Cholesterol 0mg; Calcium 9mg; Fibre 0g; Sodium 2mg.

North-East India

The regional fare of the hilly north-east is dominated by a wide range of meat, poultry and dairy foods, although freshwater fish adds variety. Vegetables, as elsewhere in the country, form a major part of the daily diet. From succulent duckling, pigeon and chicken dishes to hearty stews, vibrant vegetable snacks and fragrant rice accompaniments, the cooking of north-east India offers a colourful cornucopia of sumptuous flavours and textures.

North-East India

Seven states make up the region of north-east India. This is a picturesque, hilly country, bordering on the eastern edge of the Himalayan mountains where they tower over Nepal, Bhutan and China. These states are all landlocked – the only access to the sea is via Bangladesh or Myanmar (Burma) – and so the main focus of regional cuisine is on meat and dairy products rather than fish. However, tasty freshwater fish from the Brahmaputra River and its tributaries brings a welcome variation to the diet.

ASSAM

Perhaps the best known of the north-eastern states, because of its association with its tea crop, is Assam. Peoples of distinctly different cultures and trends of civilization settled here – the Dravidians, Indo-Mongols, Tibetans and Burmese are among those who contributed to the creation of this unique community. The soil is very fertile and the climate benign, making it perfect for growing the main food crops of tea, rice and turmeric. There are over 700 tea plantations in the state and more than half of the crop is exported to other states in India and to the rest of the world. Assam is also famous for its exquisite silk.

The food in the state is simple and nutritious, with fish and rice forming the major part of the daily diet, but vegetables are also very important. This is probably the only state in India where healthy eating is a way of life – very little fat is used in cooking and the emphasis is on fresh vegetables, plenty of greens, and pulses tempered with garlic, mustard oil and chillies. Dishes such as banana flower curry and a tomato and

lemon curry known as *tenga* are among the delicacies that the people of Assam have made their own. Another distinctive Assamese dish is *khar*, which is typically made with raw papaya, raw banana or a mixture of peas, beans and a vegetable such as marrow (large zucchini). *Khar* is believed to aid the digestion, as it includes *kharoni*, an ingredient made from burnt banana ash.

ARUNACHAL PRADESH

The smaller, more remote states that cluster around the foothills of the Himalayas include Arunachal Pradesh which, owing to its easternmost position in this region, is popularly known as 'the land of the rising sun'. It is situated directly in the shadow of the high snow-clad peaks, and its thick evergreen forests and meandering rivers make beautiful vistas.

Left *The ridge of high mountains in Cherapunji, Meghalaya, is one of the wettest places on earth.*

Above *Lush green tea gardens are a common sight in Assam, which produces much of the world's tea.*

The majority of the population here have Tibetan and Burmese ancestors, and they have maintained the culinary traditions of these countries. Meat – often lamb, goat or yak – forms the basis of many dishes, and cooks in Arunachal Pradesh do not use many spices – only garlic, ginger, chillies and aromatic herbs. A popular locally brewed drink called *apong* is made from fermented rice or millet.

MEGHALAYA

Meaning 'abode of the clouds', Meghalaya is a small, hilly state with the highest rainfall levels in the world. The warm, very wet climate is perfect for growing a large variety of fruit, vegetables, medicinal plants and spices, including rice, maize, wheat and oilseeds such as mustard and rapeseed. Despite this bounty of fruit and vegetables,

many of the local dishes are meat-based, with pork being the first choice. *Jadoh*, a spicy dish of rice and pork or liver, is consumed almost every day and Chinese food is also eaten regularly, often washed down with a local drink known as *kyat*.

MANIPUR

Once part of British India, Manipur is a culturally rich state, and its temple dance, known as the 'Manipuri Dance', is well known all over India. The food in Manipur is an eclectic mixture of fish, meat, poultry and vegetables with some pulses. Fish cooked with bamboo shoots is one of the most popular dishes, and rice is the staple here.

TRIPURA

The majority of the population in the hilly landlocked state of Tripura is Bengali, and the Bengali influence is evident in the food of the region. The area produces oil seeds, sugar cane, potatoes and pulses, although rice is the staple crop and forms the basis of the diet, along with fish cooked in mustard oil. Tripura is also well known for hand-woven cotton and intricate wooden carvings.

Right *Villagers till the earth in Arunachal Pradesh to produce the few crops that will grow there.*

NAGALAND

Bordering the states of Assam and Arunachal Pradesh and the country of Myanmar, Nagaland is a hilly state with a tribal population that is mainly Christian. Most of the hills consist of tropical and sub-tropical evergreen forests that are important for the timber trade, and local farmers produce a few staple crops in cleared areas which, together with meat, form the basis of the simple daily diet.

Above *Tripura is known for its wood carvings, some of which can be seen at Ujjayanta Palace.*

MIZORAM

Strategically positioned between Myanmar and Bangladesh, Mizoram is a beautiful state with rolling hills and huge rivers and lakes. The diet consists of meat and the few crops that can be grown locally, and the preference is for smoked, stewed and steamed meat without the addition of any spices.

Mushroom soup with green chilli and garlic

This recipe, *Khumb Ka Shorba*, is from the strikingly beautiful district of Arunachal Pradesh in the foothills of the Himalayas. It is ideal on a cold winter's night and, when made to perfection, you can taste and savour each ingredient. A good stock is essential, so it is worth paying a little extra or making your own.

SERVES 4

900ml/1½ pints/3¾ cups fresh vegetable stock or 2 vegetable stock (bouillon) cubes
250g/9oz potatoes, cubed
2.5cm/1in piece of fresh root ginger, finely grated
4 large garlic cloves, crushed to a pulp or grated
1 fresh green chilli, finely chopped (deseeded if preferred)
250g/9oz button (white) mushrooms, sliced
15ml/1 tbsp fresh coriander (cilantro) leaves, chopped
hot crusty rolls, to serve

1 Put the stock in a pan. If using stock cubes, put them in a heatproof jug and dissolve them in 900ml/1½ pints/3¾ cups hot water. Add the potatoes, ginger, garlic and chilli.

2 Bring to the boil and cook over a medium heat for 10 minutes.

3 Add the mushrooms and cook for a further 10 minutes, until the mushrooms are cooked.

4 Stir in the chopped coriander and serve immediately with hot crusty rolls.

Per portion Energy 69kcal/290kJ; Protein 3g; Carbohydrate 12g, of which sugars 1g; Fat 1g, of which saturates 0g; Cholesterol 0mg; Calcium 11mg; Fibre 2.4g; Sodium 596mg.

Fresh vegetables in chilli and ginger broth

This dish, *Oying*, originates in the scenic mountain state of Arunachal Pradesh. The cuisine of this region is simple, delicious and extremely nutritious. Most of the cooking is done without using any fat, as in this recipe, relying instead on the addition of herbs and spices to give it superb, distinctive flavours.

SERVES 4

250g/9oz/1 cup potatoes, cut into
  2.5cm/1in cubes
1–2 fresh green chillies, sliced diagonally
150g/5oz/1 cup green beans, cut into
  2.5cm/1in lengths
150g/5oz/1 cup cabbage, shredded
5ml/1 tsp salt, or to taste
10ml/2 tsp grated fresh root ginger
1 large garlic clove, crushed
150g/5oz/1 cup fresh spinach, washed
  and roughly chopped
15–30ml/1–2 tbsp fresh coriander (cilantro)
  leaves, chopped
hot crusty rolls, to serve

1 Put the potatoes in a medium pan, pour in 700ml/1¼ pints/3 cups water and bring to the boil. Add the chillies, reduce the heat to low, cover and cook for 7–8 minutes.

2 Add the green beans and cabbage, bring back to the boil, then cover and cook over a medium heat for 5 minutes.

3 Add the salt, ginger and garlic, replace the lid and continue to cook for 5 minutes.

4 Stir in the spinach and cook for a further 1–2 minutes, until it has wilted.

5 Add the coriander leaves, cook for about 1 minute, then remove from the heat and serve with hot crusty rolls.

Per portion Energy 77kcal/322kJ; Protein 3.7g; Carbohydrate 14.1g, of which sugars 4.4g; Fat 0.9g, of which saturates 0.2g; Cholesterol 0mg; Calcium 125mg; Fibre 3.7g; Sodium 66mg.

Pigeon soup

In Assam, birds such as duck and pigeon are common in everyday cooking and many households keep their own. In *Paror Soup* they are gently braised, so that the meat is tender.

SERVES 4

5ml/1 tsp cumin seeds
2.5ml/½ tsp black peppercorns
15ml/1 tbsp sunflower or light olive oil
15ml/1 tbsp butter
2 wood pigeons, prepared
2.5cm/1in piece cinnamon stick
2 brown cardamom pods
2 bay leaves
15g/½oz fresh root ginger, finely chopped
2 cloves garlic, crushed, or 10ml/2 tsp
　garlic purée
150g/5oz potatoes, peeled and cut into
　1cm/½in dice
2.5ml/½ tsp salt, or to taste
150ml/¼ pint/⅔ cup single (light) cream
warm Indian bread, to serve

1 Preheat a small, heavy pan over a medium heat and dry-roast the cumin seeds and black peppercorns for about 40 seconds, until they release their aroma. Remove from the heat. Leave to cool, then finely crush them in a mortar and pestle.

2 Heat the oil and butter in a large, heavy pan over a low-medium heat and brown the birds all over, turning them frequently using tongs. Remove and set aside.

3 Add the cinnamon, cardamom, bay leaves, ginger and garlic to the remaining fat in the pan. Fry for about a minute, then add the potatoes. Continue to cook for 1–2 minutes.

4 Return the pigeons to the pan and pour in 900ml/1½ pints/3¾ cups boiling water. Add the salt, bring to the boil, then reduce the heat to low. Half-cover the pan with a lid and simmer for 1–1¼ hours, or until the birds are tender and cooked through.

5 Remove the birds from the stock with a slotted spoon and leave until they are cool enough to handle. Remove and discard the skin, then take the meat off the bones and chop it into small chunks.

6 Skim any fat from the surface of the stock using a spoon, then remove and discard the cinnamon, cardamom and bay leaves.

7 Transfer the stock to a blender or food processor and purée until smooth. Return to the pan and add the cream and pigeon meat. Heat until piping hot, but not boiling, then ladle the soup into warmed bowls and serve with warm Indian bread.

Per portion Energy 159kcal/665kJ; Protein 11g; Carbohydrate 8g; of which sugars 1g; Fat 10g; of which saturates 5g; Cholesterol 21mg; Calcium 67mg; Fibre 0.5g; Sodium 289mg.

Batter-fried spinach leaves

In this easy-to-make dish, *Paleng Sakor Pat Bhoja*, large, very fresh spinach leaves are dipped in a spicy gram flour batter and crisp-fried in sizzling oil to give them a delectable crunchy finish. Every mouthful exudes a complex blend of chilli, cumin, nigella and turmeric that titillates the tastebuds, making these the perfect accompaniment to a cold pre-dinner drink or for an appetizer with some cooling raita.

3 Heat the oil in a wok or other suitable pan for deep-frying over a medium to high heat. To check that the oil is at the right temperature, drop a tiny piece of the batter into the hot oil. If it floats to the surface immediately without browning, then the temperature is just right. If you have a cooking thermometer, make sure that the oil is at least 180°C/350°F.

4 Using your fingertips, hold each leaf by its stem and dip it in the batter, making sure it is fully coated. The stem should also be coated with the batter.

SERVES 4

12 large spinach leaves
75g/3oz/⅔ cup gram flour (besan)
25g/1oz/2 tbsp ground rice
2.5ml/½ tsp ground turmeric
2.5ml/½ tsp chilli powder
5ml/1 tsp cumin seeds
5ml/1 tsp nigella seeds
2.5ml/½ tsp salt, or to taste
vegetable oil, for deep-frying

1 Wash the spinach leaves carefully under cold running water, taking care not to damage them. Trim the stems using a knife or scissors, leaving approximately 2.5cm/1in of stem on each leaf. Dry the leaves thoroughly on kitchen paper.

2 Sift the gram flour into a large mixing bowl and add the rest of the ingredients except the oil. Mix the dry ingredients well, then gradually add 175ml/6fl oz/¾ cup water. Continue to stir the mixture until you have a thick batter.

5 Carefully lower two or three leaves at a time into the hot oil, depending on the size of the pan. Cook them until they are golden brown and crisp; this will only take 1–1½ minutes per batch. Remove the cooked leaves with a slotted spoon and drain them on kitchen paper. Cook the remaining batches of leaves in the same way and serve immediately.

Per portion Energy 247kcal/1027kJ; Protein 3.2g; Carbohydrate 20.6g, of which sugars 0.9g; Fat 17.5g, of which saturates 1.9g; Cholesterol 0mg; Calcium 106mg; Fibre 0.9g; Sodium 21mg.

Deep-fried battered yam

Lightly coated in spiced gram flour batter and crisp-fried, these yam slices, *Kath Alur Pokora*, make a delicious appetizer before a special lunch or dinner. Yams are readily available in larger supermarkets and Asian stores, and are a good source of protein and potassium, but you could also use slices of potato or sweet potato, or a mixture of all three vegetables.

SERVES 8
1kg/2¼lb yam
5ml/1 tsp salt, or to taste
5ml/1 tsp ground turmeric
5–7.5ml/1–1½ tsp chilli powder
2.5ml/½ tsp aniseed seeds
25g/1oz/¼ cup gram flour (besan), sifted
15g/½oz/1 tbsp ground rice
vegetable oil, for deep-frying
relish of your choice, to serve

1 Peel the yam and cut into 5mm/¼in thick slices. Some yams have thin ends and are thick in the centre, so cut the bigger slices in half. Place in a bowl and soak in cold water for 30 minutes, then drain. Do not dry them as they need to remain moist.

2 Put the salt, turmeric, chilli powder, aniseed seeds, gram flour and ground rice in a large bowl and mix well with a wooden spoon. Add the sliced yam pieces and stir until they are fully coated with the spiced gram flour mixture.

3 Heat the oil in a wok or other suitable pan for deep-frying over a medium to high heat. To check that the oil is at the right temperature, drop a tiny piece of the batter into the hot oil. If it floats to the surface immediately without browning, then the temperature is just right. If you have a cooking thermometer, make sure that the oil is at least 180°C/350°F.

4 Carefully lower two or three slices of yam at a time into the hot oil, depending on the size of the pan. Fry in a single layer, taking care not to overcrowd the pan, for about 3–4 minutes or until they are crisp and golden brown.

5 Remove with a slotted spoon and drain on kitchen paper. Cook the remaining batches in the same way. Serve with a relish of your choice, such as mango chutney, a pickle or raita.

Per portion Energy 335kcal/1415kJ; Protein 3.5g; Carbohydrate 53.1g, of which sugars 1.3g; Fat 13.7g, of which saturates 1.6g; Cholesterol 0mg; Calcium 39mg; Fibre 2.4g; Sodium 4mg.

Golden yam cubes with spinach

Very popular in Assam and the rest of north-east India, this appetizing dish, *Kath Alu Paleng Sakor Torkari*, is easy to prepare and extremely nutritious. The yam is cut into small cubes and browned in perfumed, spicy mustard oil. The spinach is then added in quickly, and the yam cooks in the spinach juice.

3 Fry the ginger, garlic and green chillies in remaining oil in the pan for 1–2 minutes.

4 Stir in the cumin and add the remaining turmeric and the fried yam cubes, followed by the chopped spinach. Stir-fry until the spinach has wilted, then add the tomatoes and 200ml/7fl oz/¾ cup warm water.

5 Stir in the remaining salt and cook for 4–5 minutes, or until the water has been absorbed by the yam. Serve immediately.

SERVES 4

675g/1½lb yam
5ml/1 tsp ground turmeric
5ml/1 tsp salt, or to taste
60ml/4 tbsp mustard oil
5ml/1 tsp ginger purée
5ml/1 tsp garlic purée
2 fresh green chillies, chopped
  (deseeded if preferred)
2.5ml/½ tsp ground cumin
250g/9oz spinach, finely chopped
150g/5oz fresh tomato, finely chopped

1 Peel the yam and cut it into 1cm/½in cubes. Soak in cold water for 30 minutes, drain and dry with a cloth. Sprinkle in half the turmeric and half the salt and mix well.

2 Heat the oil in a large frying pan over a medium heat and fry the yam cubes in two or three batches, for about 5 minutes, until they are golden brown. Remove the fried yam cubes with a slotted spoon and drain on kitchen paper.

Per portion Energy 243kcal/1037kJ; Protein 5.2g; Carbohydrate 55.9g, of which sugars 3.4g; Fat 1.5g, of which saturates 0.3g; Cholesterol 0mg; Calcium 142mg; Fibre 4g; Sodium 587mg.

Spiced yam fingers

These crispy yam bites, *Kath Alu Bhoja*, are rather like French fries with a spicy coating, and are often served at informal parties as an appetizer with drinks. They are easy to make and very tasty. Yams are usually readily available in larger supermarkets, as well as in Asian and African stores.

SERVES 4

450g/1lb yam
45ml/3 tbsp sunflower oil or light olive oil
10ml/2 tsp garlic purée
2.5–5ml/½–1 tsp chilli powder
2.5ml/½ tsp ground turmeric
5ml/1 tsp salt, or to taste

5 Remove the lid and increase the heat slightly. Cook, stirring frequently, until the yam has browned. Remove from the heat and serve immediately.

4 Add the yam fingers to the pan and stir over a medium heat for 2–3 minutes. Reduce the heat slightly, cover the pan and cook for 8–9 minutes, until the yam is tender.

1 Peel the yam and slice the flesh into thin fingers to resemble French fries. Wash and dry thoroughly with a dish cloth.

2 In a large frying pan, heat the oil over a low heat. Add the garlic and fry gently until it is light brown.

3 Add the chilli powder, turmeric and salt, and stir to combine.

> ## VARIATION
> Parsnips make a good alternative to yams, if you prefer. Reduce the cooking time to 5 minutes.

Per portion Energy 209kcal/880kJ; Protein 2.2g; Carbohydrate 32.8g, of which sugars 0.9g; Fat 8.6g, of which saturates 1.1g; Cholesterol 0mg; Calcium 18mg; Fibre 1.7g; Sodium 3mg.

Egg cutlets

Cutlets of various kinds were a favourite snack item during the period of the British Raj in east and north-east India. *Andey Ka Cutless* are served with tomato ketchup, in the social and sports clubs.

MAKES 12

6 hard-boiled eggs
350g/12oz potatoes, boiled, peeled
  and mashed
45ml/3 tbsp sunflower oil or light olive oil
2.5ml/½ tsp nigella seeds
1 medium onion, finely chopped
10ml/2 tsp ginger purée
2 fresh green chillies, finely chopped
  (deseeded if preferred)
2.5ml/½ tsp ground turmeric
2.5ml/½ tsp chilli powder, or to taste
2.5ml/½ tsp garam masala
15ml/1 tbsp fresh coriander (cilantro)
  leaves, finely chopped
5ml/1 tsp salt, or to taste
sunflower oil, for deep-frying
30ml/2 tbsp plain (all-purpose) flour
1 large (US extra large) egg, beaten
75g/3oz/1½ cups fresh soft breadcrumbs
tomato ketchup or chutney, to serve

4 Add the chilli powder, garam masala, coriander and salt. Cook, stirring, for 1–2 minutes, then remove from the heat and add to the potato and egg mixture. Mix until the ingredients are well combined.

5 Divide the mixture into 12 equal portions and form into oval-shaped flat cutlets about 1cm/½in thick. Heat the oil to 180°C/350°F in a large pan suitable for deep-frying.

1 Remove the shells from the hard-boiled eggs and cut them in half. Scoop out the yolks and mash them.

2 Chop the whites finely and then mix the egg yolks and whites with the mashed potatoes in a large bowl.

3 Heat the oil over a medium heat and add the nigella seeds, followed by the onion, ginger and chillies. Fry, stirring, for 5 minutes, until the onion is soft, but not brown.

6 Dip each portion in turn in flour, then in the beaten egg, then roll them in the soft breadcrumbs so they are evenly coated all over.

7 Carefully lower four or five cutlets into the hot oil and fry for 3–4 minutes, until crisp and golden brown.

8 Lift out with a slotted spoon and drain on kitchen paper. Repeat with the other cutlets.

9 Serve immediately with tomato ketchup or chutney.

Per portion Energy 132kcal/550kJ; Protein 5g; Carbohydrate 11g, of which sugars 1g; Fat 8g, of which saturates 1g;
Cholesterol 96mg; Calcium 31mg; Fibre 1.0g; Sodium 235mg.

Egg fritters

Konir Bora are great for buffet or drinks parties as well as making a delicious first course with a salad garnish – they are also just the sort of snack to eat sitting in front of the fire on a cold, wintry evening.

MAKES 12

2 slices white bread, a day or two old, crusts removed
30–45ml/2–3 tbsp fresh coriander (cilantro) leaves and stalks
1–2 fresh green chillies, chopped (deseeded if preferred)
1cm/½in piece of root ginger, peeled and chopped
5ml/1 tsp fennel seeds
2.5ml/½ tsp salt
1 egg, beaten
4 large (US extra large) hard-boiled eggs
sunflower oil, for deep-frying
15ml/1 tbsp cornflour (cornstarch)
mixed lettuce leaves, red onion rings and diced cucumber, to garnish
chutney, to serve

1 Put the bread in a food processor and process it into crumbs. Add the coriander, chillies, ginger, fennel, salt and beaten egg. Process until the mixture is well blended, then add the hard-boiled eggs and chop them roughly using the pulse action.

2 Transfer the mixture into a bowl and make 12 equal portions. Form each into a ball and flatten with your hands to form a smooth round cake.

3 Heat the oil in a pan suitable for deep-frying over medium/high heat. Dust each cake in cornflour, shaking off any excess.

4 Arrange the lettuce leaves, onion rings and cucumber on a serving plate.

5 Fry the cakes in batches for 3–4 minutes, until crisp and golden brown.

6 Lift the cakes out with a slotted spoon and drain on kitchen paper. Arrange on the prepared plate and serve with a chutney of your choice.

VARIATION
For a rich treat, use 2 hard-boiled duck eggs instead of hen's eggs.

Per portion Energy 307kcal/1278kJ; Protein 25.1g; Carbohydrate 3.8g, of which sugars 0.1g; Fat 22g, of which saturates 6.1g; Cholesterol 745mg; Calcium 119mg; Fibre 0.1g; Sodium 299mg.

Mixed vegetables with five-spice mix

This Assamese dish, *Meeholi Bhaji*, is made with odds and ends that are already in the kitchen. It has a wonderful confetti of colours and a fabulous mingling of flavours, which are imparted by the different types of vegetables and the five-spice mix that is typical of this region. Serve with rice and a lentil dish.

SERVES 4

60ml/4 tbsp mustard oil
175g/6oz potatoes, cut into 2.5cm/1in cubes
115g/4oz carrots, cut into 2.5cm/1in cubes
150g/5oz cauliflower, divided into
 2.5cm/1in florets
2 bay leaves
5ml/1 tsp ground coriander
5ml/1 tsp ground cumin
2.5ml/½ tsp ground turmeric
2.5ml/½ tsp chilli powder
½ a small cabbage (about 200g/7oz),
 finely shredded
115g/4oz garden peas, fresh or frozen
 (boiled until tender, if fresh)
5ml/1 tsp salt, or to taste
4–5 whole fresh green chillies
2 ripe tomatoes, cut into 2.5cm/1in chunks
30ml/2 tbsp fresh coriander (cilantro)
 leaves, chopped
Plain Boiled Rice or Plain Flour Flat Bread

For the five-spice mix:
2.5ml/½ tsp black or brown mustard seeds
2.5ml/½ tsp cumin seeds
2.5ml/½ tsp fennel seeds
2.5ml/½ tsp nigella seeds
6 fenugreek seeds

1 Heat 45ml/3 tbsp of the oil in a non-stick or cast iron pan until it reaches smoking point, then reduce the heat slightly and add the potatoes and carrots.

2 Stir-fry for about 4 minutes, until they begin to brown, then remove with a slotted spoon and drain on kitchen paper. Brown the cauliflower in the remaining oil for about 3 minutes, then remove and drain.

3 Add the remaining oil to the pan and heat until smoking point is reached. Switch off the heat source and add the five-spice mix. Let it crackle and pop for about 30 seconds.

4 Add the bay leaves, coriander, cumin, turmeric and chilli powder.

5 Place the pan over a low heat and fry the spices for about 1 minute.

6 Add the browned potatoes and carrots and pour in 300ml/½ pint/1¼ cups lukewarm water. Bring it to the boil, reduce the heat to low and cover the pan.

7 Cook for 5–6 minutes, then add the cauliflower, cabbage, peas and salt.

8 Cover and simmer for 4–5 minutes, then add the chillies, tomatoes and coriander.

9 Cook, uncovered for 2–3 minutes, remove from the heat and serve with Plain Boiled Rice or Plain Flour Flat Bread.

VARIATION

You can either buy pre-mixed five-spice mix or make your own, as in this recipe.

Per portion Energy 161kcal/668kJ; Protein 3g; Carbohydrate 10g, of which sugars 4g; Fat 13g, of which saturates 2g; Cholesterol 0mg; Calcium 38mg; Fibre 2.2g; Sodium 413mg.

Cinnamon-scented cabbage with potatoes

Dishes from the north-east tend to be simple and use just a few spices, rather than the more complex mixtures that feature elsewhere in India. In this recipe, *Bondhakobi-alu Bhaji*, the oil is fragranced with cinnamon and turmeric and a little heat is provided by chillies, so that the main flavour stands out.

2 Reduce the heat to medium and pour the remaining 15ml/1 tbsp oil into the pan. Add the cinnamon and allow it to sizzle for 20 seconds.

3 Add the onion, chillies and garlic. Fry for 7–8 minutes, until the onion is lightly browned, stirring frequently.

4 Add the turmeric, cabbage, salt and fried potatoes. Stir, then reduce the heat to low, pour over 90ml/6 tbsp water and cover the pan with a lid.

5 Cook gently for about 10–15 minutes, until the potatoes are soft and the cabbage is just tender, but still has some bite. If there is a lot of fluid left, cook for a few more minutes, uncovered, over a medium heat to reduce the liquid.

SERVES 4

60ml/4 tbsp sunflower or light olive oil
1 large potato, peeled and cut into
  2.5cm/1in cubes
5cm/2in piece cinnamon stick, halved
1 large onion, thinly sliced
2–3 fresh red chillies, sliced at an angle
  (deseeded if preferred)
2 cloves garlic, crushed, or 10ml/2 tsp
  garlic purée
2.5ml/½ tsp ground turmeric
1 small white cabbage, finely shredded
5ml/1 tsp salt, or to taste
chopped tomatoes and sprigs of fresh
  coriander (cilantro), to garnish

1 Heat 45ml/3 tbsp of the oil in a frying pan over a medium-high heat. Fry the potatoes for 5 minutes, until browned. Remove with a slotted spoon and drain on kitchen paper.

6 Spoon into a warmed serving dish and serve, garnished with chopped tomatoes and coriander, as an accompaniment to any meat or chicken dish.

Per portion Energy 218kcal/902kJ; Protein 3g; Carbohydrate 18g, of which sugars 8g; Fat 15g, of which saturates 2g; Cholesterol 0mg; Calcium 60mg; Fibre 3.1g; Sodium 503mg.

Chilli and coriander cauliflower with eggs

Cauliflower was first grown in India in the 19th century and is now popular in many dishes. Instead of being boiled or steamed, the cauliflower in this dish, *Phulkobi Aru Konir Torkari*, is stir-fried with a range of spices until lightly browned. Eggs are scrambled in at the end of the cooking time to provide a contrast in texture.

SERVES 4

1 medium cauliflower, about 400g/14oz
45ml/3 tbsp sunflower or light olive oil
1.25ml/¼ tsp black mustard seeds
1.25ml/¼ tsp nigella seeds
1.25ml/¼ tsp cumin seeds
1 large red onion, finely chopped
2 fresh red chillies, sliced at an angle
  (deseeded if preferred)
2.5ml/½ tsp ground turmeric
5ml/1 tsp salt, or to taste
4 large eggs, beaten
30ml/2 tbsp chopped fresh coriander
  (cilantro)
warm Indian bread, to serve

3 Fry the mixture over medium heat for 5 minutes, then add the cauliflower florets and salt and stir-fry until the cauliflower begins to colour. Reduce the heat to low, cover the pan, and cook for 5–6 minutes until tender.

4 Mix the beaten egg and coriander together in a small bowl until well combined, then pour it over the cauliflower mixture in the pan.

5 Increase the heat slightly and stir for about 1 minute or until softly scrambled eggs coat the cauliflower florets.

6 Remove the pan from the heat and serve immediately with any warm Indian bread.

VARIATION
Mix cauliflower with broccoli for a colourful alternative.

1 Using a knife, divide the cauliflower into even-sized florets.

2 Heat the oil in a heavy, non-stick pan over a medium heat. When hot, add the mustard seeds followed by the nigella and cumin. Let the seeds crackle for 10 seconds, then add the onion and chillies. Stir-fry for 4–5 minutes, then add the turmeric.

Per portion Energy 278kcal/1155kJ; Protein 14g; Carbohydrate 13g, of which sugars 9g; Fat 20g, of which saturates 4g; Cholesterol 255mg; Calcium 97mg; Fibre 3.5g; Sodium 599mg.

Cauliflower and potato curry

This highly spiced vegetable curry, *Phoolkobi, Motor Alu Alur Jool*, is often served as a delicious vegetarian alternative for Hindu festivals on which meat is forbidden, and other special occasions.

SERVES 4

500g/1¼lb potatoes
1 small cauliflower or 350g/12oz cauliflower
  florets, with outer stalks removed
45ml/3 tbsp sunflower oil or olive oil
1 large onion, finely sliced
5ml/1 tsp ginger purée
5ml/1 tsp garlic purée
2 fresh green chillies, chopped
  (deseeded if preferred)
2.5ml/½ tsp ground turmeric
5ml/1 tsp ground coriander
175g/6oz fresh tomatoes, chopped
5ml/1 tsp salt, or to taste
115g/4oz frozen garden peas
15ml/1 tbsp chopped fresh coriander
  (cilantro), to garnish

3 Heat the oil in a large, non-stick pan over a medium–high heat and fry the potatoes in two to three batches until they are well browned and form a crust on the surface – they will look a bit like roast potatoes. Remove the potatoes from the pan with a slotted spoon and drain them on kitchen paper. Set aside.

4 In the same oil, fry the onion, ginger, garlic and chillies over a low–medium heat, stirring regularly, for about 5 minutes, until the mixture begins to brown slightly.

5 Add the ground turmeric and coriander to the onion mixture, cook for 1 minute, then add the tomatoes, fried potatoes and salt. Stir to combine.

1 Halve or quarter the unpeeled potatoes according to their size – the pieces should be quite chunky so that they do not fall apart during cooking.

2 Divide the cauliflower into florets, about 2.5cm/1in in size, then blanch them for about 2 minutes in a small pan of boiling salted water. Plunge the blanched florets straight into cold water to prevent any further cooking.

6 Pour in 400ml/14fl oz/1⅔ cups warm water. Bring to the boil, reduce the heat to low, then cover and cook for 15 minutes. Drain the cauliflower and add to the pan. Add the peas and cook for 5 minutes. Serve, garnished with coriander.

COOK'S TIP
Use a waxy variety of potato, such as Charlotte, for this recipe, as they hold their shape when cooked.

Per portion Energy 276kcal/1153kJ; Protein 9.7g; Carbohydrate 37g, of which sugars 11.6g; Fat 10.9g, of which saturates 1.5g; Cholesterol 0mg; Calcium 89mg; Fibre 6.5g; Sodium 33.8mg.

Lentil fritters in tomato sauce

This recipe comes from Assam, the land of rich natural resources and world-renowned tea. You can make the fritters, *Borar Anjar*, in advance and store them in the refrigerator, then simply reheat them in the sauce when you are ready to serve them.

SERVES 4

For the fritters:

115g/4oz/½ cup red split lentils (masoor dhal)
125g/4¼oz/½ cup yellow split lentils (mung or moong dhal)
5ml/1 tsp fennel seeds
2 fresh green chillies, roughly chopped (deseeded if preferred)
15g/½oz/¼ cup fresh coriander (cilantro) leaves and stalks
2.5ml/½ tsp salt, or to taste
1.25ml/¼ tsp bicarbonate of soda (baking soda)
vegetable oil, for deep-frying

For the sauce:

30ml/2 tbsp mustard oil
1.25ml/¼ tsp black mustard seeds
1.25ml/¼ tsp cumin seeds
1.25ml/¼ tsp fennel seeds
1.25ml/¼ tsp nigella seeds
6–8 fenugreek seeds
2 fresh green chillies, sliced lengthways (deseeded if preferred)
2 small potatoes, finely chopped or grated
2.5ml/½ tsp ground turmeric
400g/14oz canned chopped tomatoes, with their juice
2.5ml/½ tsp salt, or to taste
15ml/1 tbsp lime juice
15ml/1 tbsp chopped fresh coriander (cilantro) leaves
Plain Boiled Rice, to serve

1 To make the fritters, wash the lentils and soak them together with the mung beans for 3–4 hours. Drain and put them in a food processor. Add the remaining fritter ingredients except the oil. Add 45ml/3 tbsp water and blend the mixture until smooth.

2 Heat the oil in a wok over a medium heat. Add the fritter mixture, 5ml/1 tsp at a time and fry for 2–3 minutes, until they are golden brown. Drain on kitchen paper.

3 To make the sauce, heat the oil over a medium heat until smoking. Remove the pan from the heat and add the mustard, cumin, fennel, nigella and fenugreek seeds and the green chillies.

4 Add the potatoes to the hot oil and return the pan to the heat. Stir-fry the potatoes for about 5 minutes, until they are well browned all over.

5 Stir in the turmeric, followed by the tomatoes and salt. Pour in 300ml/10fl oz/ 1¼ cups warm water and bring to the boil. Reduce the heat to low and simmer for 3–4 minutes or until the potatoes are tender.

6 Add the fritters to the sauce and cook for 3–4 minutes. Add the lime juice and coriander leaves and remove from the heat. Serve with Plain Boiled Rice.

Per portion Energy 360kcal/1,510kJ; Protein 14g; Carbohydrate 51.3g, of which sugars 8.3g; Fat 12.3g, of which saturates 1.4g; Cholesterol 0mg; Calcium 119.2mg; Fibre 5.3g; Sodium 25.8mg.

Vegetables with roasted split mung beans

A delightful dish from Tripura with definite influences from Bengal, *Shukto* is a dish in which different types of vegetables and the roasted mung beans themselves act as the main flavouring agents. Its superb taste belies the simplicity of the spicing and cooking method. Mustard oil is preferred, but other types of cooking oil can be used if liked, though the same flavour profile will not be achieved.

SERVES 4

115g/4oz skinless split mung beans
   (mung dhal)
60ml/4 tbsp mustard oil
175g/6oz carrots, peeled and cut into batons
1 turnip, peeled and cut into bitesize pieces
115g/4oz cauliflower, divided into
   2.5cm/1in florets
3–4 whole dried red chillies
2.5ml/½ tsp ground turmeric
5ml/1 tsp salt, or to taste
2.5ml/½ tsp sugar
250g/9oz baby spinach leaves
Plain Boiled Rice, to serve

For the five-spice mix:
2.5ml/½ tsp black or brown mustard seeds
2.5ml/½ tsp cumin seeds
2.5ml/½ tsp nigella seeds
2.5ml/½ tsp fennel seeds
6 fenugreek seeds

1 Wash the mung beans in a sieve (strainer), then transfer to a large bowl and soak in cold water for 1–2 hours. Drain well.

2 Heat 15ml/1 tbsp of the oil in a non-stick pan over a medium heat until it reaches smoking point, then add the mung beans. Roast for 2–3 minutes, stirring regularly.

3 Reduce the heat to low and continue to roast for a further 3–4 minutes or until the mung beans are a shade darker. Transfer to a plate and set aside.

4 In the same pan, heat 30ml/2 tbsp of the remaining oil until smoking point is reached, then add the carrots and turnip.

5 Stir-fry the vegetables for 3–4 minutes, until they begin to brown, then remove with a slotted spoon and transfer to a plate, leaving behind the oil.

6 In the same oil, stir-fry the cauliflower florets for 3–4 minutes, until brown patches appear, then remove with a slotted spoon and add to the other browned vegetables on the plate.

7 Add the remaining oil to the pan and heat until smoking point is reached.

8 Switch off the heat source and add the five-spice mix, immediately followed by the dried red chillies and the ground turmeric. Cook for 2–3 minutes, until the chillies blacken and the five-spice mix releases its aroma.

9 Add the roasted mung beans, salt, sugar, carrots and turnips and pour in 400ml/14fl oz/1¾ cups water and bring it to the boil.

10 Reduce the heat to low, cover the pan and simmer for 10 minutes. Add the cauliflower, cover and simmer for 5 minutes.

11 Add the spinach and stir over a medium heat until the spinach has wilted. Cook, uncovered, for 2–3 minutes. Remove from the heat and serve with Plain Boiled Rice.

Per portion Energy 196kcal/809kJ; Protein 5g; Carbohydrate 9g, of which sugars 8g; Fat 16g, of which saturates 2g; Cholesterol 0mg; Calcium 156mg; Fibre 6.4g; Sodium 600mg.

Garlic-flavoured mung beans

Khar is from Assam and is always served at the beginning of a meal, as it is believed to aid digestion. Bicarbonate of soda (baking soda) replaces the traditional ingredient of banana tree trunk ashes.

SERVES 4

225g/8oz/1½ cups whole mung beans
  (sabut mung dhal)
60ml/4 tbsp mustard oil
8–10 fenugreek seeds
4–5 large garlic cloves, crushed
8cm/3in piece of fresh root ginger, grated
1 fresh red chilli, sliced diagonally
  (deseeded if preferred)
1 fresh green chilli, sliced diagonally
  (deseeded if preferred)
2.5ml/½ tsp bicarbonate of soda
  (baking soda)
5ml/1 tsp salt, or to taste
1 courgette (zucchini), finely diced
Plain Boiled Rice, to serve

4 Stir-fry for 3–4 minutes, then add the bicarbonate of soda and salt.

5 Pour in 600ml/1 pint/2½ cups warm water and bring the mixture to the boil. Reduce the heat and cook for 12–15 minutes or until the beans are tender.

1 Wash the mung beans in several changes of water, then transfer them to a large bowl, cover with cold water and soak them for 6–8 hours or overnight.

2 Heat 45ml/3 tbsp of the mustard oil over a medium heat, until it reaches smoking point. Switch off the heat and add the fenugreek. When the seeds go a shade darker, add the garlic, half the ginger and the red and green chillies.

3 Turn the heat back on to medium and stir-fry the ingredients for 1–2 minutes. Drain the soaked mung beans and add them to the pan.

6 Add the diced courgette and cook for a further 4–5 minutes. Remove the pan from the heat and stir in the remaining mustard oil and ginger. Transfer to a serving dish and serve with Plain Boiled Rice.

Per portion Energy 268kcal/1125kJ; Protein 13.5g; Carbohydrate 27g, of which sugars 1.5g; Fat 12.6g, of which saturates 1.6g; Cholesterol 0mg; Calcium 70mg; Fibre 8.8g; Sodium 13mg.

Red lentils with cumin

In a country where the vast majority of the population is vegetarian, lentils regularly form part of a meal. Called dhal, dal or daail, they are cooked with their own distinctive combination of spices to produce an utterly satisfying dish.

SERVES 4

115g/4oz/½ cup red split lentils
115g/4oz/½ cup yellow split lentils
  (moong or mung dhal)
2.5ml/½ tsp ground turmeric
5ml/1 tsp salt, or to taste
25g/1oz/2 tbsp ghee or unsalted butter
30ml/2 tbsp sunflower oil
2.5ml/½ tsp mustard seeds
2.5ml/½ tsp cumin seeds
2 dried red chillies, whole
2 bay leaves
1 small onion, finely chopped
30ml/2 tbsp coriander (cilantro) leaves,
  finely chopped
Wholemeal Flat Bread or Plain Boiled Rice

1 Wash both types of lentils thoroughly in a sieve (strainer) under cold water, then drain. Put them in a pan with the turmeric and add 1 litre/1¾ pints/4 cups water. Bring to the boil, remove any froth with a spoon, and boil for 3–5 minutes.

2 Skim off any further froth, reduce the heat to low and cover the pan. Simmer for 30–35 minutes, then stir in the salt. Stir the lentils once or twice during cooking.

3 Heat the ghee or butter and oil in a pan over a medium heat until almost smoking.

4 Turn the heat off and add the mustard and cumin seeds, followed by the chillies and bay leaves. Allow the chillies to blacken slightly, then turn the heat back up to medium.

5 Add the onion and stir-fry until the onion turns golden brown. Add all the cooked spices to the lentils and mix well.

6 Stir in the chopped coriander and remove from the heat. Serve with Wholemeal Flat Bread and/or Plain Boiled Rice.

Per portion Energy 263kcal/1110kJ; Protein 15.2g; Carbohydrate 36.6g, of which sugars 2.2g; Fat 7.4g, of which saturates 1g; Cholesterol 0mg; Calcium 49mg; Fibre 3g; Sodium 24mg.

Indian cheese balls

The Indian cheese known as paneer in the rest of the country is called sana in north-east India and Bengal. In this recipe, *Sanar Kofta*, grated Indian cheese is mixed with mashed potatoes and a few chosen spices, formed into small balls and browned before being simmered in a spicy sauce.

SERVES 4

225g/8oz/2 cups paneer (Indian cheese), coarsley grated
200g/7oz/1 cup cooked potatoes, mashed
10ml/2 tsp ginger purée
1 fresh green chilli, chopped
2.5ml/½ tsp garam masala
1 egg, beaten
30ml/2 tbsp fresh coriander (cilantro) leaves, finely chopped
7.5ml/1½ tsp salt, or to taste
60ml/4 tbsp sunflower oil or light olive oil
4 green cardamom pods, bruised
2.5cm/1in piece of cinnamon stick
1 large onion, finely chopped
5ml/1 tsp garlic purée
2.5ml/½ tsp ground turmeric
2.5–5ml/½–1 tsp chilli powder
5ml/1 tsp ground coriander
5ml/1 tsp ground cumin
150g/5oz frozen garden peas
3–4 whole fresh green chillies
Plain Boiled Rice, to serve

1 Mix together the paneer, potatoes, half the ginger, the chilli, garam masala, egg, coriander and half the salt in a bowl.

2 With dampened hands, make about 16 equal-sized balls from the mixture.

COOK'S TIP
Paneer provides as much protein per portion as meat, fish and poultry.

3 Heat 30ml/2 tbsp of the oil in a non-stick pan over a medium heat and brown the cheese balls. Drain on kitchen paper.

4 Add the remaining oil to the pan and stir in the cardamom and cinnamon. Let them sizzle for a few seconds, then add the onion and fry until it is beginning to brown.

5 Add the ginger and the garlic. Cook for 1 minute. Add the turmeric, chilli powder, coriander and cumin. Fry for 1 minute.

6 Pour in 300ml/10fl oz/1¼ cups warm water and add the remaining salt. Bring the mixture to the boil and cook over a medium heat for 2–3 minutes.

7 Add the browned cheese balls in a single layer and spoon over some of the sauce. Add the peas and whole chillies, reduce the heat to low, and cook for 5–6 minutes or until the sauce has thickened to the desired consistency. Serve with Plain Boiled Rice.

Per portion Energy 263kcal/1097kJ; Protein 12.2g; Carbohydrate 20.4g, of which sugars 8.8g; Fat 15.5g, of which saturates 3g; Cholesterol 55mg; Calcium 89mg; Fibre 2.3g; Sodium 242mg.

Duck eggs with cauliflower

Duck eggs are very popular in the north-east of India, but hen's eggs are also perfectly suitable here. This dish, *Hahor Koni Aru Phoolkobi*, was created by my mother and includes lightly spiced cauliflower florets and golden eggs accentuated with fresh chillies and coriander (cilantro) leaves.

SERVES 4

1 medium-sized cauliflower, about 450g/1lb, divided into 2.5cm/1in florets
iced water
45ml/3 tbsp sunflower oil or light olive oil
2.5ml/½ tsp black mustard seeds
5ml/1 tsp cumin seeds, lightly crushed
5ml/1 tsp coriander seeds, lightly crushed
2.5ml/½ tsp nigella seeds
1 medium onion, finely sliced
1–2 fresh green chillies, finely chopped (deseeded if preferred)
5ml/1 tsp ground turmeric
2.5ml/½ tsp salt, or to taste
30ml/2 tbsp fresh coriander (cilantro) leaves, finely chopped
4 duck eggs, beaten
Wholemeal Flat Bread and/or Plain Boiled Rice and Red Split Lentils with Mustard and Cumin, to serve

1 Blanch the cauliflower florets in boiling salted water for 3 minutes, drain, then immediately plunge in iced water.

2 Heat the oil in a non-stick wok or a frying pan over a medium heat. When hot, but not smoking, add the mustard seeds, and as soon as they pop, add the cumin, coriander and nigella seeds.

3 Let the seeds crackle for a few seconds, then add the onion and chillies and stir-fry for about 5 minutes, until the onion is soft, but not brown. Add the turmeric.

4 Drain the cauliflower florets and add them to the pan along with the salt. Stir-fry for 3–4 minutes, until the cauliflower is heated through, then add the chopped coriander and stir to combine.

5 Pour over the egg and leave it to set for 2 minutes, then stir to coat the cauliflower. Serve immediately with Wholemeal Flat Breads and/or Plain Boiled Rice and Red Split Lentils with Mustard and Cumin.

Per portion Energy 264kcal/1095kJ; Protein 16.1g; Carbohydrate 7.9g, of which sugars 4.5g; Fat 19g, of which saturates 3.5g; Cholesterol 509mg; Calcium 90mg; Fibre 2.5g; Sodium 103mg.

Indian cheese curry in milk

This recipe, *Sana Thongba*, comes from the state of Manipur and makes a satisfying meal when served with rice. It contains garden peas and potatoes along with cubes of cheese and the entire dish is cooked in milk, making it protein-rich, creamy and nutritious as well as delicious.

SERVES 4

30ml/2 tbsp sunflower oil or light olive oil
2 bay leaves
10ml/2 tsp ginger purée
10ml/2 tsp garlic purée
1 fresh green chilli, finely chopped
2.5ml/½ tsp ground turmeric
5ml/1 tsp ground coriander
2.5ml/½ tsp ground cumin
2.5ml–5ml/½–1 tsp chilli powder
200g/7oz paneer (Indian cheese)
150g/5oz frozen peas or fresh peas
250g/9oz potatoes
2.5cm/1in piece of cinnamon stick
2.5ml/½ tsp salt, or to taste
600ml/1 pint/2½ cups full-fat (whole) milk
2.5ml/½ tsp garam masala
a mixture of wild and basmati rice,
  to serve

1 Heat the oil in a large, non-stick pan over a low heat and add the bay leaves, ginger, garlic and chilli. Fry gently for 3–4 minutes, until the garlic softens but does not brown.

2 Add the turmeric, coriander, cumin and chilli powder. Stir and cook for 2 minutes.

3 Meanwhile, cut the paneer into 2.5cm/1in cubes. Set aside.

VARIATION
For a richer version, substitute half the milk with double (heavy) cream.

4 Put the peas in a bowl, cover with boiling water and leave until tender. Drain.

5 Peel the potatoes, then cut them into 2.5cm/1in chunks.

6 Reduce the heat to medium and pour the remaining 15ml/1 tbsp oil into the pan. Add the cinnamon and sizzle for 20 seconds.

7 Add the potatoes, salt and milk and stir to combine. Bring to the boil, reduce the heat to low and simmer, uncovered, for 20 minutes, stirring often.

8 Add the paneer and peas and simmer for 6–7 minutes. Stir in the garam masala and remove from the heat. Serve with a mixture of wild and basmati rice.

COOK'S TIP
Wild rice is particularly beneficial in a vegetarian diet because it is high in protein, unlike true rice, which contains incomplete proteins. It provides useful amounts of the essential amino acid, lysine, which is a building block of protein in the body. It also aids calcium absorption and is involved in the production of various hormones, enzymes and antibodies.

Per portion Energy 378kcal/1566kJ; Protein 10g; Carbohydrate 22g, of which sugars 8g; Fat 29g, of which saturates 14g; Cholesterol 50mg; Calcium 235mg; Fibre 3.6g; Sodium 413mg.

Smoked fish with onion, chilli and coriander

Fish is plentiful in north-east India and is harvested from the many rivers, ponds and lakes. As fresh fish doesn't keep for long, smoking is a great way to preserve it and many families do this themselves at home. This dish from Assam, *Pura Masor Pitika*, uses smoked mackerel served in a simple yet flavoursome marinade of red onion, chillies, coriander (cilantro), mustard oil and lime juice.

SERVES 4

400g/14oz smoked mackerel
1 small red onion, finely chopped
1–2 fresh green chillies, finely chopped
    (deseeded if preferred)
30ml/2 tbsp fresh coriander (cilantro)
30ml/2 tbsp mustard oil
juice of 1 lime
a lentil dish, a wedge of lime and Plain
    Boiled Rice, to serve

COOK'S TIP
Don't leave the fish to marinate too long or it will become mushy.

1 Remove the skin from the smoked mackerel and remove any visible bones. Using your hands, break the flesh into flakes, removing any more bones you find, and put the flakes in a bowl.

2 Add the finely chopped red onion, chillies and coriander to the bowl.

3 Whisk together the mustard oil and lime juice in a separate bowl, then pour over the fish and onion mixture. Stir with a fork to combine thoroughly, cover with clear film (plastic wrap) and set aside for 30 minutes for the flavours to mingle.

4 Serve the marinated fish with a lentil dish, a wedge of lime and Plain Boiled Rice.

Per portion Energy 452kcal/1872kJ; Protein 13g; Carbohydrate 21g, of which sugars 14g; Fat 36g, of which saturates 21g; Cholesterol 101mg; Calcium 363mg; Fibre 0.5g; Sodium 139mg.

Fish in tangy tomato sauce

Meals in Assam usually end with *Masor Tenga*, a dish made with tomatoes and lime juice along with a flavoursome sprinkling of whole spices. Any firm white-fleshed fish can be used and the selection of spices can be varied. Here, an earthy flavour is imparted by using mustard and nigella seeds. Although fresh tomatoes are more traditional, canned tomatoes have been used here to add a lovely rich colour.

SERVES 4

675g/1½lb fillets of tilapia, monkfish or
   other firm white fish
5ml/1 tsp ground turmeric
5ml/1 tsp salt, or to taste
45ml/3 tbsp mustard oil
2.5ml/½ tsp black mustard seeds
2.5ml/½ tsp nigella seeds
10–12 fenugreek seeds
2 fresh green chillies, sliced lengthways
   (deseeded if preferred)
2 small potatoes, about 200g/7oz, finely
   chopped or grated
250ml/8fl oz/1 cup warm water
400g/14oz canned chopped tomatoes with
   their juice
15ml/1 tbsp lime juice
15ml/1 tbsp chopped fresh coriander
   (cilantro) leaves
Plain Boiled Rice, to serve

1 Cut the fish fillets into 5cm/2in pieces and lay them on a large plate. Sprinkle half of the turmeric and half the salt over them and rub both gently into the flesh. Cover with clear film (plastic wrap) and set aside for 10 minutes.

2 Heat the oil in a frying pan over a medium to high heat until it starts to smoke but not burn (the oil must be very hot), then fry the fish fillets in batches until the edges turn brown. Remove the fish pieces from the pan and drain on kitchen paper.

3 Take the pan off the heat and add the mustard, nigella and fenugreek seeds, and the chillies. Return the pan to the heat and add the potatoes. Fry until the potatoes are golden brown.

4 Add the remaining turmeric and salt, and pour in 250ml/8fl oz/1 cup warm water. Bring the pan to the boil, then reduce the heat to low and cook for a further 5–6 minutes, until the potatoes are tender.

5 Add the chopped tomatoes with their juice to the pan and cook, uncovered, for 5–6 minutes. Add the fried fish pieces, stir gently, taking care not to break up the fish, and cook for 5 minutes longer.

6 Add the lime juice and chopped coriander, give them a brief stir and remove the pan from the heat. Serve the dish immediately with a large spoonful of Plain Boiled Rice.

Per portion Energy 345kcal/1445kJ; Protein 23g; Carbohydrate 28.3g, of which sugars 5.6g; Fat 16.3g, of which saturates 4.2g; Cholesterol 144mg; Calcium 105mg; Fibre 2g; Sodium 338mg.

Manipuri fish curry

The cuisine of the state of Manipur is much spicier than that found in the rest of the north-east. This fish curry, *Nga Thongba*, is cooked with both red and green chillies and intensified with mustard oil, ginger and garlic. Traditionally it is made with white fish, but this version features salmon as the oily nature of the robust fish complements the tart and hot flavours of the sauce.

SERVES 4

675g/1½lb salmon or firm white fish
   fillets, skinned
30ml/2 tbsp lime juice
5ml/1 tsp salt, or to taste
5ml/1 tsp ground turmeric
60ml/4 tbsp mustard oil
2.5ml/½ tsp black mustard seeds
2 bay leaves
1 large onion, finely chopped
2.5cm/1in fresh root ginger, grated, or
   10ml/2 tsp ginger purée
2 cloves garlic, crushed, or 10ml/2 tsp
   garlic purée
2.5–5ml/½–1 tsp chilli powder
10ml/2 tsp ground coriander
200g/7oz cannned chopped tomatoes
4 fresh green chillies, slit lengthways
   (deseeded if preferred)
30ml/2 tbsp chopped fresh coriander
   (cilantro) (optional)

> **COOK'S TIP**
> Mustard oil must be heated to a high temperature to reduce its pungency. When a haze starts to appear above the oil, turn down the heat and start cooking.

1 Cut the fish into 5cm/2in pieces. Place in a bowl and sprinkle with the lime juice, half the salt and half the turmeric. Stir to coat, then set aside for 15–20 minutes.

2 Heat 15ml/1 tbsp of the oil in a non-stick pan over a medium heat until it reaches smoking point. Turn down the heat and fry the fish in batches for 30–40 seconds on each side. Remove and set aside.

3 Add the remaining mustard oil to the pan, increase the heat to medium and wait until it reaches smoking point. Add the mustard seeds, bay leaves and finely chopped onion to the oil.

4 Fry the onion for about 5 minutes, until it begins to brown, then add the ginger and garlic purées. Cook for 2–3 minutes, stirring, then add the remaining turmeric, the chilli powder and the ground coriander.

> **VARIATION**
> If you don't have any mustard oil you can use vegetable oil, but it won't have the same flavour.

5 Add the tomatoes and 30ml/2 tbsp water. Cook until oil begins to separate, then add 30ml/2 tbsp more water and cook for a further 2–3 minutes.

6 Add the chillies, 300ml/½ pint/1¼ cups hot water and the remaining salt. Stir, add the fish and cook for 5–6 minutes.

7 Stir half the coriander into the sauce. Use the rest as a garnish, if you like.

Per portion Energy 496kcal/2061kJ; Protein 37g; Carbohydrate 12g, of which sugars 8g; Fat 35g, of which saturates 5g; Cholesterol 84mg; Calcium 94mg; Fibre 2.1g; Sodium 606mg.

Mizo chicken stew

The population of Mizoram consists of several different tribes. Living off the land, they make great use of roots, leaves and nuts. Like most tribal races in the north-east, their use of spices is very limited, although ginger, garlic and fresh chillies feature in many dishes, including this one, *Arsa Bai*. The practice of bhuna, the gentle frying of spices before the addition of the main ingredients, is absent in their cuisine.

2 Add the salt, garlic, ginger, onion, and bay leaves. Bring to the boil, reduce the heat, cover and cook for 10 minutes.

3 Add the potatoes, cover and cook for 20 minutes. Add the carrots, cover and cook for 10 minutes, until they are tender.

4 Add the cooked rice and green chillies, simmer for 5–6 minutes, then remove from the heat. Ladle into bowls and garnish with strips of ginger and tomato. Serve with extra Plain Boiled Rice or warm Indian bread.

SERVES 4–5

1 chicken, weighing approximately
  1.5kg/3lb 5oz
7.5ml/1½ tsp salt, or to taste
8 large garlic cloves, crushed
15g/½oz fresh root ginger, finely chopped
1 large onion, finely chopped
2 bay leaves
450g/1lb small potatoes, peeled
225g/8oz carrots, cut at an angle
150g/5oz/1¼ cups cooked basmati rice
3–4 fresh green chillies, slit open
  lengthways (deseeded if preferred)
fine strips of fresh root ginger and
  tomatoes, to garnish
Plain Boiled Rice, or warm Indian bread,
  to serve

1 Joint the chicken, remove the skin and trim off any excess fat. Alternatively, ask a butcher to do this for you or buy pre-jointed pieces. Put the prepared chicken into a large pan and pour in 550ml/18fl oz/2½ cups cold water.

Per portion Energy 308kcal/1303kJ; Protein 37g; Carbohydrate 32g, of which sugars 7g; Fat 4g, of which saturates 1g; Cholesterol 135mg; Calcium 49mg; Fibre 2.9; Sodium 729mg.

Tripura chicken curry

Most dishes in the tiny state of Tripura are simple yet delicious, with many being cooked in mustard oil, although sunflower oil can be used instead. As rice is the staple in this region, this curry, *To Khan*, would be enjoyed with boiled rice. The chicken pieces are traditionally cooked on the bone as this adds flavour to the sauce, while the skin and any excess fat is removed prior to cooking.

SERVES 4–6

1 chicken weighing about 1.5kg/3lb 5oz
30ml/2 tbsp lemon juice
5ml/1 tsp salt
45ml/3 tbsp mustard or sunflower oil
2–3 fresh green chillies, sliced lengthways
3 cloves garlic, crushed, or 15ml/1 tbsp
    garlic purée
4cm/1½in fresh root ginger, grated, or
    15ml/1 tbsp ginger purée
1 large onion, finely chopped
5ml/1 tsp ground turmeric
10ml/2 tsp ground cumin
2.5ml/½ tsp chilli powder
10ml/2 tsp tomato purée
sprigs of fresh coriander (cilantro), to garnish
Plain Boiled Rice, to serve

2 Heat the oil in a large, heavy frying pan over a medium heat until smoking. Remove the pan from the heat and add the chillies, garlic and ginger. Fry, stirring, for about 1 minute.

3 Return the pan to the heat, increase the heat to high and add the chicken pieces. Fry, turning them frequently, until the chicken is lightly coloured all over. Add the onion and fry for 5 minutes,

4 Add the turmeric, cumin and chilli powder. Cook for 3–4 minutes, stirring constantly. Pour in 300ml/½ pint/1¼ cups hot water. Bring to the boil, reduce the heat and cover the pan. Simmer for 30 minutes, until the chicken is tender and cooked through.

5 Stir in the tomato purée and cook for a further 3–4 minutes. Transfer to a warmed serving dish and garnish with sprigs of fresh coriander. Serve with Plain Boiled Rice.

1 Joint the chicken, remove the skin and trim off any excess fat. Alternatively, ask a butcher to do this for you or buy pre-jointed pieces. Sprinkle over the lemon juice and salt and rub into the meat. Cover and set aside for 30 minutes.

Per portion Energy 209kcal/874kJ; Protein29; Carbohydrate 1g, of which sugars 1g; Fat 11g, of which saturates 2g; Cholesterol 113mg; Calcium 29mg; Fibre 0.1g; Sodium 440mg.

Chicken with tamarind and palm sugar

The origins of this recipe, *Naram Kukhura Ko Masu*, lie in Nepal, just across the border, but it is popular among most of the tribal states in north-east India. The use of Sichuan pepper is also an external influence, drawn from neighbouring China. The tart flavour of tamarind combined with the caramel sweetness of palm sugar (jaggery) gives a pleasing sweet and sour slant to the dish.

SERVES 4

1 chicken, about 1.3kg/3lb
7.5ml/1½ tsp salt
zest and juice of 2 limes
5ml/1 tsp Sichuan peppercorns
4 green cardamom pods
10ml/2 tsp coriander seeds
5ml/1 tsp cumin seeds
2 dried red chillies
2 onions, roughly chopped
25g/1oz fresh root ginger, chopped
8 garlic cloves
60ml/4 tbsp mustard or sunflower oil
2.5cm/1in piece of cinnamon stick
2 brown cardamom pods, bruised
1 bay leaf
5ml/1 tsp ground turmeric
200g/7oz canned chopped tomatoes
4 kaffir lime leaves, shredded
30ml/2 tbsp tamarind pulp
15ml/1 tbsp palm sugar (jaggery), grated
4 fresh green chillies, halved lengthways
   (deseeded if preferred)
30ml/2 tbsp chopped fresh coriander
   (cilantro)
Plain Boiled Rice, to serve

COOK'S TIP
Palm sugar (jaggery) is an unrefined sugar made from boiled cane sugar or palm sap and is sold in large lumps. It should be slightly sticky and easy to crumble.

1 Joint the chicken, remove the skin and trim off any excess fat. Alternatively, ask a butcher to do this for you or buy pre-jointed pieces. Sprinkle with 2.5ml/½ tsp salt and the lime juice and rub these into the chicken. Set aside for 15–20 minutes. Reserve the lime zest for use later.

2 Grind the Sichuan peppercorns, cardamom, coriander, cumin and dried red chillies in a coffee grinder or mortar and pestle. Put the onion, ginger and garlic in a food processor or blender and process to a fairly smooth purée.

3 If you are using mustard oil, heat it in a large, heavy frying pan over a medium heat until it reaches smoking point. If you are using sunflower oil, heat over a medium heat until it is hot. Turn down the heat (if using sunflower oil) to medium, add the cinnamon, cardamom and bay leaf to the hot oil and let them sizzle for about 15 seconds.

4 Add the puréed onion, garlic and ginger mixture to the pan and cook for 5 minutes, stirring frequently. Add the turmeric and cook for a further 2–3 minutes.

5 Add the tomatoes to the pan and cook for 4–5 minutes, or until the oil separates from the rest of the ingredients. Add the kaffir lime leaves, reserved lime zest and marinated chicken. Stir and cook for about 5 minutes, until the chicken is opaque.

6 Pour in 300ml/½ pint/1¼ cups hot water and the remaining salt. Cover and simmer for 30 minutes or until the chicken is tender and cooked through.

7 Add the tamarind pulp, palm sugar and green chillies. Cook, uncovered for a further 2–3 minutes.

8 Stir in half the chopped coriander and sprinkle over the rest as a garnish. Serve with Plain Boiled Rice.

Per portion Energy 431kcal/1807kJ; Protein 45g; Carbohydrate 20g, of which sugars 16g; Fat 20g, of which saturates 03g; Cholesterol 169mg; Calcium 85mg; Fibre 2.3g; Sodium 911mg.

Chicken with stir-fried spices

Bhoja Murgi is north-east India's equivalent of chicken bhuna. Like many of the region's recipes, it uses fewer spices and the flavouring comes from stir-frying the onion, ginger and garlic purée for a prolonged period, which lends a delicious toasted aroma.

SERVES 4

675g/1½lb boned chicken thighs or breasts, skinned and cut into 5cm/1in cubes

juice of 1 lime

5ml/1 tsp salt, or to taste

1 large onion, roughly chopped

15g/½oz fresh root ginger, roughly chopped

6 large garlic cloves

45ml/3 tbsp sunflower or light olive oil

2.5–5ml/½–1 tsp chilli powder

2.5ml/½ tsp ground turmeric

150g/5oz canned chopped tomatoes, with their juice

5ml/1 tsp garam masala

3–4 whole fresh green chillies

30ml/2 tbsp chopped fresh coriander (cilantro)

a vegetable curry, Plain Boiled Rice and warm Indian bread, to serve

1 Put the chicken in a large mixing bowl and sprinkle with the lime juice and salt. Stir to coat the chicken, then cover and set aside for 15–20 minutes.

2 Purée the onion, ginger and garlic in a blender or food processor. Alternatively, use a large knife to very finely chop the ingredients, then scrape and crush to form a paste.

3 Heat the oil in a large, heavy frying pan over a medium-high heat and add the puréed ingredients. Cook, stirring, for about 4–5 minutes, until softened.

4 Reduce the heat to medium and continue to cook for a further 1–2 minutes, then stir in 30ml/2 tbsp water.

5 Stir-fry for 1 minute more, then add the chilli powder, turmeric and canned tomatoes. Stir-fry until the tomatoes have reached a paste-like consistency and the oil has separated from the paste.

6 Add the chicken, increase the heat to high and stir-fry for 4–5 minutes.

7 Reduce the heat to low, pour in 120ml/4fl oz/½ cup hot water and cover the pan. Cook gently for 15 minutes, then stir in the garam masala and chillies. Continue to cook, uncovered, until the sauce is very thick and the chicken is cooked through.

8 Stir in half the chopped coriander and sprinkle over the rest as a garnish. Serve with a vegetable curry, Plain Boiled Rice and some warm Indian bread.

Per portion Energy 326kcal/1364kJ; Protein 40g; Carbohydrate 8g, of which sugars 5g; Fat 16g, of which saturates 2g; Cholesterol 152mg; Calcium 52mg; Fibre 1.3g; Sodium 654mg.

Roast duckling

Although this succulent recipe, *Poora Haah*, is labelled 'roast duckling', the bird is not roasted in the traditional way – rather, it is sautéed until it takes on a rich brown colour, then simmered in a spicy sauce. The final result is a beautifully flavoured, tender dish.

SERVES 4

4 duckling portions, about 675g/
  1½lb, skinned
5ml/1 tsp salt, or to taste
30ml/2 tbsp red wine vinegar
45ml/3 tbsp sunflower oil or olive oil
1 large onion, finely chopped
10ml/2 tsp ginger purée
10ml/2 tsp garlic purée
2.5ml/½ tsp ground cumin
5ml/1 tsp ground coriander
2.5ml/½ tsp ground turmeric
2.5ml/½ tsp chilli powder
200g/7oz canned chopped tomatoes,
  with their juice
2.5ml/½ tsp garam masala
30ml/2 tbsp chopped fresh coriander
  (cilantro) leaves
Plain Boiled Rice, to serve

1 Lay the duckling portions on a large plate and rub in half the salt and all of the vinegar. Cover with clear film (plastic wrap) and set aside for 30 minutes.

2 In a large frying pan, preferably non-stick, heat the oil over a medium to high heat and brown the duckling portions until they are well coloured and a crust has formed on the surface. Remove from the pan and drain on kitchen paper. Alternatively, you could brown the duckling pieces in the oven or under a hot grill (broiler), if you wish, but you will need to first brush the duck pieces with some oil.

3 In the remaining oil, fry the onion over a medium heat until it is soft. Add the ginger and garlic purées, and stir-fry until the mixture begins to brown.

4 Add the cumin, coriander, turmeric and chilli powder. Stir-fry for 1 minute, then add the tomatoes. Stir-fry for another 4–5 minutes, or until the tomatoes are reduced to a paste-like consistency and the oil separates from the spice paste.

5 Add the duckling portions and pour in 250ml/9fl oz/1 cup warm water with the remaining salt. Bring to the boil, then reduce the heat to low and cover. Cook gently over a low heat for 40–45 minutes, until the sauce has thickened to a paste-like consistency.

6 Stir in the garam masala and half the chopped coriander. Serve, garnished with the remaining coriander and accompanied by Plain Boiled Rice.

Per portion Energy 361kcal/1510kJ; Protein 37.5g; Carbohydrate 13g, of which sugars 7.2g; Fat 21.3g, of which saturates 3.5g; Cholesterol 193mg; Calcium 67.5mg; Fibre 1.9g; Sodium 204mg.

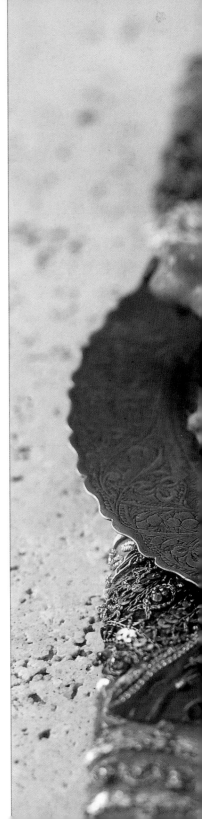

Pork with mixed beans

While a third of the beautiful state of Meghalaya is forest, there are also large areas with plentiful vegetation that are suitable for raising both cattle and pigs, and as a result pork features heavily on local menus. This hearty dish, *Tungrumbai*, combines succulent pork shoulder with a few well-chosen spices and some mixed beans to create a flavoursome and sustaining dish.

4 Bring to the boil, then lower the heat, cover and simmer for 1 hour or until the meat is tender. Add the beans and simmer for a further 10–15 minutes.

SERVES 4

675g/1½lb shoulder of pork
30ml/2 tbsp sunflower or light olive oil
1 large onion, finely chopped
8–10 garlic cloves, crushed
20g/¾oz fresh root ginger, grated
5ml/1 tsp salt, or to taste
400g/14oz canned mixed beans,
   drained and rinsed
22.5ml/1½ tbsp sesame seeds
3–4 fresh green chillies, halved lengthways
   (deseeded if preferred)
45ml/3 tbsp chopped fresh coriander
   (cilantro)
Plain Boiled Rice, to serve

1 Remove the rind from the shoulder of pork using a small, sharp knife and trim off any excess fat from the meat. Cut the meat into 2.5cm/1in cubes.

2 Heat the oil over a medium heat and add the onion. Fry until just beginning to brown. Add the pork and increase the heat to high. Stir-fry for 3–4 minutes.

3 Add the garlic and ginger to the pan. Stir-fry until the liquid evaporates and fat becomes visible. Add the salt and 550ml/18fl oz/2½ cups hot water. Stir to combine.

5 Meanwhile, heat a pan over a medium heat and dry-roast the sesame seeds until they are a shade darker. Remove from the pan, cool and grind in a coffee grinder.

6 Stir the ground sesame seeds into the pork with the green chillies and coriander. Serve with Plain Boiled Rice.

Per portion Energy 449kcal/1878kJ; Protein 42g; Carbohydrate 24g, of which sugars 8g; Fat 21g, of which saturates 5g; Cholesterol 110mg; Calcium 72mg; Fibre 5.6g; Sodium 618mg.

Smoked pork with bamboo shoots

Pork and beef are the most popular meats among the various tribes in Nagaland. The Nagas are extremely hospitable and love to welcome their guests with food, often slaughtering a pig for the occasion. In this recipe, *Bas Tenga Pura Gahori*, the pork is first marinated and would then be smoked over a wood fire – using smoked gammon recreates this flavour. The cooking process is very simple, but the result unbelievably good.

SERVES 4

675g/1½lb smoked gammon joint,
    cut into 2.5cm/1in cubes
10–12 garlic cloves, crushed
2 bay leaves
20g/¾oz fresh root ginger, grated
two 225g/8oz cans bamboo shoots
    in water
1–3 fresh green chillies, slit open
    lengthways (deseeded if preferred)
1–3 fresh red chillies, slit open lengthways
    (deseeded if preferred)
Plain Boiled Rice, to serve

3 Drain the bamboo shoots in a sieve. If they are whole, cut them into 1cm/½in thick slices and into short pieces, then add them to the pork.

4 Add both types of chillies and the remaining ginger. Cook, uncovered, for 10 minutes, then remove from the heat.

5 Place a few spoonfuls of Plain Boiled Rice in warmed individual bowls or soup plates. Top with the gammon and bamboo shoots and as much or as little of the cooking juices as you like.

VARIATION
This dish is extremely fiery, so use fewer chillies if you prefer.

1 Put the smoked gammon cubes into a pan and add 550ml/18fl oz/2½ cups water. Bring to the boil and skim off any foam that rises to the top.

2 Add the garlic and bay leaves. Reserve 5ml/1 tsp of the grated ginger and add the remainder to the pan. Cover the pan with a lid and simmer over a medium heat for 45 minutes.

Per portion Energy 246/1026kJ; Protein 31g; Carbohydrate 2g, of which sugars 1g; Fat 13g, of which saturates 4g; Cholesterol 39mg; Calcium 18mg; Fibre 0.g; Sodium 1487mg.

Indian cheese pilau

The bland taste of paneer (Indian cheese) makes it an extremely versatile ingredient, as it can absorb any flavour quite easily. The cheese is used in both sweet and savoury dishes, and in each recipe it takes on a completely different taste and flavour. This pilau rice, *Sanar Pulao*, with wonderfully fragrant yet subtle spicing, really tingles your taste buds and satisfies your soul.

SERVES 4

225g/8oz/generous 1 cup basmati rice
50g/2oz/4 tbsp ghee, or 15ml/1 tbsp
  sunflower oil and 25g/1oz/2 tbsp
  unsalted butter
225g/8oz paneer (Indian cheese), cut into
  bitesize pieces
6 green cardamom pods, bruised
4 cloves
2.5cm/1in piece of cinnamon stick
2 bay leaves
1 large onion, finely sliced
1–2 fresh green chillies, finely chopped
  (deseeded if preferred)
2.5ml/½ tsp ground turmeric
5ml/1 tsp salt, or to taste
115g/4oz frozen garden peas
25g/1oz raisins
15ml/1 tbsp toasted flaked (sliced)
  almonds, to garnish

1 Wash the rice in several changes of water by tossing and turning the grains gently in a sieve (strainer) until the water runs clear. Soak in a bowl of cold water for 30 minutes, then leave to drain in the sieve.

2 In a heavy pan, heat the ghee or oil and butter over a medium heat. Add the paneer and sauté for 2–3 minutes, until browned. Remove with a slotted spoon and drain on kitchen paper.

3 Add the cardamom, cloves, cinnamon and bay leaves to the remaining fat in the pan.

4 Allow to sizzle for a few minutes, then add the onion and green chillies. Fry for 9–10 minutes, until the onion is a caramel-brown colour, stirring regularly.

5 Add the rice and turmeric and reduce the heat to low. Stir-fry gently for 1–2 minutes, then and add the salt, browned paneer, peas and raisins.

6 Pour in 450ml/¾ pint/scant 2 cups water and bring it to the boil. Allow to boil for about 1 minute, then reduce the heat to low.

7 Cover the pan tightly and cook the pilau for 8–9 minutes. Remove from the heat and allow to stand undisturbed for 10 minutes.

8 Fluff up the rice with a fork and transfer to a serving dish. Serve, garnished with the roasted almonds.

VARIATIONS

• You can replace the paneer (Indian cheese) with an equal amount of halloumi cheese, but omit the salt in step 5.
• Replace the frozen peas with fresh broad (fava) beans, sliced green (French) beans or fresh peas, when they are in season. Or you can use other frozen vegetables, such as corn or soya beans.

Per portion Energy 55kcal/2318kJ; Protein 8g; Carbohydrate 61g, of which sugars 9g; Fat 33g, of which saturates 20g; Cholesterol 71mg; Calcium 83mg; Fibre 4.9g; Sodium 615mg.

Pilau rice with raisins

This rice dish, *Khismis Diya Pulao*, is cooked in Assamese households on special occasions. It is similar to north Indian pilau rice, but with a different blend of spices and the addition of dried fruit such as raisins or sultanas (golden raisins), which add sweetness. Rice is a part of all meals in Assam.

SERVES 4

225g/8oz/1 cup basmati rice
2.5ml/½ tsp ground turmeric
2.5ml/½ tsp salt
50g/2oz/¼ cup ghee or unsalted butter
4 green cardamom pods, bruised
2.5cm/1in piece cinnamon stick
4 cloves
1 bay leaf
1 onion, finely sliced
25g/1oz raisins
toasted flaked (sliced) almonds,
  to garnish

1 Rinse the rice in a sieve under cold running water, drain well, then transfer to a large mixing bowl. Sprinkle with the turmeric and salt, stir to combine thoroughly, then set aside.

3 Add the finely sliced onion and fry for about 7–8 minutes, stirring frequently, until it is well browned.

2 In a heavy pan, melt the ghee or butter over a low heat and add the cardamom, cinnamon, cloves and bay leaf. Allow them to sizzle for 30 seconds.

4 Reduce the heat to low and add the rice and raisins. Stir gently until the spiced butter has coated all the grains of rice.

5 Pour in 450ml/¾ pint/scant 2 cups hot water and bring to the boil. Boil, uncovered for 1–2 minutes. Reduce the heat to low, cover and cook for 7–8 minutes, until the rice is just tender. Remove from the heat and let it stand for 10 minutes. Fluff up the rice with a fork. Garnish with flaked almonds.

Per portion Energy 260kcal/11105kJ; Protein 5g; Carbohydrate 59g, of which sugars 9g; Fat 2g, of which saturates 1g; Cholesterol 0mg; Calcium 58mg; Fibre 1.4g; Sodium 255mg.

Wholemeal flat bread

These breads from Assam, called *Ruti*, are thicker than chapatis and are griddle-cooked, with oil or ghee spread over the surface. Unlike the dough for chapatis and *Phulkas*, this mixture contains a small amount of fat and warm water is used instead of cold, creating a softer, richer dough.

MAKES 8

400g/14oz/3½ cups chapati flour (atta)
  or fine wholemeal (whole-wheat) flour
5ml/1 tsp salt
30ml/2 tbsp sunflower oil or light
  olive oil
250ml/9fl oz/1 cup lukewarm water
a little extra flour for dusting
sunflower oil or light olive oil,
  for frying

1 Mix the flour and salt together in a large mixing bowl. Add the oil and work well into the flour with your fingertips. Gradually add the water and keep stirring until a soft dough is formed.

2 Transfer the dough to a flat surface and knead it for 4–5 minutes. When all the excess moisture is absorbed by the flour, wrap the dough in clear film (plastic wrap) and let it rest for 30 minutes, until doubled in size. Alternatively, make the dough in a food processor, using a dough hook and following manufacturer's instructions.

3 Divide the dough into eight equal-size balls and make flat cakes by rotating them between the palms and pressing them down.

4 Roll out each cake on a floured surface into a 13cm/5in circle.

5 Preheat a griddle over a medium heat and place a disc on it. Cook for 2 minutes, then turn it over.

6 Spread 5ml/1 tsp oil evenly on the surface and turn it over again. Cook for 2 minutes, until browned all over. Spread 5ml/1 tsp oil on the other side, turn the bread over, and cook as above until browned.

7 Keep the cooked breads hot by wrapping them in a piece of foil lined with kitchen paper. Cook the remaining flat breads in the same way. Serve with any curry.

Per portion Energy 180kcal/761kJ; Protein 6.4g; Carbohydrate 32g, of which sugars 1.1g; Fat 3.9g, of which saturates 0.5g; Cholesterol 0mg; Calcium 19mg; Fibre 4.5g; Sodium 247mg.

Deep-fried soft puffed bread

Kumol Lusi from Assam are similar to luchi from east India, but they are softer and richer. They are made with plain (all-purpose) flour and the dough is enriched with ghee and hot milk, instead of water, creating a velvety soft bread. They are perfect with any vegetable curry and are also popular with egg dishes.

MAKES 16
275g/10oz/2½ cups plain (all-purpose) flour, plus a little extra for dusting
2.5ml/½ tsp salt
1.25ml/¼ tsp sugar
15ml/1 tbsp ghee or unsalted butter
175ml/6fl oz/⅔ cup lukewarm milk
sunflower oil, for deep-frying
Parsee Spiced Omelette or South-Indian Scrambled Eggs, to serve

1 Sift the flour into a large bowl and add the salt, sugar and ghee or butter.

2 Mix the ingredients and gradually add the milk. Mix until a soft dough is formed.

3 Transfer the dough to a floured surface. Knead for 4–5 minutes. Alternatively, make the dough in a food processor, following manufacturer's instructions.

4 Wrap the dough in clear film (plastic wrap) and let it rest for 20–30 minutes.

5 Divide the dough into two equal parts and make eight equal-sized balls out of each. Flatten the balls into cakes by rotating and pressing them between your palms.

6 Dust each cake very lightly in the flour and roll them out to about 6cm/2½in circles, taking care not to tear or pierce them, as they will not puff up if damaged.

7 Place them in a single layer on a piece of baking parchment and cover with another piece of baking parchment.

8 Heat the oil in a wok or other suitable pan for deep-frying, over a medium/high heat. When the oil has a faint shimmer of rising smoke on the surface, carefully drop in one flattened dough cake. As soon as it floats, gently tap round the edges to encourage puffing.

9 When it has puffed up, turn it over and fry the other side until browned.

10 Lift out and drain on kitchen paper. Keep the fried breads on a tray in a single layer. They are best eaten fresh, although they can be reheated briefly (3–4 minutes) in a moderately hot oven.

11 Serve warm with egg dishes, such as Parsee Spiced Omelette or South-Indian Scrambled Eggs.

VARIATION
A healthier version of these breads can be made by using wholemeal (whole-wheat) flour and adding olive oil instead of ghee. This creates a wholesome taste that complements most vegetable curries, lentils, beans and peas.

Per portion Energy 72kcal/306kJ; Protein 2g; Carbohydrate 14g, of which sugars 0.9g; Fat 1.3g, of which saturates 0.6g; Cholesterol 1mg; Calcium 37mg; Fibre 0.5g; Sodium 68mg.

Plain flour flat bread

A soft dough made with strong white bread flour, ghee and warm water is what makes this Assamese flat bread, *Moidar Sukan Ruti*, so different from any other. They are dry-roasted like chapatis, but because of the fat content, they are softer and can be re-heated without drying out. They are the perfect partner for curries.

4 Cover with a damp dish towel and set aside for 30 minutes.

5 Divide the dough into 10 equal portions, then shape each into a smooth flat cakes by rotating it between your palms.

6 Place a heavy griddle or a *tawa* (the Indian cast iron griddle for making flat bread) over a medium heat.

7 Place a dough circle on the griddle and cook for 2 minutes, then turn it over with a spatula and cook for a further 2 minutes.

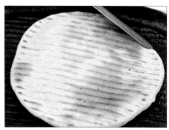

MAKES 10

400g/14oz/3½ strong white bread flour,
  plus extra for dusting
5ml/1 tsp salt
75g/3oz/6 tbsp ghee or unsalted butter,
  at room temperature
200ml/7fl oz/scant 1 cup warm water

1 In a large mixing bowl, mix together the flour and salt, then rub in the ghee or butter using your fingertips.

2 Gradually add the water and mix until a soft dough is formed.

3 Transfer the dough to a lightly floured surface and knead for about 10 minutes, until it is soft and smooth.

8 Press all around the edges of the bread with the spatula during cooking to encourage the bread to puff up and cook evenly.

9 Wrap each bread in a clean dish towel to keep it warm until you finish cooking the remaining dough circles. Serve immediately, or leave to cool and reheat in a moderate oven for 5 minutes.

Per portion Energy 204kcal/857kJ; Protein 5g; Carbohydrate 30g, of which sugars 1g; Fat 8g, of which saturates 5g; Cholesterol 21mg; Calcium 56mg; Fibre 1.5g; Sodium 198mg.

Golden potato cubes with chilli and coriander

This is a very simple, but gloriously delicious potato dish, which is often accompanied by Deep-fried Soft Puffed Bread for breakfast or high tea. Alu Bhaji can also be served as an accompaniment to a lentil dish and with any other type of bread for a satisfying vegetarian meal.

SERVES 4

60ml/4 tbsp mustard oil or sunflower oil
1 medium onion, finely chopped
1–2 fresh green chillies, finely chopped
5ml/1 tsp ground turmeric
5ml/1 tsp ground cumin
450g/1lb potatoes, peeled and chopped
3.75ml/¾ tsp salt, or to taste
250ml/8fl oz/1 cup lukewarm water
15ml/1 tbsp fresh coriander (cilantro)
   leaves, chopped
Deep-fried Soft Puffed Bread, to serve

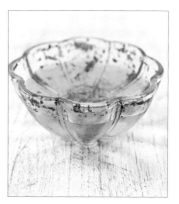

4 Stir in the coriander leaves and remove from the heat. Transfer to a serving dish and serve with Deep-fried Soft Puffed Bread and/or a lentil dish.

1 Heat the oil over a medium heat until smoking point is reached. Add the onion and chilli and fry for 7–8 minutes, stirring often, until the onion is beginning to colour.

2 Stir in the turmeric and cumin and cook for about 1 minute.

3 Add the potatoes, salt and water. Bring to the boil, reduce the heat to low, cover and cook for 12 minutes, until the potatoes are tender and have absorbed most of the water.

Per portion Energy 234kcal/973kJ; Protein 3g; Carbohydrate 22g, of which sugars 3g; Fat 15g, of which saturates 2g; Cholesterol 0mg; Calcium 22mg; Fibre 2.4g; Sodium 305mg.

Potatoes with poppy seeds

The east and north-east Indian five-spice mix transforms the simplest ingredient into a stunning dish, *Afu Guti Diya Alu*. Opulent poppy seed paste coats the potatoes, giving them a luxurious taste.

SERVES 4

30ml/2 tbsp white poppy seeds
675g/1½lb potatoes
60ml/4 tbsp mustard oil
4–5 large garlic cloves, crushed
1–2 fresh green chillies, finely chopped
2.5ml/½ tsp ground turmeric
5ml/1 tsp salt, or to taste
rotis and a curry, to serve

For the five-spice mix:
2.5ml/½ tsp black or brown mustard seeds
2.5ml/½ tsp cumin seeds
2.5ml/½ tsp fennel seeds
2.5ml/½ tsp nigella seeds
6 fenugreek seeds

1 Dry-roast the poppy seeds in a heavy pan over a medium heat. Stir constantly for about 1 minute or until they are just a shade darker. Do not allow them to become too dark.

2 Remove the poppy seeds from the pan and let them cool, then grind them in a spice or coffee mill, or in a mortar and pestle.

3 Peel the potatoes and cut them into 1cm/½in cubes. Soak them in water for 15 minutes, then drain and dry with a cloth.

4 Heat half the oil in a heavy frying pan over a medium-high heat until smoking point is reached. Add the potatoes and fry for 3–4 minutes then remove from the pan.

5 Add the remaining oil to the pan and reduce the heat. Add the five-spice mix and let it crackle and pop for 15–20 seconds. Reduce the heat to low and add the garlic and chilli. Continue to fry for 2–3 minutes, until the garlic has turned light brown.

6 Stir in the turmeric, potatoes and salt. Mix, then add 120ml/4fl oz/½ cup water and reduce the heat to low. Cover and cook for 8–10 minutes, until the potatoes are tender.

7 Add the poppy seeds and increase the heat. Stir-fry until the potatoes have absorbed any excess liquid and are coated with the poppy seeds. Serve with rotis and a curry.

Per portion Energy 265kcal/1106kJ; Protein 5g; Carbohydrate 30g, of which sugars 1g; Fat 18g, of which saturates 2g; Cholesterol 0mg; Calcium 115mg; Fibre 2.7g; Sodium 506mg.

Crushed potatoes with hard-boiled eggs

This classic dish, *Alu-Konir Pitika*, can be enjoyed any time of day as a snack, side dish or light meal. It is very easy to make, being a simple combination of mashed potatoes and chopped hard-boiled eggs flavoured with mustard oil, finely chopped shallots, green chilli and fresh coriander (cilantro) leaves.

SERVES 4

675g/1½lb potatoes
4 hard-boiled eggs, peeled
5ml/1 tsp salt, or to taste
30ml/2 tbsp mustard oil
2 shallots, finely chopped
1 fresh green chilli, finely chopped
  (deseeded if preferred)
30ml/2 tbsp fresh coriander (cilantro)
  leaves, finely chopped
julienne strips of fresh red chillies,
  to garnish
Garlic-flavoured Mung Beans and Plain
  Boiled Rice, to serve

1 Peel the potatoes, cut them into chunks, then boil them in a large pan of salted water for about 10 minutes, until they are soft. Drain well, then mash until smooth.

2 Cut the eggs in half and separate the whites from the yolks. Chop the whites.

3 Mash the yolks to a paste in a large bowl using a fork.

4 Add the potato and egg whites with all the remaining ingredients. Stir to combine.

5 Spoon the mixture in four ring moulds or small bowls, then turn out onto serving plates and garnish with the red chilli strips. Serve with Garlic-flavoured Mung Beans and Plain Boiled Rice.

Per portion Energy 150kcal/622kJ; Protein 7.2g; Carbohydrate 5.9g, of which sugars 4.2g; Fat 11.2g, of which saturates 2.1g; Cholesterol 190mg; Calcium 47mg; Fibre 1.1g; Sodium 72mg.

Fresh tomato chutney with mustard seeds

With its distinctive sweet, hot and slightly tart taste, *Bilahir Oambal* is an enticing side dish that will enhance any Indian meal. It is very easy to make and requires only a few common ingredients, and tastes far superior to any store-bought chutney. Leftovers will keep in the refrigerator for up to four weeks.

SERVES 4

30ml/2 tbsp sunflower oil or olive oil
2.5ml/½ tsp black mustard seeds
2.5ml/½ tsp nigella seeds
500g/1¼lb tomatoes, skinned and chopped
3.75ml/1¼ tsp salt, or to taste
50g/2oz palm sugar (jaggery), grated, or
  30ml/2 tbsp dark brown sugar
10ml/2 tsp ground cumin
50g/2oz/⅓ cup seedless raisins

1 Heat the sunflower or olive oil in a medium-sized, heavy pan over a medium heat. When it is hot, but not smoking, add the mustard seeds and fry for a few seconds until they start to pop.

2 Add the nigella seeds, followed by the chopped tomatoes. Stir and reduce the heat slightly. Cover the pan and cook for 5 minutes.

3 Stir in the salt, palm sugar and cumin, cover again and cook a further 5 minutes.

4 Add the raisins and cook, stirring often, for 9–10 minutes, until the chutney has thickened. Remove from the heat, cool and serve with any Indian meal.

Per portion Energy 154kcal/650kJ; Protein 1.2g; Carbohydrate 25.6g, of which sugars 25.6g; Fat 5.9g, of which saturates 0.8g; Cholesterol 0mg; Calcium 21.2mg; Fibre 1.5g; Sodium 560mg.

Coconut dumplings

These sweet dumplings, *Narikolor Malpuwa*, are redolent with the heady aroma of crushed cardamom. They are served for breakfast in Assam, but can be enjoyed as a dessert with fresh fruits and cream, or even as wonderful sweet snacks at buffet parties.

SERVES 4–5

350ml/12fl oz/1½ cups canned
  coconut milk
115g/4oz/½ cup palm sugar (jaggery),
  grated, or soft dark brown sugar
225g/8oz/2 cups plain (all-purpose) flour
a pinch of bicarbonate of soda
  (baking soda)
5ml/1 tsp ground cardamom
1.25ml/¼ tsp ground nutmeg
5ml/1 tsp nigella seeds
25g/1oz seedless raisins
sunflower oil, for deep-frying
150ml/5fl oz/⅔ cup single (light) cream
a few pomegranate seeds or other
  seasonal fruits, to garnish

1 Put the coconut milk into a small pan and grate in the palm sugar or add the dark brown sugar.

2 Place over a low heat and stir until the sugar is completely dissolved. Set aside and leave to cool.

3 Sift the flour into a mixing bowl and add the bicarbonate of soda, cardamom, nutmeg, nigella seeds and raisins. Mix well.

4 Add the cooled, sweetened coconut milk to the mixing bowl and combine until a thick batter is formed.

5 Heat the oil in a pan suitable for deep-frying over a low-medium heat until it reaches 180°C/350°F. Carefully drop in as many spoonfuls of the batter as the pan will hold in a single layer. Do not overcrowd the pan.

6 Fry the dumplings gently for 7–8 minutes, reducing the heat if necessary, until they are well browned. Lift out with a slotted spoon and drain on kitchen paper. Repeat until you have used all the batter.

7 Pour the cream into a pan and heat gently until just simmering. Add the dumplings and stir until they are well coated, and the cream has thickened slightly.

8 Remove the dumplings from the heat and leave to cool. Serve garnished with the pomegranate seeds.

Per portion Energy 393kcal/1657kJ; Protein 6.9g; Carbohydrate 66.3g, of which sugars 31.9g; Fat 12.9g, of which saturates 2.1g; Cholesterol 4mg; Calcium 161mg; Fibre 1.6g; Sodium 55mg.

Coconut balls

Snow-white coconut balls, scented with ground cardamom, are made during all kinds of festivals in the Assam and Bengal regions of India. *Narikolor Laddu* are similar to coconut ice, but the process of making them is much simpler, so they are a quick and easy alternative for a home cook. For an irresistible treat, dip some of the balls into melted, rich dark (bittersweet) chocolate and cool.

2 Reduce the heat to low and cook, stirring constantly, for 35–40 minutes or until the coconut stops sticking to the bottom and sides of the pan. Stir in the ground cardamom and remove from the heat.

3 Have a bowl of cold water ready and dip your hand in it, then pick up a lime-sized portion of the still-hot coconut mixture and place it in the palm of your hand. Shape the coconut mixture into a neat ball. Repeat with the remaining mixture.

MAKES 16

225g/8oz/1 cup desiccated (dry unsweetened shredded) coconut
250ml/8fl oz/1 cup full-fat (whole) milk
150g/5oz/¾ cup caster (superfine) sugar
5ml/1 tsp ground cardamom

COOK'S TIP
The coconut mixture needs to be still hot when you mould the balls or it will become too stiff to work. If this happens, simply reheat the mixture until it softens again.

1 Put the coconut, milk and sugar in a non-stick pan and cook over a medium heat until the sugar has dissolved, stirring frequently to prevent the milk scalding.

Per portion Energy 132kcal/551kJ; Protein 1.3g; Carbohydrate 11.5g, of which sugars 11.5g; Fat 9.3g, of which saturates 7.9g; Cholesterol 2mg; Calcium 26mg; Fibre 1.9g; Sodium 13mg.

Sweet potato dumplings

These sweet potato dumplings, *Mitha Alur Pantua*, are spiced with cinnamon and cardamom and deep-fried to a rich brown colour. They make a delicious dessert served with a dollop of whipped cream and some fresh fruit. Traditionally, the dumplings are soaked in a spiced sugar syrup, but here the sugar and spices are added to the dumpling mixture instead, making the finished dessert slightly less sweet.

MAKES 12–14

400g/14oz sweet potatoes
115g/4oz/1 cup dried full-fat milk powder
5ml/1 tsp ground cinnamon
5ml/1 tsp ground cardamom
50g/2oz/⅓ cup icing (confectioners') sugar, plus extra for dusting
30ml/2 tbsp plain (all–purpose) flour, for dusting
vegetable oil, for deep-frying
whipped cream and fresh fruit, to serve

COOK'S TIP

There are two types of sweet potato; one has cream flesh, the other orange. Either are suitable for this dessert, but when cooked the cream-fleshed variety has a drier texture, so you may need to add 15ml/1 tbsp milk or water when mashing.

---

1 Put the unpeeled sweet potatoes in a large pan and pour over just enough boiling water to cover them. Bring back to the boil, cover the pan and simmer for 12–15 minutes or until the potatoes are just tender when pierced with a knife.

2 Drain the sweet potatoes in a colander, leave until cool enough to handle, then peel off the skins, return the potatoes to the pan and mash until smooth.

3 Transfer the mashed sweet potatoes to a large mixing bowl and add the milk powder, cinnamon, cardamom and icing sugar. Mix thoroughly, cover, and chill the mixture for about 45 minutes.

4 Divide the mixture into 12 portions and mould each of these into a fat sausage shape. Lightly dust with the flour.

5 Pour about 5cm/2in of oil into a heavy pan or wok and heat until a piece of dough sizzles as soon as it hits the oil. Fry the dumplings in batches for 2–3 minutes or until well browned, turning them frequently. Drain on kitchen paper.

6 Dust with icing sugar and serve warm or cold with whipped cream and fresh fruit.

Per portion Energy 167kcal/696kJ; Protein 3g; Carbohydrate 15g, of which sugars 9g; Fat 11g, of which saturates 2g; Cholesterol 10mg; Calcium 97mg; Fibre 0.8g; Sodium 48mg.

Coconut-filled pancakes

These delicious crepe-type pancakes are light and crisp. *Pati Shepta* is a childhood favourite that is enjoyed during the Hindu festival of lights, Diwali. Freshly grated coconut is used in India, but desiccated (dry unsweetened shredded) coconut saves time and effort.

MAKES 6

For the filling:

50g/2oz/¼ cup desiccated (dry unsweetened shredded) coconut
50g/2oz/4 tbsp soft dark brown sugar
25g/1oz/1 tbsp chopped mixed nuts
250ml/8fl oz/1 cup double (heavy) cream
5ml/1 tsp ground cinnamon

For the pancakes:

2 eggs
150g/5oz/1¼ cups wholemeal (whole-wheat) flour
2.5ml/½ tsp ground cinnamon
1.25ml/¼ tsp ground clove
15ml/1 tbsp caster (superfine) sugar
200ml/7fl oz/scant 1 cup full-fat (whole) milk
melted ghee or unsalted butter, for frying
whipped cream or vanilla ice cream, to serve, (optional)

1 To make the filling, combine all the ingredients except the ground cinnamon in a small pan and place over a medium heat.

2 As soon as it begins to bubble, reduce the heat to low and let it simmer, uncovered, for 8–10 minutes, until the coconut has absorbed all the liquid. Stir regularly during the cooking time.

3 To make the pancakes, blend all the ingredients, except the ghee or butter, in a blender. Alternatively, beat together in a large bowl. Cover and set aside for 30 minutes.

4 Brush the surface of a non-stick or cast iron frying pan with some melted ghee or butter and place it over a low heat.

5 Pour about 30ml/2 tbsp of the batter into the pan, spreading it quickly to cover the surface by tilting it. Cook for about 1 minute, until the pancake is set, then continue to cook for a further 1 minute, until brown spots appear on the underside.

6 Carefully turn the pancake over with a metal spatula or fish slice. Cook the other side for about 1 minute or until brown spots appear as before.

7 Spread about 15ml/1 tbsp of the filling on one side of the pancake and roll it up. Make the rest of the pancakes the same way.

Per portion Energy 452kcal/1879kJ; Protein 9g; Carbohydrate 30g, of which sugars 15g; Fat 34g, of which saturates 20g; Cholesterol 139mg; Calcium 102mg; Fibre 4.2g; Sodium 71mg.

Black sesame seed fudge

Sesame seeds grow throughout India and they come in all shades from pale ivory to brown and black. The ivory ones are used to enrich and thicken curries, while the black seeds are used mainly in the north-east to make sweetmeats. If black seeds prove difficult to find, ivory ones can be used in this recipe, *Tilor Borfi*.

3 Add the ground sesame seeds. Stir over a medium heat for 5–6 minutes, until the mixture stops sticking to the bottom and sides of the pan.

4 Brush a 30cm/12in plate with a little oil and spread the sesame mixture on it. Push the sides in with the back of a metal spoon to make a rough square about 1cm/½in thick.

5 Rub the peanuts with a clean cloth to remove some of the salt, then split them into halves.

6 Press them gently on to the surface of the fudge, leave to cool, then chill for an hour or two before cutting into squares or diamonds and serving.

SERVES 6

350g/12oz/generous 2 cups black
  sesame seeds
5 cardamom pods, bruised
150g/5oz/⅔ cup palm sugar (jaggery),
  grated, or soft dark brown sugar
200ml/7fl oz/¾ cup water
25g/1oz roasted peanuts

1 Dry-roast the black sesame seeds and the cardamom pods in a heavy pan over a medium heat, stirring constantly, for 7–8 minutes. Transfer them to a large plate and let them cool. When cold, grind them in a food processor or coffee grinder.

2 Put the sugar into a heavy pan and add 200ml/7fl oz/¾ cup water. Place over a medium heat and bring to the boil. Cook for about 2 minutes.

COOK'S TIP

Any leftover fudge can be stored in the refrigerator for 4–5 days.

Per portion Energy 471kcal/1959kJ; Protein 11.8g; Carbohydrate 27.2g, of which sugars 26.6g; Fat 35.8g, of which saturates 5.2g; Cholesterol 0mg; Calcium 407mg; Fibre 4.9g; Sodium 13mg.

Soft mango fudge

This fruity sweetmeat is a recreation of a very old recipe by a prominent Assamese housewife called Dhanada Kumari Saikia. This version, *Aamor Haluwa*, produces a wonderfully sweet and flavoursome fudge studded with crunchy nuts, which makes the ideal end to a spicy meal.

SERVES 4–6

125g/4¼oz/scant ¾ cup caster
  (superfine) sugar
a good pinch of saffron threads, pounded
115g/4oz/½ cup ghee or unsalted butter
115g/4oz/⅔ cup semolina
50g/2oz/½ cup raw cashew nuts, chopped
115g/4oz/½ cup ground almonds
300ml/½ pint/1¼ cups sweetened mango
  purée or 2 x 400g/14oz cans of sliced
  mango, drained and puréed
30ml/2 tbsp rose water
22.5ml/1½ tbsp shelled pistachio nuts,
  lightly roasted and crushed

1 Put the sugar into a pan and add 300ml/ ½ pint/1¼ cups water. Place over a high heat and stir until the sugar has dissolved. Stir in the saffron and set aside.

2 In a heavy pan, melt the ghee or butter over a low heat, then add the semolina and cashew nuts. Cook for 5–6 minutes, stirring frequently.

3 Add the ground almonds and continue to cook, stirring, for 3–4 minutes or until the mixture is light brown and aromatic.

4 Mix the mango purée and rose water together and add to the sugar syrup. Pour the mixture into the semolina and stir over a low heat for 3–4 minutes or until it thickens and stops sticking to the bottom and sides of the pan.

5 Grease a 30cm x 18cm/12in x 7in baking tin (pan). Using a metal spoon, spread the fudge mixture into the tin. Press down firmly to level the surface.

6 Sprinkle the pistachio nuts on top and gently but firmly press them in. Leave to cool, then cut into 4cm/1½in squares. Serve at room temperature.

Per portion Energy 525kcal/2193kJ; Protein 8g; Carbohydrate 47g, of which sugars 30g; Fat 35g, of which saturates 14g; Cholesterol 54mg; Calcium 62mg; Fibre 4.6g; Sodium 18mg.

East India

Spanning mountain peaks and flood plains, both the landscapes and the weather of east India vary tremendously, and the food reflects this diversity. From sultry and sweet curries to silky cheese curd desserts, the cooking tradition provides a fabulous range of healthy, hearty and subtly delicious dishes. Spices, including the Bengali five-spice mix, create a mouthwatering mélange of tastes and aromas.

East India

The eastern states comprise Bengal, Bihar, Jharkhand and Orissa, with the former dominating the region and being home to the capital city Kolkata (formerly Calcutta). It is an area of contrasts, with the topography ranging from the precipitous uplands of the Himalayas to the verdant flood plains of the Ganges, where approximately 30 per cent of the nation's rice crops are produced. Tea is another important commodity in the region, and the beautiful town of Darjeeling produces some of the best leaves in the world.

Dairy products such as yogurt, paneer (Indian cheese) and ghee are used imaginatively to create fabulous sweet and savoury recipes. But perhaps Bengal's greatest contribution to the food heritage of India is its magnificent spectrum of desserts, which are famous all over the nation. Sweets such as *Gulab Jamoon* (fried milk puffs in sugar syrup), *Sandesh* (a kind of soft fudge made of fresh cheese), and milky cardamom- and cinnamon-scented rice pudding are among the classics that have made the reputation of Bengali cooks.

BIHAR

The wide fields of Bihar in the north of the region are dominated by the eastern sweep of the Himalayas, and by the magnificent Ganges River, which meanders slowly down from the mountains to emerge in Bangladesh (the independent Muslim state that was once part of Bengal). In landlocked Bihar, the climate is very hot in the summer and very cold in the winter, but wheat is grown here and bread is as popular as rice as a staple accompaniment to dishes.

BENGAL

The influence of Anglo-Indian food can still be found in Bengal, many years after the end of British rule. The Bengali people are proud of their own rich cultural heritage – the poet Rabindranath Tagore is one of their most famous celebrities – and Bengali cuisine is part of this artistic tradition. The use of spices was fairly minimal here until medieval times, and so the Bengalis have developed a subtle cuisine using ingredients available in their own region. Locally grown

Above *Lush green tea plantations abound on the beautiful slopes of the Himalayas in Darjeeling, West Bengal.*

spices include the major crop of the region, tea, especially in Darjeeling, as well as fresh ginger, turmeric and mustard, and the five-spice mix known as panchforon that was invented by Bengali cooks.

Plenty of fish and shellfish are caught in the Bay of Bengal, and this helped the Bengalis to create a stunning range of fish recipes, which are renowned all over India.

Below left *Sandesh, a dessert made from soft cheese that is moulded into decorative shapes, is a Bengali speciality.*
Below right *Jharkhand has a number of protected areas, including a tiger reserve.*

The daily diet in Bihar consists of rice, flat bread stuffed with spicy vegetables, lentils, raw vegetables and pickles. Thick and creamy yogurt is made by boiling buffalo's milk and then cooking it until it reduces to half its quantity, and as a result, the yogurt has a low water content and is smooth, delicious and very nutritious. The people of Bihar are very fond of ghee and tend to use it freely in cooking instead of oil. They also maintain the thrifty tradition of preserving fresh food for future use, and this is usually done by drying summer vegetables in the fierce sun or preserving them as pickles.

JHARKHAND

This relatively new state was created from the southern area of Bihar in 2000. Meaning 'land of the forests', the region is primarily situated on the Chhota Nagpur Plateau, and is rich in minerals, including iron ore, copper, graphite and limestone, among others. The abundant forests are home to a wide range of flora and fauna, and there are a number of protected areas, including a tiger reserve, which provides sanctuary for all kinds of wildlife as well as the famous endangered mammals.

With a population that traces its roots to diverse regions of India, Jharkhand does not have a particularly strong culinary footprint. Native inhabitants base their diet primarily on rice, and there are a huge number of rice dishes, including *Dhuska*,

which is made with mashed rice and pulses and served as an accompaniment to *Aloo Dum* or mutton curry. Flowers and leaves (*sag*) are notably used as vegetables to add variety to the food; the blooms plucked from the drumstick, august and jhirool plants are the most popular.

ORISSA

The state of Orissa lies in the tropical zone and enjoys equable temperatures. Rice predominates in these lower, wetter areas of east India, where the climate is ideal for its cultivation. Sugar cane, coconuts and turmeric are the other main crops. However, the state is frequently hit by calamities such as cyclones, floods and droughts, which badly affect people's livelihoods as well as threatening their lives, as the population relies heavily on agriculture.

The long coastline at the northern edge of the Bay of Bengal means that fish and shellfish are a major part of the diet, often cooked in fragrant coconut-based sauces. During the heat of the summer, a delicious cool dish consisting of fermented rice and yogurt is a great favourite as it helps to lower the body temperature.

Below *Fish and the fishing industry are a vital part of everyday life along the Bay of Bengal.*

Tangy potato canapés with mint and yogurt

Papri Chaat are a street-side snack full of amazing aromas and sensational tastes. They are easy to cook and are ideal as a light bite or appetizer. If you do not have time to make the small crisp-fried bread (papri), you can serve the potato topping on small crackers instead. In India, these are served with a yogurt sauce, a chilli-coriander chutney and tamarind chutney, but you can use any chutney you like.

SERVES 4

For the crisp-fried bread:
250g/9oz/2¼ cups gram flour (besan),
  sifted, plus extra for dusting
a pinch of bicarbonate of soda
  (baking soda)
5ml/1 tsp salt, or to taste
5ml/1 tsp chilli powder
5ml/1 tsp cumin seeds
15ml/1 tbsp dried fenugreek leaves
  (kasuri methi)
15ml/1 tbsp sunflower oil or light
  olive oil
sunflower oil, for deep-frying

For the potato topping:
450g/1lb potatoes, peeled and cut into
  bitesize pieces
2.5ml/½ tsp ground cumin
2.5ml/½ tsp chilli powder
1.25ml/¼ tsp salt
30ml/2 tbsp lime juice

To serve:
115g/4oz natural (plain) yogurt
1.25ml/¼ tsp salt
5ml/1 tsp sugar
chutneys of your choice

1 To make the crisp-fried bread, mix the gram flour, bicarbonate of soda, salt, chilli powder, cumin seeds and fenugreek leaves in a bowl. Add the oil and stir to combine. Add 120ml/4fl oz/½ cup water and mix until a dough is formed.

2 Transfer the dough to a lightly floured surface and knead it briefly, then form it into a flat circle.

3 Dust the dough with flour and roll it out to form a disc 30cm/12in in diameter and with a thickness of 2.5mm/⅛in.

4 Using a small round cookie cutter, cut out as many circles as possible, then gather up the remaining dough and roll again. Cut out into circles as before. You should have about 24 in total.

5 Heat the oil in a pan suitable for deep-frying over a medium heat. Fry the breads in two or three batches for 4–5 minutes, until they are crisp and golden brown. Drain on kitchen paper. Repeat with the remaining circles of dough.

6 To make the potato topping, boil the potatoes in boiling water for 10 minutes, until tender. Drain and leave to cool.

7 Mix the cold potato with the cumin, chilli powder, salt and lime juice.

8 Beat the yogurt with a fork and add the salt, sugar and 30ml/2 tbsp water.

9 Top each crisp-fried bread with some of the potato mixture and drizzle the yogurt sauce over it. Spoon over the chutneys and serve immediately.

Per portion Energy 410kcal/1724kJ; Protein 17g; Carbohydrate 54g, of which sugars 6g; Fat 16g, of which saturates 2g; Cholesterol 3mg; Calcium 189mg; Fibre 10.2g; Sodium 775mg.

Spiced potato cakes

These delicious Bengali deep-fried spiced potato cakes, *Alur Bora*, are traditionally enjoyed at afternoon tea – a legacy left behind by the British tea plantation owners. They are also lovely as an appetizer, and can easily be made in advance.

SERVES 4–5

30ml/2 tbsp sunflower oil or vegetable oil
2.5ml/½ tsp fennel seeds
1 medium onion, finely chopped
1–2 fresh green chillies, chopped
  (deseeded if preferred)
10ml/2 tsp ginger purée
2.5ml/½ tsp ground turmeric
30ml/2 tbsp fresh coriander (cilantro)
  leaves, chopped
5ml/1 tsp salt, or to taste
450g/1lb potatoes, boiled and mashed
15ml/1 tbsp cornflour (cornstarch)
1 large (US extra large) egg, beaten
sunflower oil, for deep-frying
Roasted Tomato Chutney, to serve

2 Put the mashed potato into a mixing bowl and add the onion mixture, stir well and add the cornflour and egg. Stir until all the ingredients are well blended.

3 Heat the oil for deep-frying in a wok or other suitable pan over a medium/high heat. Drop a tiny amount of the potato mixture into the oil to test the temperature. If the potato mixture starts sizzling and floats to the surface immediately, then the oil is at the right temperature.

1 Heat the oil in a pan over a medium heat and add the fennel seeds. Allow them to sizzle for a few seconds, then add the onion, chillies and ginger. Fry for 3–4 minutes, until the onions soften. Stir in the turmeric, coriander and salt. Remove from the heat.

4 Take 15ml/1 tbsp of the potato mixture and, with two spoons, make a rough croquette shape, then gently and carefully lower it into the hot oil.

5 Fry as many cakes as the pan will hold in a single layer without overcrowding it. Fry for 5–6 minutes, until well browned. Remove with a slotted spoon and drain on kitchen paper. Repeat with the remaining mixture. Serve with Roasted Tomato Chutney.

Per portion Energy 256kcal/1064kJ; Protein 3.8g; Carbohydrate 23.6g, of which sugars 5.7g; Fat 16.9g, of which saturates 2.3g; Cholesterol 38mg; Calcium 32mg; Fibre 2g; Sodium 421mg.

Potatoes and chickpeas in lime dressing

There is no cooking involved in making this dish, *Alu Kabli*, except boiling some potatoes, and it makes great use of storecupboard ingredients. It can be eaten as an irresistible snack, which is enjoyed in Bengal at any time of the day, and it is also ideal as an appetizer or as part of a buffet party menu.

2 Boil the potatoes in a pan of salted water for about 10 minutes, until tender, but firm. Drain and leave to cool.

3 Drain the chickpeas in a sieve (strainer) and rinse several times under cold running water. Drain well. Put them in a mixing bowl and add the potatoes.

4 Dry-roast the cumin and peppercorns in a small, heavy pan over a medium heat for about 1 minute, until they release their aroma.

5 Remove the pan from the heat and leave the spices to cool, then crush them in a mortar and pestle or put them in a plastic bag and crush them with a rolling pin. Add the mixture to the potato and chickpeas.

SERVES 4

450g/1lb waxy potatoes
400g/14oz canned chickpeas, or 400g/14oz
   dried chickpeas, soaked in water overnight
10ml/2 tsp cumin seeds
5ml/1 tsp black peppercorns
1 red onion, finely chopped
2.5ml/½ tsp chilli powder
2.5ml/½ tsp garam masala
2.5ml/½ tsp salt, or to taste
juice of 1 lime
30ml/2 tbsp fresh coriander (cilantro)
   leaves, chopped

1 Peel the potatoes and cut them into 1cm/½in cubes.

6 Reserve a little onion and add the remainder to the bowl. Add the chilli powder, garam masala, salt, lime juice and chopped coriander. Mix gently and serve topped with the reserved onion.

Per portion Energy 182kcal/771kJ; Protein 8g; Carbohydrate 24g, of which sugars 3g; Fat 3g, of which saturates 0g; Cholesterol 0mg; Calcium 65mg; Fibre 2.4g; Sodium 418mg.

Deep-fried spiced cauliflower

In this recipe, *Phoolkopir Fuluri*, tender white cauliflower florets are coated in a light gram flour batter, flavoured with aromatic cumin, nigella and fennel seeds, green chillies to add a little heat and turmeric to enrich the colour. They are then deep-fried in hot oil until golden-brown and crisp.

SERVES 4

150g/5oz/1½ cups gram flour (besan)
15ml/1 tbsp ground rice
2.5ml/½ tsp salt, or to taste
2.5ml/½ tsp cumin seeds
2.5ml/½ tsp nigella seeds
2.5ml/½ tsp fennel seeds
2.5ml/½ tsp ground turmeric
1–2 fresh green chillies, finely chopped
30ml/2 tbsp chopped fresh coriander
   (cilantro)
150g/5oz cauliflower, cut into 1cm/1½in florets
vegetable oil, for deep-frying
Roasted Tomato Chutney, to serve

1 Sift the gram flour into a large mixing bowl and add all the remaining ingredients, except the cauliflower and vegetable oil. Stir everything together to combine, then make a hollow in the middle.

2 Pour 150ml/¼ pint/⅔ cup cold water into the hollow and gradually beat it in using a wooden spoon, drawing in the flour from the sides to make a smooth batter.

3 Pour 150ml/¼ pint/⅔ cup cold water into the hollow and gradually beat it in using a wooden spoon, drawing in the flour from the sides to make a smooth batter.

4 Heat a 10cm/4in depth of oil in a deep, heavy pan suitable for deep-frying until it registers 160°C/325°F on a thermometer, or until a teaspoonful of batter dropped into the oil floats to the surface immediately without browning.

5 Dip a few cauliflower florets into the batter, coating them all over, then carefully lower these into the hot oil using a slotted spoon. Fry the florets for 5–6 minutes or until they are golden brown.

6 Lift out the hot fritters, drain on kitchen paper and keep warm while cooking the remaining cauliflower florets in the same way. Serve hot and accompany with a flavoursome chutney.

Per portion Energy 213kcal/893kJ; Protein 9g; Carbohydrate 23g, of which sugars 2g; Fat 10g, of which saturates 1g; Cholesterol 0mg; Calcium 87mg; Fibre 4.8g; Sodium 266mg.

Spicy chicken-and-egg rolls

These wickedly piquant chicken-filled tortilla rolls, *Kathi Roll*, are the Indian version of 'fast food'. Cut into small portions they make a delicious appetizer, or can be served whole for lunch.

SERVES 4

45ml/3 tbsp sunflower oil or olive oil, plus extra for brushing
1 large onion, finely chopped
10ml/2 tsp ginger purée
10ml/2 tsp garlic purée
675g/1½lb boneless chicken thighs or breast fillets, skin removed and cut into cubes
2.5ml/½ tsp ground turmeric
2.5–5ml/½–1 tsp chilli powder
7.5ml/1½ tsp ground coriander
3.75ml/¾ tsp salt, or to taste
15ml/1 tbsp lemon juice
'2.5ml/½ tsp garam masala
30ml/2 tbsp chopped fresh coriander (cilantro)
5 x 25cm/10in-diameter tortilla wraps
5 eggs

To serve:
1 medium red onion, finely sliced
15ml/1 tbsp chopped fresh coriander (cilantro)
1 fresh green chilli, finely chopped (optional)
15ml/1 tbsp lemon juice

1 Heat the oil in a frying pan over a medium heat and fry the onion for 3–4 minutes, until translucent, then add the ginger and garlic. Stir-fry until lightly browned. Add the chicken and increase the heat to high.

2 Fry for 3–4 minutes, stirring constantly, then add the turmeric, chilli powder, ground coriander, salt and lemon juice to the pan.

3 Stir-fry for a further 4–5 minutes, then stir in the garam masala and coriander. Remove from the heat but keep hot.

4 Place a heavy frying pan over a low heat and brush with oil. Beat an egg lightly. Place a tortilla wrap on the pan and spread the egg on top of this. Keep stirring and spreading the egg until it begins to set.

5 Divide the chicken mixture into five equal portions and spread a portion on one half of each tortilla.

6 Mix the red onion, coriander, chilli, if using, and lemon juice together and place on top of the chicken.

7 Roll up the tortilla in the pan, then turn it over and briefly cook to seal the join. Make the remaining rolls in the same way. Serve hot, or leave to cool completely for a packed lunch.

Per portion Energy 349kcal/1464kJ; Protein 34.7g; Carbohydrate 26.5g, of which sugars 4.9g; Fat 12.4g, of which saturates 2.3g; Cholesterol 60mg; Calcium 90mg; Fibre 2.1g; Sodium 191mg.

Meat-filled potato cakes

Created by Indian chefs during the period of the British Raj, this delicious snack, *Alur Chop*, consists of spicy minced (ground) meat packed into mashed potato casings, which are deep-fried in breadcrumbs for a lovely crunchy texture. They are perfect as an appetizer or light lunch, served with a spicy chutney.

MAKES 14

For the filling:
45ml/3 tbsp sunflower oil or olive oil
2.5ml/½ tsp black mustard seeds
2.5ml/½ tsp nigella seeds
1 large onion, finely chopped
10ml/2 tsp ginger purée
10ml/2 tsp garlic purée
2 fresh green chillies, finely chopped
   (deseeded if preferred)
350g/12oz lean minced (ground) lamb
   or beef
5ml/1 tsp ground cumin
7.5ml/1½ tsp ground coriander
2.5ml/½ tsp ground turmeric
200g/7oz canned chopped tomatoes
75g/3oz/¾ cup frozen garden peas
2.5ml/½ tsp salt, or to taste
2.5ml/½ tsp garam masala
30ml/2 tbsp chopped coriander (cilantro)

For the potato cakes:
1kg/2¼lb floury potatoes, skins left on
2.5ml/½ tsp salt, or to taste
1 large (US extra large) egg
30ml/2 tbsp milk
30ml/2 tbsp plain (all-purpose) flour
115g/4oz/2 cups golden breadcrumbs
vegetable oil, for deep-frying
salad or fruity chutney, to serve

1 Heat the oil over a medium heat. When it is hot, but not smoking, add the mustard seeds followed by the nigella seeds. Add the onion and stir-fry until translucent, then add the ginger, garlic and green chillies.

2 Add the minced meat, increase the heat slightly and stir-fry until the meat is dry and begins to brown slightly.

3 Add the ground spices and stir-fry gently for 1 minute, then add the tomatoes, peas and salt. Stir-fry over a medium heat until the tomato juice has evaporated, but the mixture is still quite moist.

4 Stir in the garam masala and chopped coriander and remove from the heat. Allow to cool, then divide into 14 equal portions.

5 Boil the potatoes with their skins on, then peel and mash them. Add the salt and mix in well, then divide the mashed potato into 14 equal portions. Beat the egg and the milk together in a separate bowl and set aside.

6 Take a portion of the mashed potato and flatten it into a neat cake, then make a depression in the centre to form a cup shape. Fill this cavity with a portion of the minced meat mixture, leaving about 5mm/¼in around the border.

7 Press the circular border together to cover the minced meat completely, seal well and gently press it down to form a neat cake that is about 1cm/½in thick.

8 Put the flour on one large, flat plate and the breadcrumbs on another. Dip each cake in the flour, then in the egg and milk mixture, then roll them carefully in the breadcrumbs, without breaking them up.

9 Heat a 10cm/4in depth of oil in a deep, heavy pan suitable for deep-frying until it registers 160°C/325°F on a thermometer, Fry the cakes for about 4–5 minutes, until they are crisp and golden brown, then drain them on kitchen paper. Serve with a salad and a fruity chutney of your choice.

Per portion Energy 270kcal/1126kJ; Protein 9.3g; Carbohydrate 23g, of which sugars 3.4g; Fat 16.3g, of which saturates 2.7g; Cholesterol 29mg; Calcium 36mg; Fibre 1.8g; Sodium 99mg.

Aubergine with boiled egg

Khagina is similar to the north-Indian dish *bharta*, but the addition of hard-boiled eggs makes all the difference in taste, texture and appearance. In days gone by, it graced many tables of the British-influenced clubs in Kolkata (formerly Calcutta) and it remains a favourite dish in most of these establishments.

SERVES 4

1 aubergine (eggplant), about 350g/12oz
45ml/3 tbsp sunflower oil or light olive oil
2.5ml/½ tsp mustard seeds
2.5ml/½ tsp fennel seeds
2.5ml/½ tsp nigella seeds
1 medium onion, finely chopped
5ml/1 tsp ginger purée
1 fresh green chilli, chopped
2.5ml/½ tsp ground turmeric
2.5ml/½ tsp ground cumin
1 ripe tomato, skinned and chopped
2 hard-boiled eggs, roughly chopped
15g/1½oz fresh coriander (cilantro) leaves
  and stalks, roughly chopped
2.5ml/½ tsp salt
strips of naan or crackers, to serve

1 Preheat the grill (broiler) to high and make two small incisions in the aubergine. Rub with oil, place 15cm/6in below the heat source and grill (broil) for 8–10 minutes, turning it over halfway through. Remove from the heat and leave to cool.

2 When the aubergine is cool enough to handle, slit it lengthways into two halves and scrape out the flesh with a knife or a spoon. Discard the skin and chop the flesh finely.

3 Heat the oil over a medium heat and add the mustard seeds; as soon as they start popping, add the fennel and nigella seeds. Sizzle for 15–20 seconds.

4 Add the onion, ginger and chilli. Stir-fry for 5–7 minutes, until the onion browns.

5 Add the turmeric and cumin and stir-fry for 30–40 seconds.

6 Add the aubergine and the tomato, and stir-fry for 1–2 minutes, then add the eggs, coriander and salt. Cook for 1 minute. Serve with strips of naan or on crackers.

VARIATION

Try topping the dish with cubes of paneer (Indian cheese) that have been stir-fried until golden.

Per portion Energy 173kcal/719kJ; Protein 6g; Carbohydrate 10.6g, of which sugars 6.6g; Fat 12.4g, of which saturates 2g; Cholesterol 95mg; Calcium 62mg; Fibre 3.2g; Sodium 44mg.

Egg do-piaza

Do-piaza broadly translates as 'two onions' or 'double onions' and some versions of this classic dish use unusually large amounts of the vegetable. Others, like this recipe, use them both in the sauce and with a garnish of golden-fried onions. Instead of hard-boiled eggs, as here, you could add ready-cooked chicken or vegetables to the sauce in their place, and reheat until piping hot.

SERVES 4

4 large (US extra large) hard-boiled eggs
2 large onions
sunflower oil, for shallow-frying
30ml/2 tbsp gram flour (besan)
1 large egg, beaten
5ml/1 tsp salt, or to taste
2.5ml/½ tsp chilli powder
2.5ml/½ tsp ground turmeric
5ml/1 tsp ground cumin
10ml/2 tsp ground coriander
30ml/2 tbsp unsalted butter
15ml/1 tbsp sunflower oil or light olive oil
200g/7oz canned chopped tomatoes
5ml/1 tsp caster (superfine) sugar
115g/4oz/¾ cup frozen peas
30ml/2 tbsp chopped fresh coriander
 (cilantro), to garnish
warm Indian bread, to serve

1 Shell the eggs and cut them in half lengthways. Thinly slice one of the onions and finely chop the other.

2 Pour about 2.5cm/1in sunflower oil into a heavy frying pan. Place over a medium heat and, when hot, add the sliced onion and fry it for 10–12 minutes, or until it is well-browned and crispy.

3 Remove from the pan with a slotted spoon. Drain on kitchen paper. Reserve the oil.

4 Put the gram flour in a bowl and whisk in 30ml/2 tbsp cold water to make a smooth paste. Stir in the egg, a little at a time, then add 1.5ml/¼ tsp each of the salt, chilli powder, turmeric, cumin and coriander.

5 Heat the remaining oil in the pan over a medium heat. Dip each egg half in the batter and fry them until browned. Remove with a slotted spoon and drain on kitchen paper.

6 In a separate pan, heat the butter and oil together over low heat and add the chopped onion. Fry for 5–6 minutes, until the onion is browned. Stir in the remaining chilli, turmeric, cumin and coriander.

7 Add half the tomatoes. Cook over medium-high heat for 2–3 minutes, then add the remaining tomatoes.

8 Cook for a further 2–3 minutes, then add 90ml/6 tbsp water, the remaining salt, the deep-fried eggs and the peas. Stir gently, reduce the heat to low, cover the pan and cook for 5 minutes.

9 Transfer to a warmed dish and garnish with the chopped coriander leaves and the deep-fried onions. Serve immediately with warm Indian bread.

COOK'S TIP
When hard-boiling eggs, put the eggs into cold water and bring to the boil. Start timing the cooking when the water boils gently, allowing 9–10 minutes, depending whether you prefer the yolks very slightly soft or completely solid. Turn or stir the eggs gently once or twice in the first minute of cooking so that the yolks stay in the middle and look attractive when cut.

Per portion Energy 333kcal/1385kJ; Protein13g; Carbohydrate 14g, of which sugars 7g; Fat 26g, of which saturates8; Cholesterol 273mg; Calcium 103mg; Fibre 3.5; Sodium 617mg.

Vegetables in ginger and cumin sauce

The original recipe for this dish was created using leftover vegetables when there were too few of any one type to make up a single dish. It was so delicious that these days a combination of fresh vegetables are specially bought just to make *Labra*. Mustard oil is used here, but sunflower or olive oil may also be used.

3 Stir in the turmeric, chilli powder and cumin. Cook for 30 seconds, then add the potatoes, butternut squash, aubergine and salt. Pour in 450ml/16fl oz/2 cups warm water and bring it to the boil. Reduce the heat to low, cover and simmer for 20 minutes.

4 Blanch the beans in boiling salted water for 30 seconds, then plunge into cold water.

5 Add the beans and tomatoes to the pan. Cook, uncovered, for 5–6 minutes over a medium heat, until the sauce thickens.

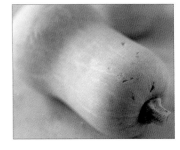

SERVES 4–5

60ml/4 tbsp mustard oil
1.25ml/¼ tsp black mustard seeds
1.25ml/¼ tsp cumin seeds
1.25ml/¼ tsp fennel seeds
1.25ml/¼ tsp nigella seeds
5–6 fenugreek seeds
2 bay leaves
1 medium onion, finely chopped
5ml/1 tsp ginger purée
2 fresh green chillies, chopped,
   (deseeded if preferred)
2.5ml/½ tsp ground turmeric
2.5ml/½ tsp chilli powder
2.5ml/½ tsp ground cumin
225g/8oz potatoes, cut into 2.5cm/1in cubes
1 small or ½ large butternut squash,
   cut into 2.5cm/1in cubes

1 large aubergine (eggplant), sliced
   lengthways and cut into 1cm/½in chunks
5ml/1 tsp salt, or to taste
75g/3oz/½ cup green beans, cut into
   2.5cm/1in lengths
75g/3oz canned chopped tomatoes,
   with their juice

1 Heat the oil in a large pan over a medium to high heat. When hot, remove from the heat and add the mustard seeds, followed by the cumin, fennel, nigella and fenugreek seeds and the bay leaves.

2 Return the pan to the heat and add the onion, ginger and chillies. Stir-fry for 5–6 minutes, until the mixture begins to brown.

Per portion Energy 190kcal/796kJ; Protein 7.2g; Carbohydrate 21.3g, of which sugars 5.5g; Fat 9.3g, of which saturates 1.4g; Cholesterol 0mg; Calcium 161mg; Fibre 3.4g; Sodium 45mg.

Cauliflower, peas and potatoes in tomato sauce

Phulkcopir Dalna is classic family fare, in which crisp white cauliflower florets join hands with cubed browned potatoes and green, tender peas in a rich chilli-tomato sauce. Mustard oil is the traditional choice, but sunflower or light olive oil can be used instead if preferred.

SERVES 4

1 small cauliflower, about 350g/12oz
60ml/4 tbsp mustard oil
450g/1lb potatoes, peeled and cut
   into 2.5cm/1in chunks
10ml/2 tsp sugar
2.5ml/½ tsp mustard seeds
5ml/1 tsp cumin seeds
5ml/1 tsp ginger purée
5ml/1 tsp garlic purée
2.5ml/½ tsp ground turmeric
5ml/1 tsp ground coriander
5ml/1 tsp ground cumin
2.5–5ml/½–1 tsp chilli powder
150g/5oz fresh tomatoes, chopped
5ml/1 tsp salt, or to taste
150g/5oz frozen garden peas
2.5ml/½ tsp garam masala
15ml/1 tbsp chopped fresh coriander
  (cilantro) leaves
Indian bread or Plain Boiled Rice, to serve

4 Add the remaining oil to the pan and sprinkle the sugar evenly over the base. As soon as it starts to caramelize, add the mustard seeds, followed by the cumin. Let them crackle and pop for a few seconds and reduce the heat to low.

5 Add the ginger and garlic and cook, stirring, for 2–3 minutes. Add the turmeric, coriander and cumin, cook for 1 minute,

6 Add the tomatoes, fried potatoes and salt, then pour in 400ml/14fl oz/1⅔ cups warm water. Bring it to the boil, reduce the heat to low, cover and cook for 15 minutes.

7 Drain the cauliflower and add to the potatoes. Add the peas, cook for 5 minutes, then stir in the garam masala and coriander. Remove from the heat and serve with Indian bread or Plain Boiled Rice.

1 Divide the cauliflower into 2.5cm/1in florets. Blanch them in a pan of salted boiling water for 2 minutes, then plunge into cold water to prevent further cooking.

2 Heat half the oil in a large, non-stick pan over a medium-high heat until smoking point is reached.

3 Add the potatoes and brown them for 3–4 minutes in several batches. Drain on kitchen paper.

Per portion Energy 293kcal/1221kJ; Protein 8g; Carbohydrate 29g, of which sugars 8g; Fat 17g, of which saturates 2g; Cholesterol 0mg; Calcium 78mg; Fibre 6.3g; Sodium 554mg.

Slow-cooked vegetables

This is a fresh-tasting, colourful curry with a good mixture of vegetables, which give varied tastes and texture. *Ghanta* makes a substantial meal for four, accompanied by naan or chapattis. Alternatively, you could serve it as an accompaniment for six people.

SERVES 4

15ml/1 tbsp white poppy seeds

10ml/2 tsp coriander seeds

2 dried red chillies

115g/4oz green beans, cut into 2.5cm/
  1in lengths

60ml/4 tbsp sunflower oil or light olive oil

250g/9oz potatoes, cut into 2.5cm/1in cubes

1.25ml/¼ tsp black mustard seeds

1.25ml/¼ tsp cumin seeds

1.25ml/¼ tsp fennel seeds

1.25ml/¼ tsp nigella seeds

4–5 fenugreek seeds

5ml/1 tsp ginger purée

1 clove garlic, crushed

2.5ml/½ tsp ground turmeric

5ml/1 tsp salt, or to taste

250g/9oz marrow (large zucchini) or
  courgettes (zucchini), cut into
  2.5cm/1in cubes

150g/5oz green cabbage, finely shredded

15ml/1 tbsp lemon juice

Plain Boiled Rice or warm Indian bread,
  to serve

1 Heat a small, heavy pan over a medium heat and dry-roast the poppy and coriander seeds and chillies for 45–50 seconds, or until they release their aroma. Remove from the pan, leave to cool and grind in a coffee grinder or mortar and pestle.

2 Blanch the green beans in boiling salted water for 30 seconds, then plunge them into cold water, to stop further cooking.

3 Heat the oil in a heavy frying pan over a medium heat, add the potatoes and cook, stirring frequently until the potatoes are brown. Remove with a slotted spoon, leaving most of the oil behind, and drain on kitchen paper.

4 Add the mustard, cumin, fennel, nigella and fenugreek seeds to the pan. Allow them to crackle and pop for 15–20 seconds, then add the ginger and garlic. Reduce the heat to low and cook until lightly browned.

5 Stir in the turmeric, fried potatoes and salt and add 250ml/8fl oz/1 cup hot water. Bring to the boil, reduce the heat, cover and cook until the potatoes are just tender.

6 Add the marrow (if using) and cook for 3–4 minutes. Add the beans, cabbage and courgettes (if using). Cook for 2–3 minutes until all the vegetables are tender. Stir in the lemon juice and ground and seed mixture. Serve with rice or bread.

Per portion Energy 213kcal/883kJ; Protein 5g; Carbohydrate 15g, of which sugars 4g; Fat 17g, of which saturates 2g; Cholesterol 0mg; Calcium 89mg; Fibre 3.0g; Sodium 501mg.

Plantain curry

In eastern India, plantains are very popular in curries or dusted with ground spices as a vegetable side dish. The earthy, squash-like flavour of the plaintain, mixed with a variety of seeds, roots and spices, gives this curry, *Kaach Koler Kari*, a delightfully different flavour, perfect for a quick dinner for family and friends. When shopping, plantains are occasionally referred to as 'raw' or 'green' bananas.

SERVES 4

5 plantains
2 medium potatoes, about 225g/8oz
45ml/3 tbsp mustard oil
1.25ml/¼ tsp black mustard seeds
1.25ml/¼ tsp cumin seeds
1.25ml/¼ tsp nigella seeds
1.25ml/¼ tsp fennel seeds
6–8 fenugreek seeds
1 fresh green chilli, chopped,
  (deseeded if preferred)
2.5cm/1in piece of fresh root ginger,
  minced (ground) or finely chopped
2.5ml/½ tsp ground cumin
2.5ml/½ tsp ground turmeric
1.25–2.5ml/¼–½ tsp chilli powder
75g/3oz fresh ripe tomato, skinned
  and chopped
3.75ml/¾ tsp salt, or to taste
2.5ml/½ tsp garam masala
sprigs of fresh coriander (cilantro),
  to garnish
Plain Boiled Rice or warm Indian bread,
  to serve

COOK'S TIP
Plantains are available in Asian and Caribbean stores, and are increasingly on sale in specialist sections of large supermarkets.

---

1 Peel the plantains with a small knife. Quarter them lengthways and cut them into 1cm/½in pieces. Put them in a bowl of cold water and set aside to soak.

2 Cut the potatoes into pieces the same size as the plantains.

3 Heat 30ml/2 tbsp of the mustard oil over a medium heat until smoke rises. Drain the plantains and dry them with a cloth. When the oil is ready, fry the plantain pieces in two batches for about 5 minutes, until they begin to brown. Drain on kitchen paper.

4 Brown the potatoes in the same oil in the frying pan for about 5 minutes, then drain on kitchen paper.

5 Add the remaining mustard oil to the frying pan and heat until smoke rises. Remove the pan from the heat and stir in the mustard, cumin, nigella, fennel and fenugreek seeds.

6 Stir in the chilli and ginger. Return the pan to the heat and stir-fry the ingredients for 25–30 seconds, then add the cumin, turmeric and chilli powder.

7 Stir everything well and add the chopped tomato. Cook for 2–3 minutes, then add the fried potatoes and salt. Stir to combine, taking care not to break up the potatoes.

8 Pour in 400ml/14oz/1⅔ cups warm water and bring it to the boil. Reduce the heat to low, cover the pan with a lid and cook for 8–10 minutes or until the potatoes are just tender when pricked with a knife.

9 Gently stir in the fried plantains and the garam masala. Cook for 2–3 minutes more or until the plantains are tender, then remove from the heat.

10 Serve, garnished with the sprigs of coriander and accompanied by Plain Boiled Rice or warm Indian bread.

Per portion Energy 340kcal/1437kJ; Protein 3.9g; Carbohydrate 63.3g, of which sugars 11.3g; Fat 9.8g, of which saturates 1.2g; Cholesterol 0mg; Calcium 32mg; Fibre 3g; Sodium 17mg.

Spiced lentil-filled pancakes

From the little-known cuisine of the state of Bihar, this recipe for pancakes filled with spiced lentils, *Pittha*, is wholesome and healthy as well as delicious. The pancakes are very versatile – they can be served as an appetizer, a hearty brunch, or as a teatime snack. They can also be frozen, then defrosted and briefly shallow-fried or steamed to reheat when needed.

MAKES 12

For the filling:
225g/8oz/1 cup split Bengal gram (channa dhal or skinless split chickpeas), washed
2 large garlic cloves, chopped
2.5cm/1in piece fresh root ginger, peeled and chopped
2 dried red chillies, chopped
1 fresh green chilli, chopped
2.5ml/½ tsp ground turmeric
2.5ml/½ tsp Asafoetida
50g/2oz/¼ cup natural (plain) yogurt
30ml/2 tbsp fresh coriander (cilantro) leaves, chopped
5ml/1 tsp salt, or to taste

For the pastry:
150g/5oz/1¼ cups chapati flour (atta) or fine wholemeal (whole-wheat) flour
150g/5oz/1¼ cups plain (all-purpose) flour, plus extra for dusting
2.5ml/½ tsp salt
200ml/7fl oz/¾ cup water
Roasted Tomato Chutney, to serve

1 Soak the split Bengal gram for 4–5 hours. Drain and put into a food processor together with the garlic, ginger and chillies. Blend to a paste, adding 30–45ml/2–3 tbsp water if necessary.

2 Put the paste into a non-stick pan with the turmeric and Asafoetida. Cook, stirring, until the mixture is dry and crumbly.

3 Remove from the heat and transfer to a mixing bowl. Add the yogurt, chopped coriander and salt and mix thoroughly. If the mixture is still slightly crumbly, add a little water until it has a paste-like consistency. Allow to cool.

4 Meanwhile, make the pastry. Mix both types of flour and the salt in a mixing bowl, then gradually add the water (the amount needed will depend on the absorbency of the flour), stirring with a spoon or using your fingers.

5 When a dough has formed, transfer it to a floured surface and knead it for about 5 minutes, until soft and pliable.

6 Wrap the dough in clear film (plastic wrap) and allow it to rest for 30 minutes, then divide it into 12 portions and make each portion into a flat cake. Keep them covered with a damp cloth while you are working on one at a time.

7 Using a rolling pin, roll out each cake into roughly a 10cm/4in circle.

8 Divide the filling into 12 equal parts and place a portion to one side of a dough circle, leaving a 1cm/½in border. Repeat until you have used all the filling and all the dough circles.

9 Moisten the edges of the dough circle with water and enclose the filling by folding over the other half, making a half-moon shape. Press to seal and crimp the edges with the back of a fork.

10 Place the pancakes on a piece of oiled baking parchment in a steamer (take care not to completely block the steam vents or the steam won't be able to circulate).

11 Steam over a pan of boiling water for 10 minutes, or until the filling and pancakes are thoroughly cooked. Serve with Roasted Tomato Chutney.

Per portion Energy 148kcal/630kJ; Protein 7.7g; Carbohydrate 29.2g, of which sugars 1.2g; Fat 0.9g, of which saturates 0.2g; Cholesterol 0mg; Calcium 43mg; Fibre 2.4g; Sodium 12mg.

Gram flour dumplings in a tomato sauce

This protein-rich dish, *Ghoomni*, is from the state of Bihar, where vegetarian food is prevalent. Gram flour (besan) is mixed with chillies and spices and made into a dough, which is poached until set and cut into slices known as *gatte*. These are then fried and simmered in a spicy sauce. Asafoetida is added to the sauce for its curative quality as gram flour is sometimes difficult to digest.

SERVES 4

For the dumplings:
300g/10½oz/generous 2½ cups gram flour
   (besan), sifted
2.5ml/½ tsp bicarbonate of soda
   (baking soda)
2.5ml/½ tsp ground turmeric
5ml/1 tsp cumin seeds
5ml/1 tsp fennel seeds
5ml/1 tsp dried red chilli flakes
2.5cm/1in piece of fresh root ginger, grated
30ml/2 tbsp fresh coriander (cilantro)
   leaves, chopped
5ml/1 tsp salt, or to taste
150g/5oz/generous ½ cup full-fat (whole)
   natural (plain) yogurt
sunflower oil, for deep-frying

For the sauce:
45–60ml/3–4 tbsp sunflower oil or light
   olive oil
2.5cm/1in piece of cinnamon stick
4 cloves
1.25ml/¼ tsp Asafoetida
1 large onion, finely sliced
10ml/2 tsp ground coriander
2.5–5ml/½–1 tsp chilli powder
2.5ml/½ tsp ground turmeric
250g/9oz canned chopped tomatoes,
   with their juice
5ml/1 tsp salt, or to taste
2.5ml/½ tsp garam masala
30ml/2 tbsp fresh coriander (cilantro)
   leaves, chopped, to garnish
Indian bread, to serve

1 Put the gram flour in a mixing bowl and add the remaining dumpling ingredients except the yogurt and oil. Mix well to combine, then add the yogurt.

COOK'S TIP
Ensure the parcels are completely sealed or they will be spoiled.

2 Add 50–75ml/2–2½fl oz/¼–⅓ cup water and mix until a soft dough is formed. The amount of water you use will depend on the type of yogurt and its water content.

3 Brush two pieces of foil with oil and place one half of the dough on it. Wrap and roll it into a cylindrical shape and seal by twisting the two ends to form a tight parcel. Repeat with the remaining dough.

4 Bring a large pan of water to the boil and place the parcels in it. Reduce the heat to medium, cover and cook for 20 minutes.

5 Remove the parcels from the water using tongs and set aside until they are cool enough to handle.

6 Remove the foil and allow the rolls to cool, then cut them in half. Cut each half into 1cm/½in slices. These could now be stored, covered, in the refrigerator for 24 hours, if you like.

7 Heat the oil in a wok or other suitable pan for deep-frying over a medium heat. Fry the dumpling slices for 3–4 minutes, until well browned. Drain on kitchen paper. Keep hot.

8 To make the sauce, heat the oil over a low heat and add the cinnamon, cloves and Asafoetida. Allow to sizzle for 20 seconds, then add the onion. Increase the heat to medium and fry the onion for 7 minutes, until soft. Add the coriander, chilli and turmeric.

9 Cook for 1 minute, then add the tomatoes. Continue to cook until the tomato juice evaporates, then add 30ml/2 tbsp water. Cook for 2 minutes, then add a further 30ml/2 tbsp water and cook for 2 minutes.

10 Add 500ml/17fl oz/generous 2 cups lukewarm water and simmer, uncovered, for 8–10 minutes. Switch off the heat and add the fried dumpling slices. Stir gently, transfer to a serving dish and garnish with coriander. Serve with any Indian bread.

Per portion Energy 457kcal/1915kJ; Protein 19g; Carbohydrate 47g, of which sugars 10g; Fat 24g, of which saturates 3g; Cholesterol 4mg; Calcium 268mg; Fibre 11.5g; Sodium 1217mg.

Cinnamon and clove-scented cheese curry

Paneer (Indian cheese) is a great source of protein and the vast majority of the Indian population thrive on this versatile ingredient. In this dish, *Channer Dalna*, melt-in-the-mouth cubes of cheese and tender pieces of potato are bathed in a fragrant spiced sauce to create a memorable vegetarian curry.

SERVES 4

60ml/4 tbsp sunflower oil or light olive oil
225g/8oz/2 cups paneer (Indian cheese),
    cut into 2.5cm/1in cubes
400g/14oz potatoes, peeled and cut into
    2.5cm/1in cubes
2.5cm/1in piece of cinnamon stick
4 green cardamom pods, bruised
4 cloves
1 large onion, finely chopped
5ml/1 tsp ginger purée
5ml/1 tsp garlic purée
2.5ml/½ tsp ground turmeric
2.5–5ml/½–1 tsp chilli powder
2.5ml/½ tsp ground cumin
5ml/1 tsp salt, or to taste
2.5ml/½ tsp garam masala
15ml/1 tbsp fresh coriander (cilantro)
    leaves, chopped
Indian bread, to serve

4 Cook for 5–6 minutes until the onion has softened, then add the ginger and garlic and fry until the onion is beginning to brown. Add the turmeric, chilli powder and cumin and cook for about 1 minute.

5 Add 30ml/2 tbsp water, and cook until the mixture is dry and the water has evaporated. Repeat this process twice more, adding 30ml/2tbsp water each time (90ml/6 tbsp water in all).

6 Add the potatoes, salt and 250ml/9fl oz/ 1 cup warm water to the pan.

7 Bring to the boil, reduce the heat to low, cover the pan and simmer for 10 minutes, stirring occasionally.

8 Add the browned paneer, stir gently to combine and increase the heat to medium. Cook, uncovered, for 6 minutes or until the sauce has thickened.

9 Stir in the garam masala and coriander. Transfer to a serving dish and serve with any Indian bread.

1 Heat half the oil in a non-stick pan over a medium heat and brown the cubes of paneer. Stand well away from the pan while frying the paneer as it tends to splutter. Drain the cubes on kitchen paper.

2 Dry the cubes of potato with a cloth and brown them in the same oil. Drain on kitchen paper.

3 Add the remaining oil to the pan. Reduce the heat to low. Add the cinnamon, cardamom and cloves. Sizzle for 30 seconds, until the cardamom pods have puffed up. Add the onion and increase the heat slightly.

VARIATION
This curry is also delicious served with Plain Boiled Rice or Yellow Rice.

Per portion Energy 280kcal/1170kJ; Protein 11.5g; Carbohydrate 28.5g, of which sugars 9.5g; Fat 14.2g, of which saturates 2.9g; Cholesterol 7mg; Calcium 85mg; Fibre 2.8g; Sodium 230mg.

Egg, potato and green pea curry

In this classic dish, *Dimer Dalna*, hard-boiled eggs and cubed boiled potatoes are flavoured with turmeric and chilli powder, then shallow-fried to a rich golden colour before being simmered in an aromatic sauce. The jade-green peas, golden eggs and potato cubes doused in a rich-red sauce create a strikingly beautiful dish. Luchi are the traditional accompaniment to this curry, but you can use any Indian bread.

SERVES 4

4 hard-boiled eggs
350g/12oz medium-sized potatoes,
  peeled and quartered
60ml/4 tbsp sunflower oil or light
  olive oil
2.5ml/½ tsp ground turmeric
2.5ml/½ tsp chilli powder
2.5cm/1in piece of cinnamon stick
4 green cardamom pods, bruised
4 cloves
2 bay leaves
1 large onion, finely chopped
5ml/1 tsp ground coriander
2.5ml/½ tsp ground cumin
1 ripe tomato, skinned and chopped
5ml/1 tsp salt, or to taste
2.5ml/½ tsp sugar
115g/4oz/1 cup frozen peas
2.5ml/½ tsp garam masala
Indian bread, to serve

1 Shell the eggs and make four small slits in each without cutting them right through.

2 Wash the potatoes to remove the starch and dry them with a cloth.

3 Heat the oil over a low heat and add 1.25ml/¼ tsp each of the turmeric and chilli powder, followed by the whole eggs.

4 Stir the eggs around for 3–4 minutes, until they are coloured by the spices and develop a light golden crust.

5 Remove the eggs with a slotted spoon and set them aside on a piece of kitchen paper to absorb any excess oil.

6 Add the potatoes to the same oil and increase the heat to medium. Stir-fry them for 4–5 minutes, until they are well browned and develop a light golden crust. Remove them with a slotted spoon, leaving behind as much oil as possible in the pan, and drain on kitchen paper.

7 Reduce the heat to low and add the cinnamon, cardamom, cloves and bay leaves to the oil remaining in the pan, and fry them for a few seconds.

8 Add the onion, increase the heat to medium, and fry for 9–10 minutes, until the onion is golden brown.

9 Reduce the heat to low, then add the ground coriander and cumin and the remaining turmeric and chilli powder.

10 Stir-fry for 1 minute, then add the tomato and continue to cook for 1–2 minutes.

11 Add the browned potatoes, salt and sugar and pour in 250ml/9fl oz/1 cup warm water. Bring the mixture to the boil, cover the pan and reduce the heat to low. Cook for 8–10 minutes, until the potatoes are almost cooked.

12 Add the peas, cover the pan and cook for 5–6 minutes longer, until the potatoes are tender and the peas are cooked.

13 Stir in the garam masala and remove from the heat. Serve with your favourite Indian bread.

COOK'S TIP

To save time, omit skinning the tomato before chopping it, although the dish will not look as good.

Per portion Energy 316kcal/1317kJ; Protein 11.9g; Carbohydrate 29g, of which sugars 9.3g; Fat 18g, of which saturates 3.1g; Cholesterol 190mg; Calcium 79mg; Fibre 4.2g; Sodium 87mg.

Chickpeas in onion-scented tomato sauce

Ghughni is the most popular street food in Kolkata. Street vendors serve it to hundreds of people every day, topped with a flat bread of some kind. It is wonderfully aromatic and packed full of protein and fibre. Traditionally, dried chickpeas are soaked and boiled until tender before cooking them in the spiced sauce, but canned chickpeas give an excellent result if you rinse them thoroughly before use.

3 Add the coriander, cumin, turmeric and chilli powder. Continue to cook for about 2 minutes, then add the tomatoes.

4 Cook for 7–8 minutes, until the tomatoes reach a paste-like consistency. Add 30–45ml/ 2–3 tbsp water during the cooking time.

SERVES 4

45ml/3 tbsp mustard oil, sunflower oil or
   light olive oil
1 large onion, finely chopped
2.5cm/1in piece of cinnamon stick
10ml/2 tsp ginger purée
10ml/2 tsp garlic purée
10ml/2 tsp ground coriander
10ml/2 tsp ground cumin
2.5ml/½ tsp ground turmeric
2.5ml/½ tsp chilli powder
150g/5oz canned chopped tomatoes
   with their juice
5ml/1 tsp salt, or to taste
675g/1½lb canned chickpeas, drained
   and well rinsed
julienne strips of fresh tomato and fresh
   red chillies, and sprigs of fresh coriander
   (cilantro), to garnish
Plain Boiled Rice and Indian bread,
   to serve

1 Heat the mustard oil over a medium heat until smoking point is reached (if using sunflower or olive oil, heat until hot) and add the onion and cinnamon stick. Stir-fry for about 15 minutes, until the onion is well browned, taking care not to burn it. Reduce the heat slightly halfway through.

2 Add the ginger and garlic and cook for 2–3 minutes.

5 Add 150ml/¼ pint/⅔ cup lukewarm water, salt and the chickpeas. Reduce the heat, cover and simmer for 5 minutes. Garnish with tomato, chilli and coriander. Serve with Plain Boiled Rice and Indian bread.

Per portion Energy 274kcal/1146kJ; Protein 10g; Carbohydrate 26g, of which sugars 5g; Fat 15g, of which saturates 2g; Cholesterol 0mg; Calcium 89mg; Fibre 1.2g; Sodium 788mg.

Stir-fried spiced lentils

In this recipe, *Bhaja Muger Dhal*, split yellow gram are stir-fried with onions, chillies and cinnamon, before the cooking liquid is added in several batches. Golden turmeric provides an assertive yet subtle background taste, and heightens the lovely colour of the lentils. As with all *dhals*, this makes an excellent accompaniment to many vegetable dishes as part of a *thali*-style feast.

SERVES 4

225g/8oz/1 cup split yellow gram (channa dhal)
45–60ml/3–4 tbsp sunflower oil or olive oil
1 large onion, finely sliced
2.5cm/1in piece of cinnamon stick
4 green cardamom pods, bruised
1 bay leaf
2.5ml/½ tsp cumin seeds
5ml/1 tsp ground turmeric
2.5–5ml/½–1 tsp chilli powder
5ml/1 tsp salt, or to taste
1 fresh green chilli, deseeded and cut into
   julienne strips, to garnish

> ## COOK'S TIP
> Do not add salt early in the cooking time or it will make the lentils tough.

1 Lentils often include tiny stones and other debris, so scan them carefully by spreading them in a large tray, then wash and drain them thoroughly.

2 Heat the oil in a large, heavy, non-stick pan and add the onion. Fry, stirring regularly, for 6–8 minutes, until browned.

3 Lift out the onion with a slotted spoon, pressing down with another spoon to squeeze excess oil back into the pan. Drain on kitchen paper.

4 In the remaining oil, sauté the cinnamon, cardamom, bay leaf and cumin seeds over a low heat for 30–40 seconds. Add the lentils and increase the heat to medium. Stir-fry for 4–5 minutes.

5 Add the turmeric and chilli powder. Stir-fry for 2–3 minutes, add the salt and 120ml/4fl oz/½ cup lukewarm water. Increase the heat slightly and stir-fry until the water has evaporated.

6 Add 120ml/4fl oz/½ cup water and repeat the process, then add another 300ml/½ pint/1¼ cups warm water, and reduce the heat to low.

7 Reserve a little fried onion as garnish and stir the rest into the lentils. Cover and cook for 12–15 minutes, until the lentils are tender. Garnish with the onion and chilli and serve.

Per portion Energy 339kcal/1427kJ; Protein 23.7g; Carbohydrate 38.6g, of which sugars 4.9g; Fat 11g, of which saturates 7g; Cholesterol 35mg; Calcium 221mg; Fibre 3.7g; Sodium 788mg.

Fish in aromatic sauce

This well-loved dish from west Bengal, *Macher Jhol*, is flavoured with mustard oil and a five-spice mix known as *panchforon* – an aromatic combination of five whole spices. It makes a healthy and satisfying meal when served with boiled rice.

SERVES 4–5

675g/1½lb fillets of tilapia or other white fish
5ml/1 tsp ground turmeric
5ml/1 tsp salt, or to taste
60ml/4 tbsp mustard oil
1.25ml/¼ tsp black mustard seeds
1.25ml/¼ tsp cumin seeds
1.25ml/¼ tsp fennel seeds
1.25ml/¼ tsp nigella seeds
5–6 fenugreek seeds
2 bay leaves
2 dried red chillies, left whole
2 fresh green chillies, chopped
2.5ml/½ tsp ground cumin
5ml/1 tsp ground coriander
75g/3oz canned chopped tomatoes
115g/4oz potatoes, cut into 1cm/½in cubes
115g/4oz aubergine (eggplant), cut into 1cm/½in cubes
50g/2oz/½ cup frozen garden peas
30ml/2 tbsp chopped fresh coriander (cilantro)
Plain Boiled Rice, to serve

1 Cut the fish fillets into 5cm/2in pieces. Place them on a large plate and gently rub in half the turmeric and half the salt. Set aside until required.

2 Heat 30ml/2 tbsp of the mustard oil in a frying pan over a medium to high heat and, when it is almost smoking, switch off the heat and immediately add the mustard seeds, followed by the cumin, fennel, nigella and fenugreek seeds. Add the bay leaves, then the dried and fresh chillies.

3 Return the pan to the heat and add the cumin, coriander and remaining turmeric. Stir over a medium heat for 30 seconds, then add the tomatoes. Cook for 4–5 minutes.

4 Add all the potato and aubergine cubes, along with about 350ml/12fl oz/1½ cups warm water and the remaining salt. Bring the liquid to the boil, then reduce the heat to low, cover and cook for 15 minutes, stirring occasionally.

5 Meanwhile, heat the remaining mustard oil in a separate large frying pan, preferably non-stick, until it is almost smoking. Fry the marinated fish pieces in batches until they are well browned on all sides, then drain on kitchen paper.

6 Add the fried fish to the tomato mixture along with the frozen peas. Cook for 4–5 minutes, until the peas are cooked, then stir in the chopped coriander and remove from the heat. Serve with Plain Boiled Rice.

Per portion Energy 242kcal/1011kJ; Protein 27.1g; Carbohydrate 7.4g, of which sugars 1.4g; Fat 11.9g, of which saturates 1.5g; Cholesterol 0mg; Calcium 184mg; Fibre 1.2g; Sodium 83mg.

Fish cooked in yogurt

Bengali weddings are elaborate affairs and fish dishes such as this often play a starring role. In this recipe, *Doi Maach*, the fish is first marinated in spicy yogurt, then stirred into a sauce.

SERVES 4

675g/1½lb firm white fish fillets, skinned
250ml/8fl oz/1 cup whole-milk natural
  (plain) yogurt
5ml/1 tsp ground turmeric
5ml/1 tsp salt, or to taste
5ml/1 tsp caster (superfine) sugar
15ml/1 tbsp lemon juice
15ml/1 tbsp gram flour (besan)
75ml/5 tbsp mustard oil
1 large onion, finely chopped
1 green chilli, finely chopped
  (deseeded if preferred)
2.5cm/1in piece of cinnamon stick
4 green cardamom pods, bruised
4 cloves
2.5cm/1in fresh root ginger, grated, or
  10ml/2 tsp ginger purée
2 cloves garlic, crushed, or 10ml/2 tsp
  garlic purée
10ml/2 tsp ground coriander
5ml/1 tsp ground cumin
2.5–5ml/½–1 tsp chilli powder
30ml/2 tbsp torn fresh coriander (cilantro),
  to garnish

1 Cut the fish into 5cm/2in pieces. Stir the yogurt, turmeric, salt, sugar, lemon juice and gram flour together in a bowl. Add the fish and mix to coat all the pieces. Cover with clear film (plastic wrap) and leave to marinate in a cool place for 20–30 minutes.

2 Heat the oil in a heavy frying pan until very hot, then turn the heat down to low (see Cook's Tip).

3 Add the onion and green chilli with the cinnamon stick, cardamom pods and cloves and cook for 4–5 minutes, stirring often, until the onion is soft, but not brown.

4 Stir in the ginger, garlic, coriander, cumin and chilli powder. Cook for about 1 minute, add 30ml/2 tbsp water and continue to fry for 2–3 minutes. Add 30ml/2 tbsp water and fry for a further 2 minutes.

5 Add the fish together with any leftover marinade. Bring to simmering point, then cook gently for 8–10 minutes, until the fish is just cooked.

6 Spoon into a warmed serving dish and sprinkle with torn coriander leaves just before serving.

COOK'S TIP
The distinctive and pungent flavour of mustard oil typifies the cuisine of Bengal and features in many dishes. It needs to be heated to a high temperature in order to reduce the pungency and to develop its nutty taste. Sunflower or light olive oil may be used in this recipe instead if you prefer a milder flavour; it is not necessary to heat them to a high temperature.

Per portion Energy 395kcal/1645kJ; Protein 36g; Carbohydrate 13g, of which sugars 10g; Fat 22g, of which saturates 3g; Cholesterol 85mg; Calcium 175mg; Fibre 1.3g; Sodium 652mg.

Fish in five-spice sauce with potatoes and peas

Macher Kalia is one of Bengal's signature dishes. It is hugely popular all over eastern India, and contains warm, fragrant cinnamon and cardamom and pungent asafoetida. Bengalis serve it with plain boiled rice, which is the best way to enjoy the blend of spices. As the recipe contains a generous amount of both potatoes and peas, there is no need to make an accompanying vegetable dish.

SERVES 4–6
675g/1½lb firm white fish fillets, such as
　cod or haddock, skinned
5ml/1 tsp ground turmeric
5ml/1 tsp salt, or to taste
75ml/5 tbsp sunflower or light olive oil
150g/5oz potatoes, cut into
　1cm/½in cubes

For the five-spice mix:
1.25ml/¼ tsp black mustard seeds
1.25ml/¼ tsp cumin seeds
1.25ml/¼ tsp fennel seeds
1.25ml/¼ tsp nigella seeds
6 fenugreek seeds
1.5ml/¼ tsp asafoetida
1 bay leaf
4 green cardamom pods, bruised
2.5cm/1in piece cinnamon stick
2 cloves garlic, crushed, or 10ml/2 tsp
　garlic purée
2.5cm/1in fresh root ginger, grated, or
　10ml/2 tsp ginger purée
2.5–5ml/½–1 tsp chilli powder
115g/4oz/¾ cup frozen peas
30ml/2 tbsp chopped fresh coriander
　(cilantro)
Plain Boiled Rice, to serve

1 Cut the fish into 5cm/2in pieces and place in a bowl. Sprinkle with half the turmeric and half the salt, then gently stir to coat all the pieces. Set aside for 10 minutes.

2 Meanwhile, heat 30ml/2 tbsp of the oil in a non-stick pan over a medium-high heat and fry the potatoes for about 5 minutes, until golden brown, stirring frequently. Lift out of the pan with a slotted spoon and drain on kitchen paper.

3 Pour a further 30ml/2 tbsp oil into the pan and fry the fish in two batches until brown. Remove from the pan with a slotted spoon, leaving any oil behind, and set aside.

4 To make the five-spice mix, heat the remaining 15ml/1 tbsp oil over a medium heat. When the oil is just smoking, add the mustard seeds, then the cumin, fennel, nigella and fenugreek. Let them crackle for 20 seconds then add the asafoetida, bay leaf, cardamom and cinnamon.

5 After a few seconds, add the garlic and ginger. Fry for about 1 minute, then add the chilli powder and the remaining turmeric, and return the fried potatoes to the pan.

6 Pour in 150ml/¼ pint/⅔ cup hot water and bring the liquid to the boil. Reduce the heat to low, cover and simmer for 10 minutes, or until the potatoes are almost tender.

7 Add the peas, the remaining salt and the fried fish. Simmer for 5 minutes, gently stirring occasionally, taking care not to break up the fish. Transfer to a serving dish and sprinkle with the chopped coriander before serving with Plain Boiled Rice.

VARIATION
Try other vegetable combinations for a change, such as potatoes and cauliflower or peas and carrots.

Per portion Energy 236kcal/984kJ; Protein 23g; Carbohydrate 6g, of which sugars 1g; Fat 14g, of which saturates 2g; Cholesterol 52mg; Calcium 26mg; Fibre 1.3g; Sodium 400mg.

Fish in spicy mustard sauce

Although it takes a little longer to roast and grind your own spices, the freshness and intensity of flavour is well worth the extra effort. Being a coastal state, fish is an integral part of the Orissan diet and is prepared and served in many different ways. In this dish, *Machcha Torkari*, warm spices including coriander, cumin and poppy seeds are made into a paste, and fresh and dried chillies add both heat and colour.

SERVES 4
675g/1½lb firm white fish fillets, skinned
5ml/1 tsp salt, or to taste
5ml/1 tsp ground turmeric
10ml/2 tsp coriander seeds
5ml/1 tsp cumin seeds
10ml/2 tsp white poppy seeds
10ml/2 tsp ready-made mustard paste
75ml/5 tbsp sunflower or light olive oil
2.5ml/½ tsp black mustard seeds
3–4 dried whole red chillies
1 large onion, finely chopped
1cm/½in fresh ginger, grated, or 5ml/1 tsp
 ginger purée
1 clove garlic, crushed, or 5ml/1 tsp
 garlic purée
200g/7oz potatoes, finely diced
2 fresh green chillies
22.5ml/1½ tbsp lemon juice
30ml/2 tbsp chopped fresh coriander
 (cilantro), to garnish
Plain Boiled Rice, to serve

VARIATION
675g/1½lb large raw prawns (shrimp) may be used instead of the fish. There is no need to pre-fry them; add to the sauce and cook for 3–5 minutes or until they are just cooked and pink all over.

1 Cut the fish into 5cm/2in pieces and place them in a single layer on a large plate. Gently rub in half the salt and half the turmeric and set aside for 20 minutes.

2 Meanwhile, preheat a small, heavy pan over a medium heat and dry-roast the coriander, cumin and white poppy seeds for about 45 seconds, or until they smell aromatic. Remove the pan from the heat, leave the seeds to cool, then grind to a powder in a coffee grinder.

3 Put the ground dry spices in a small bowl with the mustard paste and stir to combine, adding 15–30ml/1–2 tbsp cold water to make a paste.

4 Heat half the oil in a large, heavy frying pan over a medium heat and brown the fish in two batches. Remove the fish from the pan with a slotted spoon, leaving any oil behind, and drain well on kitchen paper. Set aside.

5 Add the remaining oil to the pan and when hot, add the mustard seeds and the whole dried chillies. Allow the chillies to blacken slightly, then add the chopped onion and cook, stirring frequently, for about 8 minutes, until lightly browned.

6 Add the ginger, garlic and potatoes and continue to cook for 2–3 minutes.

7 Stir in 450ml/¾ pint/scant 2 cups hot water. Bring to the boil, then reduce the heat to low, cover and cook for 12 minutes, until the potatoes are almost tender.

8 Stir in the spice paste and whole green chillies, and simmer for 2–3 minutes. Add the fish, cover and cook for 4–5 minutes or until the fish is just cooked and opaque.

9 Transfer to a serving dish. Sprinkle with lemon juice and garnish with chopped fresh coriander. Serve immediately with Plain Boiled Rice.

Prawn pilau

Bengal is renowned for its fish and shellfish, and this pilau, *Chingrir Pulao*, combines abundant, tasty prawns (shrimp) with a simple preparation method, making this a favourite among locals. A meal in itself, the dish also fits easily into a spread that includes meat, poultry and vegetable dishes as well.

SERVES 4

275g/10oz/1⅓ cups basmati rice
60ml/4 tbsp sunflower oil or olive oil
5cm/2in piece of cinnamon stick, halved
6 green cardamom pods, bruised
4 cloves
2 bay leaves, crumpled
1 large onion, finely sliced
10ml/2 tsp ginger purée
1 fresh green chilli, finely chopped
(deseeded if preferred)
2.5ml/½ tsp ground turmeric
5ml/1 tsp salt, or to taste
5ml/1 tbsp chopped fresh coriander (cilantro)
250g/9oz cooked and peeled
prawns (shrimp)
sprigs of fresh coriander, to garnish (optional)

1 Wash the basmati rice in several changes of cold water and soak for 20 minutes. Drain in a sieve.

2 Heat the oil in a heavy pan over a low heat and add the cinnamon, cardamom pods, cloves and bay leaves. Stir-fry the ingredients gently for 25–30 seconds and then add the onion.

3 Increase the heat to medium, and fry until the onion is beginning to brown, around 7–8 minutes, stirring regularly to prevent the spices from burning.

4 Add the ginger purée and finely chopped chilli and continue to fry for 3–4 minutes, stirring, until the onion is well browned.

5 Add the turmeric, salt, chopped coriander, prawns and the soaked and drained basmati rice. Stir gently to combine everything. Stir-fry for 2–3 minutes, then pour in 475ml/16fl oz/2 cups hot water. Bring this to the boil and let it cook, uncovered, for 2–3 minutes. Reduce the heat to low, cover the pan tightly and cook for another 7–8 minutes.

6 Remove from the heat and let the dish stand for 5–6 minutes to absorb the flavour. Fluff up the pilau with a fork and transfer it to a serving dish. Garnish with sprigs of coriander, if you like.

VARIATION
You could use chicken or fish fillets in place of the prawns (shrimp).

Per portion Energy 440kcal/1835kJ; Protein 17.9g; Carbohydrate 64.1g, of which sugars 5.6g; Fat 12.4g, of which saturates 1.3g; Cholesterol 122mg; Calcium 94mg; Fibre 1.4g; Sodium 123mg.

Chicken with poppy seeds in chilli sauce

Bengalis make good use of locally grown spices such as ginger, turmeric, mustard and chillies, and the cuisine includes spice combinations not found in other parts of India. White poppy seeds are a popular addition and, in this dish, *Murgi Posto*, they are roasted and ground and used to thicken the spicy sauce.

SERVES 4

675g/1½lb boned chicken skinless thighs
  or breast fillets
juice of 1 lime
5ml/1 tsp salt, or to taste
60ml/4 tbsp sunflower or light olive oil
2.5cm/1in piece of cinnamon stick
4 green cardamom pods, bruised
4 cloves
1 large onion, finely chopped
2 fresh green chillies, finely chopped
  (deseeded if preferred)
3 garlic cloves, crushed, or 15ml/1 tbsp
  garlic purée
2.5ml/½ tsp ground turmeric
2.5ml/½ tsp chilli powder
30ml/2 tbsp white poppy seeds
1 fresh green chilli, thinly sliced, to garnish
warm Indian bread, to serve

1 Cut the chicken into 2.5cm/1in cubes, put in a bowl and sprinkle with the lime juice and half the salt. Stir to coat, then cover and leave to marinate for 30 minutes.

2 Heat the oil in a large, heavy frying pan over a low heat and add the cinnamon, cardamom and cloves. Let them sizzle for a few seconds, then add the onion and chillies and increase the heat to medium. Cook the mixture, stirring frequently, for about 5 minutes, until the onion is soft and translucent, but not brown.

3 Add the chillies and garlic and continue to cook until the onion begins to brown.

4 Stir in the turmeric and chilli powder, followed by the chicken. Cook, stirring, for about 10 minutes, until the chicken is opaque, then add the remaining salt and 200ml/7fl oz/scant 1 cup hot water. Bring to the boil, cover and simmer for 20 minutes.

5 Meanwhile, dry-roast the poppy seeds in a small, heavy pan over a medium heat until the seeds begin to crackle and smell aromatic. Take care not to let them burn.

6 Pour into a small bowl, leave to cool and grind to a fine powder in a coffee grinder.

7 Sprinkle the toasted, ground poppy seeds over the chicken, then stir and cook uncovered for a few minutes, until the sauce has thickened.

8 Transfer to a warmed serving dish and garnish with green chilli slices. Serve with warm Indian bread.

Per portion Energy 321kcal/1341kJ; Protein 38g; Carbohydrate 0g, of which sugars 0g; Fat 19g, of which saturates 3g; Cholesterol 152mg; Calcium 42mg; Fibre 0.1g; Sodium 623mg.

Chicken with creamed coconut

In India, chicken curry has a special place on the family dining table and at dinner parties, and Bengal is no exception. The word *malai* means 'cream', and this can mean either dairy or coconut cream. Both are abundant in Bengal, and are used imaginatively to create fabulous dishes such as this one, *Murgir Malai Kari*.

3 Add the onion, turn up the heat a little, and fry gently for about 5 minutes, until soft but not brown. Add the ginger, garlic, turmeric and chilli powder and continue to fry until the onions are lightly browned.

4 Add the chicken and fry, turning often, for 8–10 minutes, until opaque all over. Add the remaining salt, creamed coconut and 175ml/6fl oz/¾ cup hot water, or the coconut cream without the water. Bring to the boil, cover and simmer for 35–40 minutes or until the chicken is cooked through.

5 Transfer to a warmed serving dish. Serve with Butter-drenched Milk Breads or Plain Boiled Rice.

SERVES 4

675g/1½lb chicken joints on the bone, skinned
30ml/2 tbsp lemon juice
5ml/1 tsp salt, or to taste
60ml/4 tbsp sunflower or light olive oil
2.5cm/1in piece of cinnamon stick
4 green cardamom pods, bruised
4 cloves
1 large onion, finely chopped
2.5cm/1in fresh root ginger, grated, or 10ml/2 tsp ginger purée
2 cloves garlic, crushed, or 10ml/2 tsp garlic purée
2.5ml/½ tsp ground turmeric
2.5–5ml/½–1 tsp chilli powder
75g/3oz creamed coconut, chopped, or 175ml/6fl oz/¾ cup coconut cream
Butter-drenched Milk Breads or Plain Boiled Rice, to serve

1 Cut each chicken leg joint into two pieces, i.e. into thighs and drumsticks, and cut the breast joints in half. Rub all over with lemon juice and sprinkle with half of the salt. Cover and set aside to marinate.

2 Meanwhile, heat the oil in a large, heavy pan over a low heat. Add the cinnamon, cardamom and cloves and fry for 1–2 minutes, until the cardamom pods puff up.

VARIATION
The chicken in this curry is cooked on the bone, but you could use boneless meat, and reduce the cooking time to 20 minutes.

Per portion Energy 412kcal/1714kJ; Protein 32g; Carbohydrate 2g, of which sugars 2g; Fat 31g, of which saturates 14g; Cholesterol 124mg; Calcium 20mg; Fibre 0.1g; Sodium 604mg.

Chicken curry Anglo-Indian style

This recipe, Murjir Jhol, uses plenty of curry powder to give it a real kick. When made with pieces of chicken on the bone, it becomes a beautifully classic 'Anglo-Indian' curry with a thick, aromatic sauce, and is best served with a helping of plain boiled rice to moderate the spicy flavours.

SERVES 4

675g/1½lb chicken leg or breast joint
  pieces on the bone, skinned
2.5ml/½ tsp ground turmeric
15ml/1 tbsp plain (all-purpose) flour
5ml/1 tsp salt, or to taste
1 large onion, roughly chopped
2.5cm/1in piece of fresh root ginger, grated
4–5 garlic cloves, roughly chopped
60ml/4 tbsp sunflower oil or olive oil
22ml/1½ tbsp curry powder
2.5ml/½ tsp chilli powder (optional)
175g/6oz fresh tomatoes, chopped
30ml/2 tbsp chopped coriander (cilantro)

1 Separate the chicken legs from the thighs. If you are using breast meat, cut each one into three pieces. Mix the turmeric, flour and salt together and rub this mixture into the chicken. Set aside.

2 Put the onion, ginger and garlic in a food processor to make a purée; alternatively, you can pound them together into a paste using a mortar and pestle.

3 Heat the oil in a medium, heavy pan and add the puréed or pounded ingredients. Cook over a medium heat, stirring regularly, for 8–10 minutes.

4 Add the curry powder and chilli powder, if using, to the pan and cook, stirring, for 2–3 minutes. Add around 30ml/2 tbsp water and continue to cook for a further 2–3 minutes.

5 Add the chicken pieces to the pan, increase the heat to medium-high and stir until the chicken begins to brown. Add 425ml/15fl oz/1¾ cups warm water, bring it to the boil, cover and reduce the heat to low. Cook for another 35–40 minutes.

6 Add the tomatoes. Cook for 2–3 minutes longer, then stir in the chopped coriander and serve with Plain Boiled Rice.

Per portion Energy 392kcal/1632kJ; Protein 24.3g; Carbohydrate 12.5g, of which sugars 7.3g; Fat 27.6g, of which saturates 5.8g; Cholesterol 135mg; Calcium 67mg; Fibre 2.6g; Sodium 108mg.

Chicken pilau

Added to Bengal cuisine by the Mughals, this moist chicken dish has a long list of ingredients, but it is easy to make and the final result is well worth the effort. *Murgir Pulao* tastes best when served hot and sprinkled with crunchy toasted almonds, which add flavour and texture as well as looking attractive.

SERVES 4

275g/10oz/1⅓ cups basmati rice
10ml/2 tsp coriander seeds
5ml/1 tsp cumin seeds
1–3 dried red chillies, chopped
10 black peppercorns
30ml/2 tbsp white poppy seeds
15ml/1 tbsp sesame seeds
45ml/3 tbsp sunflower oil or olive oil
1 medium onion, finely sliced
10ml/2 tsp ginger purée
10ml/2 tsp garlic purée
2.5ml/½ tsp ground turmeric
450g/1lb skinned, halved chicken
  thigh fillets
75g/3oz/⅓ cup thick set natural (plain)
  yogurt, whisked
5ml/1 tsp salt, or to taste
15ml/1 tbsp ghee or unsalted butter
2.5cm/1in piece of cinnamon stick
6 green cardamom pods, bruised
6 cloves
2 star anise
2.5ml/½ tsp salt, or to taste
15ml/1 tbsp toasted flaked (sliced)
  almonds, to garnish

COOK'S TIP
It is important to use the correct proportions of rice and water when making a pilau, so measure these carefully. You should also exactly follow the timings given.

1 Wash the rice in several changes of water and soak it for 20 minutes. Leave to drain.

2 Preheat a small, heavy pan over a medium heat and add the coriander and cumin seeds. Dry-roast for 25–30 seconds.

3 Add the chillies, peppercorns, poppy and sesame seeds to the pan. Stir them for 25–30 seconds, then transfer to a bowl. When cooled, grind in a coffee grinder or with a mortar and pestle until fine. Set aside.

4 Heat the oil in a heavy pan over a medium heat, then add the onion. Fry for about 5 minutes, until the onion is soft. Add the ginger and garlic and fry for a further 3–4 minutes. Add the turmeric and chicken, and increase the heat slightly. Cook until the chicken has changed colour.

5 Add half the yogurt to the pan and cook for 2–3 minutes, stirring. Add the remaining yogurt and continue to cook for a further 2–3 minutes.

6 Add the ground ingredients and the salt, and reduce the heat to medium. Cook for 2–3 minutes. Pour in 75ml/2½fl oz/⅓ cup water, reduce the heat to low and cook for another 5 minutes or until the liquid has evaporated, stirring. Remove from the heat.

7 In a separate pan, heat the ghee or butter over a low heat and add the cinnamon, cardamom, cloves and star anise. Stir-fry until the cardamom pods have puffed up. Add the rice and salt and stir to combine.

8 Pour in 475ml/16fl oz/2 cups warm water, bring it to the boil and let it boil for 1 minute. Reduce the heat to low, cover the pan tightly and cook for 7–8 minutes.

9 Switch off the heat, remove the lid and pile the cooked chicken on top of the rice. Cover the pan and let it stand for 20 minutes.

10 Gently mix the rice and the chicken with a metal spoon and serve immediately, garnished with toasted almonds.

Lamb in ginger and yogurt

Yogurt is commonly used in marinades as a tenderizing ingredient, but in Bengali cuisine it is often used in larger quantities to make a sauce. In this recipe, *Doi Diya Mangsho*, the meat is slowly cooked in yogurt until almost dry.

SERVES 4

675g/1½lb boned leg of lamb
10ml/2 tsp gram flour (besan)
200ml/7fl oz/scant 1 cup Greek (US strained plain) yogurt
2.5ml/½ tsp ground turmeric
4cm/1½in fresh root ginger, grated, or 15ml/1 tbsp ginger purée
2 cloves garlic, crushed, or 10ml/2 tsp garlic purée
5ml/1 tsp chilli powder, or to taste
45ml/3 tbsp mustard oil or sunflower oil
1 large onion, finely chopped
5ml/1 tsp salt, or to taste
10ml/2 tsp ground coriander
10ml/2 tsp ground cumin
2.5ml/½ tsp caster (superfine) sugar
4 whole fresh green chillies
15ml/1 tbsp chopped fresh mint
15ml/1 tbsp chopped fresh coriander (cilantro)
2.5ml/½ tsp garam masala
sprigs of fresh mint and fine strips of fresh red chillies, to garnish

1 Trim any excess fat from the lamb and cut it into 2.5cm/1in cubes.

2 Combine the gram flour and yogurt in a bowl, then add the turmeric, ginger, garlic and chilli powder. Stir in the lamb, cover the bowl and set aside for 30–35 minutes.

3 In a heavy pan, heat the mustard oil to smoking point and then turn down the heat to medium and add the onion (if using sunflower oil, heat to medium). Fry, stirring frequently, until the onion is lightly browned all over.

4 Add the meat and increase the heat to medium-high. Fry for 3–4 minutes or until the meat changes colour.

5 Reduce the heat to low, cover the pan with a tight-fitting lid and cook the meat for 35–40 minutes, shaking the pan occasionally. Remove the lid, add the salt and cook for 8–10 minutes, stirring frequently.

6 Stir in the coriander, cumin and sugar. Continue to cook, stirring frequently, for 4–5 minutes or until the oil separates from the spice paste.

7 Add 150ml/¼ pint/⅔ cup hot water and the whole chillies. Cook for 5 more minutes. Stir in the chopped mint and coriander and the garam masala.

8 Spoon into a warmed serving dish and serve, garnished with sprigs of mint and fine strips of red chilli.

Per portion Energy 481kcal/2002kJ; Protein 40g; Carbohydrate 15g, of which sugars 10g; Fat 30g, of which saturates5; Cholesterol 135mg; Calcium 131mg; Fibre 2.0g; Sodium 1142mg.

Lamb in tamarind sauce

Bengalis often add small quantities of sugar to their savoury dishes as this enhances the flavours of other ingredients, but in this recipe, *Tetuler Mangsho*, slightly more sugar is used and, together with tamarind and chilli, produces a delicious sweet, sour and hot taste.

SERVES 4

675g/1½lb boned leg of lamb
120ml/4fl oz/½ cup whole-milk natural (plain) yogurt
10ml/2 tsp gram flour (besan)
5ml/1 tsp ground turmeric
10ml/2 tsp ground cumin
5ml/1 tsp ground coriander
2.5–5ml/½–1 tsp chilli powder
10ml/2 tsp ready-made mustard
5ml/1 tsp salt, or to taste
45ml/3 tbsp sunflower oil or light olive oil
2.5cm/1in piece cinnamon stick
3 brown cardamom pods, bruised
4 cloves
1 bay leaf
1 large onion, finely chopped
1cm/½in fresh root ginger, grated, or 10ml/2 tsp ginger purée
2 cloves garlic, crushed, or 10ml/2 tsp garlic purée
15ml/1 tbsp caster (superfine) sugar
45ml/3 tbsp tamarind pulp
15ml/1 tbsp chopped fresh coriander (cilantro)
sprigs of fresh mint, to garnish
warm Indian breads, to serve

1 Remove any excess fat from the meat and cut it into 2.5cm/1in cubes.

2 Whisk the yogurt and gram flour together in a bowl. Stir in the turmeric, cumin, coriander, chilli powder, mustard and salt. Add the meat and stir to coat, then cover and leave to marinate for 30 minutes.

3 In a heavy pan, heat the oil over a low heat and add the cinnamon, cardamom, cloves and bay leaf. Let them sizzle for 30 seconds. Add the onion and fry for about 5 minutes, until soft but not brown.

4 Add the ginger and garlic and fry for 2 minutes more, then add the meat and cook for 5 minutes, stirring frequently.

5 Reduce the heat to low, cover the pan tightly with a lid and simmer the curry for 45 minutes or until the meat is tender, stirring occasionally.

6 Add the sugar and tamarind pulp, stir to combine and simmer for 5 minutes more. Stir in the chopped coriander and garnish with sprigs of fresh mint. Serve with warm Indian breads.

> **COOK'S TIP**
> It is important to use a tight-fitting lid for the pan, as the meat is cooked entirely in its own juices. If you do not have a tight lid, cover the pan with double thickness of foil first and then put the lid on.

Per portion Energy 483kcal/2016kJ; Protein 39g; Carbohydrate 25g, of which sugars 20g; Fat 26g, of which saturates 2g; Cholesterol 130mg; Calcium 0140mg; Fibre 2.0g; Sodium 1019mg.

Marinated lamb rib chops

Mutton, rather than lamb, is the traditional choice for this Muslim-influenced dish, which originated in the kitchens of one of the Mughal rulers near Kolkata (formerly Calcutta). However, this recipe for *Rezala* uses lamb rib chops, as the cooking time is quicker and they are also easier to get hold of in most supermarkets. Warming and sustaining, this makes a delectable meal when served with chunks of fresh naan or some rice.

SERVES 4

675g/1½lb lamb rib chops
15ml/1 tbsp red wine vinegar
5ml/1 tsp salt, or to taste
pinch of saffron threads, pounded
15ml/1 tbsp hot milk
1 large onion, roughly chopped
5cm/2in piece fresh root ginger,
   roughly chopped
4–5 garlic cloves, roughly chopped
4 cloves
2.5ml/½ tsp black peppercorns
4 green cardamom pods
5cm/2in piece cinnamon stick, halved
60ml/4 tbsp sunflower oil or olive oil
1 large onion, finely sliced
175g/6oz/¾ cup natural (plain) yogurt,
   whisked until smooth
10ml/2 tsp gram flour (besan)
50g/2oz/4 tbsp butter, softened
2.5ml/½ tsp ground fennel
2.5ml/½ tsp dried ginger powder
3–4 fresh red chillies
2.5ml/½ tsp freshly grated nutmeg
2.5ml/½ tsp sugar
15ml/1 tbsp rose water
naan or Plain Boiled Rice, to serve

1 Put the lamb chops in a large mixing bowl and rub in the vinegar and salt. Set aside.

2 Put the saffron and the hot milk in a small bowl and leave to infuse (steep) while you prepare the other ingredients.

3 Purée the onion, ginger and garlic in a blender or food processor. Put in a bowl and add a little water to make a thin paste, then add the cloves, peppercorns, cardamom and cinnamon. Mix well.

4 Pour the marinade over the meat. Stir to coat thoroughly, then cover the bowl with clear film (plastic wrap) and leave to marinate for at least 3–4 hours or overnight in the refrigerator. Bring the meat to room temperature before cooking.

5 Heat the oil over a medium to high heat and fry the sliced onions until they are browned. Remove them with a slotted spoon, squeezing out as much excess oil as possible by pressing them to the side of the pan with the spoon.

6 In the remaining oil, fry the marinated lamb chops for 4–5 minutes, stirring frequently. Reduce the heat to low, cover and cook for 5–7 minutes.

7 Meanwhile, mix the yogurt, gram flour and butter together in a small pan and place over a low heat. Cook for 3–4 minutes, stirring constantly.

8 Add the yogurt mixture to the lamb chops in the pan. Stir in the fennel and ginger. powder and cover the pan. Cook for about 45–50 minutes, until the chops are tender.

9 Add the chillies along with the nutmeg and sugar. Cook for 1–2 minutes longer, then add the saffron milk and rose water. Stir well, remove from the heat and serve immediately with naan or some Plain Boiled Rice.

VARIATION
If you choose to use mutton instead of lamb in this dish, simply increase the cooking time in Step 8 to 1 hour 15 minutes.

Per portion Energy 610kcal/2529kJ; Protein 31.2g; Carbohydrate 7.4g, of which sugars 5g; Fat 51.1g, of which saturates 21.7g; Cholesterol 141mg; Calcium 124mg; Fibre 0.4g; Sodium 219mg.

Spiced vegetables over rice

Tarkari Bhate, is one of many tasty Bengali dishes made using steamed vegetables and lentils, which are spiced up and served with rice. The distinctive taste in Bengali cuisine comes from mustard oil.

SERVES 4

115g/4oz carrots, peeled and cut into
  bitesize pieces
1 small turnip, peeled and cut into
  bitesize pieces
½ small green cabbage
45ml/3 tbsp mustard oil, plus extra for
  drizzling (optional)
2.5ml/½ tsp black or brown
  mustard seeds
2.5ml/½ tsp cumin seeds
2 whole dried red chillies
1–2 fresh green chillies, chopped
  (deseeded if preferred)
115g/4oz baby spinach leaves
2.5ml/½ tsp salt, or to taste
Plain Boiled Rice, to serve

2 Heat the oil in a frying pan until smoking point is reached. Switch off the heat, then add the mustard seeds followed by the cumin, dried chillies and fresh chillies.

3 Cook for 25–30 seconds, then add the steamed vegetables, spinach and salt.

1 Place the carrots, turnip and cabbage in an electronic steamer, or in a steamer basket placed over a pan of simmering water, and steam until tender but firm.

4 Stir until the spinach has wilted, then remove from the heat.

5 Put the cooked rice in a serving dish and serve topped with the spiced vegetables. Bengalis sprinkle extra mustard oil on the vegetables, but this is optional.

Per portion Energy 345kcal/1452kJ; Protein 6g; Carbohydrate 55g, of which sugars 6g; Fat 13g, of which saturates 1g; Cholesterol 0mg; Calcium 109mg; Fibre 5.5g; Sodium 305mg.

Vegetable pilau

Local climate and soil conditions mean that rice flourishes in Bengal, and it has become the staple diet of the people who live there. This colourful creation, *Torkarir Pulao*, made with basmati rice and fresh produce, is ideal as a vegetarian main meal. The choice of vegetables can be varied according to seasonal availability.

SERVES 4

225g/8oz/generous 1 cup basmati rice
60ml/4 tbsp sunflower oil or light olive oil
25g/1oz raw cashew nuts
25g/1oz seedless raisins
4 green cardamom pods, bruised
2.5cm/1in piece of cinnamon stick
4 cloves
2 bay leaves
1 large onion, finely sliced
5ml/1 tsp ginger purée
5ml/1 tsp garlic purée
1–2 fresh green chillies, chopped
  (deseeded if preferred)
2.5ml/½ tsp ground turmeric
75g/3oz/½ cup carrots, cut into sticks
110g/4oz baby corn, halved
75g/3oz/½ cup green beans, cut into
  2.5cm/1in lengths
5ml/1 tsp salt, or to taste
50ml/2fl oz/3 tbsp single (light) cream

1 Wash the rice in a sieve (strainer) in several changes of water until it runs clear, then soak in a bowl of cold water for 20–30 minutes. Drain and set aside.

2 In a heavy pan, heat the oil over a medium/low heat and brown the cashew nuts. Drain on kitchen paper.

VARIATION
Try blanched almonds or unsalted peanuts instead of cashew nuts.

3 Add the raisins to the oil in the pan and fry until puffed up. Drain on kitchen paper.

4 Add the cardamom, cinnamon, cloves and bay leaves to the oil and let them sizzle until the cardamoms have puffed up.

5 Add the onion, ginger, garlic and chillies, increase the heat and fry for 10 minutes, until the onion is brown, stirring regularly.

6 Stir in the turmeric and add all the vegetables and the salt. Stir and cook for 2–3 minutes.

7 Add the rice and stir-fry for 2–3 minutes, then pour in 450ml/16fl oz/1¾ cups hot water and bring it to the boil. Boil steadily for 2 minutes, then reduce the heat to low.

8 Pour the cream over the rice and cover the pan. Cook for 10–12 minutes. Remove from the heat and leave, undisturbed, for 8–10 minutes. Fluff up the rice and serve, garnished with the nuts and raisins.

Per portion Energy 410kcal/1705kJ; Protein 8.1g; Carbohydrate 60.9g, of which sugars 12.5g; Fat 14.9g, of which saturates 2g; Cholesterol 0mg; Calcium 55mg; Fibre 3g; Sodium 343mg.

Buttered rice with spiced stock

Rice is eaten throughout India, but is most popular in areas where heavy rainfall results in thriving rice crops. This wonderful dish, *Ghee Bhat*, is cooked in ghee with aromatic spices. The flavour of this rice is rich, but still mild enough to go with any vegetable curry.

SERVES 4

225g/8oz/generous 1 cup basmati rice
50g/2oz/4 tbsp ghee or unsalted butter
25g/1oz raw cashew nuts
15ml/1 tbsp seedless raisins
1 large onion, finely sliced
2.5cm/1in piece of cinnamon stick
4 cloves
2 bay leaves
5ml/1 tsp salt, or to taste

1 Put the rice in a sieve (strainer) and wash it thoroughly under cold running water, then transfer it to a large bowl, cover with cold water and leave to soak for 20 minutes. Leave to drain in the sieve.

2 Melt half the ghee or butter over a low heat, then brown the cashew nuts. Drain on kitchen paper and set aside.

3 Add the raisins to the pan and stir until they are plump. Remove from the pan, drain on kitchen paper and set aside.

4 Add the remaining ghee or butter to the pan and add the onion. Increase the heat to medium and fry, stirring, until well browned.

5 Remove any excess fat by pressing the onions to the side of the pan, then lift them out and drain them on kitchen paper.

6 Reduce the heat to low and add the cinnamon, cloves and bay leaves. Sizzle for 10–15 seconds, then add the drained rice and cook for 2 minutes. Pour in 450ml/16fl oz/ scant 2 cups hot water, add the salt, bring to the boil and cook for 2 minutes.

7 Reduce the heat to very low, cover and cook for 7–8 minutes. Switch off the heat and leave, undisturbed, for 7–8 minutes.

8 Fluff up the rice with a fork and mix in half the fried onions. Reserve a few cashews and raisins and mix the remainder into the rice.

9 Transfer to a serving dish and garnish with the remaining onion, cashews and raisins.

Per portion Energy 369kcal/1537kJ; Protein 5.8g; Carbohydrate 57.4g, of which sugars 9.6g; Fat 13g, of which saturates 5.9g; Cholesterol 0mg; Calcium 44mg; Fibre 1.8g; Sodium 6mg.

Chilli and ginger yogurt rice

Doi Bhat can be served at room temperature as well as hot. The rice is first boiled, then tossed in a seasoned oil with mustard seeds, ginger and fresh coriander (cilantro) and finally mixed with yogurt. Ideally, mustard oil should be used for this dish, but you can substitute sunflower oil if you prefer.

SERVES 4

275g/10oz/1¼ cups basmati rice
5ml/1 tsp butter
3.75ml/¾ tsp salt
30ml/2 tbsp mustard oil
2.5ml/½ tsp black mustard seeds
1.25ml/¼ tsp asafoetida
5ml/1 tsp grated fresh root ginger
1–2 fresh red chillies, finely chopped
 (deseeded if preferred)
15ml/1 tbsp chopped fresh coriander
 (cilantro)
175ml/6fl oz/¾ cup whole-milk natural
 (plain) yogurt, whisked

COOK'S TIP
To ensure a tight seal, put a double layer of foil over the pan before adding a tightly fitting lid.

1 Rinse the rice thoroughly in a sieve under cold running water, then transfer to a bowl and soak it in cold water for 20 minutes. Drain well.

2 In a medium pan, bring 550ml/18fl oz/ 2½ cups of water to the boil. Add the butter, salt and drained rice. Bring to the boil and let it boil steadily for 2 minutes.

3 Reduce the heat to low and cover the pan tightly. Cook for 8–9 minutes, then remove from the heat. Let the pan stand undisturbed for 10 minutes.

4 Meanwhile, heat the mustard oil to smoking point (this is unnecessary if you substitute sunflower oil), turn the heat to low and add the mustard seeds, followed by the asafoetida, ginger and chilli. Fry until the ginger begins to brown.

5 Stir the chopped coriander into the onion mixture and pour this over the cooked rice. Stir briefly, then add the yogurt and gently mix everything together until it is thoroughly combined. Transfer to a serving dish and serve hot or at room temperature.

Per portion Energy 376kcal/1589kJ; Protein 8g; Carbohydrate 63g, of which sugars4; Fat 12g, of which saturates 3g; Cholesterol 7mg; Calcium 130mg; Fibre 0.3g; Sodium 390mg.

Lemon-laced rice with cardamom

Bengali lemon-laced rice, *Lebur Bhat*, is rather different from the version that is cooked in southern India. It has a more prominent lemon flavour, which smells and tastes wonderfully refreshing. Bay leaves, cardamom, cinnamon and cloves are commonly used in east India to flavour rice dishes.

SERVES 4

225g/8oz/generous 1 cup basmati rice
30ml/2 tbsp mustard oil
2.5ml/½ tsp black mustard seeds
2.5cm/1in piece of cinnamon stick
4 cardamom pods, bruised
2 cloves
1 bay leaf
25g/1oz seedless raisins
5ml/1 tsp salt, or to taste
5ml/1 tsp sugar
45ml/3 tbsp freshly squeezed
  lemon juice

3 Place the pan back over a medium heat and add the drained rice and raisins. Add the salt and sugar and cook, stirring, for 2 minutes. Pour in 450ml/16fl oz/scant 2 cups hot water and bring it to the boil.

4 Add the lemon juice, stir and reduce the heat to low. Cover and cook for 7–8 minutes without lifting the lid. Switch off the heat and leave, undisturbed, for 8–10 minutes. Fluff up the rice with a fork and serve.

1 Wash the rice until the water runs clear and then soak it for 20 minutes. Leave to drain in a sieve (strainer).

2 In a heavy pan, heat the oil until it is smoking. Remove from the heat and add the mustard seeds (covering the pan if necessary to prevent the mustard seeds from jumping out of the pan). Add the cinnamon, cardamom, cloves and bay leaf and let them sizzle for a few seconds.

Per portion Energy 294kcal/1228kJ; Protein 5.4g; Carbohydrate 52.9g, of which sugars 5.4g; Fat 6.8g, of which saturates 0.7g; Cholesterol 0mg; Calcium 28mg; Fibre 0.1g; Sodium 498mg.

Wheat-flour flat bread with spiced greens

In the state of Bihar, situated near west Bengal, this fabulous spicy wheat-flour flat bread, *Bathuway Ki Roti*, is made with locally grown greens that are difficult to get hold of anywhere else. However, you can use spinach, which makes an easy and delicious alternative. This healthy flat bread is very tasty and makes the perfect accompaniment to many Indian vegetarian dishes.

MAKES 10

250g/9oz spinach leaves
450g/1lb/4 cups chapati flour (atta) or
    fine wholemeal (whole-wheat) flour, plus
    extra for dusting
5ml/1 tsp salt
2.5ml/½ tsp aniseed
30ml/2 tbsp sunflower oil or light olive oil
sunflower oil, for shallow-frying

1 Put the spinach in a large bowl or pan and pour over boiling water to cover it completely. Leave it to soak for 2 minutes, then drain, refresh with cold water and drain again. Squeeze out as much water as possible, but make sure that the spinach remains quite moist.

2 Place the spinach in a food processor and chop it finely, but do not process it to a purée.

3 Mix the flour, salt and aniseed in a bowl. Add 15ml/1 tbsp of the oil and mix well, then stir in the spinach.

4 Gradually add 200ml/7fl oz/¾ cup water and mix until a soft dough is formed. You may not need all the water as the spinach leaves will release their own moisture into the flour, so add a little at a time.

5 Transfer to a flat surface, add the remaining oil and knead the dough for 3–4 minutes. Cover with a damp dish towel and let it rest for 15–20 minutes.

6 Divide the dough into two equal parts and pinch off or cut each half into five equal portions. Form into balls and flatten each one into a smooth, round cake.

7 Dust each cake in the flour and roll out to approximately an 18cm/7in circle.

8 Preheat a griddle over a medium heat and place a flat bread on it. Cook for 30–40 seconds, then turn it over. Spread 5ml/1 tsp of oil on the surface of the bread and turn it over again.

9 Cook until brown patches appear underneath, checking by lifting the bread with a metal spatula or a fish slice.

10 Spread 5ml/1 tsp oil on the second side, turn it over and cook until brown patches appear.

11 Repeat until all the dough circles are cooked. Serve immediately.

COOK'S TIP

Place the cooked bread on one end of a long piece of foil lined with kitchen paper. Cover with the other end to keep it hot while you cook the remaining breads. Stack the cooked breads in the foil, covering each time you add one.

Per portion Energy 166kcal/700kJ; Protein 6.4g; Carbohydrate 29.2g, of which sugars 1.3g; Fat 3.4g, of which saturates 0.4g; Cholesterol 0mg; Calcium 60mg; Fibre 4.6g; Sodium 36mg.

Griddle-cooked flaky bread

A speciality from Dhaka, the capital of Bangladesh, this flaky bread, *Dhakai Parota*, is highly addictive! The dough is rolled, spread with ghee or unsalted butter, and then folded and re-rolled until several thin layers are formed, which puff up when the bread is cooked.

6 Sprinkle a little flour on top of the fat and, starting at the centre of the disc, make a slit to the edge of the disc. Roll from one side of the cut to the other, to make a cone. Press down to make a cake again.

7 Roll it out again, spread with ghee or butter as before, and repeat the process of sprinkling flour and making a cone. Press this down again and roll it out to a 13cm/5in diameter disc known as a *parota*.

8 Preheat a heavy cast iron or similar griddle over a medium heat and place a rolled disc on it. Allow the disc to cook for 2 minutes, then turn it over. Spread 5ml/ 1 tsp ghee or butter evenly on the surface and immediately turn it over again. Cook for an additional 2 minutes until the bread is browned all over underneath.

MAKES 8

450g/1lb/4 cups plain (all-purpose) flour,
plus extra for sprinkling
2.5g/½ tsp salt
115g/4oz ghee or unsalted butter
200ml/7fl oz/¾ cup warm water

1 Sift the flour into a large bowl and rub in the salt and 15ml/1 tbsp of the ghee or butter. Gradually add the water and mix until a dough is formed.

2 Transfer the dough to a lightly floured pastry board or work surface, and knead for 5–6 minutes, until it is soft and pliable.

3 Cover the bowl with a damp cloth and set the dough aside for 30 minutes to rest, until doubled in size.

4 Divide the dough into eight equal-sized balls and make each one into a flat cake by turning it between the your palms and pressing it down.

5 Roll each cake into a 13cm/5in diameter disc and spread about 2.5ml/½ tsp ghee or butter on the surface.

9 Spread 5ml/1 tsp ghee on the uncooked side. Turn it over and cook as above, until browned. Remove and place on a wire rack. Cook the remaining *parotas* the same way.

Per portion Energy 293kcal/1232kJ; Protein 5.4g; Carbohydrate 43.7g, of which sugars 0.9g; Fat 12g, of which saturates 7.5g; Cholesterol 32mg; Calcium 81mg; Fibre 1.7g; Sodium 228mg.

Deep-fried puffed bread

Crunchy and delicious, *Luchis* are always made for Indian weddings and many other special occasions, served with meat curries or vegetable dishes and used to scoop up the juices, providing a contrast to the soft ingredients. Allow three or four breads per person, but make spares – they will be eaten!

MAKES 16

275g/10oz/2½ cups plain (all-purpose) flour, plus a little extra for dusting
2.5ml/½ tsp nigella seeds
2.5ml/½ tsp salt
1.25ml/¼ tsp sugar
15ml/1 tbsp ghee or butter
175ml/6fl oz/¾ cup lukewarm water
sunflower oil, for deep-frying

1 Sift the flour into a large bowl and mix in the nigella seeds, salt and sugar. Rub in the ghee or butter. Gradually add the water and mix until a stiff dough is formed.

2 Transfer to a lightly floured surface and knead for 5 minutes, until the dough is soft and pliable. Cover the bowl with a damp cloth and leave to rest for 20 minutes.

3 Divide the dough into two equal parts and make eight equal-sized balls out of each. Press down between your palms to make flat cakes. Cover with a damp cloth.

4 Heat the oil in a wok over a medium to high heat. While the oil is heating, start rolling out the breads by dusting each ball very lightly in flour. Roll out to 7.5cm/3in discs, taking care not to tear or pierce them, as they will not puff up if damaged.

5 Place the discs in a single layer on a piece of baking parchment and cover with another sheet of baking parchment.

6 When the oil has a faint shimmer of rising smoke, carefully drop in one disc. As soon as it floats, gently tap around the edges to encourage puffing.

7 When it has puffed up, turn it over and fry the other side until browned. Drain on kitchen paper. Keep the breads in a single layer while you make the rest. Serve fresh, or they can be re-heated for 2 minutes in a hot oven.

Per portion Energy 121kcal/506kJ; Protein 1.6g; Carbohydrate 13.4g, of which sugars 0.3g; Fat 7.2g, of which saturates 1.3g; Cholesterol 2mg; Calcium 24mg; Fibre 0.5g; Sodium 8mg.

Spicy egg-filled flaky bread

This wonderful flaky bread, *Dimer Parota*, can easily steal the centre stage as it is packed full of protein, fibre and vitamins. Delicious served warm from the oven, any leftovers make an ideal accompaniment to a vegetable curry, or you could cut the bread into small pieces and serve it as an appetizer at drinks parties.

MAKES 8

275g/10oz/2½ cups wholemeal
　(whole-wheat) flour
175g/6oz/½ cup plain (all-purpose) flour,
　plus extra for dusting
2.5ml/½ tsp salt
5ml/1 tsp baking powder
30ml/2 tbsp sunflower oil or light olive oil
115g/4oz/½ cup full-fat (whole) natural
　(plain) yogurt, beaten
150ml/¼ pint/⅔ cup warm water
sunflower oil, for shallow frying

For the filling:

3 large (US extra large) eggs, beaten
1 small red onion, finely chopped
1 fresh red chilli, finely chopped
　(deseeded if preferred)
30ml/2 tbsp fresh coriander (cilantro)
　leaves, finely chopped
1.25ml/¼ tsp salt

3 Transfer the dough to a lightly floured surface and knead it for about 10 minutes, until it is soft and pliable. Cover the dough with clear film (plastic wrap) and set aside for 30 minutes.

4 To make the filling, mix together all the ingredients and set aside.

1 Put both types of flour into a large mixing bowl and work in the salt and baking powder. Add the oil and yogurt and mix with your fingertips.

2 Gradually add the water and combine until a soft dough is formed.

> ### COOK'S TIP
> These delicious stuffed breads are ideal for a packed lunch or a snack on the go.

5 Divide the dough into eight equal portions, shape into balls and flatten to round cakes. Lightly dust one cake in the flour and roll it out to a 18cm/7in circle. Keep the remaining cakes covered while you are working.

6 Preheat a heavy griddle or a non-stick frying pan over a medium heat, then place the dough circle on it and dry-roast each side of the bread for about 30 seconds.

7 Drizzle about 5ml/1 tsp oil around the edges and cook for a futher 1 minute or until brown patches appear on the underside. You can lift the bread slightly to check.

8 Turn it over and spread about 30ml/2 tbsp of the filling mixture on the cooked side. Reduce the heat slightly and drizzle 5ml/1 tsp oil around the edges.

9 When the egg mixture has lightly set, and the second side of the bread has brown patches, fold the bread in half and cook until the egg has fully set. Do not worry if some egg spills out, it will soon set.

10 Keep the cooked bread wrapped in a clean dish towel while you repeat the process with all the dough balls.

Per portion Energy 291kcal/1223kJ; Protein 10g; Carbohydrate 41g, of which sugars 2g; Fat 11g, of which saturates 11g; Cholesterol 2mg; Calcium 98mg; Fibre 3.9g; Sodium 289mg.

Peas and potatoes in tomato sauce

The Bengali community takes great pride in this simple but exquisite dish, *Alu Matarer Dalna*, in which plump fresh peas with turmeric-tinged potatoes float in a rich tomato sauce. The sharp lemony taste of cardamom, musky ginger and warm cumin produce an unforgettable flavour combination.

3 Place the pan over a low heat and allow the cardamom pods to puff up, then add the cumin, coriander, turmeric and chilli powder.

4 Cook for about 1 minute, then add the tomatoes. Increase the heat slightly and cook until the tomato pieces are broken up.

5 Sprinkle over 30ml/2 tbsp water and continue to cook for 2–3 minutes. Repeat this process once more and cook until the tomatoes reach a paste-like consistency and the oil begins to float on the surface.

SERVES 4

60ml/4 tbsp mustard oil or sunflower oil
450g/1lb potatoes, peeled and cut into
  2.5cm/1in cubes
10ml/2 tsp sugar
4 green cardamom pods, bruised
2 cloves
10ml/2 tsp ground cumin
5ml/1 tsp ground coriander
2.5ml/½ tsp ground turmeric
2.5–5ml/½–1 tsp chilli powder
115g/4oz canned chopped tomatoes,
  with their juice
5ml/1 tsp salt, or to taste
115g/4oz frozen garden peas
2.5ml/½ tsp garam masala
15ml/1 tbsp lemon juice
fresh root ginger, peeled and cut into
  julienne strips, and sprigs of fresh
  coriander (cilantro), to garnish
Indian bread or boiled rice, to serve

1 Heat half the mustard oil in a frying pan over a medium-high heat until smoking point is reached (if using sunflower oil, heat until hot). Add the potatoes and fry for 4–5 minutes, until the edges brown. Drain on kitchen paper.

2 Heat the remaining oil until it begins to smoke. Remove from the heat and add the sugar. As soon as it begins to caramelize, add the cardamom pods and cloves.

6 Add the potatoes, salt and 250ml/8fl oz/ 1 cup water. Bring to the boil, reduce the heat to low and cook for 10 minutes.

7 Add the peas and cook for 5–7 minutes or until the potatoes are tender and the sauce has thickened.

8 Stir in the garam masala and lemon juice, and garnish with the ginger and fresh coriander. Serve with bread or rice.

Per portion Energy 254kcal/1061kJ; Protein 5g; Carbohydrate 26g, of which sugars 5g; Fat 16g, of which saturates 2g; Cholesterol 0mg; Calcium 28mg; Fibre 4.0g; Sodium 519mg.

Sweet rice flour and coconut mini bread

The people of the eastern state of Orissa makes this sweetmeat, *Kakara*, for festive occasions. Roasted coconut is normally used as a filling that is enclosed in a flat bread-like dough and then deep-fried. To save time and effort, in this recipe the coconut is added to the dough instead of being used as a filling.

SERVES 6–8

150g/5oz palm sugar (jaggery) or soft dark
  brown sugar
5ml/1 tsp freshly ground black pepper
5ml/1 tsp fennel seeds
5ml/1 tsp ground cinnamon
2.5ml/½ tsp salt
150g/5oz/1¼ cups plain (all-purpose) flour,
  plus extra for dusting
150g/5oz/1¼ cups ground rice
75g/3oz desiccated (dry unsweetened
  shredded) coconut
sunflower oil or ghee, for deep-frying

1 Cut the palm sugar into small pieces and put these into a pan. Add 150ml/¼ pint/⅔ cup water and place over a medium heat.

2 Let the sugar dissolve, stir, then add the pepper, fennel, cinnamon and salt. Stir, then add the flour, ground rice and coconut.

3 Stir until a dough has formed, then remove from the heat. Cover with a damp dish towel and let it cool completely.

4 Knead the dough gently on a lightly floured surface for about 8 minutes, until it is smooth and pliable, then divide it into two equal pieces.

5 Roll out each half on a floured surface to a thickness of about 5mm/¼in. Stamp out rounds using a 7.5cm/3in cookie cutter. Gather up any remaining dough, roll it out and cut as before.

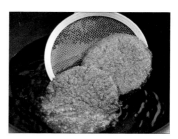

6 Heat the ghee or oil in a wok or other suitable pan for deep-frying over a medium heat and fry the bread in batches, until browned on both sides.

7 Drain on kitchen paper, leave to cool and serve as a teatime treat or with after-dinner coffee. Keep any leftover bread in an airtight container. They will keep well for 4–5 days.

Per portion Energy 325kcal/1363kJ; Protein 4g; Carbohydrate 48g, of which sugars 18g; Fat 14g, of which saturates 6g; Cholesterol 0mg; Calcium 59mg; Fibre 2.7g; Sodium 142mg.

Courgettes and potatoes in coconut milk

This simple but delicious Orissan dish, *Potala Rasa*, is traditionally cooked with a vegetable known as parwal, which belongs to the same family as squash and cucumber. Courgettes (zucchini) make an excellent substitute, but do take care not to overcook them or they will be mushy.

SERVES 4

450g/1lb courgettes (zucchini)
350g/12oz potatoes
60ml/4 tbsp sunflower oil or light olive oil
1 large onion, finely chopped
10ml/2 tsp ginger purée
5ml/1 tsp ground turmeric
5ml/1 tsp ground cumin
2.5–5ml/½–1 tsp chilli powder
400ml/14fl oz/1⅔ cups canned
  coconut milk
5ml/1 tsp salt, or to taste
2.5ml/½ tsp garam masala
Plain Boiled Rice or Indian bread,
  to serve

1 Trim the courgettes and halve them lengthways. Cut each half into about 2.5cm/1in chunks. Peel the potatoes and cut them into 2.5cm/1in chunks.

2 Heat half the oil in a frying pan over a medium-high heat, then add the potatoes and cook for about 3–4 minutes, until browned. Drain on kitchen paper.

3 Brown the courgettes for 2–3 minutes in the same oil, then drain on kitchen paper.

4 Reduce the heat to medium and add the remaining oil. Add the onion and fry for about 8 minutes, until the onion is soft, then add the ginger.

5 Continue to fry for 2 minutes, then add the turmeric, cumin and chilli powder.

6 Cook the spices for about 1 minute, then add the coconut milk, salt and the browned vegetables. Simmer, uncovered, for 10–12 minutes, until the vegetables are tender.

7 Stir in the garam masala and remove from the heat. Transfer to a serving dish and serve with Plain Boiled Rice or bread.

Per portion Energy 132kcal/555kJ; Protein 5g; Carbohydrate 27g, of which sugars g; Fat 1g, of which saturates 0g; Cholesterol 0mg; Calcium 88mg; Fibre 2.3g; Sodium 618mg.

Potatoes with coriander and sun-dried mango

In this recipe, *Aloo Chokha*, cubed potatoes are adorned with crushed coriander seeds, red and green chillies and fresh coriander (cilantro) leaves. Sun-dried mango powder, known as amchur, has a lovely sour flavour and is sold in Asian shops. If amchur proves difficult to find, lime juice can be substituted.

SERVES 4

60ml/4 tbsp sunflower oil or light olive oil
1 large onion, finely sliced
1–2 fresh green chillies, chopped
 (deseeded if preferred)
1–2 dried red chillies, sliced into 2–3 pieces
10ml/2 tsp coriander seeds, crushed
5ml/1 tsp ground cumin
2.5ml/½ tsp ground turmeric
450g/1lb potatoes, cut into 2.5cm/1in cubes
5ml/1 tsp salt, or to taste
5ml/1 tsp sun-dried mango powder
 (amchur) or 15ml/1 tbsp lime juice
30ml/2 tbsp fresh coriander (cilantro)
 leaves, chopped
a lentil dish and/or a vegetable curry, and
 any Indian bread, to serve

1 Heat the oil over a medium heat. Fry the onion with the chillies for 6–7 minutes, until the onion is beginning to brown.

2 Add the coriander and fry for 1 minute. Add the cumin and turmeric and fry for 1 minute.

3 Add the potato cubes and the salt and stir to combine everything thoroughly. Pour in 250ml/9fl oz/1 cup warm water and bring it to the boil.

4 Reduce the heat to low, cover the pan with a tight-fitting lid and cook for 12–15 minutes, until the potatoes are tender and all the water has been absorbed.

5 Stir in the mango powder or lime juice and chopped coriander, and remove from the heat. Serve with a lentil dish and/or a vegetable curry, accompanied by any Indian bread.

Per portion Energy 237kcal/990kJ; Protein 4.2g; Carbohydrate 29.7g, of which sugars 8.5g; Fat 12.2g, of which saturates 1.5g; Cholesterol 0mg; Calcium 47mg; Fibre 2.9g; Sodium 509mg.

Roasted tomato chutney

This delicious chutney recipe, *Tomato Achar*, comes from Darjeeling, with definite influences from Nepal, across the northern border. The Nepalese would roast the tomatoes over a wood fire, which imparts an unforgettable flavour. The tomatoes are then combined with chillies and spices and made into a purée.

MAKES 225G/8OZ

675g/1¼lb ripe tomatoes
30ml/2 tbsp sunflower oil or light olive oil
1–2 fresh green chillies, chopped
  (deseeded if preferred)
1cm/½in piece of fresh root ginger, peeled
  and chopped
1 clove garlic, chopped
30ml/2 tbsp fresh coriander (cilantro)
  leaves, chopped
2.5ml/½ tsp salt, or to taste

1 Preheat the oven to 190°C/375°F/Gas 5. Halve the tomatoes widthways.

2 Put the tomato halves in a roasting pan and drizzle the oil over them. Shake to coat with the oil, then place in the centre of the oven and roast for 20 minutes, or until softened and cooked.

3 Remove the tomatoes from the oven, leave them to cool and then peel off and discard the skins.

4 Place the tomatoes in a blender or food processor along with all the remaining ingredients and purée until smooth.

5 This chutney is best eaten fresh, although it can be stored in sterilized jars (*see* Cook's Tip) in the refrigerator for up to 1 week.

COOK'S TIP

The easiest way to sterlize jars is to put them in the dishwasher. Alternatively, place washed, dried jars in an oven heated to 120°C/ 250°F/Gas ½ and bake for about 15 minutes.

Per portion Energy 334kcal/1395kJ; Protein 6.4g; Carbohydrate 23.1g, of which sugars 22.8g; Fat 24.7g, of which saturates 3.3g; Cholesterol 0mg; Calcium 149mg; Fibre 9.5g; Sodium 80mg.

Cardamom and rose-scented mango drink

Sherbat is the generic name for fruit-based drinks made with milk or water, and this one, *Amer Sherbat*, includes a touch of spice to make it extra special. Ready-to-use mango purée is sold in Indian stores, but canned mangoes that have been drained and puréed can also be used.

SERVES 4–6

450g/1lb canned mango pulp or
  2 x 425g/15oz cans of sliced
  mangoes, drained
600ml/1 pint/2½ cups full-fat (whole) milk
45–60ml/3–4 tbsp sugar
5ml/1 tsp ground cardamom
30ml/2 tbsp rose water (optional)
sprigs of fresh mint, to garnish

3 Add 300ml/½ pint/1¼ cups cold water and the rose water, if using. Mix well and chill the *sherbat* in the refrigerator.

4 Pour the chilled drink into stemmed glasses, if you like, and serve garnished with the mint.

1 Put the mango pulp or slices into a food processor and add the milk, sugar and the ground cardamom.

2 Blend everything together until smooth, then transfer to a jug (pitcher).

VARIATION

For a healthier alternative, you can use skimmed or semi-skimmed (low-fat) milk if you wish.

Per portion Energy 790kcal/3344kJ; Protein 18g; Carbohydrate 147g, of which sugars 145g; Fat 19g, of which saturates 12g; Cholesterol 63mg; Calcium 595mg; Fibre 13.1g; Sodium 206mg.

Sweet and salty lime drink

In Bengal this drink is known as *Lebur Sharbat* and it is very refreshing during the heat of the oppressive summer months. Many different varieties of lemon and lime are available in east India and you can use either citrus fruit, or a combination of both, according to your preference.

2 Add the lime juice to the jug and stir well to combine. Chill in the refrigerator for about 1 hour.

3 When you are ready to serve the drink, crush some ice by placing ice cubes in a clean dish towel and crushing them with a rolling pin.

4 Line individual glasses with the crushed ice and pour in the lime drink. Garnish with the slices of lime and serve immediately.

SERVES 4

30–45ml/2–3 tbsp caster (superfine) sugar
5ml/1 tsp salt
600ml/1 pint/2½ cups cold water
juice of 2 limes
ice cubes
4 slices of lime, to garnish

VARIATION

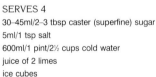

This refreshing drink would also be delicious made with freshly squeezed grapefruit juice.

1 Put the sugar, salt and water in a large jug (pitcher) and stir with a spoon until the sugar has completely dissolved.

Per portion Energy 46kcal/194kJ; Protein 50g; Carbohydrate 12g, of which sugars 12g; Fat 0g, of which saturates 0g; Cholesterol 0mg; Calcium 3mg; Fibre 0.0g; Sodium 492mg.

Milky cardamom coffee

Indian food and drink are well known for their enticing aroma and captivating flavours. Tea and coffee, flavoured with aromatic herbs and spices, are popular all over the country, although the spicing does vary from one region to another. *Elaichi Coffee* makes a delicious hot drink during the winter months.

SERVES 4

8 green cardamom pods, bruised
600ml/1 pint/2½ cups water
300ml/½ pint/1¼ cups milk
instant coffee and sugar, to taste

1 Put the cardamom pods and the water into a pan and bring to the boil.

2 Reduce the heat to low, cover the pan and simmer for 5–6 minutes, to allow the flavours to infuse the water.

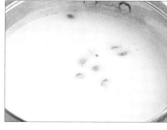

3 Add the milk and bring the liquid to the boil again.

4 Remove the cardamom pods with a slotted spoon and discard them.

5 Put instant coffee and sugar to taste into individual cups and pour over the milky mixture. Stir and serve immediately.

VARIATION

This fragrant coffee is equally enjoyable served chilled in the summer, and in India it is often served in tall glasses with a scoop of vanilla ice-cream as a luxurious form of iced coffee when part of afternoon tea.

Per portion Energy 70kcal/293kJ; Protein 3g; Carbohydrate 9g, of which sugars 9g; Fat 3g, of which saturates 2g; Cholesterol 11mg; Calcium 92mg; Fibre 0.0g; Sodium 34mg.

Cardamom tea

This Bengali version, *Cha*, of the much-loved spiced tea that is drunk all over the country, has the exotic aroma of cardamom, and is rich and fragrant rather than warming – perfect with a mid-morning snack or for afternoon tea. It also makes an excellent alternative to coffee after a meal.

SERVES 3–4

450ml/16fl oz/scant 2 cups water
20ml/4 tsp leaf tea, preferably Darjeeling
5–6 green cardamom pods, bruised
300ml/10fl oz/1¼ cups milk
sugar, to taste

VARIATION
If you do not have Darjeeling, you can use Assam, Ceylon or English Breakfast tea instead.

1 Put the water, tea and cardamom pods into a pan and bring to the boil.

2 Reduce the heat to low and simmer for 6–8 minutes.

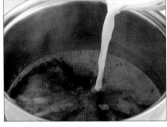

3 Add the milk to the pan and increase the heat slightly. Simmer, uncovered, for 5–6 minutes, until the tea has turned a pinkish-brown colour.

4 Add more milk to taste. Strain into cups, add sugar to taste and serve.

COOK'S TIP
As well as being thirst-quenching, tea contains health-boosting antioxidants, which may help the body combat illnesses such as cancer and heart disease.

Per portion Energy 42kcal/177kJ; Protein 2.9g; Carbohydrate 4.6g, of which sugars 3.8g; Fat 1.6g, of which saturates 0.8g; Cholesterol 4mg; Calcium 95mg; Fibre 0g; Sodium 42mg.0

Tender cheese balls in saffron-cream sauce

This dessert, *Channer Payesh*, is absolutely delicious. Traditionally, the milk is reduced to the consistency of evaporated milk by simmering and stirring constantly over a long period of time. To reduce time and effort, rice flour and double (heavy) cream have been used here to create the same effect.

SERVES 4

227g/8oz paneer (Indian cheese)
2.5ml/½ tsp ground cinnamon
2.5ml/½ tsp ground cardamom
50g/2oz/¼ cup caster (superfine) sugar,
  plus 15ml/1 tbsp
large pinch of saffron, pounded
15ml/1 tbsp hot milk
600ml/1 pint/2½ cups full-fat (whole) milk
30ml/2 tbsp rice flour
4 green cardamom pods, bruised
3 cloves
2.5cm/1in piece cinnamon stick
1 bay leaf
25g/1oz/⅙ cup raisins
25g/1oz/¼ cup cashew nuts, chopped
150ml/¼ pint/⅔ cup double (heavy) cream
slices of mango or papaya, to serve

COOK'S TIP
You can make the balls a day in advance, then keep them chilled until required.

1 Crumble the paneer into a bowl and add the cinnamon, cardamom and 15ml/1 tbsp of the sugar. Stir together, then knead the mixture until it is smooth and shape it into balls the size of large cherries.

2 Crumble the saffron into a small bowl and pour over the hot milk. Leave to soak for a few minutes.

3 Brush a heavy pan with a little oil and pour in the milk. Sprinkle over the rice flour and whisk until the rice flour is incorporated into the milk.

4 Place the pan over a medium heat and add the spices and bay leaf. Stir and cook until the milk begins to bubble, then stir in the raisins, cashew nuts and the remaining 50g/2oz/¼ cup caster sugar.

5 Add the soaked saffron, reduce the heat to low and cook, stirring, for 15 minutes or until the milk has thickened.

6 Add the cream and cook for 5 minutes more. Carefully add the cheese balls to the sauce and gently simmer for 5 minutes. Remove from the heat and serve hot or at room temperature with slices of mango or papaya.

Per portion Energy 452kcal/1872kJ; Protein 13g; Carbohydrate 21g, of which sugars 14g; Fat 36g, of which saturates 21g; Cholesterol 101mg; Calcium 363mg; Fibre 0.5g; Sodium 139mg.

Milk balls in cardamom-scented syrup

This dish, *Golap Jamun*, is traditionally made with two dairy products known as khoya (reduced solidified milk) and chenna (cottage cheese), both of which are time-consuming to make. Full-cream (whole) milk powder or skimmed milk powder mixed with single (light) cream are good, quick alternatives.

MAKES 16

5ml/1 tsp saffron threads, pounded
30ml/2 tbsp hot milk
175g/6oz/1¼ cups full-cream (whole) milk powder, or skimmed milk powder mixed with 150ml/5fl oz/½ cup single (light) cream
75g/3oz/½ cup semolina
10ml/2 tsp plain (all-purpose) flour
5ml/1 tsp ground cardamom
5ml/1 tsp baking powder
40g/1½oz/3 tbsp ghee or unsalted butter, melted
150ml/5fl oz/½ cup milk
350g/12 oz/1¾ cups granulated (white) sugar
8 green cardamom pods, bruised
900ml/1½ pints/3½ cups water
sunflower oil, for deep-frying
whipped double (heavy) cream mixed with 30ml/2 tbsp rose water, and seasonal fresh fruits, to serve

1 Soak the pounded saffron in the hot milk for 10–12 minutes.

2 In a bowl, mix together the full-cream milk powder or skimmed milk powder and cream, semolina, flour, cardamom and baking powder. Rub in the ghee or butter.

3 Add the milk and the saffron threads, including the milk in which they were soaked.

4 Mix until a soft dough is formed, then transfer to a flat surface and knead for about 5 minutes, until smooth.

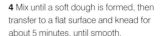

5 Divide the dough into two equal parts and form eight balls out of each. Rotate them between your palms to make them as smooth as possible, without any cracks.

6 Put the sugar, cardamom pods and water in a pan and bring to the boil. Stir until the sugar has dissolved. Turn the heat down and simmer for 6–8 minutes. Remove from the heat and set aside

7 Heat the oil in a pan over a low heat and deep-fry the balls until they are a dark brown colour. They will sink, but should start floating after a few minutes. If they do not, ease them away from the base of the pan.

8 Remove with a slotted spoon and lower into the syrup. Fry the next batch in the same way. Leave them all soaking for 2 hours before serving with the cream and fruit.

Per portion Energy 219kcal/917kJ; Protein 1.6g; Carbohydrate 28.1g, of which sugars 24.6g; Fat 11.9g, of which saturates 4.1g; Cholesterol 10mg; Calcium 58mg; Fibre 0.1g; Sodium 58mg.

Steamed sweet yogurt

Hugely popular in Bengal, this yogurt, *Bhapi Doi*, makes a delicious dessert on its own or accompanied by other treats such as Silky Soft Cheese Fudge. It is also scrumptious served with seasonal fresh fruits such as Indian mango, summer fruits or ripe peaches. This version is a quick and easy dessert option.

MAKES 16

150g/5oz/⅔ cup natural (plain) yogurt
400g/14oz can evaporated milk
400g/14oz can sweetened condensed milk
2.5ml/½ tsp ground cardamom
fresh fruit, to serve

1 Preheat the oven to 120°C/250°F/Gas ½. Put the yogurt in a large bowl and whisk it until it is smooth and glistening.

2 Add the remaining ingredients to the bowl and continue to whisk until everything is well blended.

3 Brush a 23cm/9in square baking dish with a little melted butter and pour the mixture into it.

4 Fill a roasting pan or an ovenproof dish with hot water to the a depth of about 1cm/½in. Set the baking dish inside.

5 Bake the mixture in the centre of the preheated oven for 30 minutes, or until it is lightly set. Remove from the oven and allow it to cool.

6 The dessert will become more firm as it cools. Remove the dish from the water bath. Transfer to the refrigerator and chill for 30–40 minutes, before serving with some fresh fruit of your choice.

COOK'S TIP
Children will love this dessert, and it is a good source of calcium.

Per portion Energy 470kcal/1980kJ; Protein 18.5g; Carbohydrate 68.7g, of which sugars 68.7g; Fat 15.3g, of which saturates 9.45g; Cholesterol 57mg; Calcium 625mg;

Silky soft cheese fudge

With its snow-white appearance, subtle sweetness and refined taste, *Sandesh* is best enjoyed with a cup of tea or coffee. This basic recipe can be used to make variations of the traditional sweet (candy), which comes in different shapes and sizes, tastes and textures. Home-made cheese is essential for the recipe, so don't be tempted to cut corners and use a store-bought version as it won't taste the same.

SERVES 4

vegetable oil, for brushing
2.2 litres/4 pints/10 cups full-fat
  (whole) milk
juice of 1½ lemons
45ml/3 tbsp caster (superfine) sugar
1.25ml/¼ tsp ground cardamom
15ml/1 tbsp melted butter, for greasing
15ml/1 tbsp pistachio nuts, chopped
fresh fruit, to serve

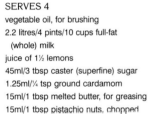

1 First make the cheese. Lightly brush a non-stick pan with oil (this will prevent the milk from sticking to the bottom) and pour in all the milk. Place over a medium heat and bring to the boil, watching it carefully to prevent it boiling over the top of the pan. When the milk begins to rise, add the lemon juice and reduce the heat to low.

2 Let the milk bubble until the whey has separated from the curdled milk. This will become obvious within a minute or so, as the milk becomes watery and the curds float on the top.

3 Strain the curdled milk through a piece of muslin (cheesecloth) placed over a large bowl and tie up the ends loosely, leaving the curds intact. Place the cloth in a sieve (strainer) and position back over a bowl.

4 Leave the curds to drain for 20 minutes, then place them on a pastry board or other flat surface, and discard the watery whey that will have collected in the bowl below the sieve.

5 Using your hands, knead the curds for 8–10 minutes until the cheese is soft and smooth. At first, the mixture will be crumbly, but as you continue to knead it, using the knuckles and the heel of the hand, it will soon become smooth.

6 Place the cheese in a non-stick pan and add the sugar. Place the pan over a very low heat and cook, stirring continuously, for 8–10 minutes, or until the cheese stops sticking to the base and sides of the pan.

7 Stir in the ground cardamom and remove the pan from the heat.

8 Grease a plate with a little melted butter and spread the cheese mixture on it. Shape it into a 15cm/6in square, about 1cm/½in thick.

9 Spread the chopped pistachio nuts on top and press them down gently. Let the mixture cool completely and then cut it into 5cm/2in squares.

10 Serve the fudge on its own as a snack with tea or coffee, or with fresh fruits such as slices of fresh mango, ripe peaches or chunks of pineapple, as a dessert.

COOK'S TIPS

• You can use this recipe, up to the end of Step 5, to make your own delicious cheese to spread on bread or for use in all manner of curd tarts and other desserts.
• To store the cheese, place it in an airtight container and keep it in the refrigerator for up to 3 days.

Per portion Energy 107kcal/449kJ; Protein 4.6g; Carbohydrate 9.6g, of which sugars 9.6g; Fat 5.9g, of which saturates 3.4g; Cholesterol 19mg; Calcium 161mg; Fibre 0.1g; Sodium 81mg.

South India

The tart flavours of tamarind, lime and mango are used to complement the combinations of spices that are favoured in south Indian cuisine. Rice and coconut grow prolifically in the warm, humid conditions and coconut milk and cream are a recurring theme in the many luscious curries on offer. Being a mainly coastal area, fish and shellfish feature strongly on the menu, and are transformed into a range of tantalizing treats.

South India

The four states of Andhra Pradesh, Tamil Nadu, Karnataka and Kerala make up the region of south India. Foreign traders and explorers have often landed on these shores over the centuries, attracted by the promise of a lucrative trade in exotic and costly items such as spices and silks. They inevitably brought outside influences with them, which have had an impact on all aspects of life in the area, including food. The result is a varied and exotic cuisine that reflects the wealth of ingredients on offer to local cooks.

KARNATAKA

The name of this state is derived from the word 'Karunadu', which means 'lofty land'. Much of Karnataka is on the high plateau that lies between the western and eastern 'Ghats', precipitous mountains that run along the western and eastern coasts of peninsular India. The rest of the state lies along a 300km (186-mile) stretch of coastline with smooth, sandy beaches that are popular with tourists.

Numerous crops grow in this diverse landscape, including tea and coffee, which are produced in huge, lush plantations on the western coast. Rice, millet, groundnut and sesame, along with other agricultural crops, are also abundant. Farther inland, deep forests of much sought-after ebony, cedar and sandalwood trees cover the slopes of the western Ghats, providing timber that is perfect for furniture-making.

Above *Coffee and rice are two of the staple crops grown on lush plantations in the Kodagu (Coorg) region of Karnataka.*

Above *A wide range of fresh vegetables are on offer at colourful street markets in Andhra Pradesh, such as this one in Puttaparthi.*

Sandalwood, used for incense, is perhaps the most valuable commodity, although the area also produces more than 85 per cent of the country's raw silk.

A mainly vegetarian state, Karnataka offers a wealth of exciting dishes based on rice, lentils, vegetables and dairy products. With the exception of fish, which is eaten in abundance in the coastal towns and villages, most of the non-vegetarian dishes originated in the beautiful hilly region of Coorg, the homeland of the warrior community. Their meat, chicken and pork dishes, like those of Andhra Pradesh, have been influenced by both Hindu and Muslim styles of cooking and are among the finest in India.

ANDHRA PRADESH

Situated on the eastern seaboard, Andhra Pradesh has quite a different climate from Karnataka, with the humidity of the monsoon making it ideally suited to rice

production, earning it the nickname the 'granary of the south'. Cotton, tobacco and pulses are also grown in huge quantities and exported all over the world.

The twin cities of Hyderabad and Secunderabad make up the municipality of Hyderabad, which is one of the largest metropolises in India. It is a beautiful place, with stately architecture and shops displaying colourful uncut precious stones, softly glistening pearls of different shades and delicate filigree work on pure silver.

The cuisine of Andhra Pradesh owes much of its unique nature among the southern states to the influence of both Muslim and Mughal cooking, dating back to the invaders who fought over this land from the 14th century onwards. Unlike the other southern states, Andhra Pradesh has

Right *The stunning palm-fringed coastline of Kerala is famous both for its beaches and its many spice plantations.*

more meat-eaters than vegetarians. Mouthwatering kebabs and biryanis are a speciality in this part of the country and are famous all over India. Chillies – including the famed Guntur red chillies, which are known for their pungency – are one of the main crops of this region, and hot mixtures such as lime pickle are a favourite side dish.

KERALA

Representing only 1.8 per cent of the total area of India, Kerala is the smallest state of south India. This strip of land along the Arabian Sea leads right to the southernmost tip of India, and has a beautiful coastline that stretches 590km (367 miles). Kerala's most prized possession, along with its beautiful sandy beaches, is its fabulous spice plantations, where crops of cardamom, cinnamon, cloves, chillies and peppercorns, among others, are grown in abundance. As a producer of such valuable spices, the area has long been visited by traders, including the Romans, Chinese, Syrians and Arabs.

The cuisine of Kerala is very light and refreshing, using locally grown coconut and exotic spices. Every part of this nut is

Above Idlis, *served on a green banana leaf, are very popular in Tamil Nadu. Traditionally the banana leaf would be fed to cows after the meal.*

used, from the milk to the flesh, and not forgetting the husk, which makes a good, tough building material. The fine, delicate flavour of the pure white flesh and the coconut cream permeates both sweet and savoury Keralan recipes.

Fish and seafood feature prominently in the Hindu homes, whereas delicious meat and poultry dishes are a speciality of the Muslims, Christians and the Jews. Most dishes are generally healthy, with minimum use of fat and maximum use of fresh ingredients, including the many tropical fruits, such as cashews, mangoes, bananas, and jackfruit, that thrive in the area.

TAMIL NADU

The history of the picturesque state of Tamil Nadu, on the south-eastern coast, is one of occupation by the Dravidian people, who are supposedly the descendants of the ancient Indus Valley civilization. Indications of people living and farming in this warm, wet

land go back 6,000 years, and the Dravidian Tamil language is at least 2,000 years old. In later centuries Tamil Nadu became part of the European trade routes and a focus for the East India Trading Company.

The food in Tamil Nadu is almost all vegetarian, partly for the purely practical reason that meat deteriorates quicker than vegetarian food in the muggy heat, and partly for religious reasons, as the majority of the population are Hindu or Jainist. Soft, fluffy *idlis* (rice dumplings), crispy, paper-thin *dosas* (rice pancakes) filled with spicy potatoes, and colourful vegetable and lentil dishes are all presented on emerald-green banana leaves. The food tends to contain a lot of fiery chillies; perhaps because this is where these now ubiquitous fruits were first introduced to the country by the traders from the New World. Locally grown spices such as curry leaves, tamarind, coriander, cumin and nutmeg, as well as many others, also have a strong presence.

Tomato and coriander soup

Based on a recipe from southern India, this soup, *Rasam*, is traditionally served in a cup to accompany a meal. However, it is rather a novel idea to serve this in shot glasses or coffee cups as an appetizer. Fresh curry leaves provide the main flavour here, but if you cannot obtain them, use the dried ones instead.

2 Add the tomatoes and pour in 300ml/ ½ pint/1¼ cups hot water. Bring it to the boil, add the salt and sugar, cover and reduce the heat to low.

3 Simmer for 15–20 minutes, cool slightly, then process in a blender or food processor. Push through a sieve (strainer) into the pan.

4 Reheat the soup gently until it is just simmering. Garnish with the coriander leaves and serve immediately.

SERVES 4
30ml/2 tbsp sunflower oil or light olive oil
2 cloves garlic, crushed
1cm/½in piece of fresh root ginger, peeled and grated
2 dried red chillies, finely snipped
2.5ml/½ tsp black peppercorns, crushed
8 fresh or 10 dried curry leaves
600g/1lb 6oz chopped fresh tomatoes or canned chopped tomatoes
5ml/1 tsp salt
5ml/1 tsp sugar
30ml/2 tbsp fresh coriander (cilantro) leaves, to garnish

1 Heat the oil in a pan over a low heat, then add the garlic, ginger, chillies, peppercorns and curry leaves and fry for 2–3 minutes, until the garlic and ginger have browned and the chillies have blackened a little.

COOK'S TIP
Fresh curry leaves are often available from Asian stores. The best way to preserve them is to wash them, then pat them dry with kitchen paper and freeze them in a single layer. Once frozen, transfer them to an airtight freezer bag and use them direct from the freezer, as required.

Per portion Energy 101kcal/421kJ; Protein 2g; Carbohydrate 7g, of which sugars 6g; Fat 8g, of which saturates 1g; Cholesterol 0mg; Calcium 24mg; Fibre 1.2g; Sodium 1043mg.

Tamarind-flavoured lentil broth

Pigeon peas, known as *toor* or *tuvar dhal*, are one of the most widely used ingredients in southern India. This spicy dish, *Rasam*, originates in the hot region of Tamil Nadu, and is served in small cups to accompany a meal. The spices cool down the body in summer, but the dish is equally good in the winter.

SERVES 4

75g/3oz/⅓ cup pigeon peas (toor or
  tuvar dahl)
5ml/1 tsp salt, or to taste
2–3 whole fresh green chillies
6–8 curry leaves
7.5ml/1½ tsp cumin seeds
2.5ml/½ tsp black peppercorns
30ml/2 tbsp sunflower oil or olive oil
2.5ml/½ tsp black mustard seeds
2.5ml/½ tsp asafoetida
1.25–2.5ml/¼–½ tsp chilli powder
1 small ripe tomato, finely chopped
15ml/1 tbsp fresh coriander (cilantro)
  leaves, chopped
22.5ml/1½ tbsp tamarind or 30ml/2 tbsp
  lemon juice

1 Wash the pigeon peas and place them into a medium pan.

2 Add 1.5 litres/2½ pints/6¼ cups hot water, the salt, chillies and curry leaves. Place over a medium heat and gradually bring to the boil. Reduce the heat to low. Simmer for 35–40 minutes.

3 Meanwhile, put the cumin seeds and the peppercorns in a plastic bag and crush them using the end of a rolling pin.

4 Strain the soup through a sieve positioned over a bowl, then push the peas back into the broth through the sieve using the back of a spoon. Mix well.

5 Heat the oil in a small pan until almost smoking. Remove from the heat and add the mustard seeds, followed quickly by the asafoetida and chilli powder.

6 Stir the crushed cumin seeds and peppercorns into the spices and oil, then return the pan to the heat, add the tomato and cook for 1 minute.

7 Pour the seasoned oil into the soup, add the chopped coriander and tamarind or lemon juice, stir and serve immediately.

Per portion Energy134kcal/560kJ; Protein 5.7g; Carbohydrate 13.7g, of which sugars 1g; Fat 6.8g, of which saturates 0.8g; Cholesterol 0mg; Calcium 24mg; Fibre 1.1g; Sodium 11mg.

Spiced chicken soup

There are many recipes for this Anglo-Indian soup, *Mulligatanny*, which became popular during colonial days and would have been familiar to all Britons living during the Imperial Raj. *Mulliga* means 'pepper', and *tanni* is 'water', so the literal translation is 'pepper water'.

SERVES 4

30ml/2 tbsp sunflower or light olive oil
30ml/2 tbsp butter
1 poussin, cut into pieces, skin removed
1 small onion, chopped
2.5cm/1in fresh root ginger, grated, or
    10ml/2 tsp ginger purée
2 cloves garlic, crushed, or 5ml/1 tsp
    garlic purée
115g/4oz/1 cup mushrooms, sliced
115g/4oz white cabbage, chopped
5ml/1 tsp salt, or to taste
5ml/1 tsp ground cumin
5ml/1 tsp ground coriander
2.5ml/½ tsp ground turmeric
10ml/2 tsp ground black pepper,
    or to taste
15ml/1 tbsp finely chopped fresh
    coriander (cilantro)
strips of toasted naan, to serve

4 Mix the cumin, coriander, turmeric and black pepper together with 15ml/1 tbsp water to make a paste.

5 Heat the remaining oil and butter in a small frying pan over a low heat. Add the spice paste and cook for 2–3 minutes, then stir into to the soup.

6 Bring the soup back to the boil and simmer for 2–3 minutes to ensure it is piping hot.

7 Stir the chopped coriander into the soup, and ladle into warmed bowls. Serve with strips of toasted naan.

1 Heat half the oil and half the butter in a heavy pan over a medium heat. Add the poussin, onion, ginger, garlic, mushrooms and cabbage. Fry for 5 minutes until beginning to brown, stirring frequently.

2 Pour in 1.2 litres/2 pints/4 cups hot water and add the salt. Bring to the boil, reduce the heat and cover the pan. Gently simmer for 30 minutes.

3 Lift out the poussin and set aside. Purée the soup in batches in a blender and return to the pan with the pieces of poussin.

Per portion Energy 191kcal/794kJ; Protein 14g; Carbohydrate 2g, of which sugars 1g; Fat 15g, of which saturates 5g; Cholesterol 55mg; Calcium 22mg; Fibre 0.3g; Sodium 573mg.

Batter-fried peppers

If your taste buds ever crave a change from Onion Bhajiyas try these sweet (bell) peppers, *Mirchi Bhaje*, which are cut into rings, dipped in a spiced batter and deep-fried until crisp and brown.
They make a wonderful snack, a delicious appetizer or a tasty canapé piled high to serve with drinks.

MAKES 15

1 green (bell) pepper
1 red (bell) pepper
1 yellow (bell) pepper
200g/7oz/1¾ cups gram flour (besan)
a pinch of bicarbonate of soda
  (baking soda)
5ml/1 tsp fennel seeds
5ml/1 tsp cumin seeds
5ml/1 tsp coriander seeds, lightly crushed
2.5ml/½ tsp ground turmeric
3.75ml/¾ tsp salt, or to taste
1–3 fresh green chillies, finely chopped
  (deseeded if preferred)
sunflower oil or light olive oil, for
  deep-frying

1 Wash the peppers, pat dry with kitchen paper and then cut them widthways into 5mm/¼in-wide rings. Remove and discard the seeds and the bitter white membrane. Set aside.

2 Sift the gram flour into a large mixing bowl, lifting the sieve (strainer) up high.

3 Add all the remaining ingredients except the oil. Mix well and gradually add 200ml/7fl oz/¾ cup water. Stir thoroughly to make a thick batter.

4 Heat the oil in a pan suitable for deep-frying over a medium heat until it reaches 180°C/350°F on a thermometer. To measure the temperature without a thermometer, drop about 1.25ml/¼ tsp of the batter into the hot oil. If it floats up to the surface immediately without turning brown, then the oil is at the right temperature.

5 Ensure the pepper rings are well coated with the spiced batter, then add them one by one to the hot oil without overcrowding the pan, as this will result in soggy rings.

6 Fry until they are crisp and golden brown. Drain on kitchen paper and repeat with the remaining pepper rings.

Per portion Energy 104kcal/433kJ; Protein 2.3g; Carbohydrate 11.4g, of which sugars 2.6g; Fat 5.7g, of which saturates 0.6g; Cholesterol 0mg; Calcium 11mg; Fibre 1.8g; Sodium 2mg.

Coconut kebabs

In India, these little morsels, *Nariyal Ke Kabab*, are made from grated fresh coconut. To make life easier, this recipe uses desiccated (dry unsweetened shredded) coconut moistened with milk to replenish some of its richness. They make an ideal appetizer served with chutney and a glass of cold beer or white wine.

MAKES 16

150g/5oz desiccated (dry unsweetened shredded) coconut
150ml/¼ pint/⅔ cup full-fat (whole) milk, heated until warm
2 large slices of white bread, crusts removed
75g/3oz/⅔ cup gram flour (besan)
1–3 fresh green chillies, roughly chopped (deseeded if preferred)
2.5cm/1in piece of fresh root ginger, peeled and roughly chopped
1 large garlic clove, peeled and roughly chopped
15ml/1 tbsp fresh coriander (cilantro) leaves and stalks, roughly chopped
2.5ml/½ tsp chilli powder, or to taste
3.75ml/¾ tsp salt, or to taste
1 medium onion, finely chopped
sunflower oil, for shallow-frying
chutney, to serve

1 Put the desiccated coconut in a large mixing bowl and pour over the warm milk. Set aside for 10 minutes for the coconut to absorb the milk and rehydrate slightly. Cut the bread into small pieces.

2 Place all the ingredients, except the onion and the oil, in a food processor and blitz for a few seconds, until you have a smooth paste.

3 Transfer the mixture to a bowl and add the onion. Mix thoroughly and divide the mixture into 16 balls, each the size of a lime.

4 Flatten the coconut balls to form 16 smooth, round cakes. If the mixture sticks to your fingers, moisten your palms with cold water between cakes.

5 Pour enough oil in a frying pan to measure about 1cm/½in in depth, and heat over a high heat.

6 Fry the kebabs in batches, without overcrowding the pan, for 3–4 minutes on each side, until browned all over.

7 Lift out the kebabs with a slotted spoon, drain on kitchen paper and keep warm while you fry the remaining kebabs. Serve with a chutney of your choice.

Per portion Energy 121kcal/502kJ; Protein 3g; Carbohydrate 8g, of which sugars 2g; Fat 9g, of which saturates 6g; Cholesterol 1mg; Calcium 34mg; Fibre 3.1g; Sodium 125mg.

Onion bhajiyas

Kanda Bhaje is one of the most popular snacks in India, and indeed the rest of the world, and it comes from the mainly vegetarian state of Karnataka. Bhajiyas are delicious served with chutney.

SERVES 4–6

150g/5oz/1¼ cups gram flour (besan)
25g/1oz ground rice
5ml/1 tsp salt, or to taste
a pinch of bicarbonate of soda (baking soda)
2.5ml/½ tsp ground turmeric
5ml/1 tsp ground cumin
5ml/1 tsp cumin seeds
2.5ml/½ tsp Asafoetida
2 fresh green chillies, finely chopped
  (deseeded if preferred)
450g/1lb onions, sliced into half rings
  and separated
15ml/1 tbsp fresh coriander (cilantro) leaves
  and stalks, finely chopped
sunflower oil or light olive oil, for deep-frying
chutney, to serve (optional)

1 Sift the flour into a large mixing bowl and add the ground rice, salt, bicarbonate of soda, turmeric, ground cumin, cumin seeds and Asafoetida.

2 Mix these dry ingredients together thoroughly, then add the chillies, onion rings and coriander.

COOK'S TIPS
• If the oil is not hot enough the bhajiyas will be soggy.
• Maintaining a steady temperature is important to ensure that the centre of each bhajiya is cooked and the outside turns brown.

3 Gradually pour in 200ml/7fl oz/¾ cup water and mix until a thick batter is formed and all the ingredients are well coated.

4 Heat the oil in a pan suitable for deep-frying over a medium heat until it reaches 180°C/350°F on a thermometer. To measure the temperature without a thermometer, drop about 1.25ml/¼ tsp of the batter into the hot oil. If it floats up to the surface immediately without turning brown, then the oil is at the right temperature.

5 Lower about 15ml/1 tbsp of the onion batter mixture at a time into the hot oil, in a single layer. Avoid overcrowding the pan as this will lower the temperature of the oil and the bhajiyas will not crisp up.

6 Reduce the heat slightly and continue to cook until the bhajiyas are golden brown and crisp. This should take 8–10 minutes.

7 Drain on kitchen paper and serve on their own or with a chutney of your choice.

Per portion Energy 284kcal/1181kJ; Protein 5.1g; Carbohydrate 27g, of which sugars 4.7g; Fat 18g, of which saturates 1.9g; Cholesterol 0mg; Calcium 38mg; Fibre 3.3g; Sodium 5mg.

South Indian scrambled eggs

This is a supremely scrumptious dish and can be served in smaller quantities on small crackers with drinks, or as an appetizer spread on hot buttered toast and served with a garnish of salad. A south Indian dish, it is known locally as *Mutta Ulathiyathu.*

2 Add the turmeric, curry leaves and coconut to the pan and stir to combine.

3 Cook for 1 minute, then pour in 120ml/ 4fl oz/½ cup water. Cook over a low heat for about 10 minutes, until the coconut has absorbed most of the water.

4 Add the beaten eggs and salt, then cook for 2–4 minutes, stirring constantly until the required consistency is achieved. Remove from the heat and serve on crackers or hot buttered toast.

SERVES 4

30ml/2 tbsp sunflower oil or light
  olive oil
1 large onion, finely chopped
2 fresh red chillies, chopped (deseeded
  if preferred)
2.5ml/½ tsp ground turmeric
6–8 curry leaves
50g/2oz desiccated (dry unsweetened
  shredded) coconut
4 large (US extra large) eggs, beaten
salt, to taste
small crackers or hot buttered toast,
  to serve

1 Heat the oil in a medium pan over a moderate heat and fry the onion and chillies for 8–10 minutes, until soft and pale brown.

Per portion Energy 285kcal/1180kJ; Protein 11g; Carbohydrate 11g, of which sugars 8g; Fat 23g, of which saturates 10g; Cholesterol 251mg; Calcium 77mg; Fibre 4.4g; Sodium 297mg.

Rice with aubergine, coconut and cashews

This recipe, *Vangi Bhat*, is from the coastal state of Karnataka where people generally eat a range of vegetarian and seafood dishes cooked with coconut. This makes a delicious and substantial vegetarian main course. Serve with cucumber raita for a balanced meal.

SERVES 4

225g/8oz/generous 1 cup basmati rice
1 large aubergine (eggplant)
50g/2oz/4 tbsp ghee or unsalted butter
2.5cm/1in piece of cinnamon stick
5 cloves
1 large onion, finely sliced
5ml/1 tsp salt, or to taste
5ml/1 tsp garam masala
30ml/2 tbsp fresh coriander (cilantro)
  leaves, finely chopped
30ml/2 tbsp desiccated (dry unsweetened
  shredded) coconut, ground until fine
30ml/2 tbsp cashew nuts
cucumber raita, to serve

1 Wash the rice until the water runs clear. Soak in a bowl of cold water for 20 minutes and leave to drain in a sieve (strainer).

2 Cut the aubergine into quarters lengthways, then cut each quarter into 1cm/½in chunks. Soak in a bowl of cold salted water for 15–20 minutes, then rinse well.

3 Melt the ghee or butter in a heavy pan over a low heat, then add the cinnamon and cloves. Let them sizzle for 25–30 seconds.

4 Add the onion. Increase the heat slightly to medium and fry for 9–10 minutes, stirring occasionally, until the onion begins to turn a golden-brown colour.

5 Add the drained rice, aubergine, salt, garam masala and half the chopped coriander. Stir-fry gently for 2–3 minutes, then add 450ml/¾ pint/scant 2 cups lukewarm water.

6 Bring the water to the boil, reduce the heat to low, cover the pan tightly and cook for 8–9 minutes.

7 Remove the pan from the heat and scatter the coconut and cashew nuts on top. Replace the lid and leave the pan to stand for 8–10 minutes.

8 Fluff up the rice with a fork and transfer it to a serving dish. Serve garnished with the remaining chopped coriander and with some raita to accompany it.

Per portion Energy 461kcal/1932kJ; Protein 8g; Carbohydrate 62g, of which sugars 9g; Fat 22g, of which saturates 13g; Cholesterol 35mg; Calcium 72mg; Fibre 5.9g; Sodium 1000mg.

Rice pancakes filled with spiced potatoes

Crispy rice pancakes filled with spiced potatoes and served with coconut chutney are a popular breakfast or brunch dish in south India. This version of *Masala Dosai* is simplified for cooks with limited time in the kitchen and is easy and quick to put together – perfect for a light snack or appetizer.

MAKES 8

For the pancakes:
75g/3oz/⅔ cup plain (all-purpose) flour
110g/4oz/⅔ cup semolina
110g/4oz/⅔ cup ground rice
2.5ml/½ tsp salt, or to taste
150g/5oz/⅔ cup natural (plain) yogurt
sunflower oil or light olive oil, for cooking
  the pancakes

For the filling:
600g/1¼lb potatoes
60ml/4 tbsp sunflower oil or light
  olive oil
2.5ml/½ tsp black mustard seeds
2.5ml/½ tsp cumin seeds
1.25ml/¼ tsp fenugreek seeds
1 large onion, finely sliced
1–3 fresh green chillies, finely chopped
  (deseeded if preferred)
2.5ml/½ tsp ground turmeric
5ml/1 tsp ground coriander
5ml/1 tsp ground cumin
5ml/1 tsp salt, or to taste
30ml/2 tbsp fresh coriander (cilantro)
  leaves, chopped

1 To make the pancakes: mix all the dry ingredients in a large mixing bowl. Make a well in the centre of the ingredients.

2 Beat the yogurt in a bowl until smooth, then blend with 450ml/16fl oz/scant 2 cups water. Gradually add the blended yogurt to the dry ingredients, beating well with a wire whisk.

3 Place a heavy non-stick griddle (23cm/9in wide) or frying pan over a medium heat and add 10ml/2 tsp oil. Brush the oil quickly all over the surface and allow to heat up for a few minutes.

4 Using a measuring jug (cup), pour about 125ml/4fl oz/½ cup of the batter on to the griddle, spread it quickly and evenly and let the mixture set for 2 minutes.

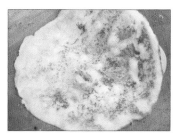

5 Sprinkle 15ml/1 tbsp water around the edges, wait for 15–20 seconds, then turn the pancake over with a metal spatula or a fish slice.

6 Cook for a further 2–3 minutes or until brown patches appear underneath. Cook the remaining pancakes the same way and place on a wire rack in a single layer.

7 For the filling: boil the potatoes in their skins to stop them going mushy. Cool, peel and cut them into 2.5cm/1in cubes. You can also cook them in advance and store them in the refrigerator.

8 Heat the oil over a medium heat. When hot, but not smoking, add the mustard seeds, followed by the cumin and fenugreek seeds.

9 Add the onion and green chillies and stir-fry for 8–9 minutes or until the onions are a light golden colour. Add the turmeric, coriander and cumin. Cook for 1 minute.

10 Add the cooked potatoes and salt to the spice mixture and stir until the potatoes are heated through.

11 Stir in the coriander leaves and remove from the heat. Divide the potato filling into eight equal portions.

12 Place the griddle used to cook the pancakes over a low heat. Lay a pancake on it, put a portion of the potato filling on one side, roll it up and heat through for about 1 minute.

13 Place the rolled pancake in a very low oven while you finish making all of them, but do not leave them too long or they will become dry.

VARIATION
You could subsitute the potato with sweet potato or parsnip for a sweet and spicy alternative.

Per portion Energy 279kcal/1172kJ; Protein 7.1g; Carbohydrate 49.1g, of which sugars 6g; Fat 7.1g, of which saturates 1.1g; Cholesterol 0mg; Calcium 83mg; Fibre 2.2g; Sodium 29mg.

Stuffed meat patties

These fragrant, melt-in-the mouth kebabs, *Shikampuri Kebab*, originated in Shikampur, near Hyderabad. The meat is flavoured with spices, almonds and coconut, and yellow split gram are used as a binding agent. They are then shaped into patties and filled with a flavoursome stuffing before being shallow-fried.

SERVES 4

500g/1¼lb minced (ground) lamb or beef
115g/4oz/½ cup yellow split gram
   (channa dhal)
25g/1oz blanched almonds
25g/1oz desiccated (dry unsweetened
   shredded) coconut
30ml/2 tbsp sunflower oil or olive oil
1 medium onion, roughly chopped
5cm/2in piece of fresh root ginger, chopped
6 large garlic cloves, roughly chopped
2 dried red chillies, torn into pieces
2.5cm/1in piece of cinnamon stick, crushed
seeds of 6 green cardamom pods
4 cloves
8–10 black peppercorns
5ml/1 tsp cumin seeds
5ml/1 tsp salt
7.5ml/1½ tbsp lemon juice
15g/½oz coriander (cilantro) leaves and stalks
2 large (US extra large) eggs
22.5ml/1½ tbsp cornflour (cornstarch)
vegetable oil, for shallow frying
mint leaves, to garnish
Plain Boiled Rice, to serve

For the filling:
1 small onion, chopped
1 small tomato, chopped
1 fresh green chilli, finely chopped
30ml/2 tbsp coriander (cilantro), chopped

1 Put the minced meat and the lentils in a pan and add 300ml/½ pint/1¼ cups water. Bring to the boil, reduce the heat to medium and cook, uncovered, for 10–12 minutes.

2 Add the almonds and coconut to the pan, reduce the heat and continue to simmer for about 10 minutes, until the lentils are tender but not mushy. Turn the heat up and cook for 5–6 minutes, until dry and crumbly. Remove from the heat and leave to cool.

3 Heat the oil in a small pan over a medium heat and fry the onion, ginger, garlic and red chillies for 6–7 minutes, until browned.

4 Finely grind the cinnamon, cardamom seeds, cloves, peppercorns and cumin seeds in a coffee grinder.

5 Put the fried onion and ground spices in a food processor and add the cooked meat, salt, lemon juice, coriander and one egg. Add the ground ingredients and process until well blended.

6 Divide the mixture into 16 equal portions. Have a bowl of cold water ready, moisten your palms and mould each portion of the kebab mixture into a miniature cup shape.

7 Mix all the ingredients for the filling in a bowl and divide into 16 equal portions.

8 Fill the hollow in each kebab with a little of the filling mixture and cover it completely with the meat, then flatten it slightly to form a 2.5cm/1in thick cake.

9 Blend the cornflour with a little water in a small bowl, then add the remaining egg and beat well to form a smooth paste. Pour enough oil into a frying pan to measure about 1cm/½in in depth, and heat over a medium to high heat.

10 Dip each kebab in the cornflour and egg mixture and fry in batches until they are well browned, about 2–3 minutes on each side. Remove with a slotted spoon and drain on kitchen paper.

11 Garnish with fresh onion rings, sliced cucumber and tomato, lime wedges and sprigs of fresh mint and serve immediately, accompanied by Plain Boiled Rice.

Per portion Energy 488kcal/2033kJ; Protein 27.9g; Carbohydrate 25.7g, of which sugars 3.7g; Fat 31.2g, of which saturates 7.4g; Cholesterol 238.5mg; Calcium 86.8mg; Fibre 3.1g; Sodium 140mg.

Cauliflower braised with chilli

In this dish, *Ambat*, which is a classic example of the delicious, healthy cuisine of Karnataka, florets of cauliflower are simmered in rich coconut milk, teamed with lightly browned red onion. It goes well with plain boiled basmati rice.

SERVES 4

45ml/3 tbsp sunflower oil or light olive oil
2.5ml/½ tsp fenugreek seeds
1–2 dried red chillies, chopped
1 cauliflower, divided into 1cm/½in florets
400ml/14fl oz/1½ cups canned
  coconut milk
5ml/1 tsp salt, or to taste
1 red onion, finely sliced
22.5ml/1½ tbsp tamarind juice or
  lime juice
Plain Boiled Rice, to serve

1 In a small pan, heat 10ml/2 tsp of the oil over a low heat and add the fenugreek and chillies. Stir them around until they are just a shade darker. Leave to cool.

2 Meanwhile, blanch the cauliflower in a large pan of lightly salted boiling water for 2 minutes, then drain and return to the pan.

3 Crush the fenugreek and chillies to a paste with the oil in which they were fried using a mortar and pestle.

4 Add the coconut milk and salt. Leave it to bubble without a lid over a very low heat.

5 Heat the remaining oil over a medium heat and fry the onion for 5 minutes, until golden. Add the onion, together with the oil, to the cauliflower. Stir and increase the heat slightly.

6 Add the fenugreek and chilli paste to the cauliflower with the tamarind or lime juice. Simmer for 1–2 minutes, remove from the heat and serve with Plain Boiled Rice.

Per portion Energy 153kcal/636kJ; Protein 5.9g; Carbohydrate 10.6g, of which sugars 9.5g; Fat 9.9g, of which saturates 1.5g; Cholesterol 0mg; Calcium 64mg; Fibre 2.9g; Sodium 124mg.

South Indian fried eggs

This delicious vegetarian dish, *Dakshini Andey*, originates from Kerala and is based on a recipe known locally as 'egg roast'. The 'roast' is, in fact, hard-boiled eggs, which are fried with spices until browned. This version includes potatoes to make a more substantial meal.

3 Heat the oil over a low heat in a non-stick frying pan, and add the cumin, chilli powder and turmeric, followed by the eggs. Stir for 2–3 minutes, until the eggs have developed a light crust. Add salt and remove from the pan. Keep hot while you fry the potatoes.

4 In the same oil, fry the potatoes over a medium heat, stirring regularly until they begin to brown. Add salt to taste.

5 Return the eggs to the pan and stir in the coriander. Remove from the heat and serve.

SERVES 4

350g/12oz waxy potatoes
4 hard-boiled eggs, shelled
30ml/2 tbsp sunflower oil or light olive oil
2.5ml/½ tsp ground cumin
1.25ml/¼ tsp chilli powder
1.25ml/¼ tsp ground turmeric
salt, to taste
30ml/2 tbsp fresh coriander (cilantro)
  leaves, finely chopped

COOK'S TIP
Slitting the eggs enables the spices to permeate them fully.

1 Parboil the potatoes without skinning them, then cool, peel and cut them into wedges.

2 Make four slits lengthways on each egg, taking care not to cut them right through.

Per portion Energy 199kcal/831kJ; Protein 8.5g; Carbohydrate 15.8g, of which sugars 1.1g; Fat 12g, of which saturates 2.4g; Cholesterol 190mg; Calcium 43mg; Fibre 0.9g; Sodium 81mg.

Lentils in chilli-infused coconut milk

Flavoursome lentils are combined with deep green spinach and rich coconut milk to create this simple but unforgettable dish, *Dali Ambat*. Plenty of protein and fibre in the lentils make it an excellent vegetarian main course. Serve this with boiled basmati rice for a satisfying meal.

SERVES 4

200g/7oz red split lentils
250g/9oz spinach, fresh or frozen, chopped
5ml/1 tsp ground turmeric
45ml/3 tbsp sunflower oil or light olive oil
2 dried red chillies, snipped
2.5ml/½ tsp fenugreek seeds
200ml/7fl oz/scant 1 cup canned
    coconut milk
30ml/2 tbsp tamarind juice
1 small onion, finely chopped
Plain Boiled Rice, to serve

1 Wash the lentils in a sieve (strainer) in several changes of water. Drain, transfer to a pan and pour over 750ml/1¼ pints/3 cups water. Place over a high heat and bring it to the boil.

2 Boil, uncovered, for 8–9 minutes, then reduce the heat to low. Cover and simmer for 25–30 minutes, until the lentils are soft.

3 Add the spinach and turmeric, cover and simmer for 10–12 minutes.

4 Meanwhile, heat 15ml/1 tbsp of the oil in a frying pan over a low heat and fry the chillies and fenugreek seeds gently until they are a shade darker. Take care not to burn them or they will taste bitter.

5 Remove the spices from the heat, leave to cool, then crush them to a fine paste with a mortar and pestle or the back of a spoon, along with the flavoured oil.

6 Add the spice paste to the lentils and pour in the coconut milk. Add the tamarind juice, stir well and simmer for 5–7 minutes. Remove from the heat and keep hot.

7 In a separate pan, heat the remaining oil over medium heat and fry the onion for 8–10 minutes, until it begins to brown. Stir the onion into the lentils, remove from the heat and serve with Plain Boiled Rice.

Per portion Energy 319kcal/1342kJ; Protein 15g; Carbohydrate 39g, of which sugars 11g; Fat 13g, of which saturates 2g; Cholesterol 0mg; Calcium 166mg; Fibre 8.1g; Sodium 163mg.

Lentil and aubergine curry

A really perfect partner dish for Steamed Rice Cakes this curry, *Sambhar*, is equally delicious with boiled basmati rice and, interestingly, with crusty white bread, too. The choice of vegetables used in the dish is flexible – in this version aubergine (eggplant) and tomatoes are used. Pigeon peas are now widely available from most Indian shops.

SERVES 4

225g/8oz/1 cup pigeon peas (toor dhal)
2.5ml/½ tsp ground turmeric
1 large aubergine (eggplant), quartered
    lengthways and cut into 2.5cm/1in pieces
7.5ml/1½ tsp salt, or to taste
15ml/1 tbsp coriander seeds
5ml/1 tsp cumin seeds
1–4 dried red chillies, broken up
2.5ml/½ tsp black peppercorns
2.5ml/½ tsp black mustard seeds
225g/8oz fresh tomatoes, chopped
30ml/2 tbsp tamarind juice or the juice
    of 1 lime
30ml/2 tbsp fresh coriander (cilantro)
    leaves and stalks, finely chopped

1 Put the peas in a large pan and add the turmeric and 1.2 litres/2 pints/5 cups cold water. Bring to the boil, then reduce the heat to medium and cook for 3–4 minutes or until all the foam subsides from the surface. Reduce the heat to low, cover the pan and cook for 20 minutes.

2 Add the aubergine and salt, re-cover the pan and continue to cook for a further 8–10 minutes or until the aubergine is tender when prodded with a fork.

3 Meanwhile, preheat a small, heavy pan over a medium heat. Reduce the heat to low and add the coriander, cumin, dried chillies, peppercorns and mustard seeds. Stir and dry-roast for 30 seconds, until they begin to release their aroma.

4 Remove the spices from the pan and leave them to cool, then grind finely in a coffee or spice grinder. Add the spice mix to the lentils.

5 Stir in the tomatoes and tamarind or lime juice. Simmer for 2–3 minutes. Add the chopped coriander, remove from the heat and serve immediately.

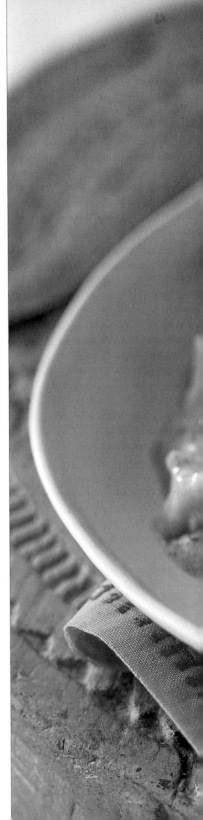

Per portion Energy 215kcal/914kJ; Protein 15.5g; Carbohydrate 36.2g, of which sugars 3.1g; Fat 2.1g, of which saturates 0.3g; Cholesterol 0mg; Calcium 69.8mg; Fibre 4.8g; Sodium 28mg.

Fish in tamarind-laced coconut milk

Both fish and coconut are found in abundance in and around the southern Indian coastline. Recipes such as this one, *Meen Molee*, are best made using white, firm-textured fish such as tilapia, monkfish or sole. However, it is just as successful when using large prawns (shrimp). The coconut adds a richness to the dish.

3 Add the ginger, garlic and green chillies, and cook for 5–6 minutes, until light golden.

4 Add the chilli powder and turmeric, cook for 30 seconds, then pour in the coconut milk and add the creamed coconut or coconut cream. Add the remaining salt and lemon juice, and stir until the creamed coconut has dissolved.

5 Add the fish. Simmer for 7 minutes or until the sauce has thickened. Garnish with coconut flakes. Serve with Plain Boiled Rice.

SERVES 4

675g/1½lb fillet of tilapia or any other firm
    white fish
30ml/2 tbsp lemon juice
5ml/1 tsp salt, or to taste
15ml/3 tbsp sunflower oil or olive oil
1 large onion, finely chopped
10ml/2 tsp ginger purée
5ml/1 tsp garlic purée
2 fresh green chillies, finely chopped,
    (deseeded if preferred)
2.5ml/½ tsp chilli powder
2.5ml/½ tsp ground turmeric
400ml/14oz/1⅔ cups canned coconut milk
45ml/3 tbsp creamed coconut, cut into
    small pieces, or coconut cream
toasted coconut flakes, to garnish
Plain Boiled Rice, to serve

1 Cut the fish into 5cm/2in pieces and lay them out on a large plate. Rub in half the lemon juice and half the salt. Set aside.

2 Heat the oil over medium heat, then add the onion and fry 5–6 minutes, until the onion is soft, but not brown.

Per portion Energy 366kcal/1528kJ; Protein 33.6g; Carbohydrate 13.7g, of which sugars 11.4g; Fat 20g, of which saturates 9.1g; Cholesterol 0mg; Calcium 269mg; Fibre 1.4g; Sodium 208mg.

Mackerel in coconut milk

Mackerel is a popular fish in the south of India and its firm texture makes it ideal for curries. This dish, *Ayila Vattichathu*, comes from Chennai and has the contrasting tastes of tart tamarind and sweet, creamy coconut. Here the mackerel is cooked on the bone, which adds to the flavour of the dish.

SERVES 4

675g/1½lb cleaned mackerel
30ml/2 tbsp sunflower oil or light olive oil
2.5ml/½ tsp black mustard seeds
1 small onion, finely chopped
10ml/2 tsp garlic purée
5–10ml/1–2 tsp chilli powder
2.5ml/½ tsp ground turmeric
5ml/1 tsp salt, or to taste
75g/3oz creamed coconut, chopped, or
   250ml/8fl oz/1 cup coconut cream
8–10 curry leaves
30–45ml/2–3 tbsp tamarind juice
Plain Boiled Rice, to serve

4 Pour 250ml/8floz/1 cup boiling water into the pan if using creamed coconut. Don't add water if using coconut cream. Add the creamed coconut or coconut cream, curry leaves and tamarind juice. Heat, stirring , until the creamed coconut has dissolved.

5 Carefully place the fish in the broth in a single layer, cover and gently simmer for 6–7 minutes, or until the fish is cooked.

6 Ladle on to warmed plates or bowls, and serve with Plain Boiled Rice.

1 Cut the fish into thick steaks about 5cm/2in thick, then cut into chunks.

2 Heat the oil in a large, shallow frying pan over a medium heat and add the mustard seeds. As soon as they start to pop, add the onion and fry until it begins to brown.

3 Add the garlic and cook for a minute, then stir in the chilli powder, turmeric and salt.

Per portion Energy 543kcal/2253kJ; Protein 33g; Carbohydrate 10g, of which sugars 9g; Fat 42g, of which saturates 12g; Cholesterol 91mg; Calcium 49mg; Fibre 0.3g; Sodium 612mg.

Mussels in spicy garlic and tamarind sauce

The vast coastline of southern India is one of the best sources of seafood in the country. The people of Kerala, at its southernmost tip, thrive on the daily local catch and use shellfish imaginatively in everyday family meals. Once prepared, mussels are extremely quick to cook. This dish, *Kakkaerachi Oolarthu*, can be served as a main course, or would make a fabulous appetizer for eight people.

SERVES 4

2kg/4½lb mussels
2.5ml/½ tsp salt
3.75ml/¾ tsp ground turmeric
2 thick slices of lemon
60ml/4 tbsp sunflower oil or light olive oil
2.5ml/½ tsp black mustard seeds
3–4 dried red chillies
1 large onion, finely chopped
2 cloves garlic, crushed, or 5ml/2 tsp
  garlic purée
5ml/1 tsp black peppercorns, crushed
10–12 curry leaves
30ml/2 tbsp tamarind juice
chopped fresh red chillies, to garnish

1 Wash the mussels in several changes of water to make sure all the grit is removed. Pull off any beards and barnacles and wash them again.

2 Tap any open mussels sharply with the back of the knife. If they won't close, throw them away.

3 Pour 600ml/1 pint/2½ cups water into a large pan. Add the salt, turmeric and lemon slices and bring it to the boil.

4 Transfer the mussels to the pan, cover and reduce the heat slightly.

5 Cook for exactly 5 minutes, then strain the stock through a sieve set over a bowl.

6 Remove the lemon slices and return the mussels to the pan, discarding any that have not opened. Cover the pan with the lid to keep the mussels warm.

7 In a separate pan, heat the oil over a medium heat until it starts to smoke, and add the mustard seeds. As soon as they start popping, add the chillies and allow them to blacken slightly.

8 Add the onion and garlic to the pan and cook, stirring, for 5–6 minutes, until the onions begin to brown.

9 Add the strained stock, crushed black peppercorns and curry leaves to the onion mixture. Boil, uncovered, over a medium heat for 5–6 minutes.

10 Divide the mussels between warmed soup bowls and ladle over some of the broth. Garnish with chopped red chillies and serve immediately.

COOK'S TIP

In southern Indian cooking, curry leaves replace the northern practice of using fresh coriander (cilantro). Curry leaves have a distinct flavour and aroma. They can be bought fresh or dried; the fresh ones can be frozen.

Per portion Energy 551kcal/2310kJ; Protein 62g; Carbohydrate 23g, of which sugars 9g; Fat 24g, of which saturates 4g; Cholesterol 205mg; Calcium 22mg; Fibre 0.9g; Sodium 1699mg.

Prawns in a poppy seed and cashew sauce

The food of Andhra Pradesh is generally hot and spicy as a result of the large amounts of chillies used, but this rich and aromatic dish, *Jhinge Ki Kadi*, is more characteristic of north Indian cuisine, due to Mughal influences in this part of southern India. Once you have all the ingredients ready, this recipe can be cooked and served in less than 20 minutes, making it perfect food for a party.

1 Mix the prawns, lemon juice and turmeric together in a bowl. Set aside for 15 minutes.

2 Put the almonds in a heatproof bowl and pour over 150ml/¼ pint/⅔ cup boiling water. Leave to soak for 15 minutes.

3 Preheat a small, heavy pan over a medium heat and dry-roast the poppy seeds until they begin to crackle gently.

4 Remove the pan from the heat, leave the spices to cool, then grind in a coffee grinder.

5 Heat the oil in a heavy pan over a medium heat and fry the onion for about 5 minutes, until it is soft but not brown. Add the ginger, garlic and green chillies. Continue cooking for 2–3 minutes.

6 Add the chilli powder, salt, cream and prawns. Stir and cook gently for 2 minutes. Pour in 200ml/7floz/scant 1 cup hot water. Reduce the heat to low, cover the pan and cook for 4–5 minutes.

7 Put the almonds, along with the water in which they were soaked, in a blender or food processor and blend to form a purée.

8 Add the almond purée to the prawns with the ground poppy seeds. Stir well and simmer, uncovered, for 2–3 minutes or until the prawns are pink and cooked.

9 Ladle the soup into warmed bowls and serve immediately garnished with fine strips of red and green chillies.

SERVES 4

500g/14lb raw tiger prawns (jumbo shrimp), peeled and deveined (*see* Cook's Tip)
45ml/3 tbsp lemon juice
2.5ml/½ tsp ground turmeric
50g/2oz/½ cup blanched almonds
30ml/2 tbsp white poppy seeds
60ml/4 tbsp sunflower or light olive oil
1 large onion, finely chopped
2.5cm/1in fresh root ginger, grated, or 10ml/2 tsp ginger purée
2 cloves garlic, crushed or 10ml/2 tsp garlic purée
1–3 fresh green chillies, finely chopped (deseeded if preferred)
2.5–5ml/½–1 tsp chilli powder
5ml/1 tsp salt, or to taste
75ml/2½floz/⅓ cup double (heavy) cream
fine strips of fresh red and green chillies, to garnish

COOK'S TIP
To devein prawns (shrimp): Locate the black vein that runs along the back and make a slit either side of it. Remove with the tip of the knife.

Per portion Energy 426kcal/1766kJ; Protein 27g; Carbohydrate 7g, of which sugars 5g; Fat 36g, of which saturates 9g; Cholesterol 269mg; Calcium 254mg; Fibre 1.8g; Sodium 745mg.

Mixed seafood in coconut broth

This popular and tasty dish, *Cassoulet De Fruits De Mer*, hails from the once French-occupied region of Pondicherry; the recipe itself comes courtesy of Mehernosh Modi, one of the most talented Indian chefs in England. It is delicious when accompanied by basmati rice.

SERVES 4

500g/1¼lb mixture of white fish fillets and
   assorted seafood, such as prawns
   (shrimp), mussels, scallops, crab claws,
   and squid
10ml/2 tbsp sunflower oil or plain olive oil
10–12 curry leaves
1 medium onion, finely chopped
200ml/7fl oz/¾ cup canned coconut milk
10ml/2 tsp lemon juice
salt to taste

For the purée:
4 dried red chillies
2.5cm/1in piece of fresh root ginger,
   roughly chopped
3–4 garlic cloves, roughly chopped
10ml/2 tsp coriander seeds
5ml/1 tsp cumin seeds
2.5ml/½ tsp ground turmeric
6 black peppercorns
15ml/1 tbsp malt vinegar
sprigs of fresh coriander (cilantro),
   to garnish
Plain Boiled Rice, to serve

1 Shell, trim, devein and clean the seafood as required (*see* Fish and Shellfish in the Introduction chapter for further preparation instructions).

2 Grind the chillies, ginger, spices and other purée ingredients to a coarse paste in a food processor or blender, or use a mortar and pestle.

3 Heat the oil in a medium-sized shallow pan and add the curry leaves, followed by the chopped onion. Stir-fry over a medium heat for 4–5 minutes, until the onion is translucent, then add the puréed ingredients and sauté gently for 2 minutes.

4 Add the seafood, but not the white fish. Stir gently and cook for 2 minutes more.

5 Pour in the coconut milk, bring it to the boil, then add the white fish. Lower the heat and simmer for 5–7 minutes, until the white fish is opaque and cooked through.

6 Add the lemon juice and salt and stir gently. Serve garnished with sprigs of fresh coriander and accompanied by Plain Boiled Rice.

Per portion Energy 218kcal/913kJ; Protein 25.3g; Carbohydrate 13g, of which sugars 8.1g; Fat 7.7g, of which saturates 1g; Cholesterol 58mg; Calcium 64mg; Fibre 1.4g; Sodium 136mg.

Kerala chicken stew

In this dish, *Ishtoo*, chicken on the bone is slow-cooked in a sumptuous, rich coconut broth to produce a wonderful, warming stew that is packed with flavour and is very nutritious. In Kerala, where the recipe comes from, it is normally served with *appam*, a plain rice flour pancake, but it is also good accompanied by plain boiled basmati rice, which soaks up the tangy, green chilli infused saffron.

SERVES 4

675g/1½lb chicken leg or breast portions
  on the bone
60ml/4 tbsp sunflower oil or olive oil
2.5cm/1in piece of cinnamon stick
6 cardamom pods, bruised
4 cloves
12–15 curry leaves
1 large onion, finely chopped
10ml/2 tsp ginger purée
10ml/2 tsp garlic purée
2 fresh green chillies, sliced at an angle
2.5ml/½ tsp ground turmeric
400g/14fl oz/1½ cups canned coconut milk
5ml/1 tsp salt, or to taste
500g/1¼lb medium potatoes,
175g/6oz/1½ cups frozen garden peas
Plain Boiled Rice, to serve

1 Remove the skin from the chicken joints, cut each of them into two pieces, then cover and set aside.

2 Heat the oil in a large pan over a low heat and add the cinnamon, cardamom pods, cloves and curry leaves.

3 Sauté the spices for 25–30 seconds, until they release their aroma, then add the chopped onion to the pan. Increase the heat to medium and fry until the onion is soft but not browned, approximately 5–6 minutes,

4 Add the ginger, garlic and chillies and cook for 2–3 minutes longer to allow the flavours to blend.

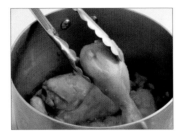

5 Add the turmeric, stir well, then add the skinned chicken pieces. Increase the heat from medium to high and cook for about 5 minutes, until the chicken browns all over.

6 Pour in the coconut milk and add the salt, stir and mix well. Reduce the heat to low, cover and simmer for 15–20 minutes.

7 Halve the potatoes and pour in 250ml/ 8fl oz/1 cup warm water. Bring to the boil, reduce the heat to low, then cover and cook for 20 minutes more, or until the chicken is cooked and the potatoes are tender.

8 Add the peas, cook for 5 minutes longer, then serve with Plain Boiled Rice.

Per portion Energy 552kcal/2309kJ; Protein 40g; Carbohydrate 43.6g, of which sugars 16g; Fat 25.5g,of which saturates 6.9g; Cholesterol 192.5mg;Calcium 104.5mg; Fibre 5.4g; Sodium 271mg.

Chettinad chicken

This recipe, *Kozhi Varatha Kosambuk*, comes from the trading community in the region known as Chettinad. The curry is quite fiery as it uses both chillies and black pepper, but you can reduce these to suit your palate. The chicken is cooked with distinct aromatic spices such as fennel, cloves, star anise, fresh ginger, cumin and cardamom pods for a unique flavour. Creamy-white poppy seeds help to thicken the sauce.

SERVES 4

4 large chicken quarters, about 1kg/2¼lb
    in total, skinned
juice of ½ lemon
5ml/1 tsp salt, or to taste
30ml/2 tbsp white poppy seeds
25g/1oz/¼ cup desiccated (dry
    unsweetened shredded) coconut
5ml/1 tsp fennel seeds
5ml/1 tsp cumin seeds
5ml/1 tsp coriander seeds
2 whole dried red chillies, torn into pieces
10–12 black peppercorns
2.5cm/1in piece cinnamon stick, broken
    into smaller pieces
2 cloves
2 green cardamom pods
45ml/3 tbsp sunflower oil or light olive oil
1 large onion, finely chopped
2.5cm/1in fresh root ginger, grated, or
    10ml/2 tsp ginger purée
2 cloves garlic, crushed, or 10ml/2 tsp
    garlic purée
2.5–5ml/½–1 tsp chilli powder
2.5ml/½ tsp ground turmeric
1 star anise
2 tomatoes, chopped
10–12 curry leaves
toasted flaked coconut, to garnish
Plain Boiled Rice, to serve

VARIATIONS
• As with most Indian recipes, the chicken is cooked on the bone to add flavour to the finished dish. You can use boneless chicken thighs or chunks of breast meat if you prefer, but you will need to reduce the cooking time in Step 8 to 5 minutes and use just 175ml/ 6floz/¾ cup water.
• If you can't take the heat, reduce the amount of chilli used.

---

1 Cut the chicken into smaller portions, separating legs from thighs. If using breasts, cut each one into three pieces. Rub with the lemon juice and salt and set aside for 15–20 minutes.

2 In a small, heavy pan, dry-roast the poppy seeds and the coconut until they are a shade darker. Remove from the heat, transfer to a small bowl and leave to cool.

3 In the same pan, dry-roast the whole spices for about 1 minute, until they release their aroma.

4 Allow the spices to cool, then mix them with the roasted poppy seeds and coconut. Grind the mixture in a coffee grinder in batches and set aside.

5 Using the same pan, heat the oil over a medium heat and add the onion. Fry, stirring frequently, until soft, then add the ginger and garlic.

6 Continue to fry for about 5 minutes, until the onion begins to brown, then stir in the chilli powder and turmeric.

7 Turn up the heat to medium-high, add the chicken pieces and fry, turning frequently, for about 5 minutes, until opaque.

8 Pour in 300ml/½ pint/1¼ cups hot water and add the star anise. Bring to the boil, reduce the heat to low, cover and cook for 15 minutes.

9 Add the ground spice and coconut mixture, tomatoes and curry leaves. Stir to combine, then cover the pan and cook for a further 15–20 minutes or until the chicken is tender.

10 Remove the lid and let the sauce reduce for a few minutes, if necessary, until it is thick. Transfer to a serving dish, garnish with flaked coconut and serve with Plain Boiled Rice.

Per portion Energy 375kcal/1572kJ; Protein 45g; Carbohydrate 7g, of which sugars 6g; Fat 23g, of which saturates 6g; Cholesterol 169mg; Calcium 157mg; Fibre 2.2g; Sodium 163mg.

Chicken in a coconut and cashew nut sauce

Unlike its north Indian counterpart, this chicken korma recipe, *Hyderabadi Murgh Korma*, calls for creamy coconut milk counterbalanced by spicy chilli, and subtle flavour notes are added with a sprinkling of nutmeg and mace. Ghee is traditionally used for making this dish, as it lends an extra depth of flavour, but unsalted butter or oil can be substituted if you prefer a healthier option.

SERVES 4

50g/2oz/½ cup raw cashew nuts
200g/7oz/¾ cup thick set natural
  (plain) yogurt
10ml/2 tsp gram flour (besan)
10ml/2 tsp ginger purée
10ml/2 tsp garlic purée
2.5ml/½ tsp ground turmeric
2.5–5ml/½–1 tsp chilli powder
5ml/1 tsp salt, or to taste
675g/1½lb skinned chicken breast fillets,
  cut into 5cm/2in cubes
75g/3oz/6 tbsp ghee or unsalted butter
2.5cm/1in piece of cinnamon stick
6 green cardamom pods, bruised
6 cloves
2 bay leaves
1 large onion, finely chopped
15ml/1 tbsp sesame seeds,
  finely ground
200ml/7fl oz/¾ cup canned coconut milk
1.25ml/¼ tsp freshly grated nutmeg
1.25ml/¼ tsp ground mace
Plain Boiled Rice and Cumin and Saffron
  Wholemeal Flat Bread

1 Soak the cashew nuts in 150ml/5fl oz/
⅔ cup boiling water for 20 minutes.

COOK'S TIP
Do not pour over the spiced butter until just before serving.

2 Whisk the yogurt and gram flour together until smooth (do this thoroughly, otherwise the yogurt will curdle). Stir in the ginger, garlic, turmeric, chilli powder and salt.

3 Pour the marinade over the chicken. Stir to coat. Cover and leave for 30–35 minutes.

4 Reserve 5ml/1 tsp of ghee or butter and melt the remainder in a pan over a low heat. Add the cinnamon, cardamom, cloves and bay leaves. Let these sizzle until the cardamom pods have puffed up.

5 Add the onion and increase the heat slightly. Sauté for 5 minutes until translucent, then stir in the ground sesame seeds.

6 Add the marinated chicken, increase the heat to medium-high and cook for about 5 minutes until the chicken changes colour. Pour in the coconut milk and 150ml/5fl oz/ ⅔ cup warm water. Bring this to the boil, reduce the heat to low, cover and simmer for 20 minutes or until the chicken is tender.

7 Meanwhile, purée the cashews with the water in which they were soaked and add to the chicken. Simmer, uncovered, for 5–6 minutes, until the sauce thickens.

8 Melt the reserved ghee or butter in a small pan. Add the grated nutmeg and ground mace, then cook gently for about 30 seconds. Pour the spiced butter over the chicken and stir to mix well. Serve with Plain Boiled Rice and Cumin and Saffron-scented Wholemeal Flat Bread.

Per portion Energy 398kcal/1671kJ; Protein 46.4g; Carbohydrate 19.1g, of which sugars 12.5g; Fat 16g, of which saturates 3.8g; Cholesterol 76mg; Calcium 195mg; Fibre 2.1g; Sodium 265mg.

Slow-cooked chicken with basmati rice

Biryani is one of India's most renowned dishes. Often cooked for festivals, it may be served with other dishes, but essentially takes centre stage itself. Biryanis are traditionally flavoured with fragrant spices, but are never overly hot. *Hyderabadi Kaachi Biryani* is considered to be one of the finest versions of this dish, with a subtle blend of spices that intermingle as it is slowly cooked in the oven.

SERVES 4

For the chicken:
100ml/3½floz/scant ½ cup whole-milk
  natural (plain) yogurt
675g/1½lb boneless chicken breasts or
  thighs, or a combination, skinned
large pinch of saffron, pounded
30ml/2 tbsp hot milk
10ml/2 tsp sesame seeds
15ml/1 tbsp white poppy seeds
10ml/2 tsp coriander seeds
½ mace blade
2.5ml/½ tsp black peppercorns
3 green cardamom pods
2.5cm/1in piece of cinnamon stick,
  broken into smaller pieces
3 cloves
2.5ml/½ tsp freshly grated nutmeg
75g/3oz ghee or 30ml/2 tbsp oil and
  30ml/2 tbsp unsalted butter
1 large onion, finely sliced
2.5cm/1in fresh root ginger, grated, or
  10ml/2 tsp ginger purée
2 cloves garlic, crushed, or 10ml/2 tsp
  garlic purée
5ml/1 tsp salt, or to taste

For the rice:
450g/1lb/2 cups basmati rice, washed
  and drained
2 bay leaves
2 x 5cm/2in pieces of cinnamon
  stick, halved
2 star anise
4 cloves
4 green cardamom pods, bruised

1 Whisk the yogurt in a large bowl until it is smooth. Cut the skinned chicken pieces into 5cm/2in chunks and add them to the bowl. Stir well to completely coat the meat with the yogurt. Cover and set aside.

2 Crumble the saffron into a heatproof bowl and pour over the hot milk. Leave to soak while you prepare the rest of the dish.

3 In a small, heavy pan, dry-roast the sesame, poppy and coriander seeds, mace, peppercorns, cardamom pods, cinnamon and cloves over a low-medium heat for about 1 minute.

4 Allow the spices to cool, then grind in a coffee grinder with the nutmeg, until fine.

5 In a heavy pan, large enough to hold the chicken and the rice together, melt the ghee, or oil and butter, over a medium heat. Add the onions and fry for 8–10 minutes, stirring regularly, until lightly browned.

6 Remove half the onion and set aside. Reduce the heat to low and add the ground spices, ginger and garlic. Continue to cook for 2–3 minutes, stirring.

7 Add the chicken pieces and salt. Cook, stirring frequently, for 2 minutes, then add the yogurt and gently mix. Turn off the heat and cover the pan with a lid.

8 Preheat the oven to 180°C/350°F/Gas 4. For the rice, bring a large pan of salted water to the boil and add the bay leaves, cinnamon, star anise, cloves and cardamom pods.

9 Add the rice and let it boil steadily for 2 minutes. Drain the rice without discarding the whole spices, then pile it on top of the chicken. Dot the surface of the rice with the saffron milk, making sure you add any remaining strands of saffron.

10 Soak a piece of greaseproof paper, large enough to sit on top of the rice, in water, then squeeze it out. Place it on top of the rice.

11 Soak a clean dish towel in cold water and wring it out. Place this loosely on top of the greaseproof paper and cover the pan with a piece of foil. Place the pan lid on top.

12 Cook in the centre of the oven for 1 hour. Switch off the oven and leave the biryani for a further 30 minutes.

13 Meanwhile, return the reserved softened onion to a small, heavy frying pan over a medium heat. Cook for 5–6 minutes, stirring regularly, until very soft and a deep golden-brown colour.

14 Transfer the biryani to a warmed serving dish and garnish with the fried onions.

Per portion Energy 832kcal/3507kJ; Protein 49g; Carbohydrate 104g, of which sugars 6g; Fat 29g, of which saturates 15g; Cholesterol 208mg; Calcium 208mg; Fibre 1.4g; Sodium 654mg.

Madras meat curry

The Christian and Muslim communities of Madras (now Chennai) have an excellent range of meat and poultry dishes. Goat or mutton is the natural choice of ingredient for *Attu Erachi Kari,* but lamb on the bone is also ideal for this intensely flavoured dish.

SERVES 4

675g/1½lb boned leg of lamb, fat trimmed
  and cut into 2.5cm/1in cubes
30ml/2 tbsp red wine vinegar
5ml/1 tsp ground turmeric
10ml/2 tsp garlic purée
10ml/2 tsp ginger purée
10ml/2 tsp chilli powder
15ml/1 tbsp tomato purée (paste)
5ml/1 tsp salt, or to taste
5ml/1 tsp black peppercorns
5ml/1 tsp coriander seeds
5ml/1 tsp cumin seeds
2.5ml/½ tsp black mustard seeds
1.25ml/¼ tsp fenugreek seeds
20 curry leaves
25g/1oz/⅓ cup desiccated (dry
  unsweetened shredded) coconut
60ml/4 tbsp sunflower oil or light olive oil
2.5cm/1in piece of cinnamon stick, halved
2 black cardamom pods
4 cloves
1 large onion, finely chopped
Plain Boiled Rice, to serve

1 Put the meat in a large non-metallic bowl and add the vinegar, turmeric, garlic, ginger, chilli powder, tomato purée and salt. Mix thoroughly, cover the bowl with clear film (plastic wrap) and leave to marinate for 4–5 hours.

2 Put the marinated meat into a heavy pan and add 150ml/5fl oz/⅔ cup water.

3 Bring the meat to a slow simmer, cover and cook until the water evaporates. Stir the mixture during cooking so that the meat does not stick to the bottom of the pan.

4 Preheat a small, pan over a low heat. Add the peppercorns, coriander, cumin, mustard and fenugreek seeds, and curry leaves. Stir until the spices release their aroma, then add the coconut. Stir-fry until the coconut is lightly browned. Leave to cool, then grind them in a coffee grinder.

5 Heat the oil over a medium heat and add the cinnamon, cardamom and cloves. Leave to sizzle for 30 seconds, then add the onion and cook for 7 minutes or until brown.

6 Add the ground ingredients and cook, stirring, for 1 minute, then add the cooked meat. Add 150ml/5fl oz/⅔ cup warm water, cover and simmer for 10 minutes. Take the pan off the heat. The sauce should be thick. Serve with Plain Boiled Rice.

Per portion Energy 524kcal/2180kJ; Protein 37.6g; Carbohydrate 13.8g, of which sugars 7.4g; Fat 36g, of which saturates 13.8g; Cholesterol 133mg; Calcium 65mg; Fibre 2.6g; Sodium 160mg.

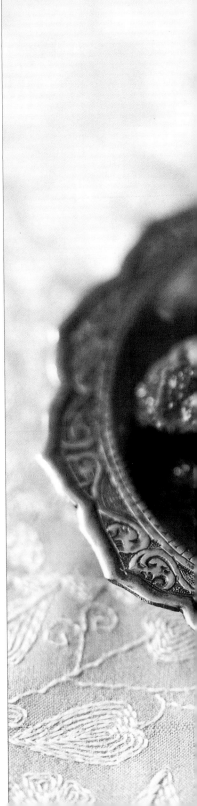

Coorgi lamb curry

Cooked with southern spices, this lamb curry, *Coorgi Gosht Ki Kari*, is deliciously different from the curries served in Indian restaurants in the West. Cumin, coriander, black peppercorns and mustard seeds are roasted and mixed with vinegar to add a sharp yet subtle flavour.

SERVES 4

675g/1½lb boned leg or shoulder of lamb
45ml/3 tbsp sunflower oil or light olive oil
2.5cm/1in piece of cinnamon stick
3 brown cardamom pods, bruised
4 cloves
2 bay leaves
4cm/1½in fresh root ginger, grated, or
    15ml/1 tbsp ginger purée
3 cloves garlic, crushed, or 15ml/1 tbsp
    garlic purée
2.5ml/½ tsp ground turmeric
2.5–5ml/½–1 tsp chilli powder
5ml/1 tsp salt, or to taste
15ml/1 tbsp coriander seeds
10ml/2 tsp cumin seeds
2.5ml/½ tsp mustard seeds
5ml/1 tsp black peppercorns
30ml/2 tbsp red wine vinegar
45ml/3 tbsp creamed coconut, roughly
    chopped, or coconut cream
toasted flaked coconut, to garnish
warm Indian bread or Plain Boiled Rice,
    to serve

1 Trim off any excess fat from the lamb and cut it into 2.5cm/1in cubes.

2 In a heavy pan, heat the oil over a low heat and add the cinnamon, cardamom pods, cloves and bay leaves.

3 Let them sizzle gently for 30 seconds, then add the ginger and garlic.

4 Cook the ginger and garlic for a minute, then stir in the turmeric and chilli powder.

5 Add the meat and increase the heat to medium-high. Stir and cook for 5 minutes, turning the pieces over with tongs, until the meat has changed colour.

6 Stir in the salt, pour in 250ml/8floz/1 cup hot water and bring to the boil. Reduce the heat to low, cover the pan and cook gently for 30 minutes.

7 Meanwhile, in a small, heavy pan, dry-roast the coriander, cumin and mustard seeds and the peppercorns for 1 minute, until the seeds begin to crackle. Leave to cool, then grind in a coffee grinder.

8 Transfer the spices to a bowl and stir in the vinegar to make a paste. Add the spice paste to the meat. Stir well, cover the pan with a lid and simmer for 15–20 minutes, or until the meat is tender.

9 Add the creamed coconut or coconut cream and stir until the creamed coconut has dissolved. Simmer, uncovered, for 6–8 minutes or until the sauce has thickened.

10 Serve garnished with the flaked coconut and accompanied by any warm Indian bread or Plain Boiled Rice.

Per portion Energy 397kcal/1649kJ; Protein 35g; Carbohydrate 1g, of which sugars 1g; Fat 29g, of which saturates 5g; Cholesterol 127mg; Calcium 32mg; Fibre 0.0g; Sodium 602mg.

Minced lamb pilau

This quick and easy pilau, *Tahari*, is traditionally made with minced (ground) mutton or lamb, but beef can also be used to ring the changes without altering the complex combination of spices. Colourful, nutritious and packed with flavour, it makes a great dinner party dish and can be easily scaled up to feed a crowd.

SERVES 4

For the minced meat:
500g/1¼lb lean minced (ground) lamb
50g/2oz/¼ cup natural (plain) yogurt
45ml/3 tbsp sunflower oil or olive oil
1 large onion, finely sliced
10ml/2 tsp ginger purée
10ml/2 tsp garlic purée
2 fresh green chillies, finely chopped
5ml/1 tsp ground cumin
7.5ml/1½ tsp ground coriander
2.5ml/½ tsp ground turmeric
2.5ml/½ tsp salt, or to taste
2.5ml/½ tsp garam masala
75ml/3fl oz/5 tbsp single (light) cream

For the rice:
250g/9oz/1¼ cups basmati rice, washed
  and soaked for 20 minutes
pinch of saffron threads, pounded
10ml/2 tbsp hot milk
25g/1oz/2 tbsp ghee or unsalted butter
2.5cm/1in piece of cinnamon stick
5 cardamom pods, bruised
4 cloves
2 star anise
2 bay leaves
5ml/1 tsp salt, or to taste
2 hard-boiled eggs, quartered,
  to garnish

1 In a non-stick pan, cook the minced lamb over medium to high heat until the juices evaporate and the lamb is beginning to brown. Add the yogurt and cook over a low heat for 2–3 minutes, then remove from the heat and set aside.

2 Heat the oil over a medium heat and add the sliced onion. Stir-fry for about 5 minutes, until the onion is well browned. Add the ginger, garlic and chillies, and stir-fry for 2 minutes, then add the cumin, coriander and turmeric.

3 Stir-fry for an additional 30 seconds, then add the browned meat and 150ml/5fl oz/ ⅔ cup of warm water.

4 Cook for 2–3 minutes, then add the salt, garam masala and cream. Cook for a further 2–3 minutes, then remove from the heat and keep warm.

5 Drain the rice in a colander. Soak the saffron strands in the hot milk in a bowl.

6 For the rice, melt the ghee or butter over a low heat. Add the cinnamon, cardamom, cloves, star anise and bay leaves. Stir-fry until the cardamom pods have puffed up.

7 Add the drained rice and salt to the pan, stir to mix and pour in 550ml/18fl oz/2½ cups hot water. Bring back to the boil and boil steadily for 2 minutes, until the surface water has almost evaporated.

8 Reduce the heat to low and sprinkle the saffron milk randomly over the surface.

9 Spread the spiced minced meat on top, making sure you cover all the grains of rice. Cover and cook for 6–7 minutes, keeping the heat as low as possible. Remove the pan from the heat and let the pilau stand undisturbed for 15 minutes.

10 Gently stir with a metal spoon to mix the spiced minced meat and rice, transfer to a serving dish and garnish with the quartered hard-boiled eggs.

Per portion Energy 609kcal/2544kJ; Protein 24.4g; Carbohydrate 79.6g, of which sugars 18.2g; Fat 21.5g, of which saturates 5.5g; Cholesterol 57mg; Calcium 70.2mg; Fibre 3.4g; Sodium 156mg.

Chickpea pilau

Basmati rice cooks to perfect, separate, fluffy grains and is considered by many to be the finest rice. In this pilau, *Kabooli*, the rice is subtly spiced with cinnamon, cardamom and cloves and combined with nutty chickpeas, fresh coriander (cilantro) and mint. Serve with a raita or a vegetable curry for a healthy meal.

SERVES 4

225g/8oz/1 cup basmati rice
50g/2oz/¼ cup ghee or unsalted butter
1 large onion, finely sliced
2.5cm/1in piece cinnamon stick
6 green cardamom pods, bruised
6 cloves
10–12 black peppercorns
5ml/1 tsp ground coriander
2.5ml/½ tsp ground cumin
2.5ml/½ tsp chilli powder
2.5ml/½ tsp ground turmeric
2 tomatoes, chopped
400g/14oz/large can chickpeas, drained
  and rinsed
5ml/1 tsp salt, or to taste
30ml/2 tbsp finely chopped fresh
  coriander (cilantro)
15ml/1 tbsp finely shredded
  fresh mint
raita, to serve

1 Wash the rice in several changes of water. Transfer to a large bowl, cover with more cold water and leave to soak for about 20 minutes. Drain.

2 Melt the ghee or butter in a heavy frying pan over a low-medium heat. Add the onion and fry for 6 minutes, until well browned, stirring frequently. Remove from the pan with a slotted spoon, leaving as much oil as possible behind in the pan. Set aside.

3 Add the cinnamon, cardamom, cloves and black peppercorbs to the pan, cook for 30 seconds, then stir in the coriander, cumin, chilli powder and turmeric.

4 Cook for about 1 minute, then add the tomatoes, chickpeas, rice and salt. Stir, then pour in 550ml/18floz/2½ cups hot water. Bring to the boil and let it cook, uncovered, for 2 minutes.

5 Reduce the heat to low, cover, and cook for 9–10 minutes. Switch off the heat. Let the pan stand undisturbed for 10–15 minutes.

6 Add the fresh coriander and mint, and fluff up the rice with a fork. Transfer to a serving dish, garnish with the fried onion and serve with raita or a vegetable curry.

Per portion Energy 434kcal/1829kJ; Protein 11g; Carbohydrate 66g, of which sugars 5g; Fat 16g, of which saturates 9g; Cholesterol 35mg; Calcium 71mg; Fibre 1.5g; Sodium 509mg.

Pilau rice with coconut and coriander pesto

A fabulous flavour triangle is created when fresh coriander (cilantro), mint leaves and green chillies combine in this sumptuous pilau, *Chatni Pulao*, which can be a vegetarian meal in itself when served with a raita. The pesto sauce used here is not dissimilar to the Italian version, although the Indian recipe does not contain pine nuts, and includes coconut to add richness.

SERVES 4

225g/8oz/generous 1 cup basmati rice
25g/1oz/⅓ cup desiccated (dry unsweetened shredded) coconut
3 garlic cloves, roughly chopped
2.5cm/1in piece of fresh root ginger, roughly chopped
15g/½oz fresh coriander (cilantro) leaves and stalks, roughly chopped
15g/½oz fresh mint leaves and stalks, roughly chopped
1–2 fresh green chillies, roughly chopped (deseeded if preferred)
50g/2oz/4 tbsp ghee, or 25g/1oz/2 tbsp unsalted butter and 30ml/2 tbsp sunflower oil or light olive oil
25g/1oz raw cashew nuts
2.5cm/1in piece of cinnamon stick
4 cardamom pods, bruised
4 cloves
1 medium onion, finely sliced
75g/3oz/½ cup green beans, cut into 2.5cm/1in pieces
75g/3oz/½ cup peas, frozen and thawed, or pre-cooked fresh ones
5ml/1 tsp salt, or to taste

1 Wash the rice in a sieve (strainer) in several changes of water until it runs clear, then soak in a bowl of cold water for 20–30 minutes. Drain and set aside.

2 Put the coconut in a large heatproof bowl, then pour over 150ml/5fl oz/⅔ cup boiling water. Leave to soak for 10 minutes.

3 Transfer the rehydrated coconut to a blender or food processor with the water in which it was soaked. Add the garlic, ginger, coriander, mint and chillies, and blend until smooth. Alternatively, you can pound the ingredients to a smooth paste using a large mortar and pestle. Set aside.

4 Melt the ghee or butter and oil in a heavy pan over a low heat. Add the cashew nuts and stir-fry for about 2 minutes, until browned. Take care not to let them burn. Drain on kitchen paper.

5 In the same pan, stir-fry the cinnamon, cardamom and cloves for 30 seconds.

6 Add the onion to the pan, increase the heat to medium and fry the onions for about 10 minutes, until they are golden brown, stirring regularly.

7 Add the drained rice, stir to combine and cook for 1–2 minutes.

8 Add the ground coconut mixture. Stir-fry for 2–3 minutes.

9 Add the beans, peas and salt. Pour in 450ml/16fl oz/scant 2 cups warm water, bring to the boil, cover and reduce the heat to low.

10 Cook for 8–9 minutes without lifting the lid and then switch off the heat. Let the pan stand undisturbed for 10 minutes, fluff up the rice with a fork and serve.

Per portion Energy 418kcal/1736kJ; Protein 8.2g; Carbohydrate 56g, of which sugars 5.8g; Fat 18g, of which saturates 9.4g; Cholesterol 0mg; Calcium 76mg; Fibre 3.8g; Sodium 10mg.

Lemon-laced rice

Naranga Choru is very popular all over India. Its mild flavour makes it a good accompaniment to any spicy curry and it makes a change from plain basmati rice. The dish also looks beautiful, with a pale yellow background providing the perfect foil for black mustard seeds, curry leaves and roasted cashew nuts. The cashew nuts add both flavour and texture, and the crunch adds an extra dimension to the rice.

SERVES 4

225g/8oz/1¼ cups basmati rice
10ml/2 tbsp sunflower oil or olive oil
2.5ml/½ tsp black mustard seeds
10–12 curry leaves
25g/1oz cashew nuts, broken
2.5ml/½ tsp ground turmeric
5ml/1 tsp salt, or to taste
30ml/2 tbsp lemon juice

1 Wash and rinse the rice two or three times in cold water, or until the water runs clear. Soak for 15–20 minutes, then rinse and drain it in a sieve. Heat the oil in a non-stick pan over a medium heat.

2 When the oil is hot, add the mustard seeds, curry leaves and cashew nuts. Let them sizzle for 15–20 seconds.

3 Add the rice, turmeric and salt to the pan. Stir-fry for 2–3 minutes, then add 475ml/16fl oz/2 cups hot water and the lemon juice. Stir once, bring to the boil and continue to boil for about 2 minutes. Cover the pan tightly, reduce the heat and simmer gently for an additional 7–8 minutes.

4 Remove the pan from the heat and leave to stand, for 6–7 minutes. Fork through and serve as an accompaniment to any curry.

Per portion Energy 345kcal/1440kJ; Protein 6.9g; Carbohydrate 57.4g, of which sugars 0.4g; Fat 9.5g, of which saturates 1.4g; Cholesterol 0mg; Calcium 22mg; Fibre 0.2g; Sodium 20mg.

Turmeric-tinged rice with fried onion

Originating in the state of Karnataka, *Birinji* is a fairly uncomplicated rice dish comprising fragrant spiced rice and sweet caramelized onions. Southern Indians thrive on rice, unlike the people in the north, where the staple is bread. This rice recipe is ideal with any vegetable curry or lentil dish.

SERVES 4

225g/8oz/generous 1 cup basmati rice
45ml/3 tbsp sunflower oil or light olive oil
4 green cardamom pods, bruised
4 cloves
2.5cm/1in piece of cinnamon stick
5ml/1 tsp ground turmeric
5ml/1 tsp salt, or to taste
1 large onion, finely sliced
2.5cm/1in piece of fresh root ginger,
   finely grated
2 cloves garlic, crushed
2–3 fresh green chillies, sliced at
   an angle

1 Wash the rice in a sieve (strainer) in several changes of water, until the water runs clear, then soak in a bowl of water for 20–30 minutes. Drain and set aside.

2 Heat 15ml/1 tbsp of the oil over a low heat in a heavy pan. Add the cardamom, cloves and cinnamon and let them sizzle for 15–20 seconds.

3 Stir in the turmeric and immediately follow with the drained rice. Stir-fry the rice for 2–3 minutes, then pour in 450ml/¾ pint/ scant 2 cups lukewarm water.

4 Add the salt and bring the water to the boil. Reduce the heat to very low, cover the pan with a lid and cook very gently for 8–9 minutes.

5 Meanwhile, heat the remaining oil in a separate pan over a medium heat. Add the onion, ginger, garlic and chillies. Fry for 9–10 minutes, until the onion is caramel-brown, stirring regularly.

6 When the rice is cooked, switch off the heat and allow it to stand undisturbed for 10 minutes. Stir in the fried onion and serve.

Per portion Energy 307kcal/1290kJ; Protein 4g; Carbohydrate 49g, of which sugars 0g; Fat 12g, of which saturates 1g; Cholesterol 0mg; Calcium 15mg; Fibre 1.2g; Sodium 497mg.

Coconut rice

This snow-white basmati rice dish, speckled with black mustard seeds and dotted with red chilli pieces, looks quite stunning, and it tastes as good as it looks. *Thengai Sadam* is best served with a simple lentil dish or a vegetable curry, as it is quite rich and very flavoursome.

SERVES 4

225g/8oz/generous 1 cup basmati rice
5ml/1 tsp salt, or to taste
50g/2oz/⅔ cup desiccated (dry unsweetened shredded) coconut
125ml/4fl oz/½ cup milk
30ml/2 tbsp sunflower oil or light olive oil
50g/2oz/½ cup raw cashew nuts
2.5ml/½ tsp black mustard seeds
15ml/1 tbsp split Bengal gram (channa dhal or skinless split chickpeas)
2–3 dried red chillies
8–10 curry leaves

1 Wash the rice until the water runs clear. Transfer to a bowl, cover with cold water and leave to soak for 20 minutes, then leave to drain in a sieve (strainer).

2 Put the rice into a heavy pan. Pour in 450ml/16fl oz/scant 2 cups hot water. Stir in the salt and bring it to the boil. Let it boil for 2 minutes, then turn the heat down to very low, cover and cook for 8 minutes. Remove from the heat and let the pan stand undisturbed for 8–10 minutes.

3 Meanwhile, put the coconut into a small pan and add the milk. Stir over a low-medium heat for about 5 minutes, until the coconut has absorbed all the milk.

4 Heat the oil in a small pan over a low heat and brown the cashew nuts. Drain on kitchen paper.

5 In the same pan, increase the heat to medium and, when the oil is hot but not smoking, add the mustard seeds, split Bengal gram, chillies and curry leaves. Cook until the chillies blacken slightly.

6 Pour the entire contents of the pan over the cooked rice and add the coconut and cashew nuts. Gently mix with a fork to fluff up the rice and combine the ingredients, then serve.

Per portion Energy 436kcal/1813kJ; Protein 9.3g; Carbohydrate 51.7g, of which sugars 3.1g; Fat 21.2g, of which saturates 9.4g; Cholesterol 4mg; Calcium 56mg; Fibre 2.3g; Sodium 58mg.

Butter-drenched milk breads

These flat breads, *Roghani Roti*, are very rich and so delicious! As the name suggests, they are flavoured with butter, which also gives them a lovely golden colour, and the dough is mixed together with cream. Traditionally made with wholemeal (whole-wheat) flour, you can use white flour if you prefer.

3 Pour the cream into the hollow with 120ml/4floz/½ cup warm water and the saffron milk.

4 Mix together to a dough, then knead on a lightly floured surface for 5–6 minutes until smooth. Cover with clear film (plastic wrap) and leave to rest for 20–30 minutes.

5 Divide the dough into ten equal pieces and shape into balls. Flatten each into a disc between the palms of your hands, then cover with a slightly damp dish towel to prevent them drying out.

6 Dust each of the dough balls lightly in flour and roll out to a circle about 15cm/6in in diameter, using a rolling pin.

MAKES 10

pinch of saffron, pounded
30ml/2 tbsp hot milk
450g/1lb/4 cups wholemeal (whole-wheat) flour, plus extra for dusting
5ml/1 tsp salt, or to taste
50g/2oz/¼ cup butter
150ml/¼ pint/⅔ cup single (light) cream
vegetable oil, for brushing

1 Crumble the saffron into a small bowl, pour over the hot milk and leave to soak for 15–20 minutes.

2 Sift the flour and salt into a large bowl, adding any bran left in the sieve. Rub in the butter with your fingers and thumbs until the mixture resembles fine breadcrumbs. Make a hollow in the middle.

7 Heat a heavy griddle or large, shallow frying pan over a medium heat. When hot, place one of the breads on it and cook for 30–40 seconds. Turn it over, brush generously with oil and turn it over again. Cook for a further 30–40 seconds, until brown patches appear on the underside.

8 Brush the uncooked side of the bread with some oil, turn the bread over and cook for about 60–90 seconds, until brown patches appear and the bread is cooked through.

9 Keep the cooked breads hot by wrapping in foil lined with kitchen paper, while cooking the remaining breads.

Per portion Energy 275kcal/1150kJ; Protein 6g; Carbohydrate 29g, of which sugars 1g; Fat 16g, of which saturates 5g; Cholesterol 19mg; Calcium 35mg; Fibre 4.1g; Sodium 234mg.

Fresh green chillies in coconut sauce

Mirchi Ka Salan is one of the signature dishes of Hyderabad. It is usually made with whole fresh green chillies, which are gently cooked then added to a fragrant spiced sauce. You can use milder red chillies or mini sweet (bell) peppers, which are often available at Asian stores, if you prefer.

SERVES 4

400g/14oz whole fresh green chillies or
  mini sweet (bell) peppers
15ml/1 tbsp sesame seeds
15ml/1 tbsp white poppy seeds
5ml/1 tsp coriander seeds
2–3 dried red chillies, cut into small pieces
25g/1oz desiccated (dry unsweetened
  shredded) coconut
30ml/2 tbsp sunflower oil or light olive oil
5ml/1 tsp cumin seeds
5ml/1 tsp ginger purée
1 clove garlic, crushed, or 5ml/1 tsp garlic
  purée
2.5ml/½ tsp ground turmeric
2.5ml/½ tsp salt, or to taste
2.5ml/½ tsp caster (superfine) sugar
50g/2oz roasted, salted peanuts, crushed
30ml/2 tbsp tamarind juice or lemon juice
a biryani or pilau dish, to serve

1 Bring a pan of lightly salted water to the boil. Trim the chillies or mini peppers, add to the pan and simmer for 5 minutes. Drain, then plunge into cold water to prevent further cooking. Drain again.

2 In a small, heavy pan, dry-roast the sesame, poppy and coriander seeds and the dried chillies for 30 seconds.

3 Add the coconut. Continue to roast, stirring, until the ingredients are a shade darker. Cool, then grind in a coffee grinder until fine-textured.

4 Heat the oil in a heavy frying pan over a medium heat and add the cumin seeds. Let them sizzle for about 30 seconds, then add the ginger and garlic. Fry until they begin to brown, then add the turmeric and the ground spices. Cook for 30 seconds.

5 Add the chillies or peppers to the pan with the salt, sugar and 250ml/8floz/1 cup warm water. Bring to the boil, cover and simmer for 10 minutes.

6 Remove the lid, add the crushed peanuts and cook for 3–4 minutes, until the sauce thickens slightly.

7 Stir in the tamarind or lemon juice, remove the pan from the heat and transfer to a serving dish. Serve immediately with a biryani or pilau dish.

Per portion Energy 251kcal/1039kJ; Protein 7g; Carbohydrate 12g, of which sugars 11g; Fat 22g, of which saturates 6g; Cholesterol 0mg; Calcium 112mg; Fibre 1.9g; Sodium 313mg.

Tamarind-laced vegetables in coconut sauce

The wonderful hot, creamy and sour flavours in this vegetarian main course, *Avial*, make it very popular in southern India, where it is normally served with rice. Any combination of vegetables – peas, beans, cauliflower and other green vegetables – works very well.

SERVES 4

125g/4½oz green beans, cut into
  2.5cm/1in lengths
200g/7oz carrots, cut into 1cm/½in thick circles
225g/8oz potatoes, cut into 2.5cm/1in cubes
1 small aubergine (eggplant), quartered
  lengthways and cut into 2.5cm/1in pieces
2.5ml/½ tsp ground turmeric
5ml/1 tsp salt, or to taste
200g/7oz cauliflower, divided into
  1cm/½in florets
10ml/2 tsp cumin seeds
50g/2oz/⅔ cup desiccated (dry
  unsweetened shredded) coconut
2–3 fresh green chillies, chopped
200ml/7fl oz/¾ cup buttermilk
10ml/2 tbsp tamarind or lemon juice
10ml/2 tbsp sunflower oil or olive oil
2.5ml/½ tsp black mustard seeds
2.5ml/½ tsp cumin seeds
2–3 whole dried red chillies
6–8 curry leaves
1.25ml/¼ tsp asafoetida
15ml/1 tbsp fresh coriander (cilantro),
  chopped
Plain Boiled Rice, to serve

1 Put the green beans, carrots, potatoes and aubergine into a large pan and add 350ml/12fl oz/1½ cups hot water. Add the turmeric and salt. Bring to the boil, reduce the heat to low and cover the pan. Cook for 5–6 minutes, then add the cauliflower. Cover.

2 Cook for 5 minutes, until everything apart from the aubergine is tender but firm.

3 Meanwhile, heat a small, heavy pan over a medium heat. Dry-roast the cumin seeds for 30–40 seconds. Remove from the heat and dry-roast the coconut and green chillies until the coconut is lightly browned.

4 Leave to cool slightly, then grind in a coffee grinder or blender until fine-textured.

5 Add the ground roasted ingredients, buttermilk and tamarind or lemon juice to the vegetables. Cook gently for 4–5 minutes, then remove from the heat.

6 Heat the oil in a small pan over a medium heat. When it is hot, but not smoking, add the black mustard seeds, followed by the cumin seeds, dried red chillies, curry leaves and asafoetida.

7 Cook for 3–4 minutes, until the chillies are blackened, then pour the entire contents of the pan over the vegetables. Stir in the chopped coriander and remove the pan from the heat. Let the curry stand, covered, for 5–6 minutes. Serve with Plain Boiled Rice.

Per portion Energy 252kcal/1050kJ; Protein 7.55g; Carbohydrate 22.5g, of which sugars 10.7g; Fat 15.5g, of which saturates 7.7g; Cholesterol 1.75mg; Calcium 119mg; Fibre 6.1g; Sodium 57mg.

Green beans with mustard, curry leaf and coconut

In Kerala, *thoren* is a very popular side dish, and it simply means stir-fried finely chopped or shredded vegetables cooked in a spice-perfumed oil. The fresh colours of the vegetables in this version, *Payaru Thoren*, along with all their nutrients, are preserved because of the quick-cooking method.

SERVES 4

450g/1lb whole green beans, fresh
  or frozen
30ml/2 tbsp sunflower oil or light olive oil
2.5ml/½ tsp black or brown mustard seeds
2.5ml/½ tsp cumin seeds
1 dried red chilli, snipped
8–10 curry leaves, fresh or dried
2.5ml/½ tsp salt, or to taste
15ml/1 tbsp desiccated (dry unsweetened
  shredded) coconut

1 Trim the beans, then blanch them in a large pan of lightly salted boiling water for 2 minutes.

2 Drain the beans, then plunge them immediately into cold water to prevent further cooking. If you are using frozen beans, it is not necessary to blanch them.

3 Heat the oil in a frying pan over a medium heat. When hot, but not smoking, add the mustard seeds.

4 As soon as the seeds start popping, add the cumin, chillies and curry leaves.

5 Allow the chillies to blacken slightly, then add the blanched beans and the salt. Stir-fry for 2–3 minutes, then cover the pan tightly and reduce the heat to low.

6 Cook the beans in their own juices for 10–12 minutes, until tender, but still firm. Stir the beans once or twice during the cooking time.

7 Add the coconut, mix well and remove from the heat. Serve immediately.

Per portion Energy 118kcal/487kJ; Protein 3g; Carbohydrate 4g, of which sugars 3g; Fat 11g, of which saturates 3g; Cholesterol 0mg; Calcium 52mg; Fibre 4.2g; Sodium 248mg.

Potatoes in coconut milk with garlic-infused butter

These potatoes, *Batata Ghashi*, are so fabulously tasty that you won't believe how simple they are to make. The only thing to remember is that you will need to pre-boil the potatoes in their skins and leave to cool completely before adding them to the sauce. Serve with flat bread for scooping up the juices.

SERVES 4

500g/1lb 2oz waxy potatoes
30ml/2 tbsp sunflower oil or light olive oil
30ml/2 tbsp ground coriander
2.5ml/½ tsp ground turmeric
2.5–5ml/½–1 tsp chilli powder
400ml/14fl oz/1½ cups canned coconut milk
5ml/1 tsp salt, or to taste
22.5ml/1½ tbsp tamarind juice or lime juice
15ml/1 tbsp ghee or unsalted butter
4–5 large garlic cloves, crushed
flat bread, to serve

1 Boil the potatoes in their skins. Cool and peel them, then cut into 2.5cm/1in cubes.

2 Heat the oil over a low heat and add the coriander, turmeric and chilli powder. Stir and cook for about 1 minute.

3 Add the potatoes, coconut milk and salt. Stir well and bring to a slow simmer. Cook for 6–8 minutes. Add the tamarind or lime juice.

4 Meanwhile, melt the ghee or butter over a low heat and add the garlic. Fry until it is lightly browned but do not allow it to darken.

5 Stir the garlic butter mixture into the potatoes, remove from the heat and serve immediately with any flat bread.

Per portion Energy 207kcal/870kJ; Protein 3.2g; Carbohydrate 26.8g, of which sugars 6.5g; Fat 10.6g, of which saturates 2.9g; Cholesterol 0mg; Calcium 46mg; Fibre 1.3g; Sodium 617mg.

Mung beans with ginger, chilli and lime

Mung beans (whole moong dhal) are available in many larger supermarkets and health food stores. Traditionally, they are soaked and sprouted before cooking. The sprouted beans are a good source of vitamin C. Unsprouted ones are equally delicious, and they are served raw as a snack, topped with chopped onion, Bombay Mix and a dash of lime juice or, as in this recipe U*sal*, cooked with aromatics to create a side dish.

SERVES 4
175g/6oz mung beans (whole
  moong dhal)
30ml/2 tbsp sunflower oil or light
  olive oil
2.5ml/½ tsp black or brown
  mustard seeds
1 large onion, finely chopped
2.5cm/1in piece of fresh root ginger,
  finely grated
2 fresh red chillies, sliced at an angle
5ml/1 tsp ground turmeric
2.5ml/½ tsp salt, or to taste
juice of 1 lime
a vegetable curry, to serve

1 Wash the mung beans in a sieve (strainer), then soak them in a bowl of cold water for 4–5 hours. Drain, then put them in a pan and add 300ml/½ pint/1¼ cups water.

2 Place over a high heat and bring to the boil. Reduce the heat to low, partially cover the pan and cook for 6–7 minutes, until the froth settles down.

3 Reduce the heat to low, cover and simmer for 15–17 minutes. The beans should be tender by now and most of the water will have been absorbed. Remove from the heat and keep hot.

4 Heat the oil in a frying pan over a high heat until smoking point is reached. Switch off the heat and add the mustard seeds, followed by the onion, ginger and chillies.

5 Turn the heat on to medium and fry the onion for 6–8 minutes, until it begins to colour. Add the turmeric and continue to cook for a further 1 minute.

6 Add the onion mixture to the lentils along with the salt and lime juice. Stir, transfer to a serving dish and serve with a vegetable curry.

Per portion Energy 106kcal/437kJ; Protein 2g; Carbohydrate 7g, of which sugars 8g; Fat 5g, of which saturates 1g; Cholesterol 0mg; Calcium 29mg; Fibre 3.4g; Sodium 251mg.

Crisp-fried okra in spicy yogurt dressing

Okra is an acquired taste, or rather texture, but is a very popular vegetable all over India and is cooked in many ways. Quick-cooking it, using a stir-frying or deep-frying method, retains its glutinous nature. This recipe, *Bhindi Pachadi*, includes a yogurt dressing, but you can also serve the deep-fried okra on its own as a side dish, sprinkled with salt, chilli and cumin.

SERVES 4–6

5ml/1 tsp coriander seeds
5ml/1 tsp cumin seeds
1 dried red chilli, snipped
225g/8oz/1 cup full-fat (whole) natural
  (plain) yogurt
2.5ml/½ tsp sugar
225g/8oz okra, cut into discs about
  3mm/⅛in thick
2.5ml/½ tsp salt, or to taste
2.5ml/½ tsp ground turmeric
sunflower oil for deep-frying

4 Mix the okra with the salt and turmeric in a small bowl. Heat the oil in a wok until the surface starts to sizzle.

5 Add the okra to the pan in batches and fry for 2–3 minutes, until crisp and golden brown. Lift out with a slotted spoon and drain on kitchen paper. Repeat with the remaining okra.

6 Just before serving, add the fried okra to the spiced yogurt and mix well. Sprinkle the reserved spices on top and serve.

1 Dry-roast the coriander, cumin and chilli for 1 minute, until they release their aroma.

2 Remove the spices from the pan and leave to cool, then crush them finely with a mortar and pestle or a rolling pin.

3 Beat the sugar into the yogurt. Reserve a little of the ground spices and add the rest to the yogurt. Cover with clear film (plastic wrap) and refrigerate until required.

Per portion Energy 106kcal/438kJ; Protein 3g; Carbohydrate 3g, of which sugars 3g; Fat 10g, of which saturates 2g; Cholesterol 5mg; Calcium 116mg; Fibre 1.7g; Sodium 184mg.

Pineapple salad

Golden pineapple cubes coated with coconut and yogurt and tempered with mustard, chilli and curry leaves make a delightful side dish. Although usually served as an accompaniment, *Pachadi* can be enjoyed as a wonderfully fragrant main dish when served with some boiled rice.

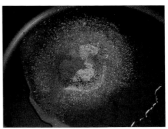

4 In a small, non-stick pan or a steel ladle, heat the oil over a medium heat. When the oil is hot, but not smoking, add the mustard seeds, followed by the green chilli and curry leaves. Allow the seeds to crackle for about 30 seconds.

SERVES 4

1 small pineapple
2.5ml/½ tsp ground turmeric
5ml/1 tsp salt, or to taste
25g/1oz/2 tbsp white sugar
25g/1oz/⅓ cup desiccated (dry unsweetened shredded) coconut
50g/2oz/¼ cup natural (plain) yogurt
30ml/2 tbsp sunflower oil or light olive oil
2.5ml/½ tsp black mustard seeds
1 fresh green chilli, finely chopped
8–10 curry leaves, fresh or dried
curry and rice, to serve

1 Remove the base from the pineapple, then stand it on its end and slice down the skin to remove it. Remove the eyes and cut the flesh into quarters. Remove the central core, then cut the flesh into 1cm/½in wedges.

2 Put the pineapple into a pan with the turmeric, salt and sugar. Add 400ml/14fl oz/1½ cups water, cover and cook over a medium heat for 12–15 minutes, until the pineapple is tender. Leave to cool.

3 Grind the coconut in a coffee grinder. Add to the pineapple with the yogurt.

5 Add to the pineapple mix and serve with any curry and some rice.

Per portion Energy 190kcal/796kJ; Protein 7.2g; Carbohydrate 21.3g, of which sugars 5.5g; Fat 9.3g, of which saturates 1.4g; Cholesterol 0mg; Calcium 161mg; Fibre 3.4g; Sodium 45mg.

Coconut chutney

In traditional Tamil Nadu style, this chutney, *Thengai Thuvaiyal*, is fiery hot. Through the pungency of the heat, you can savour the wonderful flavour and mellow taste of the chillies, with the sweet undertone of coconut and the distinctive tang of tamarind. A real explosion of flavours in your mouth!

SERVES 4–5

75g/3oz/1 cup desiccated (dry
   unsweetened shredded) coconut
1–2 fresh green chillies, chopped
   (deseeded if preferred)
2.5ml/½ tsp salt, or to taste
2.5ml/½ tsp sugar
15ml/1 tbsp natural (plain) yogurt
1cm/½in piece of fresh root ginger,
   roughly chopped
22.5ml/1½ tbsp tamarind juice or lime juice
15ml/1 tbsp sunflower oil or light olive oil
2.5ml/½ tsp black mustard seeds
6–8 curry leaves
1 dried red chilli, chopped

3 Heat the oil in a small wok or a steel ladle over a medium heat. When hot, but not smoking, add the mustard seeds, followed by the curry leaves and red chilli.

4 Allow the seeds to crackle and the chilli to blacken slightly, then switch off the heat. Pour the entire mixture over the chutney. Mix well and serve at room temperature.

1 Put the coconut in a bowl and pour in enough boiling water to just cover it. Set aside for 15–20 minutes.

2 Transfer the coconut to a blender and add the chillies, salt, sugar, yogurt, ginger and tamarind or lime juice. Blend until the ingredients are mixed to a smooth purée, then transfer to a serving bowl.

Per portion Energy 133kcal/548kJ; Protein 1.9g; Carbohydrate 4.1g, of which sugars 2g; Fat 12.3g, of which saturates 8.4g; Cholesterol 0mg; Calcium 20mg; Fibre 2.1g; Sodium 9mg.

Steamed rice cakes

These lovely rice cakes are popular all over the southern states of India, and are usually served with Lentil, Tomato and Aubergine Curry. Two types of Idlis are made: one type uses a fermented rice and lentil mixture, and is rather time-consuming to prepare; the other version, as here, uses semolina to make the cakes, which are then steamed in *idli* moulds. You can also use an egg poacher and a steamer.

MAKES 18
275g/10oz/1½ cups semolina
5ml/1 tsp baking powder
2.5ml/½ tsp bicarbonate of soda
  (baking soda)
2.5ml/½ tsp crushed dried chillies
1.25ml/½ tsp salt, or to taste
400ml/14fl oz/1⅔ cups soda water
275g/10oz/1¼ cups thick set natural
  (plain) yogurt

COOK'S TIP
These rice cakes should be eaten fresh from the steamer.

1 Place the semolina, baking powder, bicarbonate of soda, crushed dried chillies and salt in a large mixing bowl and mix together well with a wooden spoon to thoroughly combine.

2 Gradually add the soda water and mix thoroughly. Beat the yogurt until smooth and add it to the semolina mixture. Whisk until you have a smooth, thick paste.

3 Brush the egg poachers with oil, then place 22.5ml/1½ tbsp of the mixture into each. Steam for about 10 minutes.

4 Ease the rice cakes away from the egg poachers and keep them warm while you steam the remaining cakes in the same way.

Per portion Energy 62kcal/264kJ; Protein 2.4g; Carbohydrate 13g, of which sugars 1.1g; Fat 0.4g, of which saturates 0.1g; Cholesterol 0mg; Calcium 32mg; Fibre 0.3g; Sodium 15mg.

Semolina pancakes with buttermilk

Suji Ki Roti are fairly thick pancakes, which combine the fabulous flavours of finely chopped onion, green chilli, coriander (cilantro) leaves and the musky scent of root ginger. The batter is made with buttermilk or diluted yogurt, making it a healthy choice when served alongside an egg dish. This is often eaten with South Indian Scrambled Eggs, but the pancakes are also delicious on their own.

MAKES 12

300g/10½oz/scant 2 cups semolina
5ml/1 tsp salt, or to taste
2.5ml/½ tsp bicarbonate of soda
  (baking soda)
5ml/1 tsp cumin seeds
1 small onion, finely chopped
1cm/½in piece of fresh root ginger, grated
2 fresh red chillies, finely chopped
  (deseeded if preferred)
30ml/2 tbsp fresh coriander (cilantro)
  leaves, finely chopped
400ml/14fl oz/1⅔ cups buttermilk, or 150g/
  5oz/generous ½ cup natural (plain) yogurt
  blended with 300ml/½ pint/1½ cups water
sunflower oil or light olive oil,
  for shallow-frying
South Indian Scrambled Eggs, to serve

1 Place the semolina, salt, bicarbonate of soda and cumin seeds in a large mixing bowl and stir to combine.

2 Add the remaining ingredients, except the buttermilk or diluted yogurt and oil, and stir to combine thoroughly.

3 Add the buttermilk or diluted yogurt. Stir until a thick paste of a spreading consistency is formed.

4 Spread 10ml/2 tsp oil on an iron griddle or a small, heavy non-stick frying pan and heat over a medium-low heat.

5 Put one heaped tablespoon of the pancake mixture in the pan and gently spread it around to form a pancake with a diameter of 7.5cm/3in. Cover with a lid and cook for 2 minutes, until the top is set.

6 Spread 5ml/1 tsp oil on the uncooked side and turn it over with a palette knife. Cook, uncovered, for 2 minutes or until the pancake is set. Cook, tossing and turning, for a further 2–3 minutes, until browned. Keep the cooked pancakes warm while you cook the remaining batter in the same way. Serve warm.

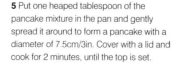

Per portion Energy 341kcal/1447kJ; Protein 12g; Carbohydrate 65g, of which sugars 6g; Fat 6g, of which saturates 1g; Cholesterol 2mg; Calcium 145mg; Fibre 2.9g; Sodium 696mg.

Rice and wheat pancakes

These indulgent pancakes, *Achappam*, are enriched with coconut milk and egg. Traditionally, they are made in small metal ring moulds, but you can use large moulds instead. They are delicious on their own, or you can serve them drizzled with thick yogurt and clear honey.

MAKES 18

110g/4oz/1 cup plain (all-purpose) flour
110g/4oz/⅔ cup ground rice
110g/4oz/1 cup caster (superfine) sugar
5ml/1 tsp ground cardamom
22.5ml/1½ tbsp sesame seeds
2 large (US extra large) eggs
400ml/14fl oz/1½ cups canned
   coconut milk
sunflower oil, for shallow-frying

1 Sift the flour into a mixing bowl and add the ground rice, sugar, cardamom and sesame seeds. Mix well.

2 Beat the eggs and slowly add the coconut milk while beating, until well blended.

3 Pour the egg and coconut milk mixture into the flour and ground rice, and stir until you have a thick batter.

4 Pour enough oil into a large frying pan to cover the base to about 1cm/½in depth and place over a low heat. Put a 5cm/2in steel ring mould in the pan and pour in enough batter to come halfway up the mould.

5 After about 2–3 minutes, when the batter is set, carefully turn it over (the top will not be completely set at this stage) and continue to cook until it is golden brown on both sides.

6 Drain on kitchen paper while you make the remaining pancakes in the same way. Serve with yogurt and honey, if you wish, or fresh berries and cream, or simply spread with a little butter while warm.

COOK'S TIP

The pancakes can be made in advance and frozen. Reheat in a moderate oven for a few minutes.

Per portion Energy 110kcal/463kJ; Protein 2.1g; Carbohydrate 17.1g, of which sugars 7.6g; Fat 4g, of which saturates 0.6g; Cholesterol 21mg; Calcium 32mg; Fibre 0.3g; Sodium 33mg.

Cardamom-scented banana fudge

Halwa is the generic Indian name for any sweetmeat cooked with sugar and a hint of spice to a soft fudge consistency. When made with freshly grated coconut and mashed banana, this *Balehannu Halwa* is divine. It is quicker to use desiccated (dry unsweetened shredded) coconut, lightly cooked in milk, than fresh coconut.

SERVES 4–5

115g/4oz/1⅓ cups desiccated (dry
  unsweetened shredded) coconut
200ml/7fl oz/¾ cup full-fat (whole) milk
4–5 semi-ripe bananas
75g/3oz/6 tbsp ghee or unsalted butter
25g/1oz seedless raisins
50g/2oz raw cashew nuts, chopped (optional)
110g/4oz/1 cup granulated (white) sugar
5ml/1 tsp ground cardamom
2.5ml/½ tsp freshly grated nutmeg
25g/1oz pistachio nuts, crushed (optional)
15ml/1 tbsp toasted coconut flakes

1 Place the coconut and milk in a pan and stir over a medium heat until the coconut has absorbed all the milk. Remove from the heat and set aside.

2 Mash the bananas in a large bowl with a potato masher or fork.

3 Melt the ghee or butter in a frying pan over a low heat, then add the mashed banana and coconut. Stir and cook for 4–5 minutes.

4 Add the raisins, cashew nuts and sugar, and increase the heat to medium. Continue to cook, stirring all the time, for 15–17 minutes until the mixture reaches a soft fudge-like consistency.

5 Add the cardamom and grated nutmeg, and mix well.

6 Brush a 30cm/12in plate with some melted butter and spread the fudge on it, shaping it into a 15cm/6in square. Sprinkle the pistachio nuts and coconut flakes on the surface and press them down firmly.

7 Allow to cool, then chill for 2–3 hours. Cut into squares or diamonds and serve.

VARIATIONS
• Ripe mango can be used instead of banana in this recipe.
• Toasted sunflower seeds make a good alternative to nuts.

Per portion Energy 572kcal/2386kJ; Protein 6.9g; Carbohydrate 53.2g, of which sugars 49.4g; Fat 38.3g, of which saturates 21.2g; Cholesterol 6mg; Calcium 79mg; Fibre 4.8g; Sodium 89mg.

Apricot dessert

This mouthwatering dessert, *Khubani Ka Meetha*, is simplicity itself. Traditionally, fresh apricots are cooked in sugar until they are soft, then cooled and served with a dollop of whipped cream. A spicy note is added by cooking the fruit with star anise and cloves. Dried, ready-to-eat apricots can also be used, as here.

SERVES 4

500g/1¼lb dried ready-to-eat apricots
4 cloves
2 star anise
115g/4oz/½ cup caster (superfine) sugar
lightly whipped double (heavy) cream,
 to serve
30–45ml/2–3 tbsp toasted pistachio nuts,
 lightly crushed, to garnish

1 Put the apricots into a pan with 750ml/
1¼ pints/3 cups water, the cloves and the
star anise, and bring to the boil. Reduce
the heat to low, cover the pan and simmer
for 15 minutes, or until the apricots are soft.
Stir at least twice during this time to ensure
even cooking.

2 Remove the spices from the pan and
discard them. Remove half of the apricots
with a slotted spoon and set aside. Purée
the remainder, along with the cooking
juices, and return the purée to the pan.
Add the whole apricots.

3 Add the sugar and stir to combine
thoroughly. Cook gently for 3–4 minutes,
then remove from the heat and allow to
cool for 30 minutes.

4 Put into individual serving dishes and top
with some whipped cream. Sprinkle with
the crushed pistachio nuts and serve.

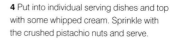

Per portion Energy 306kcal/1305kJ; Protein 5.2g; Carbohydrate 74.4g, of which sugars 74.4g; Fat 0.8g, of which saturates 0g; Cholesterol 0mg; Calcium 106mg; Fibre 7.9g; Sodium 19mg.

Rose-scented mango dessert

This dessert, *Aam Ka Mitha*, is best made with the Indian variety of mangoes known as Alphonso. They are available fresh in Indian stores during the mango season (May–August), but are also sold in cans, sliced or puréed. Canned standard mangoes from supermarkets work well, too.

2 Add the curd cheese, honey and rose water to the bowl or blender. Blitz until well blended and smooth.

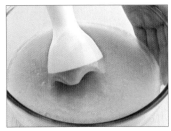

3 Arrange alternate layers of kiwi cubes and pomegranate seeds in serving dishes, and top with the mango mixture.

4 Chill for at least 30 minutes, then sprinkle the ground cardamom or nutmeg on top and serve.

SERVES 4

2 x 425g/15oz cans Alphonso mangoes
225g/8oz/1 cup curd (farmer's) cheese
22.5ml/1½ tbsp honey
30ml/2 tbsp rose water
4 kiwi fruits, cut into cubes
the seeds of ½ pomegranate
1.25ml/¼ tsp ground cardamom or nutmeg

> **VARIATION**
> Low-fat curd cheese can be used, if preferred.

1 Put the mangoes along with the syrup into a food processor, or use a bowl and stick blender, and purée until smooth.

Per portion Energy 230kcal/980kJ; Protein 9g; Carbohydrate 44g, of which sugars 43g; Fat 3g, of which saturates 2g; Cholesterol 9mg; Calcium 113mg; Fibre 6.2g; Sodium 176mg.

Mangoes in cardamom-scented coconut cream

This dessert, *Aam Ka Rasayana*, is a delight for mango-lovers. It is easy to make and refrigerates well for a few days, so it is perfect as a make-ahead dessert for a dinner party. Unrefined palm sugar (jaggery) is traditionally used, but you could use soft dark brown sugar instead.

SERVES 4

2 large or 4 small mangoes
75g/3oz/1 cup desiccated (dry
  unsweetened shredded) coconut
425ml/15fl oz/1½ cups full-fat (whole) milk
5 green cardamom pods, bruised
115g/4oz palm sugar (jaggery), grated,
  or soft dark brown sugar
1.25ml/¼ tsp freshly grated nutmeg
strawberries or other seasonal fruit
sprigs of fresh mint, to decorate

1 Peel the mango and slice off the two large pieces on either side of the stone, then the two thinner sides. Remove the skin, then cut all the slices into bitesize pieces and set aside. Scrape off all the flesh next to the stone and reserve.

2 Put the coconut into a pan and add 300ml/10fl oz/1 cup of the milk, the cardamom and sugar. Bring to the boil, reduce the heat to low and simmer for 5 minutes.

3 Remove from the heat and cool slightly, then purée until smooth in a blender, along with the reserved mango scrapings.

COOK'S TIP
You can also prepare the mango flesh by scoring the two large side slices into cubes, then inverting the skin to make a 'hedgehog' and slicing the cubes from the skin.

4 Strain the coconut purée, pushing as much of the milk through a sieve (strainer) as possible.

5 Return the solid coconut to the blender and add the remaining milk. Blend until smooth and push it through a sieve as before. Discard the solid coconut left in the sieve.

6 Combine both the milk mixtures and add the grated nutmeg.

7 Put the chopped mango into a bowl and add the sweetened, spiced coconut milk. Mix well and chill for several hours.

8 Serve in stemmed glasses layered with sliced strawberries.

Per portion Energy 349kcal/1467kJ; Protein 5.3g; Carbohydrate 49.2g, of which sugars 48.8g; Fat 16g, of which saturates 12.7g; Cholesterol 15mg; Calcium 153mg; Fibre 5.2g; Sodium 67mg.

Saffron- and rose-scented rice pudding

Even if rice pudding does not usually appeal to you, do not dismiss this one! It is quite different from the rice pudding made in the Western world. The richness of saffron, the fragrance imparted by the cardamom, nutmeg and rose water, and the crunchiness of the toasted nuts, make this pudding pure ambrosia. Serve *Pal Payasam* on its own, or team it with a fresh fruit, such as mango, to complement the delicate flavours.

SERVES 4

a good pinch of saffron strands, pounded

1.2 litres/2 pints/5 cups full-fat (whole) milk

25g/1oz/2 tbsp ghee or unsalted butter

6 green cardamom pods, bruised

2.5cm/1in piece of cinnamon stick

2 bay leaves

75g/3oz/⅓ cup basmati rice, washed

30–45ml/2–3 tbsp granulated (white) sugar

25g/1oz broken cashew nut pieces (optional)

45ml/3 tbsp double (heavy) cream

15ml/1 tbsp rose water

a few fresh rose petals, washed, to garnish

1 Soak the saffron in the milk and set aside while preparing the other ingredients.

2 Melt the ghee or butter gently in a pan over a low heat and add the cardamom, cinnamon and bay leaves. Let them sizzle for 25–30 seconds.

3 Add the rice, the saffron-flavoured milk and the saffron. Bring this to the boil and reduce the heat to low.

4 Add the sugar and cashew nuts. Let the mixture bubble gently for 45–50 minutes, stirring frequently. Remove from the heat, then add the cream and rose water.

5 Serve in pretty ice cream dishes or bowls, garnished with the rose petals.

Per portion Energy 445kcal/1852kJ; Protein 12.5g; Carbohydrate 42.6g, of which sugars 26.8g; Fat 26g, of which saturates 14.6g; Cholesterol 71mg; Calcium 363mg; Fibre 0.2g; Sodium 235mg.

Vermicelli dessert

This deliciously rich dessert, *Seviyan Ka Zarda*, is a speciality of the Muslim community and it is just one dessert among the fantastic spread of elaborate dishes served during the festival of Eid al-Fitr. The vermicelli is fried until browned and crunchy, then added to a cardamom-scented sugar syrup with an assortment of nuts and raisins, and gently simmered until all the syrup has been absorbed.

SERVES 4

50g/2oz/¼ cup granulated (white) sugar
5 green cardamom pods, bruised
50g/2oz/¼ cup ghee or unsalted butter
15ml/1 tbsp shelled pistachio nuts
15ml/1 tbsp cashew nuts,
   roughly chopped
15ml/1 tbsp toasted flaked almonds
115g/4oz plain vermicelli
2.5ml/½ tsp ground cinnamon
2.5ml/½ tsp freshly grated nutmeg
25g/1oz raisins

1 Put the sugar in a medium pan and pour in 300ml/½ pint/1¼ cups water. Add the cardamom pods, bring to the boil and simmer gently for 8–10 minutes.

2 Meanwhile, melt the ghee or butter in a heavy frying pan over a low heat and add the pistachio and cashew nuts. Cook, stirring, for 3–4 minutes, until golden.

3 Lift the nuts out of the pan using a slotted spoon, leaving the fat behind, and put them in a small bowl. Stir in the almonds and leave to cool.

5 Add the vermicelli to the sugar syrup with the cinnamon, nutmeg and raisins. Stir for about 5 minutes, until the vermicelli has softened and absorbed all the syrup.

4 Break up the vermicelli and fry it in the same fat that the nuts were cooked in, in batches, until golden brown.

6 Reserve some of the nut mixture and stir the remainder into the vermicelli. Transfer to a serving dish and top with the nuts.

Per portion Energy 321kcal/1336kJ; Protein 4g; Carbohydrate 41g, of which sugars 18g; Fat 18g, of which saturates 9g; Cholesterol 35mg; Calcium 23mg; Fibre 0.5g; Sodium 21mg.

Central India

Situated at the heart of the country, the central region of India is home to a long tradition of royal cooking as well as a strong agricultural economy that produces a wealth of local ingredients. From creamy kormas and crunchy spiced potatoes to delectable snacks and sweet treats delicately flavoured with spices, nuts and seeds, the cuisine holds many delicious surprises, with a tantalizing range of special dishes fit for a feast.

Central India

Central India is made up of one large state, Madhya Pradesh. This area is completely landlocked, with the Arabian Sea bordering the state of Gujarat to the west, and the Bay of Bengal bordering the state of Orissa to the east. The countryside is made up of beautiful rolling hills rising to 600m (2,000ft) – where primeval forests flourish and ancient temples and palaces still stand – and fertile valleys containing lakes and rivers that teem with freshwater fish and provide water for the many crops that are grown.

Madhya Pradesh sits at the northern edge of the Deccan plateau, a huge area of volcanic basalt that stretches across the whole central and southern part of India. This rock was laid down in thick layers and the subsequent nutrient-rich volcanic soil has enabled the state to establish a hugely successful agricultural economy.

The region has been a witness to the major external and internal influences that have been instrumental in shaping the country's culture and cuisine over the centuries. The state is a typical example of the diverse nature of Indian culture: beautiful Hindu and Sikh temples and Muslim mosques grace the region, with all the different religions and races now coexisting in relative harmony after the major upheavals of the 20th century.

The economy of central India relies mainly on agriculture. This fertile state is blessed by regular weather patterns – a hot

Above *Cotton grows extremely well in the predictable climate of Madhya Pradesh, and it is one of the major exports of the region.*

summer from April to June, followed by the relief of torrential monsoon rains in July and August – which enable the farmers to plan which crops to grow and when to plant and harvest them. The main food crops are rice, wheat, sorghum and coarse millet, usually grown for the local markets. The typical flat bread of the region, made of sorghum, has become popular all over India. Oilseeds, cotton, sugar cane and soya beans are the main commercial crops, all of which are exported all over the world as well as being eaten locally. Although rice is a common ingredient in central Indian cooking, wheat is the preferred staple in the drier western areas, and is used to make a range of delicious breads.

Left *The area around the state capital, Bohar, is surrounded by forest-covered hills and there are numerous lakes in the valleys.*

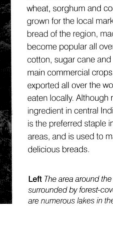

Right *One of many temples in the region, the Vishvanatha temple in Khajuraho dates back to 1002CE and is dedicated to the god Shiva.*

The main cities are Bhopal, Indore and Gwalior. Bhopal, the state capital, is situated in a beautiful area surrounded by lakes and hills, and is home to the third largest mosque in the world, Taj-ul-Masjid. In the days of British domination, the state was ruled by various Indian princes, all of whom maintained strong loyalty to the British. Even now, in the 21st century, all three of the major cities still have Indian princes and princesses living in their palaces, and the traditions of an exotic royal cuisine are maintained among the wealthy.

The cuisine of Madhya Pradesh owes much to the nearby states of Gujarat, Rajasthan and Bihar, with their emphasis on the kind of dishes that best suit hot, dry areas. The luxurious dishes served for royal banquets, with edible gold and silver decorations, are not part of most people's everyday diet, of course. However, the daily food of central India does include plenty of variety in terms of the different spices, nuts and seeds that are added to the basic meat, fish and vegetables. The people also love snacks, often dainty morsels of vegetables deep-fried to perfection in a spicy batter, or tasty sweet cakes flavoured with cashew nuts.

Left *Wheat is one of the staple crops, and the lush green fields are often overlooked by ancient temples, such as this one in Orchha.*

Above *Street food, especially deep-fried snacks such as patties and samosas, is extremely popular in the towns and cities.*

Mashed turnip with cumin, ginger and chillies

Turnips are very low in calories and they provide plenty of dietary fibre. *Shalgam Ka Bharta* is a quick recipe for which you can roast and mash the turnips in advance and spice them up just before serving. It has amazing depth of flavour and can be eaten as a simple vegetarian meal or with meat and poultry dishes.

SERVES 4

675g/1½lb turnips
60ml/4 tbsp sunflower oil or light olive oil
2.5ml/½ tsp cumin seeds
2.5ml/½ tsp nigella seeds
1 medium onion, finely chopped
2.5cm/1in piece of root ginger, finely grated
1–2 fresh green chillies, finely chopped
  (deseeded if preferred)
2.5ml/½ tsp ground turmeric
2.5ml/½ tsp ground fennel
2.5ml/½ tsp salt, or to taste
30ml/2 tbsp coriander (cilantro) leaves
  and stalks, finely chopped

> ### COOK'S TIP
> If the turnips are really young and fresh, with soft skins, then you do not need to peel them.

1 Preheat the oven to 200°C/400°F/Gas 6. Peel the turnips and cut them into 2.5cm/1in cubes. (*See also* Cook's Tip)

2 Put the turnips in a roasting pan and add 15ml/1 tbsp of the oil. Rub it well into the turnips with your fingertips. Position the pan just above the centre of the oven and roast the turnips for 20 minutes or until they are tender and brown.

3 Remove from the oven and leave to cool for a few minutes, then mash them roughly with a fork or in the food processor, using the pulse action.

4 In a heavy sauté or frying pan, heat the remaining oil over a medium heat and add the cumin and nigella seeds. Let them sizzle for 15–20 seconds.

5 Add the onion, ginger and chillies. Fry them for 6–7 minutes, stirring regularly, then add the turmeric and fennel.

6 Stir-fry for 1 minute, then add 30–45ml/ 2–3 tbsp water. Stir-fry until all of the water evaporates and repeat this process of adding and evaporating water once more.

7 Add the mashed turnips and salt. Stir-fry for 4–5 minutes, reducing the heat slightly, if necessary.

8 Stir in the coriander leaves and remove from the heat. Serve immediately.

Per portion Energy 198kcal/822kJ; Protein 3g; Carbohydrate 13g, of which sugars 11g; Fat 16g, of which saturates 2g; Cholesterol 0mg; Calcium 110mg; Fibre 5g; Sodium 275mg.

Wild fig kebabs

In India, wild figs are used for this recipe, *Goolar Kabab*, but when these are not available dried ones can be used instead. Split Bengal gram (channa dhal) and figs are ground together and combined with fresh root ginger, garlic, chillies and garam masala to produce these wonderfully fragrant kebabs.

MAKES 15

250g/9oz/1½ cups dried figs, chopped
250g/9oz/1½ cups split Bengal gram
   (channa dhal or skinless split chickpeas)
5ml/1 tsp salt, or to taste
2.5cm/1in piece of fresh root ginger, chopped
2 large garlic cloves, chopped
1 small onion, chopped
2.5ml/½ tsp ground turmeric
1 fresh green chilli, chopped
   (deseeded if preferred)
2.5ml/½ tsp chilli powder
2.5ml/½ tsp ground cumin
2.5ml/½ tsp garam masala
juice of 1 lemon
sunflower oil, for shallow-frying
fresh coriander (cilantro) sprigs, to garnish
chutney, to serve

1 Put the figs, split Bengal gram, salt, ginger, garlic and onion into a pan and add 425ml/14fl oz/1¾ cups water. Bring it to the boil, reduce the heat to low and simmer, uncovered, for 25–30 minutes until the water has been absorbed.

2 Cool slightly, then add the turmeric, green chilli, chilli powder, cumin, garam masala and lemon juice.

> ## COOK'S TIP
> Figs are native to Asia, Africa and southern Europe, and are a good source of iron and calcium.

3 Blend the ingredients in a food processor until they are finely chopped and well combined. Transfer to a mixing bowl, cover with clear film (plastic wrap) and chill in the refrigerator for 1 hour.

4 Shape the mixture into 15 equal balls and flatten each one into a neat, round cake.

5 Heat the oil in a large frying pan over medium heat and fry the kebabs in batches on low/medium heat for about 2 minutes on each side, until they are a rich brown colour on both sides.

6 Drain on kitchen paper, garnish with coriander and serve with chutney.

Per portion Energy 139kcal/585kJ; Protein 5.2g; Carbohydrate 21.1g, of which sugars 10.7g; Fat 4.4g, of which saturates 0.5g; Cholesterol 0mg; Calcium 59mg; Fibre 2.5g; Sodium 17mg.

Green pea kebabs

Only fresh peas are used in India for making these delectable kebabs, Hare Mattar Ke Kabab, but this recipe uses frozen ones for convenience. These are cooked and lightly crushed, and boiled and mashed potatoes are added for binding. The spicing is simple, delicious and quite fragrant.

3 Dry-roast the coriander and cumin seeds in a small pan over a medium heat for about 1 minute, until they release their aroma. Allow to cool, then crush them in a mortar and pestle or place them in a plastic bag and crush them with a rolling pin. Add to the potato mixture and stir to combine.

4 Melt the ghee or butter in a pan and add the onion and chillies. Cook for 6 minutes, until softened, then add the garlic.

5 Cook for about 1 minute, then add the garam masala. Remove from the heat and add to the potato/pea mixture along with the salt, breadcrumbs, flour and egg. Stir to combine. Cover and chill for 30 minutes.

6 Divide the mixture into 12 equal portions and flatten them to form round cakes.

MAKES 12
350g/12oz frozen garden peas
175g/6oz boiled potatoes, mashed
5ml/1 tsp coriander seeds
5ml/1 tsp cumin seeds
30ml/2 tbsp ghee or unsalted butter
1 large onion, finely chopped
2–3 fresh red chillies, finely chopped
10ml/2 tsp garlic purée
2.5ml/½ tsp garam masala
5ml/1 tsp salt, or to taste
65g/2½oz/1 cup soft fresh breadcrumbs
45ml/3 tbsp plain (all-purpose) flour
1 egg, beaten
sunflower oil, for shallow-frying
Roasted Tomato Chutney, to serve

1 Cook the peas in a pan of boiling water for about 5 minutes, until tender, then drain, transfer to a bowl and mash with a fork.

2 Add the mashed potatoes, stir well to combine and set aside.

7 Heat the oil in a frying pan and fry the kebabs in batches for about 3–4 minutes on each side, until browned all over. Serve with Roasted Tomato Chutney.

Per portion Energy 128kcal/535kJ; Protein 4g; Carbohydrate 12g, of which sugars 2g; Fat 8g, of which saturates 2g; Cholesterol 25mg; Calcium 31mg; Fibre 2.7g; Sodium 225mg.

Yogurt and gram flour kebabs

Yogurt and gram flour (besan) are two extremely healthy ingredients, offering protein, vitamins and minerals in abundance. These kebabs, *Dahi Ke Kabab*, are easy to make and, served with flavoursome chutney, they are deliciously moreish. They are also great topped with tomato salsa.

MAKES 14

400g/14oz/3½ cups gram flour (besan)
5ml/1 tsp salt, or to taste
1.25ml/¼ tsp Asafoetida
5ml/1 tsp ground turmeric
2.5cm/1in piece of fresh root ginger,
  finely grated
4 cloves garlic, finely choped
2 fresh green chillies, finely chopped
  (deseeded if preferred)
2.5–5ml/½–1 tsp dried chilli flakes
5ml/1 tsp garam masala
1 red onion, finely chopped
10ml/2 tsp dried fenugreek leaves
30ml/2 tbsp fresh coriander (cilantro)
  leaves, chopped
250g/9oz/generous 1 cup Greek
  (US strained plain) yogurt
sunflower oil, for deep-frying
Sweet Tamarind Chutney, to serve

1 Put the gram flour in a non-stick frying pan and add the salt, Asafoetida, turmeric, ginger, garlic, both types of chilli and the garam masala.

2 Mix well, then add the onion, fenugreek leaves, coriander and yogurt, and stir to combine well.

3 Place the frying pan over a low heat and stir the mixture until a sticky paste is formed. Continue to cook for about 2–3 minutes, then remove the pan from the heat and set aside until cool enough to handle.

4 Grease your palms and divide the mixture into 14 equal portions. Rotate them between your palms and flatten them to a smooth round cake about 5mm/¼in thick.

5 Heat the oil over a low-medium heat in a wok or other suitable pan for deep-frying.

6 Reduce the heat to low and fry the kebabs for about 3 minutes on each side, until well browned all over.

7 Lift out with a slotted spoon and drain on kitchen paper. Serve immediately with Sweet Tamarind Chutney.

Per portion Energy 158kcal/661kJ; Protein 7g; Carbohydrate 16g, of which sugars 2g; Fat 8g, of which saturates 2g; Cholesterol 3mg; Calcium 80mg; Fibre 4.0g; Sodium 165mg.

Golden mung bean patties

These delicious morsels, *Mung Ke Tikkia*, are made of skinless split mung beans (mung dhal) that are ground to a paste and cooked with spices, until the mixture reaches a mashed potato-like consistency. This is then formed into small, round cakes and deep-fried until crisp and golden brown.

MAKES 12

250g/9oz/1½ cups skinless split mung
  beans (mung dhal), soaked for 4 hours
2.5cm/1in piece of fresh root ginger, chopped
1–2 dried red chillies, chopped
5ml/1 tsp ground turmeric
15ml/1 tbsp fresh coriander (cilantro)
  leaves, chopped
1 fresh green chilli, finely chopped
50g/2oz natural (plain) yogurt
3.75ml/¾ tsp salt, or to taste
vegetable oil, for deep-frying
chutney, to serve

1 Drain the beans and transfer to a food processor with the ginger and red chillies. Grind to a coarse consistency.

2 Transfer the bean paste to a non-stick pan over a low heat. Add the turmeric and cook, stirring, until the mixture is dry and slightly crumbly. Remove from the heat and add all the remaining ingredients, except the oil.

3 Mix thoroughly and make 12 equal balls, then flatten them into neat, round cakes.

4 Heat the vegetable oil in a wok or other pan suitable for deep-frying over a low/medium heat. Fry the patties in several batches for 2–3 minutes, until they are golden brown.

6 Remove with a slotted spoon and drain on kitchen paper while you cook the rest of the patties. Serve with any chutney.

Per portion Energy 148kcal/620kJ; Protein 5.4g; Carbohydrate 12.6g, of which sugars 0.8g; Fat 8.9g, of which saturates 1g; Cholesterol 0mg; Calcium 22mg; Fibre 1g; Sodium 12mg.

Parsnip patties

Central India is famous for its varied snacks, which Indians adore. Originally made from turnip (hence their Indian name, *Shalgam Tikki* – *shalgam* means 'turnip'), these delectable little morsels use parsnips instead. The sweetness of this root vegetable works well with the pungency of chillies and ginger.

MAKES 14

10ml/2 tbsp sunflower oil or olive oil
675g/1½lb parsnips, peeled and chopped
1 large onion, roughly chopped
2.5cm/1in piece of fresh root ginger,
  roughly chopped
2–3 fresh green chillies, finely chopped
  (deseeded if preferred)
1 large slice of white bread (one or two
  days' old)
1 large (US extra large) egg
2.5ml/½ tsp garam masala
3.75ml/¾ tsp salt, or to taste
15g/½oz fresh coriander (cilantro) leaves
  and stalks, roughly chopped
vegetable oil, for shallow-frying
mango chutney, to serve

1 Heat the oil in a frying pan and add the parsnips. Stir-fry over a medium heat until the edges of the parsnips have been tinged with a medium-to-dark brown colour, being careful not to burn them.

2 Add the onion, ginger and chillies. Stir-fry for 3–4 minutes, then remove from the heat.

3 Soak the bread in cold water, then squeeze out all the liquid. Put the damp bread and the egg in a food processor or blender and blend until smooth. Add the parsnips, garam masala, salt and fresh coriander. Using the pulse action, blend all of the ingredients until smooth.

4 Transfer the mixture to a bowl and chill for 35–40 minutes. Divide into 14 equal portions and flatten into 5mm/¼in-thick cakes.

5 Cover the base of a frying pan to about 1cm/½in depth with oil and place on a medium heat. Fry the parsnip patties in batches until they are well browned on both sides. Drain on kitchen paper and serve immediately with mango chutney.

Per portion Energy 125kcal/521kJ; Protein 2g; Carbohydrate 9.9g, of which sugars 4.7g; Fat 8.9g, of which saturates 1.1g; Cholesterol 14mg; Calcium 35mg; Fibre 3g; Sodium 22mg.

Crispy gram flour rounds

Papris are a very popular snack in central India, especially during the festival of colours (Holi), which is celebrated throughout the country in the spring. The predominant flavour and aroma comes from the small amount of pungent dried fenugreek (kasuri methi) used. Serve with Raita or a spicy fruit chutney.

SERVES 24

225g/8oz/2 cups gram flour (besan),
  sifted, plus extra for dusting
a pinch of bicarbonate of soda
  (baking soda)
5ml/1 tsp salt, or to taste
5ml/1 tsp chilli powder
5ml/1 tsp cumin seeds
15ml/1 tbsp dried fenugreek leaves
  (kasuri methi)
15ml/1 tbsp sunflower oil or light olive oil
vegetable oil, for deep-frying

1 In a mixing bowl, mix the gram flour, bicarbonate of soda, salt, chilli powder, cumin seeds and fenugreek leaves.

2 Make a well in the centre, add the oil and mix well.

3 Add 125ml/4fl oz/½ cup water and mix until a dough is formed.

4 Transfer to a lightly floured surface and knead it briefly, then form the dough into a large flat cake.

5 Dust with a little flour and roll out thinly to a 30cm/12in circle about 2.5mm/⅛in thick.

6 Using a round cookie cutter, cut out as many small circles as possible, then gather up the remaining dough and roll again. Cut out into circles as before. You should end up with about 24 small circles.

7 Heat the oil in a wok or other suitable pan for deep-frying over a medium heat. Fry the rounds in hot oil in two or three batches, until they are crisp and golden brown.

8 Drain on kitchen paper and serve. Once fried, they will keep well in an airtight container for up to a week.

> **COOK'S TIP**
> Fenugreek is thought to both inhibit and alleviate arthritis.

Per portion Energy 358kcal/1498kJ; Protein 7.7g; Carbohydrate 37.3g, of which sugars 1.2g; Fat 21g, of which saturates 2.6g; Cholesterol 0mg; Calcium 28mg; Fibre 5.1g; Sodium 3mg.

Mung beans with mustard, ginger and yogurt

This dish, *Khatte Sabut Mung*, comprises green mung beans with flecks of red chillies, spiced with mustard, fresh root ginger and cumin, and served with a creamy yogurt sauce. The sauce is made with just yogurt, with no added water or stock, and it is important that it is whisked well beforehand to prevent it curdling.

SERVES 4

225g/8oz/1¼ cups whole mung beans
  (sabut mung dhal)
60ml/4 tbsp sunflower oil or light olive oil
5ml/1 tsp cumin seeds
2 whole dried red chillies
1 medium onion, finely chopped
2.5cm/1in piece of fresh root ginger, grated
1 fresh green chilli, finely chopped
  (deseeded if preferred)
2.5ml/½ tsp ground turmeric
5ml/1 tsp salt, or to taste
200g/7oz/scant 1 cup Greek (US strained
  plain) yogurt
15ml/3 tsp English (hot) mustard
15ml/1 tbsp lime juice
Ginger and Cumin Puffed Bread with
  Spinach, to serve

1 Wash the mung beans, then drain and soak in water for 6–8 hours or overnight. Drain the beans and put them in a pan with 450ml/15fl oz/scant 2 cups water. Bring to the boil and skim off any froth.

2 Cook on a medium heat for 12–15 minutes. Stir as the water evaporates, reduce the heat to low and cook for 5 minutes longer. The beans should remain whole and about 30–45ml/2–3 tbsp liquid should remain. Remove from the heat and set aside.

3 Heat the oil over a medium heat and add the cumin seeds and red chillies. Allow the chillies to blacken. Add the onion, ginger and green chilli.

4 Stir-fry for 5–7 minutes, until the onion begins to brown. Add the turmeric, salt and the beans, and stir to combine thoroughly.

5 Whisk the yogurt until smooth, then add to the bean mixture.

6 Reduce the heat to low, add the mustard and cook for 4–5 minutes. Stir in the lime juice and remove from the heat.

7 Serve with Ginger and Cumin-flavoured Puffed Bread with Spinach.

Per portion Energy 334kcal/1403kJ; Protein 17.3g; Carbohydrate 39.1g, of which sugars 10.8g; Fat 13.5g, of which saturates 1.8g; Cholesterol 1mg; Calcium 190mg; Fibre 10.2g; Sodium 57mg.

Savoury sago with chilli, coconut and peanut

Sago is a very underused ingredient, and this recipe, known as *Sabudana Khichdi*, will surprise as well as delight your palate. It is delicious and very quick to make once you have soaked, drained and rinsed the sago. It makes a very satisfying main meal and the peanuts add plenty of protein to the dish.

SERVES 4

275g/10oz sago

200g/7oz potatoes

25g/1oz/2 tbsp unsalted butter

15ml/1 tbsp sunflower oil or light olive oil

5ml/1 tsp cumin seeds

1 medium onion, finely chopped

2 fresh green or red chillies, chopped (deseeded if preferred)

50g/2oz desiccated (dry unsweetened shredded) coconut

salt, to taste

115g/4oz roasted, unsalted peanuts, crushed

30ml/2 tbsp fresh coriander (cilantro) leaves, chopped

1 Soak the sago in water for 45 minutes, then drain and rinse. Leave to drain.

2 Peel the potatoes, then cut them into 2.5cm/1in dice. Soak for about 10 minutes, then drain and dry with a clean dish towel.

3 Heat the butter and oil over a medium heat and add the cumin seeds.

4 When they pop, add the potatoes and onion. Cook them for about 8 minutes, until they begin to brown slightly. Add the chillies and coconut, and cook, stirring, for about 1 minute.

5 Pour in 120ml/4fl oz/½ cup water and cook for 6 minutes, until the potatoes are tender.

6 Add the sago and salt to the pan. Stir and cook for 5 minutes, stirring frequently until the sago is heated through.

7 Add the crushed peanuts and the chopped coriander. Stir to mix well, remove from the heat and transfer to a serving dish. Serve immediately.

Per portion Energy 567kcal/2384kJ; Protein 10g; Carbohydrate 81g, of which sugars 5g; Fat 25g, of which saturates 10g; Cholesterol 0mg; Calcium 47mg; Fibre 6.1g; Sodium 111mg.

Turnips in yogurt sauce

Fresh turnips are available in supermarkets throughout the year. Try to find small ones as they have a delicate, slightly sweet taste. As a main course *Shalgam Ka Salan* merits the use of ghee, which enriches the dish, but you could use oil instead if you prefer.

SERVES 4

5–6 turnips (about 500g/1¼lb), peeled
275g/10oz potatoes
115g/4oz/½ cup full-fat (whole) natural (plain) yogurt
10ml/2 tsp gram flour (besan), sifted
50g/2oz ghee or unsalted butter
1 large onion, finely sliced
10ml/2 tsp ginger purée
1–2 fresh green chillies, finely chopped (deseeded if preferred)
5ml/1 tsp ground coriander
2.5ml/½ tsp ground cumin
2.5ml/½ tsp chilli powder
2.5ml/½ tsp ground turmeric
5ml/1 tsp salt, or to taste
2.5ml/½ tsp sugar
2.5ml/½ tsp garam masala
30ml/2 tbsp fresh coriander (cilantro) leaves, finely chopped

1 Quarter the turnips. Cut each quarter into four smaller pieces. Peel the potatoes and cut them to the same size as the turnips.

2 Whisk the yogurt and gram flour together and set aside.

COOK'S TIP
If the turnips are really young and tender, with soft skins, then they may not require peeling.

3 Heat half the ghee or butter over a medium heat and brown the turnips, stirring them frequently, until they have a light crust. Drain on kitchen paper. Brown the potatoes in the same way and drain.

4 Add the remaining ghee or butter to the pan and reduce the heat to low. Fry the onion, ginger and green chillies for about 5 minutes, until the onion is golden brown.

5 Add the coriander, cumin, chilli powder and turmeric, and cook for about 1 minute.

6 Add the vegetables and the yogurt mixture. Add the salt, sugar and 50ml/2fl oz/ 3 tbsp water. Reduce the heat to low, cover and cook for 20 minutes, stirring often.

7 Stir in the garam masala and coriander. Serve with any Indian bread.

Per portion Energy 317kcal/1326kJ; Protein 7.9g; Carbohydrate 39.6g, of which sugars 17g; Fat 15.6g, of which saturates 6.7g; Cholesterol 3mg; Calcium 194mg; Fibre 6.3g; Sodium 61mg.

Figs in spiced yogurt

Anjeer Ka Salan is an excellent tastebud reviver with its savoury, sweet, sour and hot tastes combined in one. Dried ready-to-eat figs are easily available in supermarkets and health food shops, making this an all-year-round classic. This dish is especially good served as an appetizer.

2 Whisk the yogurt in a small bowl until it is smooth, then set aside. This helps prevent it curdling during cooking.

3 Melt the ghee or butter in a frying pan over a low heat and fry the onion for 5–6 minutes, until soft and translucent.

4 Add the coriander, turmeric and chilli powder and cook for about 1 minute. Add the fig pieces and the salt and stir-fry for 2–3 minutes. Add the yogurt, stir well, cover the pan tightly and cook for 4–5 minutes.

5 Stir in the lemon juice and garam masala. Serve hot or at room temperature.

SERVES 4–6
400g/14oz dried ready-to-eat figs
250g/9oz/generous 1 cup thick natural (plain) yogurt
50g/2oz/4 tbsp ghee or unsalted butter
1 large onion, finely chopped
15ml/1 tbsp ground coriander
2.5ml/½ tsp ground turmeric
7.5ml/1½ tsp chilli powder, or to taste
5ml/1 tsp salt, or to taste
15ml/1 tbsp lemon juice
2.5ml/½ tsp garam masala

1 Soak the figs in a bowl of salted water for 10–15 minutes, then rinse well. (*See* Cook's Tip). Slice each fig into three pieces and set aside.

COOK'S TIPS
• Some dried figs have added sugar in them, and soaking them in salted water eliminates this. There is no need to soak ones that have no added sugar.

Per portion Energy 315kcal/1352kJ; Protein 6g; Carbohydrate 47g, of which sugars 46g; Fat 13g, of which saturates 7g; Cholesterol 34mg; Calcium 304mg; Fibre 9.8g; Sodium 489mg.

Spinach in clove-infused yogurt sauce

The strong flavour of spinach is perfectly matched by the pungent sweetness of cloves in this unusual dish, *Palak-dahi Ki Kari*, which can be served hot or at room temperature. The yogurt should be thick-set, preferably Greek (US strained plain), so it doesn't split when heated.

SERVES 4

400g/14oz spinach, fresh or frozen
  (thawed if frozen)
200g/7oz/scant 1 cup Greek
  (US strained plain) yogurt
5ml/1 tsp gram flour (besan)
45ml/3 tbsp sunflower oil or light olive oil
2.5cm/1in piece cinnamon stick
5 cardamom pods, bruised
1 large onion, finely sliced
4 cloves garlic, crushed to a pulp
10ml/2 tsp fresh root ginger, finely grated
2 fresh red chillies, chopped
  (deseeded if preferred)
3.75ml/¾ tsp salt, or to taste
10ml2 tsp ghee or unsalted butter
5 whole cloves
Plain Boiled Rice and a lentil dish,
  to serve

1 Put the spinach in a large heatproof bowl, pour over boiling water and stir until the leaves have wilted.

2 Drain the spinach and rinse in cold water, then squeeze out as much water as possible. If you are using thawed frozen spinach, simply squeeze out the excess water. Chop the spinach finely.

3 Whisk the yogurt and the gram flour together in a small bowl and set aside.

4 Heat the oil in a frying pan over a low heat and add the cinnamon and cardamom.

5 When the cardamom pods puff up, add the onion. After a few minutes, add the garlic, ginger and chillies, and increase the heat. Fry for 8–10 minutes, until the ingredients are brown, stirring regularly.

6 Add the spinach and salt and cook for 4–5 minutes, until heated through. Add the yogurt and 75ml/2½fl oz/⅓ cup water. Stir well, cover the pan cook for 3–4 minutes.

7 Switch off the heat source and keep the pan covered.

8 Melt the ghee or butter and add the cloves. When they start sizzling, switch off the heat and cook for 25–30 seconds.

9 Pour the oil over the spinach, stir and cover. Let it stand for 10–15 minutes, then serve with Plain Boiled Rice and a lentil dish.

Per portion Energy 237kcal/980kJ; Protein 7g; Carbohydrate 8g, of which sugars 6g; Fat 20g, of which saturates 7g; Cholesterol 15mg; Calcium 256mg; Fibre 0.9g; Sodium 379mg.

Corn kernels in yogurt and gram flour sauce

Golden gram flour (besan) sauce, spiced with cumin and coriander and accentuated with chillies, mingles with the sweet, milky taste of corn kernels to create this enticing dish, *Makki Ke Dane Ki Kari*. Canned corn kernels can be used instead of frozen ones, but drain and rinse them well beforehand.

SERVES 4

150g/5oz/⅔ cup full-fat (whole) natural (plain) yogurt
30ml/2 tbsp gram flour (besan), sifted
45ml/3 tbsp sunflower oil or light olive oil
2.5ml/½ tsp black mustard seeds
2.5ml/½ tsp cumin seeds
1 medium onion, finely chopped
5ml/1 tsp ginger purée
5ml/1 tsp garlic purée
10ml/2 tsp ground coriander
2.5ml/½ tsp ground turmeric
2.5–5ml/½–1 tsp chilli powder
400g/14oz/2¼ cups frozen corn, thawed
5ml/1 tsp salt, or to taste
10ml/2 tsp ghee or unsalted butter
2.5ml/½ tsp garam masala
30ml/2 tbsp fresh coriander (cilantro) leaves, finely chopped
julienne strips of fresh tomato, to garnish
Ginger and Cumin Puffed Bread with Spinach, or Butter-flavoured Rice with Spiced Stock, to serve

1 Mix the yogurt and gram flour together well in a large bowl and set aside.

2 Heat the oil in a heavy frying pan over a medium heat and add the mustard seeds. As soon as they begin to pop, add the cumin seeds and let them sizzle for a few seconds to release their fragance.

3 Add the onion and stir-fry for 5–6 minutes, until translucent. Add the ginger and garlic and stir-fry for about 1 minute.

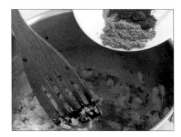

4 Reduce the heat to low and add the coriander, turmeric and chilli powder. Fry gently for 30–40 seconds, then add the yogurt mixture and cook for 3–4 minutes, stirring constantly.

5 Add the corn, salt and 200ml/7fl oz/¾ cup warm water. Cook until the sauce begins to bubble, then cover the pan and simmer over a low heat for 15–20 minutes.

6 In a small pan or a steel ladle, melt the ghee or butter over a low heat and add the garam masala.

VARIATION

You can use fresh corn when it is in season. Remove the green outer leaves, stand the corn on its end and run a sharp knife down the side to slice off the kernels. You will need 6–8 corn cobs, depending on their size.

7 Stir and cook for about 30 seconds, then pour the spiced butter over the corn, making sure that none of the garam masala is left behind.

8 Stir in the coriander and remove from the heat. Transfer to a serving dish and garnish with julienne strips of tomato. Serve with Ginger and Cumin-scented Puffed Bread or Butter-flavoured Rice with Spiced Stock.

Per portion Energy 258kcal/1068kJ; Protein 6.9g; Carbohydrate 16.7g, of which sugars 7.6g; Fat 18.7g, of which saturates 5.6g; Cholesterol 5mg; Calcium 84mg; Fibre 3.2g; Sodium 1165mg.

Clove-infused stuffed aubergines

Small, slim aubergines (eggplants) are used to make this traditional dish, *Baingan Ke Lonj*. The aubergines are sliced along most of their length, leaving them joined at the top, and these cavities are stuffed with a spicy onion paste tempered with clove and cinnamon. The aubergines are then tied shut and gently simmered in an onion sauce. This dish goes well with rice, bread or lentils.

SERVES 4

400g/14oz small, slim aubergines
  (eggplants)
60ml/4 tbsp sunflower oil or light
  olive oil
1 large onion, finely chopped
10ml/2 tsp ginger purée
1–2 fresh green chillies, finely chopped
  (deseeded if preferred)
5ml/1 tsp salt, or to taste
5ml/1 tsp ground turmeric
2.5ml/½ tsp chilli powder
5ml/1 tsp ground coriander
2.5ml/½ tsp ground cumin
2.5ml/½ tsp garam masala
4 cloves
1cm/½in piece of cinnamon stick
1 fresh tomato
sprigs of fresh coriander (cilantro),
  to garnish
wedges of lime, to garnish
rice and/or *Phulkas* and a lentil dish,
  to serve

1 Trim off the stalks from the aubergines. Cut them lengthways from the bottom to the top, leaving about 1cm/½in uncut at the top end so there are two conjoined slices that can be opened up and stuffed. Take care not to slice all the way along the length or the dish will not work.

2 Carefully place the aubergines in a large bowl of salted water and soak for 15–20 minutes. This helps remove any bitterness.

3 Meanwhile, heat half the oil over a medium heat and add the onion, ginger and chillies. Stir-fry for 4–5 minutes, until the onion is soft.

4 Reduce the heat to low and add half the salt, along with the turmeric, chilli powder, coriander and cumin. Cook for 1 minute, then stir in the garam masala and remove from the heat.

5 Drain the aubergines, rinse them and dry with a clean dish towel.

6 Stuff the aubergines with the onion mixture, using about 5ml/1 tsp of mixture per aubergine. Tie them up with a piece of thread in a criss-cross fashion. Reserve any remaining onion mixture.

7 Heat the remaining oil in a large pan over a low heat. Add the cloves and cinnamon. Let them sizzle for a few seconds, then add the aubergines and the remaining salt.

8 Increase the heat to medium and cook the aubergines, stirring, for 3–4 minutes. Add any reserved onion mixture and pour in 500ml/18fl oz/2 cups warm water. Bring it to the boil, reduce the heat to low, cover the pan and cook for 20 minutes.

9 Cut the tomato into quarters, remove the seeds and finely slice each piece into julienne strips, for a garnish.

10 At the end of the cooking time, remove the lid and cook, uncovered, for a few minutes longer, if necessary, to reduce the sauce. There should be very little liquid left and the thickened spice paste should coat the aubergines.

11 Remove the pan from the heat and carefully remove the threads holding the aubergines together, keeping them intact. Serve each aubergine with some of the sauce, accompanied by rice and/or *Phulkas* and a lentil dish of your choice.

Per portion Energy 188kcal/779kJ; Protein 3.9g; Carbohydrate 15.6g, of which sugars 9g; Fat 13g, of which saturates 1.6g; Cholesterol 0mg; Calcium 59mg; Fibre 3.8g; Sodium 9mg.

Tomatoes stuffed with paneer

These stuffed tomatoes, *Tamatar Ka Dulma*, are delicious served hot or cold. The stuffing is made from grated Indian cheese, spiced with cumin, ginger and chilli, while raisins and pistachio nuts provide a varied texture and taste. Peas may be used instead of pistachios.

SERVES 4

8 firm, medium tomatoes
15ml/1 tbsp sunflower oil or olive oil
2.5ml/½ tsp cumin seeds
1cm/½in cube of fresh root ginger,
   finely grated
1–2 fresh green chillies, finely chopped
   (deseeded if preferred)
15ml/1 tbsp raw pistachio nuts
15ml/1 tbsp seedless raisins
1.25ml/¼ tsp ground turmeric
2.5ml/½ tsp ground cumin
115g/4oz paneer (Indian cheese), grated,
   or halloumi cheese, crumbled
2.5ml/½ tsp salt, or to taste
30ml/2 tbsp double (heavy) cream
30–45ml/2–3 tbsp finely chopped fresh
   coriander (cilantro)
Potatoes in Mustard Oil with Sesame
   Seeds, to serve

4 Add the pistachio nuts, raisins, turmeric and ground cumin. Cook for 1–2 minutes, then add all the remaining ingredients. Mix well and remove from the heat.

5 Divide the mixture into eight and use to fill the cavities of the tomatoes. Place the reserved slices on top and arrange the tomatoes on a greased roasting pan. Tightly cover the pan with a piece of strong foil.

1 Slice off the tops of the tomatoes and scoop out the seeds and pulp. Keep the sliced tops, but discard the pulp.

2 Preheat the oven to 190°C/375°F/Gas 5. In a small pan, heat the oil over a medium heat and add the cumin seeds.

3 Fry them gently for 15–20 seconds, then add the ginger and chillies and fry for a further 1 minute.

6 Bake in the centre of the oven for about 15 minutes until the flesh of the tomatoes are softening, but before they collapse.

7 Serve the tomatoe hot or at room temperature, with Potatoes in Mustard Oil with Toasted Sesame Seeds.

Per portion Energy 167kcal/700kJ; Protein 6.8g; Carbohydrate 12g, of which sugars 10.6g; Fat 11.1g, of which saturates 3.8g; Cholesterol 13.2mg; Calcium 52.3mg; Fibre 2.6g; Sodium 151mg.

Rice vermicelli with peas

Indian vegetarian cuisine is incredibly varied and ranges from dishes that require lengthy preparation to quick ones such as this, *Sewian Pulao*. Rice vermicelli – very fine noodles – need little cooking. Here they are cooked with peas and tomatoes and served with peanuts.

SERVES 4

250g/9oz rice vermicelli
45ml/3 tbsp sunflower oil or light
  olive oil
15ml/1 tbsp ghee or unsalted butter
2.5ml/½ tsp black mustard seeds
2.5ml/½ tsp cumin seeds
2–3 dried red chillies
1 large onion, finely sliced
1 garlic clove, crushed, or 5ml/1 tsp
  garlic purée
2.5cm/1in fresh root ginger, grated,
  or 10ml/2tsp ginger purée
1–2 fresh green chillies, finely chopped
  (deseeded if preferred)
2.5ml/½ tsp chilli powder
175g/6oz/1 cup frozen peas
2 tomatoes, chopped
2.5ml/½ tsp garam masala
2.5ml/½ tsp salt, or to taste
25g/1oz/¼ cup roasted salted peanuts,
  roughly chopped
15ml/1 tbsp chopped fresh coriander
  (cilantro), to garnish

1 Put the rice vermicelli in a large heatproof bowl and pour over enough boiling water to cover it. Leave to soak for 5 minutes, then drain in a sieve and return to the bowl.

2 Cover the vermicelli with plenty of cold water and leave to soak for 15 minutes. Drain again in a sieve, return to the bowl and cut the vermicelli into shorter lengths, with kitchen scissors.

3 While the vermicelli is soaking, heat the oil and ghee or butter over a medium heat in a large, heavy frying pan. Add the mustard seeds and, when they start to pop, add the cumin and dried chillies. Cook for 2 minutes, stirring frequently, then add the onion and fry until softened.

4 Add the garlic, ginger and green chillies to the pan, then continue to fry until the onion is well browned.

5 Stir in the chilli powder, peas and 75ml/ 5 tbsp hot water. Cook for 3 minutes, then stir in the chopped tomatoes, vermicelli and garam masala.

6 Add with salt, then stir to combine well. Cook for 2–3 minutes, until heated through. Transfer the vermicelli mixture to a warmed serving dish, sprinkle with roughly chopped peanuts, then garnish with coriander. Serve immediately.

Per portion Energy 464kcal/1931kJ; Protein 11g; Carbohydrate 62g, of which sugars 7g; Fat 20g, of which saturates 5g; Cholesterol 11mg; Calcium 60mg; Fibre 3.9g; Sodium 289mg.

Fish with aromatic basmati rice

Madhya Pradesh does not have a distinct style of cooking of its own and many dishes are based on those of its neighbouring states. This popular recipe, *Machchi Biryani*, originated in Uttar Pradesh and has been adapted to suit local ingredients. It is essential to use firm white fish fillets in this dish.

SERVES 4

large pinch of saffron threads, pounded
30ml/2 tbsp hot milk
450g/1lb basmati rice
675g/1½lb firm white fish fillets, such as cod,
  pollock, monkfish or sea bream, skinned
30ml/2 tbsp lemon juice
2.5ml/½ tsp ground turmeric
2.5ml/½ tsp chilli powder
5ml/1 tsp salt
60ml/4 tbsp sunflower oil or light olive oil
1 large onion, finely chopped
2.5cm/1in fresh root ginger, grated,
  or 10ml/2 tsp ginger purée
2 fresh green chillies, thinly sliced at
  an angle (deseeded if preferred)
10ml/2 tsp ground coriander
5ml/1 tsp ground fennel
2 tomatoes, coarsely chopped
115g/4oz/¾ cup frozen peas
2.5cm/1in piece of cinnamon stick
6 green cardamom pods, bruised
6 cloves
2 bay leaves
large pinch of salt
15ml/1 tbsp chopped fresh coriander
  (cilantro), to garnish

1 Crumble the saffron into a small bowl. Pour over the hot milk and leave to soak while you prepare the other ingredients.

2 Rinse the rice in a sieve under cold running water, then transfer it to a bowl, cover with plenty of cold water and leave to soak for 20–30 minutes.

3 Pat the fish dry with kitchen paper. Cut into 2.5cm/1in cubes and sprinkle with lemon juice, turmeric, chilli powder and half the salt. Rub in. Set aside for 10 minutes.

4 Preheat the oven to 160°C/325°F/Gas 3. Pour 2 litres/3½ pints/8 cups of water into a large pan and bring to the boil.

5 Heat half the oil in a large, non-stick frying pan over a medium-high heat and brown the fish in batches. Remove and set aside.

6 Add the remaining oil to the pan and fry the onion over a medium heat until golden-brown, stirring frequently. Add the ginger, chillies, ground coriander and fennel. Cook, stirring, for 30 seconds. Add 30ml/2 tbsp water. Cook until the liquid has evaporated, then add the tomatoes and peas.

7 Add 45 ml/3 tbsp water, the remaining salt and the fried fish. Stir and cook for about 5 minutes to allow most of the liquid to evaporate. Remove from the heat. Cover.

8 While the fish is cooking, add the cinnamon stick, cardamom, cloves, bay leaves and a large pinch of salt to the pan of boiling water. Drain the soaked rice, add to the pan and bring back to the boil. Cook uncovered for 6 minutes, then drain in a large sieve.

9 In a casserole dish or Dutch oven large enough to hold the rice and fish together, spoon in just enough of the rice to cover the bottom, then dribble over some of the saffron (both milk and saffron strands).

10 Place a layer of the fish mixture on top, and cover with another layer of rice and sprinkle over some more saffron. Continue to layer until you have used up all the fish, rice and saffron, ending with a layer of rice.

11 Cover the dish tightly with a double piece of foil held in place by the casserole lid. Cook for 25 minutes. Remove from the heat and leave to stand for 10 minutes. Garnish with coriander, then serve.

Per portion Energy 325kcal/1356kJ; Protein 34g; Carbohydrate 10g, of which sugars 6g; Fat 17g, of which saturates 2g; Cholesterol 78mg; Calcium 73mg; Fibre 2.7g; Sodium 313mg.

Fish kebabs

Kebabs are very popular in India, whether made with chunks of marinated meat or fish, or with minced (ground) ingredients that are shaped into balls. Small, flat fish patties are also known as *kababs*. These ones, *Machchi Kabab*, contain fragrant spices and fresh herbs.

SERVES 4

15ml/1 tbsp sunflower oil or light olive oil
1 onion, roughly chopped
1cm/½in fresh root ginger, roughly chopped
4 garlic cloves, roughly chopped
2–4 dried red chillies, torn into pieces
5ml/1 tsp ground cumin
1.25ml/¼ tsp ground cloves
450g/1lb firm white fish fillets, such
   as cod or pollock, skinned and
   roughly chopped
1 egg
2.5ml/½ tsp salt, or to taste
30ml/2 tbsp chopped fresh mint
45ml/3 tbsp chopped fresh coriander
   (cilantro)
bunch of spring onions (scallions), green
   part only, finely chopped
sunflower oil, for shallow frying
baby salad leaves and Roasted Tomato
   Chutney, to serve

1 Heat the oil in a heavy frying pan over a medium heat and fry the onion, ginger, garlic and chillies for 5 minutes, until the onion is lightly browned. Add the cumin and cloves, stir and remove from the heat.

2 Blitz the fish, egg and salt in a food processor until roughly chopped, then add the onion mixture and process until fairly smooth. Transfer the mixture to a bowl.

3 Add the mint, coriander and spring onions to the fish mixture. Mix thoroughly and shape into 12 equal-sized round cakes, each about 1cm/½in thick.

4 Heat the oil in a frying pan over a medium heat and fry the cakes in batches for about 3 minutes. Carefully turn over the kebabs with a palette knife and cook for a further 3 minutes on the other side, until they are lightly browned all over and cooked through.

5 Drain on kitchen paper. Serve with baby salad leaves and some chutney.

COOK'S TIP
If time allows, cover the fish mixture with clear film (plastic wrap) and chill in the refrigerator for 1 hour to let the flavours mingle and develop.

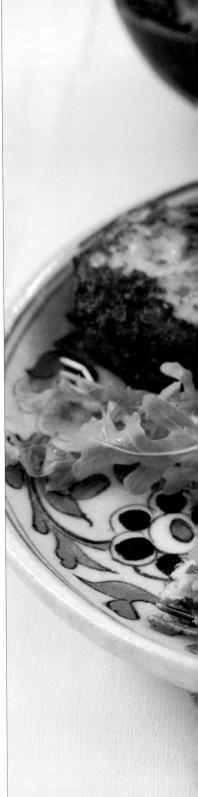

Per portion Energy 241/1004kJ; Protein 24g; Carbohydrate 5g, of which sugars 3g; Fat14, of which saturates 2g; Cholesterol 110mg; Calcium 51mg; Fibre 0.8g; Sodium 341mg.

Fish baked with cardamom

This fish recipe, *Dum Machchi*, is cooked by sealing the ingredients in a heavy roasting pan with a tight-fitting lid made from several layers of foil, so that the steam and flavour cannot escape and fish remains moist and delicate. Try it with Basmati Rice with Caramelized Sugar.

SERVES 4

675g/1½lb tilapia or monkfish fillets, or any other firm, white fish
7.5ml/1½ tbsp lemon juice
5ml/1 tsp salt
2.5cm/1in piece of cinnamon stick, broken up
seeds of 6 green cardamom pods
5ml/1 tsp cumin seeds
10ml/2 tsp coriander seeds
15ml/1 tbsp white poppy seeds
15ml/1 tbsp sesame seeds
60ml/4 tbsp sunflower oil or olive oil
1 large onion, finely chopped
10ml/2 tsp garlic purée
10ml/2 tsp ginger purée
2.5–5ml/½–1 tsp chilli powder
2.5ml/½ tsp ground turmeric
115g/4oz/½ cup thick set natural (plain) yogurt, whisked
2 medium tomatoes, sliced
30–45ml/2–3 tbsp chopped coriander (cilantro) leaves
Basmati Rice with Caramelized Sugar, to serve

3 In a small pan, heat the oil over a medium heat and add the onion. Fry until it is soft and translucent, but not brown. Add the garlic and ginger to the pan, continue to fry for 2 minutes, then stir in the ground ingredients, chilli powder and turmeric.

4 Cook, stirring constantly, for 1 minute, then add the remaining salt and the yogurt. Mix thoroughly and remove the pan from the heat.

1 Cut the fish fillets into 5cm/2in pieces and sprinkle with the lemon juice and half the salt. Set aside for 20 minutes. Preheat the oven to 160°C/325°F/Gas 3.

2 Grind the cinnamon, cardamom seeds, cumin, coriander, poppy and sesame seeds in a coffee grinder until finely ground. Set aside.

5 In a roasting pan (15cm x 30cm/6in x 12in), spread half the onion mixture, half the tomatoes and half the chopped coriander. Arrange the fish on top in a single layer. Carefully spread the remaining onion mix, coriander and tomatoes over the fish.

6 Cover the pan with a piece of foil, sealing the edges. Bake for 35–40 minutes. Transfer to a dish and strain the juices over. Serve with Basmati Rice with Caramelized Sugar.

Per portion Energy 353kcal/1473kJ; Protein 36.2g; Carbohydrate 17.8g, of which sugars 10.6g; Fat 15.9g, of which saturates 2.3g; Cholesterol 0.2mg; Calcium 320mg; Fibre 2.2g; Sodium 126mg.

Tilapia with fenugreek sauce

The slightly bitter flavour of fenugreek combines well with other spices and both the tiny tan-coloured seeds and soft green leaves are used extensively in Indian cooking. Take care not to overcook the fish in this dish, *Methi Machchi*, or it will toughen; the pieces should be just opaque.

SERVES 4

675g/1½lb tilapia fillets, skinned
juice of 1 lime
5ml/1 tsp salt, or to taste
60ml/4 tbsp sunflower oil or light olive oil
5ml/1 tsp fenugreek seeds
2.5ml/½ tsp black mustard seeds
2.5cm/1in fresh root ginger, grated, or
    10ml/2 tsp ginger purée
1 garlic clove, crushed, or 10ml/2 tsp
    garlic purée
2.5ml/½ tsp ground turmeric
5ml/1 tsp ground cumin
10ml/2 tsp ground coriander
2.5ml/½ tsp chilli powder
115g/4oz canned chopped tomatoes,
    with their juice
10ml/2 tsp dried fenugreek leaves
    (kasuri methi), crushed
julienne strips of fresh root ginger and
    fresh green chilli, to garnish
Plain Boiled Rice, to serve

1 Cut the fish into 5cm/2in pieces and sprinkle with the lime juice and half the salt. Set aside for 15–20 minutes.

2 Meanwhile, heat the oil in a heavy frying pan over a medium heat and add the fenugreek seeds. Allow them to darken and flavour the oil, then remove and discard the seeds, retaining the oil. Add the mustard seeds and reduce the heat to low when they start popping.

3 Add the ginger, garlic, turmeric, cumin, coriander and chilli powder. Fry gently for about 2 minutes, then add the tomatoes and fenugreek leaves.

4 Increase the heat and stir-fry until the tomatoes reach a paste-like consistency and the oil separates from the paste.

5 Pour in 120ml/4fl oz/½ cup warm water and stir in the remaining salt. Cook for 3–4 minutes, then add the fish.

6 Simmer for 5–6 minutes, or until the fish is just cooked. Garnish with the ginger and chilli strips and serve with Plain Boiled Rice.

COOK'S TIP
Tilapia has delicate, very white flesh and a subtle flavour. Other white fish fillets may be substituted.

Per portion Energy 285kcal/1189kJ; Protein 31g; Carbohydrate 1g, of which sugars 1g; Fat 18g, of which saturates 2g; Cholesterol 0mg; Calcium 221mg; Fibre 0.2g; Sodium 0595mg.

Prawn korma

This luscious recipe, *Jhinge Ka Korma*, comes from Bhopal, the capital of the central provinces, which is well known for its fabulous fish and shellfish dishes. The almonds and yogurt, along with poppy and sesame seeds, contrast with the hot chilli, garlic and ginger.

SERVES 4

50g/2oz/½ cup blanched almonds
500g/1¼lb raw peeled or frozen king
  prawns (jumbo shrimp), deveined
10ml/2 tbsp lemon juice
2.5ml/½ tsp ground turmeric
15ml/1 tbsp white poppy seeds
15ml/1 tbsp sesame seeds
150g/5oz/⅔ cup whole-milk natural
  (plain) yogurt
7.5ml/1½ tsp gram flour (besan)
60ml/4 tbsp sunflower oil or olive oil
1 large onion, finely chopped
10ml/2 tsp ginger purée
10ml/2 tsp garlic purée
1 fresh chilli, finely chopped (deseeded
  if preferred)
1.25–2.5ml/¼–½ tsp chilli powder
5ml/1 tsp salt, or to taste
15ml/1 tbsp toasted flaked (sliced)
  almonds, to garnish
Basmati Rice with Caramelized Sugar,
  to serve

1 Soak the almonds in 150ml/5fl oz/⅔ cup boiling water and set aside for 20 minutes.

2 In a large mixing bowl, mix the prawns, lemon juice and turmeric together. Cover with clear film (plastic wrap) and set aside.

3 Grind the poppy and sesame seeds in a coffee grinder or blender until they are finely ground. Whisk the yogurt and gram flour together and set aside.

4 In a heavy pan, heat the oil over a medium heat and add the finely chopped onion. Fry gently for 5–6 minutes, until the onion is soft and translucent.

5 Add the ginger, garlic, chilli, ground poppy and sesame seeds, and the chilli powder. Cook for 2–3 minutes, stirring, then add the prawns, salt and the whisked yogurt. Reduce the heat to low, cover the pan and cook for another 3–4 minutes.

6 Meanwhile, purée the almonds with the water in which they were soaked in a food processor or blender, and then add this to the prawns. Stir to mix well and cook for a further 5–6 minutes or until the prawns have curled up at the ends.

7 Transfer to a serving dish and garnish with the toasted almonds. This dish goes particularly well with Basmati Rice with Caramelized Sugar.

Per portion Energy 143kcal/601kJ; Protein 20.4g; Carbohydrate 5.4g, of which sugars 2.7g; Fat 4.8g, of which saturates 0.7g; Cholesterol 195mg; Calcium 168mg; Fibre 0.6g; Sodium 230mg.

Royal-style chicken korma

The presence of royal households in central India established the practice of preparing luxurious food that is now widespread. There are many types of korma, which is a technique rather than a dish. With its savoury cashew sauce, this *Murgh Korma Shahi* recipe is different in taste from the kormas of south India.

SERVES 4

675g/1½lb boned chicken thighs or
   breast fillets, skinned and cut into
   5cm/2in pieces
75g/3oz/⅓ cup whole-milk natural
   (plain) yogurt
10ml/2 tsp gram flour (besan)
5ml/1 tsp salt
10ml/2 tsp ginger purée
10ml/2 tsp garlic purée
60ml/4 tbsp ghee or unsalted butter
2.5cm/1in piece of cinnamon stick
1 large onion, finely sliced
2.5ml/½ tsp ground turmeric
15ml/1 tbsp ground coriander
2.5ml/½ tsp chilli powder, or to taste
50g/2oz/½ cup raw unsalted cashew nuts,
   soaked in boiling water for 15 minutes
150ml/5fl oz/⅔ cup double (heavy) cream
2.5ml/½ tsp ground cardamom
2.5ml/½ tsp ground mace
flat bread, to serve

3 Add the turmeric, coriander and chilli powder, stir-fry for 1 minute, then add the marinated chicken to the pan.

4 Increase the heat slightly and stir-fry the ingredients for about 3–4 minutes or until the chicken changes colour.

5 Pour in 300ml/½ pint/1¼ cups warm water, bring it to the boil, reduce the heat to low, cover and simmer for 15 minutes.

1 Put the chicken in a large bowl. Beat the yogurt and the gram flour together and add to the chicken. Add the salt, ginger and garlic, and mix. Cover with clear film (plastic wrap) and leave for 1 hour.

2 Heat the ghee or butter in a heavy pan over a medium heat and add the cinnamon, followed by the onion. Stir-fry for 5–6 minutes, until the onion is soft and translucent.

6 Drain the cashew nuts and purée them in a food processor or blender with the cream. Add to the chicken. Simmer for 2–3 minutes.

7 Stir in the ground cardamom and mace. Remove from the heat. Serve with flat bread.

Per portion Energy 343kcal/1450kJ; Protein 54g; Carbohydrate 18g, of which sugars 10.7g; Fat 6.8g, of which saturates 2.6g; Cholesterol 151mg; Calcium 66mg; Fibre 1.8g; Sodium 197mg.

Chicken in saffron sauce

The origins of this recipe, *Murgh Kalai Kesari*, go back to the Mughal era and the ingredients used certainly evoke a time of wealth. Here the sauce is enriched with saffron and freshly made almond purée.

SERVES 4

50g/2oz blanched almonds
675g/1½lb boned chicken thighs or
    breast fillets, skinned and cut into
    5cm/2in cubes
10ml/2 tsp garlic purée
10ml/2 tsp ginger purée
5ml/1 tsp ground cumin
7.5ml/1½ tsp ground coriander
2.5–5ml/½–1 tsp crushed dried chillies
1 large onion, finely chopped
75g/3oz/⅓ cup full-fat (whole) natural
    (plain) yogurt
10ml/2 tsp gram flour (besan)
4 whole cloves
4 green cardamom pods, split at the
    top of each pod
2.5cm/1in piece of cinnamon stick
25g/1oz ghee or unsalted butter
300ml/½ pint/1¼ cups full-fat (whole) milk
2.5ml/½ tsp saffron strands, pounded
    and soaked in 15ml/1 tbsp hot milk
2.5ml/½ tsp garam masala
1–2 fresh green chillies, deseeded and
    cut into julienne strips, to garnish
naan, to serve

1 Put the almonds in a small heatproof bowl and pour over 150ml/5fl oz/⅔ cup boiling water. Set aside for 20 minutes.

2 Put the chicken, garlic, ginger, cumin, coriander, crushed chillies and onion in a large, heavy pan. Beat the yogurt and gram flour together in a bowl until smooth, then add to the pan.

3 Add the cloves, cardamom and cinnamon, and place the pan over a medium heat. Stir until the contents begin to sizzle. Reduce the heat to low, cover the pan and cook for 20–25 minutes, stirring occasionally.

4 Remove the lid and increase the heat to high. Cook until the liquid is reduced to a thick, batter-like consistency, stirring often.

5 Add the ghee or butter and stir-fry the chicken for 3–4 minutes, or until the fat rises to the surface of the mixture.

6 Purée the almonds with the water in which they were soaked in a blender or food processor. Add this to the pan.

7 Add the milk, and saffron and the soaking milk. Stir and bring it to the boil. Reduce the heat and simmer, uncovered, for 5–6 minutes. Add the garam masala. Transfer to a serving dish and garnish with the strips of green chilli. Serve immediately with pieces of naan.

Per portion Energy 554kcal/2321kJ; Protein 75.6g; Carbohydrate 5.1g, of which sugars 4.7g; Fat 25.9g, of which saturates 12.2g; Cholesterol 255mg; Calcium 146mg; Fibre 0.8g; Sodium 792mg.

Marinated whole chicken with lamb stuffing

Although this may seem an unusual combination, the two different meats work extremely well together, with the spicy lamb juices soaking into the chicken, both flavouring and making it beautifully tender and succulent. To make *Zaffrani Murgh Musallam*, a bird is first skinned and marinated overnight in a saffron-scented yogurt, before being filled with a stuffing made from richly spiced lamb, and roasted.

SERVES 4–6

For the marinade:
large pinch of saffron threads, pounded
30ml/2 tbsp hot milk
60ml/4 tbsp natural (plain) yogurt
2.5cm/1in fresh root ginger, grated, or
  10ml/2 tsp ginger purée
2 cloves garlic, crushed, or 10ml/2 tsp
  garlic purée
2.5ml/½ tsp ground cardamom
2.5ml/½ tsp freshly grated nutmeg
2.5ml/½ tsp salt, or to taste
1.3kg/3lb chicken

For the stuffing and sauce:
225g/8oz lean minced (ground) lamb
1–2 fresh green chillies, finely chopped
1cm/½in fresh root ginger, grated, or
  5ml/1 tsp ginger purée
1 clove garlic, crushed, or 5ml/1 tsp
  garlic purée
10ml/2 tsp ground cumin
2.5ml/½ tsp garam masala
15ml/1 tbsp finely chopped fresh mint
30ml/2 tbsp chopped fresh coriander (cilantro)
2.5ml/½ tsp salt, or to taste
25g/1oz unsalted butter
15ml/1 tbsp gram flour (besan)
fresh mint sprigs and fine strips of fresh
  red chilli, to garnish
pilau, to serve

1 For the marinade, soak the saffron in the milk for 10 minutes. Stir in the yogurt, ginger, garlic, cardamom, nutmeg and salt.

2 Skin the chicken and lightly score the legs, thighs and the breasts with a knife.

3 Brush the marinade over the chicken, cover and refrigerate for 6–8 hours. Bring to room temperature before cooking. Pre-heat the oven to 180°C/350°F/Gas 4.

4 For the stuffing, mix together the lamb, chillies, ginger, garlic, cumin, garam masala, mint, half the coriander and salt. Fill the cavity and the neck end of the chicken with the stuffing, packing it tightly.

5 Place the chicken in a roasting tin and cover with a lid or a loose covering of foil. Roast in the centre of the oven for 1 hour.

6 Melt the butter in a small pan. Remove the lid or foil from the chicken and baste with the pan juices, then pour over the butter. Cook for a further 30 minutes, basting again with the juices after 15 minutes.

7 Transfer the chicken to a warmed serving dish, cover with foil and leave to rest.

8 Strain the pan juices into a jug and make up to 300ml/½ pint/1¼ cups with water. Blend the gram flour with a little water in the pan in which you melted the butter, then stir in the stock. Cook over a medium heat, stirring, until thickened. Stir in the remaining chopped coriander. Serve in a warmed jug.

9 Carve the chicken and garnish with mint and chilli. Serve with the sauce and a pilau.

Per portion Energy 216kcal/910kJ; Protein 33g; Carbohydrate 2g, of which sugars 0g; Fat 9g, of which saturates 3g; Cholesterol 135mg; Calcium 24mg; Fibre 0.3g; Sodium 578mg.

Chicken with spinach sauce

In this recipe, *Murgh-saag Masala*, succulent breast meat, tinged golden with turmeric, is cooked in a mildly spiced mixture with fresh spinach leaves, which wilt to make a vibrant green sauce. Briefly marinating the chicken in lime juice helps to tenderize the meat as well as adding a slight sharpness to the finished dish.

SERVES 4–6

1kg/2¼lb chicken breasts, skinned
juice of 1 lime
5ml/1 tsp salt, or to taste
60ml/4 tbsp sunflower oil or light olive oil
1 large onion, finely chopped
2.5cm/1in fresh root ginger, grated, or
   10ml/2 tsp ginger purée
4 cloves garlic, crushed, or 20ml/4 tsp
   garlic purée
2.5ml/½ tsp ground turmeric
10ml/2 tsp ground cumin
2.5ml/½ tsp chilli powder
25g/1oz ghee or unsalted butter
1 dried red chilli, finely chopped
2.5ml/½ tsp cumin seeds
450g/1lb fresh spinach, washed, drained
   and coarsely chopped
2.5ml/½ tsp garam masala
4 tomatoes, peeled and diced,
   to garnish
warm Indian bread, to serve

1 Cut each chicken breast lengthways into two pieces. Sprinkle with the lime juice and salt. Set aside for 15–20 minutes.

2 Meanwhile, heat the oil over a medium heat and fry the onion until it begins to brown. Add the ginger and half the garlic and continue to fry for further 2 minutes. Reduce the heat to low and add the turmeric, cumin and chilli powder. Cook for a few seconds.

3 Add the chicken to the pan and cook, turning occasionally until the outside of the meat is opaque. Pour in 75ml/2½fl oz/⅓ cup water and bring to the boil. Cover the pan with a lid and simmer gently for 15 minutes.

4 In a separate pan, melt the ghee or butter over a low heat and fry the remaining garlic, the chilli and the cumin seeds for 1 minute.

5 Add the spinach and increase the heat to high. Stir until the spinach has wilted. Add the chicken and cook for 10 minutes, until cooked. Stir in the garam masala, then garnish with the tomatoes and serve with warm Indian bread.

COOK'S TIP
It is common to add garam masala at the end of the cooking time, as it loses flavour if cooked too long.

Per portion Energy 351kcal/1469kJ; Protein 43g; Carbohydrate 7g, of which sugars 5g; Fat 17g, of which saturates 5g; Cholesterol 128mg; Calcium 164mg; Fibre 2.8g; Sodium 543mg.

Minced lamb in yogurt sauce

Both minced (ground) lamb and chicken are used in India to make kebabs, spicy fillings, or cooked with rice to make quick-and-easy pilaus. In this dish, *Dahi Ka Kheema*, minced lamb is flavoured with cardamom, cinnamon and cloves.

SERVES 4

60ml/4 tbsp sunflower oil or light olive oil
2.5cm/1in piece of cinnamon stick
2 brown cardamom pods, bruised
4 green cardamom pods, bruised
5 cloves
1 large onion, finely chopped
2.5cm/1in fresh root ginger, grated, or
  10ml/2 tsp ginger purée
2 cloves garlic, crushed, or 10ml/2 tsp
  garlic purée
675g/1½lb lean minced (ground) lamb
200ml/7fl oz/scant 1 cup whole-milk
  natural (plain) yogurt
10ml/2 tsp gram flour (besan)
10ml/2 tsp ground cumin
2.5ml/½ tsp ground turmeric
2.5–5ml/½–1 tsp chilli powder
2 whole fresh green chillies
2 whole fresh red chillies
2.5ml/½ tsp garam masala
sprigs of fresh mint, to garnish
warm Indian bread, to serve

1 Heat the oil over a low heat in a heavy frying pan. Add the cinnamon, both types of cardamom pods and the cloves.

2 Let the spices sizzle for about 30 seconds, then add the chopped onion. Increase the heat to medium and fry, stirring frequently, until the onion is just beginning to brown. Add the ginger and garlic and continue to fry for about 5 minutes, until the onion is soft and lightly browned.

3 Add the minced lamb and increase the heat slightly. Stir and cook, breaking up the meat with a wooden spoon, for about 5 minutes, until the meat is brown and most of the cooking juices have evaporated.

4 Blend the yogurt and gram flour together in a small bowl, then stir in the cumin, turmeric and chilli powder.

5 Add to the mince and stir for 1 minute, then pour in 175ml/6fl oz/¾ cup hot water. Bring to the boil, reduce the heat to low and simmer, uncovered, for 10 minutes.

6 Add the whole chillies and cook for 3–4 minutes, then stir in the garam masala. Garnish with mint and serve with warm Indian bread.

Per portion Energy 460kcal/1914kJ; Protein 39g; Carbohydrate 11g, of which sugars 8g; Fat 30g, of which saturates 3g; Cholesterol147mg; Calcium 141mg; Fibre 1.2g; Sodium 47mg.

Saffron-scented rice with fragrant lamb curry

Hailing from Afghanistan, this superb dish, *Biryani Khaiberi*, features lamb cooked in a fragrant sauce with saffron-scented rice. The meat and rice are part-cooked, then combined in layers and baked in a tightly sealed pan in the oven, creating an irresistible flavour and texture.

SERVES 4–5

675g/1½lb boned leg of lamb, cut into
  2.5cm/1in cubes
50g/2oz/¼ cup natural (plain) yogurt, whisked
5ml/1 tsp salt
75g/3oz ghee or unsalted butter
2 large onions, finely sliced
10ml/2 tsp ginger purée
10ml/2 tsp garlic purée

For the ground spice mix:
10ml/2 tsp coriander seeds, finely ground
5ml/1 tsp cumin seeds, finely ground
2.5cm/1in piece of cinnamon stick,
  finely ground
4 cardamom pods, finely ground
4 cloves, finely ground
15ml/1 tbsp white poppy seeds,
  finely ground
¼ of a whole nutmeg, crushed and ground

For the rice:
2.5ml/½ tsp saffron strands, pounded
30ml/2 tbsp hot milk
2.5cm/1in piece of cinnamon stick
4 cardamom pods, bruised
4 cloves
2 star anise
2 bay leaves
10ml/2 tsp salt, or to taste
350g/12oz/1¾ cups basmati rice, washed
  and drained
15ml/1 tbsp ghee or unsalted butter, melted

1 Mix the lamb, yogurt and salt in a bowl. Cover and set aside for 20–30 minutes.

2 Melt the ghee or butter over a medium heat and add the onion. Fry, stirring, until the onion is well browned. Turn off the heat and remove the onion with a slotted spoon. Drain on kitchen paper.

3 Return the pan to the heat. Add the ginger and garlic and fry for 1 minute. Combine all the ingredients for the ground spice mix.

4 Add the ground spice mix and stir-fry for 1–2 minutes, then add the lamb. Stir and cook over medium heat for 2–3 minutes, then remove from the heat and set aside.

5 For the rice, soak the saffron in the hot milk and set aside for 10 minutes. Preheat the oven to 160°C/ 325°F/Gas 3.

6 Boil 1.5 litres/2½ pints/6¼ cups water in a large pan and add the cinnamon, cardamom, cloves, star anise, bay leaves, salt and rice. Boil steadily for 2–3 minutes to partially cook the rice, then drain the rice in a sieve, reserving the whole spices.

7 Spread the lamb evenly in a heavy, ovenproof pan or casserole. Top with half the fried onion and pile the rice on top, with the whole spices.

8 Sprinkle the saffron milk and melted ghee or butter over the top.

9 Soak a large piece of baking parchment and a dish towel in water, then squeeze them out. Place the paper on top of the rice and the towel on top of the paper. Seal the pan with a double thickness of foil and cover this with the pan or casserole lid.

10 Cook in the centre of the oven for 1 hour. Switch off the oven and leave the pan or casserole inside the oven for 30 minutes.

11 Remove the pan or casserole from the oven and stir the mixture with a metal spoon to mix the rice and meat together and to fluff up the grains of rice. Transfer the biryani to a serving dish and garnish with the reserved fried onion.

Per portion Energy 769kcal/3208kJ; Protein 43.6g; Carbohydrate 67.6g, of which sugars 14.5g; Fat 36.2g, of which saturates 15g; Cholesterol 142mg; Calcium 134mg; Fibre 2.6g; Sodium 252mg.

Lamb in rose-scented almond sauce

Pasanda Badam Kari is typical of the elegant and rich creamy dishes brought to India by the Mughals. They also introduced the use of floral essences in both sweet and savoury cuisine. Here, a sprinkling of rose water adds a distinctive yet delicate aroma to tender slices of lamb braised in a saffron sauce that is thickened with a fresh almond purée. It makes the perfect dish for a special occasion.

SERVES 4

large pinch of saffron threads, pounded
30ml/2 tbsp hot milk
25g/1oz/¼ cup blanched almonds
675g/1½lb boned leg of lamb
75ml/5 tbsp natural (plain) yogurt
10ml/2 tsp gram flour (besan)
60ml/4 tbsp sunflower oil or light olive oil
1 large onion, finely chopped
2 fresh green chillies, finely chopped
2.5ml/1in fresh root ginger, grated, or
  10ml/2 tsp ginger purée
2 cloves garlic, crushed, or 10ml/2 tsp
  garlic purée
2.5ml/½ tsp ground turmeric
10ml/2 tsp ground cumin
5ml/1 tsp ground coriander
2.5–5ml/½–1 tsp chilli powder
5ml/1 tsp salt, or to taste
150ml/¼ pint/⅔ cup double (heavy) cream
2.5ml/½ tsp garam masala
30ml/2 tbsp rose water
toasted flaked (sliced) almonds,
  to garnish
Pilau Rice with Raisins, to serve

1 Crumble the saffron into a small bowl. Pour over the hot milk and leave to soak.

2 Put the almonds in another bowl and pour over 150ml/¼ pint/⅔ cup boiling water. Set aside for about 20 minutes. Purée the almonds with their liquid in a blender or using a hand-held blender, until smooth.

3 Trim any fat from the meat, then place it on a chopping board and cover it with greaseproof paper. Gently bash it with a meat mallet or a wooden rolling pin to flatten the meat evenly until it is about 5mm/¼in thick. Cut the lamb into thin slices, about 2.5cm/1in long.

4 Stir the yogurt and gram flour together in a small bowl until smooth.

5 Heat the oil in a heavy frying pan over a medium heat, add the onion and fry until soft, but not brown, stirring frequently. Add the green chillies, ginger and garlic and cook for 2 minutes, then add the dry spices and cook for 1 minute, stirring.

> **COOK'S TIP**
> If you don't have a meat mallet, you can use the base of a heavy pan or a rolling pin to pound the meat.

6 Add the meat to the pan and cook, stirring, for 1–2 minutes, until it is lightly browned. Stir in the yogurt and gram flour mixture and cook, stirring, for a further 2–3 minutes, until most of the moisture evaporates and the fat separates from the spice paste.

7 Pour in 150ml/¼ pint/⅔ cup hot water and season with salt. Bring to the boil, cover the pan with a lid and reduce the heat to low.

8 Cook the curry, stirring occasionally, for 35 minutes, then stir in the almond purée, the saffron with its soaking liquid, and the cream. Cover and simmer for a further 10–12 minutes or until the meat is tender. Stir in the garam masala and rose water.

9 Transfer to a warmed serving dish or individual plates, scatter with toasted flaked almonds and serve with Pilau Rice with Raisins.

Per portion Energy 669kcal/2775kJ; Protein 40g; Carbohydrate 10g, of which sugars 6g; Fat 53g, of which saturates 21g; Cholesterol 177mg; Calcium 128mg; Fibre 1.6g; Sodium 620mg.

Lamb in mango sauce

Aam Ka Gosht is a Mughal delicacy. It has a pleasant sweet-and-sour taste combined with a heady bouquet of spices, and contains mangoes cooked in a fragrant sugar syrup. As fresh mangoes can sometimes be difficult to find out of season, this recipe uses dried, ready to eat ones, available all year round.

SERVES 4

675g/1½lb boned leg of lamb
60ml/4 tbsp sunflower oil or olive oil
1 large onion, finely chopped
10ml/2 tsp ginger purée
10ml/2 tsp garlic purée
5ml/1 tsp ground turmeric
10ml/2 tsp ground cumin
2.5–5ml/½–1 tsp chilli powder
50g/2oz/¼ cup thick set natural (plain) yogurt
10ml/2 tsp gram flour (besan)
5ml/1 tsp salt, or to taste
2 firm, ripe tomatoes, skinned and chopped
115g/4oz dried ready-to-eat mango
2.5ml/½ tsp garam masala
22.5ml/1½ tbsp red wine vinegar
30ml/2 tbsp coriander (cilantro) chopped
warm naan, to serve

1 Trim all visible fat from the meat using a sharp knife, then cut it into 5cm/2in cubes and set aside.

2 In a heavy pan, heat the oil over a medium heat and add the onion. Fry for 3–4 minutes, stirring constantly, then add the ginger and garlic.

3 Fry the ginger and garlic for 3–4 minutes, then add the turmeric, cumin and chilli powder. Stir-fry for 30 seconds, then add 45ml/3 tbsp water. Stir-fry until the water has completely evaporated.

4 Add another 45ml/3 tbsp water to the pan and again stir fry until evaporated. Repeat one more time. Meanwhile, whisk the yogurt and the gram flour together

5 Add the meat to the pan and stir in the yogurt and gram flour mixture. Reduce the heat to low, cover the pan and cook for around 40–45 minutes.

6 Add the salt, tomatoes and mango. Simmer, uncovered, for 10–12 minutes, or until the sauce has thickened and has a gravy-like consistency.

7 Stir in the garam masala, vinegar and half of the chopped coriander. Transfer to warmed serving bowls and garnish with the remaining chopped coriander. Serve with warm naan.

Per portion Energy 534kcal/2230kJ; Protein 38.8g; Carbohydrate 23.6g, of which sugars 17g; Fat 32.6g, of which saturates 10.8g; Cholesterol 133mg; Calcium 98mg; Fibre 3.8g; Sodium 176mg.

Carrot and green pea pilau

Central Indian food is an amalgamation of recipes from the neighbouring states. This recipe, *Gajjar-Mattar Ke Pulao*, though cooked elsewhere, is richer than others, perhaps as a result of the influence of a Royal household. Because of this it is more suitable as a main course than as an accompaniment.

SERVES 4

225g/8oz/generous 1 cup basmati rice
a good pinch of saffron threads, pounded
15ml/1 tbsp hot milk
2.5cm/1in piece of cinnamon stick
2 star anise
175ml/6fl oz/¾ cup full-fat (whole) milk
5ml/1 tsp salt, or to taste
5ml/1 tsp cumin seeds
10ml/2 tsp coriander seeds
5ml/1 tsp black peppercorns
50g/2oz/4 tsp ghee or unsalted butter
10ml/2 tsp ginger purée
1 fresh green chilli, chopped
  (deseeded if preferred)
175g/6oz carrots, cut into batons
110g/4oz frozen garden peas
4 cloves
4 green cardamom pods, bruised
15ml/1 tbsp seedless raisins
15ml/1 tbsp slivered almonds
raita, to serve

3 Put the rice in a heavy pan and add the steeped saffron with its soaking milk, along with the cinnamon stick and star anise.

4 Add the milk and pour in 300ml/½ pint/ 1¼ cups water and half the salt. Bring it to the boil, reduce the heat to very low, cover and cook for 7-8 minutes. Remove from the heat and let it stand, undisturbed, for 10 minutes.

8 Stir-fry the carrots over a medium heat for 3–4 minutes, then add 50ml/2fl oz/¼ cup water. Cover and cook over a low heat until the carrots are almost tender.

9 Add the peas, the remaining salt and the ground spices, then cover and cook for 5–6 minutes. Remove from the heat.

1 Wash the rice until the water runs clear, then soak for 20–30 minutes. Drain well.

2 Soak the saffron in the hot milk and leave to infuse for 10 minutes.

5 Meanwhile, heat a small, heavy pan over a medium heat, then add the cumin, coriander and peppercorns and dry-roast for about 1 minute, until they release their aroma, stirring constantly.

6 Remove from the pan and leave to cool, then crush them to a fine powder with a mortar and pestle. Set aside.

7 Heat half the ghee or butter in a frying pan over a low heat and add the ginger and green chilli. Cook for 1 minute, then add the carrots.

10 Fluff up the rice with a fork and add the cooked vegetables. Using a fork or a flat wooden spoon, stir them around gently to mix the vegetables without breaking them up, then cover the pan.

11 Melt the remaining ghee or butter over a low heat and add the cloves, cardamom, raisins and almonds. Stir and cook until the cardamom pods and the raisins swell up and the nuts are a light brown colour.

12 Transfer the pilau to a serving dish and sprinkle the spiced butter evenly on top. Garnish with the cardamom, raisins and almonds. Serve with a raita.

VARIATIONS
• Replace the carrot batons with thick strips of pumpkin.
• Garnish with fried onions instead of cardamom, raisins and almonds.

Per portion Energy 422kcal/1772kJ; Protein 8g; Carbohydrate 63g, of which sugars 12g; Fat 17g, of which saturates 10g; Cholesterol 42mg; Calcium 104mg; Fibre 5.2; Sodium 534mg.

Ginger and cumin puffed bread with spinach

This delectable bread, *Palak Puri*, from the Indore area is gently aromatic, and its flavours mingle happily with any vegetable curry. Traditionally, the dough is divided into small portions and each puri is rolled out individually, but in order to save time, you can roll out larger portions and cut them into smaller circles with a metal cutter. The crisp fried breads are divine with all manner of curries.

MAKES 20

100g/3½oz fresh spinach leaves
300g/10oz/2½ cups chapati flour (atta) or
    fine wholemeal (whole-wheat) flour, plus
    extra for dusting
2.5ml/½ tsp aniseed
2.5ml/½ tsp salt
5ml/1 tsp ginger purée
2.5ml/½ tsp chilli powder
25g/1oz butter
30ml/1fl oz/2 tbsp water
sunflower oil, for deep-frying

1 Put the spinach in a heatproof bowl and pour over enough boiling water to cover. Stir to ensure that all the leaves are immersed in the water. Leave them soaking for 2 minutes, then drain and refresh in cold water.

2 Squeeze out as much excess water as possible from the spinach and chop the leaves finely with a large knife or in a food processor, in short bursts, taking care not to reduce the spinach to a purée.

3 Put the flour in a mixing bowl and add the aniseed, salt, ginger and chilli powder. Mix well and rub in the butter.

4 Add the chopped spinach and 30ml/1fl oz/2 tbsp water, and mix until a soft dough is formed.

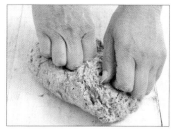

5 Transfer the dough to a flat surface and knead for 3–4 minutes.

6 Cover with a damp dish towel and set aside for 30 minutes.

7 Divide the dough into two equal parts and pinch off or cut ten equal portions from each. Form into balls and flatten to smooth, round cakes.

8 Dust the cakes lightly with flour and roll each one out to a 7.5cm/3in circle, taking care not to tear or pierce them as they will not puff up if damaged. Place them in a single layer on baking parchment and cover with another piece of parchment.

9 Heat the oil in a wok or other pan suitable for deep-frying. When the oil has a faint shimmer of rising smoke on the surface, carefully drop in one cake. As soon as it rises to the surface, gently tap round the edges to encourage puffing.

10 When it has puffed up, turn it over and fry the other side until browned. Drain on kitchen paper.

11 Keep the fried puris on a baking tray in a single layer while you cook the remaining dough. They are best eaten fresh, though they can be re-heated for 2–3 minutes in a hot oven. Serve with any curry.

COOK'S TIP
The oil should measure at least 180°C/350°F on a thermometer when you add the dough.

Per portion Energy 58kcal/247kJ; Protein 2.1g; Carbohydrate 9.8g, of which sugars 0.4g; Fat 1.5g, of which saturates 0.7g; Cholesterol 3mg; Calcium 15mg; Fibre 1.5g; Sodium 17mg.

Mung bean and wholewheat flat bread

Mah Ki Roti is traditionally made with sprouted mung beans, which can take time, but there are sprouting kits available, which make it easier. Sprouting enhances the nutritional value of the beans, but the recipe can be made without sprouting them if you wish. The delicious bread is bursting with health-giving qualities, and has a wholesome taste and unique texture.

MAKES 8

150g/5oz whole mung beans
  (sabut mung dhal)
5ml/1 tsp salt
1 medium onion, roughly chopped
15ml/1 tbsp fresh coriander (cilantro)
  leaves and stalks
30ml/2 tbsp sunflower oil or light olive oil
325g/11oz/2¾ cups strong wholemeal
  (whole-wheat) bread flour, plus extra
  for dusting
75ml–100ml/2½–3½fl oz/¼–⅓ cup water
ghee or unsalted butter, for shallow-frying

1 Wash the mung beans and soak them in a bowl of warm water. As the water cools, replace it with more warm water and leave the bowl in a warm place. During the sprouting time (*see* packet instructions), change the water 3–4 times.

2 Drain the beans and place them in a food processor.

COOK'S TIP

Some larger supermarkets and health food stores sell sprouted mung beans. If you wash and soak the beans in warm water and change the water as it gets cold, they will sprout faster. Leave it in a warm place, for 24–36 hours, and then they will be ready for use.

3 Add the salt, onion, coriander and oil to the food processor and blend until a fine, granular consistency is achieved. Add the flour and blend to combine.

4 Transfer to a bowl. Gradually add the water and mix until a soft dough is formed. Take care not to use all the water at once as the amount needed will depend on the absorbency level of the flour you are using, and you don't want the dough to be too wet.

5 Transfer the dough to a flat surface and knead it for 2–3 minutes, adding a little flour if it is too sticky. Cover with clear film (plastic wrap) and set aside to rest for 30 minutes. Alternatively, make the dough in a food processor, using a dough hook and following manufacturer's instructions.

6 Divide the dough into eight equal portions and flatten each of them into a smooth round cake. Dust each cake with a little flour.

7 Roll each portion out to a circle 13cm/5in in diameter. Keep the rest covered.

8 Place a heavy griddle over a low-medium heat and dry-roast the flat bread for 30–40 seconds on each side. Spread 5ml/1 tsp of ghee or butter on the surface and turn it over. Cook until the underside is browned.

9 Spread the surface with the ghee or butter and flip it over. Cook until browned. Wrap it in a clean dish towel until you finish cooking all the bread. Serve with any curry.

Per portion Energy 195kcal/821kJ; Protein 6g; Carbohydrate 28g, of which sugars 28g; Fat 7g, of which saturates 2g; Cholesterol 7mg; Calcium 26mg; Fibre 4.8g; Sodium 249mg.

Cumin and saffron flat bread

Bhopali Roti is a rich bread with a superb taste and flavour that does not
need to be supported by a spicy curry – its attractive appearance and
blend of spices make it good enough to eat on its own. Cumin and
saffron are the key ingredients, but the addition of chillies and
coriander (cilantro) make it even more aromatic.

MAKES 12

50g/2oz raw unsalted cashew nuts
pinch of saffron, pounded
5ml/1 tsp cumin seeds
350g/12oz/3 cups chapati flour,
  plus extra for dusting
115g/4oz/⅔ cup ground rice
2.5ml/½ tsp salt
1 fresh green chilli, finely chopped,
  (deseeded if preferred)
15ml/1 tbsp fresh coriander (cilantro)
  leaves, finely chopped
15ml/1 tbsp ghee or unsalted butter
15ml/1 tbsp sunflower oil or olive oil
vegetable oil, for cooking

1 Put the cashew nuts and saffron in a
heatproof bowl and pour over 100ml/3½fl oz/
scant ½ cup boiling water. Leave to soak for
15 minutes.

2 Dry-roast the cumin seeds in a small
heavy pan for 1 minute. Remove from the
pan, leave to cool, then crush in a mortar
and pestle.

3 In a large mixing bowl, mix the chapati
flour, ground rice, salt, chilli, coriander and
crushed cumin together. Rub in the ghee
or butter using your fingertips.

4 Purée the cashew nuts and saffron with
their soaking water in a blender or food
processor, then add this to the flour.

5 Mix together with your fingertips, then
gradually add 120ml/4fl oz/½ cup warm
water. Mix until a dough is formed, then
transfer to a lightly floured board and knead
for 4–5 minutes until the dough is pliable.
Cover with a cloth and rest for 30 minutes.

6 Divide into 12 balls, rotating between your
palms to make them smooth. Flatten into
cakes 1cm/½in thick. Dust with flour and roll
out to 15cm/6in discs. Preheat a heavy
griddle or frying pan over medium heat.

7 Place on the griddle or pan and cook for
2 minutes. Turn over and spread the lightly
cooked side with 5ml/1 tsp oil.

8 Cook until brown patches appear on the
underside, then turn over and spread the
other side with 5ml/1 tsp oil. When the
underside is lightly browned, turn again and
cook for a further 1–2 minutes. Serve hot.

Per portion Energy 169kcal/710kJ; Protein 5.4g; Carbohydrate 27.3g, of which sugars 0.9g; Fat 4.8g, of which saturates
1.3g; Cholesterol 3mg; Calcium 15mg; Fibre 2.8g; Sodium 22mg.

Spiced gram flour flat bread

Besan Ki Roti is the ideal bread for anyone who needs to avoid gluten, as they are made with gram flour (besan), which is produced from ground chickpeas rather than wheat. The dough is kneaded together with grated onion, Asafoetida and chillies, then griddle-roasted, which gives a delicious aroma and a nutty taste.

MAKES 8

400g/14oz/3½ cups gram flour (besan),
  sifted, plus extra for dusting
5ml/1 tsp nigella seeds
2.5ml/¼ tsp Asafoetida
5ml/1 tsp salt, or to taste
1 medium onion, peeled
1 fresh green chilli, finely chopped
  (deseeded if preferred)
45ml/3 tbsp coriander (cilantro) leaves,
  finely chopped
sunflower oil, for cooking

1 Put the gram flour in a mixing bowl, then add the nigella seeds, Asafoetida and salt. Grate the onion, then add to the flour with the chilli and coriander.

2 Mix well, then gradually add 100ml/3½fl oz/ 7 tbsp water until a dough forms.

3 Transfer the dough to a flat surface and knead it for a couple of minutes with gentle pressure, turning it around frequently. If the dough sticks to your fingers, add a little oil.

4 Divide the dough into eight equal portions and flatten them into round cakes.

5 Dust each cake in the flour, then roll them out to circles of about 13cm/5in diameter with a rolling pin.

6 Preheat a griddle over a low/medium heat and place a flat bread on it.

7 Cook the bread for about 1 minute, then spread 15ml/1 tbsp oil around the edges. Continue to cook for 30–40 seconds or until browned.

8 Turn the bread over and cook the second side until browned. Transfer to a plate lined with kitchen paper and keep warm while you repeat with the remaining breads.

Per portion Energy 237kcal/1002kJ; Protein 4.5g; Carbohydrate 39.2g, of which sugars 0.4g; Fat 8.1g, of which saturates 0.9g; Cholesterol 0mg; Calcium 21mg; Fibre 6g; Sodium 1mg.

Rice bread with fresh ginger

Chawal Ki Roti is an excellent way of using up leftover cooked rice. Combined with rice flour, oil and yogurt, then flavoured with fresh ginger and coriander (cilantro), the dough is simple to make. The breads are usually cooked on a *tava* – a flat iron griddle pan – but a heavy frying pan can be used instead.

MAKES 8

225g/8oz/2 cups rice flour
115g/4oz/1 cup cold cooked rice
2.5ml/½ tsp chilli powder
2.5ml/½ tsp salt, or to taste
15ml/1 tbsp finely chopped fresh
  coriander (cilantro)
2.5cm/1in fresh root ginger, grated, or
  10 ml/2 tsp ginger purée
15ml/1 tbsp sunflower oil or olive oil,
  plus extra for brushing
120ml/4fl oz/½ cup thick set natural
  (plain) yogurt

COOK'S TIP

When shaping the breads, gently pat and stretch the dough between your palms. Because rice is gluten-free, the dough won't be stretchy and elastic like normal bread dough, so it isn't possible to roll it out with a rolling pin.

---

1 Put the rice flour and cooked rice in a large mixing bowl and stir together. Add the chilli, salt and coriander and stir again to combine. Make a hollow in the centre of the mixture.

2 Blend the ginger with the oil and yogurt in a jug, then stir in 75ml/5 tbsp warm water. Pour the mixture into the hollow in the dry ingredients and stir with a wooden spoon until a dough is formed.

3 Lightly knead the dough for 1–2 minutes in the bowl. Divide the mixture into eight pieces, then shape each into a ball and set aside.

4 Preheat a heavy griddle or frying pan over a medium heat. Smear a little oil in your hands and pat and stretch each dough ball gently between your palms into a 15cm/6in circle; it doesn't matter if it is not perfectly round.

5 Place on the griddle or pan and cook for 2–3 minutes. Turn over and brush the lightly cooked side with 5ml/1 tsp oil. Cook until brown patches appear on the underside, then turn over and brush the other side with 5ml/1 tsp oil. Press down on the thicker edges to ensure it cooks evenly.

6 When the underside is lightly browned with dark brown patches, turn again and cook for a further 1–2 minutes. Serve hot.

Per portion Energy 152kcal/637kJ; Protein 3g; Carbohydrate 28g, of which sugars 1g; Fat 3g, of which saturates 1g; Cholesterol 2mg; Calcium 40mg; Fibre 0.6g; Sodium 138mg.

New potatoes in yogurt sauce

Dum Aloo is a rich side dish, which can also be served as a main course with any Indian bread. The final cooking is done using the dum (steam cooking) method, which involves tightly sealing the pan with foil and a lid and cooking over a very low heat.

SERVES 4

15ml/1 tbsp white poppy seeds
60ml/4 tbsp sunflower oil or light olive oil
675g/1½lb new potatoes, par-boiled
  and peeled
1 large onion, finely sliced
75g/3oz/⅓ cup full-fat (whole) natural
  (plain) yogurt
5ml/1 tsp ginger purée
2.5–5ml/½–1 tsp chilli powder
5ml/1 tsp ground coriander
5ml/1 tsp ground cumin
5ml/1 tsp salt, or to taste
2.5ml/½ tsp garam masala
Indian bread, to serve

1 Grind the poppy seeds in a coffee grinder or mortar and pestle and set aside. In a heavy pan, heat the oil over a medium heat and fry the potatoes in two batches until well browned. Drain on kitchen paper.

2 When cool enough to handle, prick the potatoes with a cocktail stick (toothpick).

3 In the same oil, fry the onion until it is a pale golden colour. Press the onion to the side of the pan to remove any excess oil, then transfer to kitchen paper to drain.

4 Blend the yogurt, poppy seeds and fried onion in a blender to form a smooth purée, then set aside.

5 In the remaining oil in the pan, fry the ginger over a low heat for 1 minute, then add the chilli powder, coriander and cumin. Stir-fry for 30–40 seconds, then add the purée.

6 Cook until the mixture begins to bubble, then add the browned potatoes, salt and garam masala. Cover the pan with a piece of foil and press it all the way round the edge to seal. Put the lid on and reduce the heat to very low.

7 Cook for about 30 minutes, until the potatoes are tender and the sauce has thickened. Serve with any Indian bread.

Per portion Energy 322kcal/1346kJ; Protein 7.2g; Carbohydrate 41.7g, of which sugars 10.8g; Fat 15.3g, of which saturates 2.3g; Cholesterol 2mg; Calcium 116mg; Fibre 3.8g; Sodium 41mg.

Papaya and yogurt drink

Papaya and yogurt make a very healthy combination, and this drink, *Papita Lassi*, is an ideal way to start the day or revive the body and senses in the afternoon. Rose water adds an exotic touch, but you could omit it or replace it with orange blossom water if you prefer.

SERVES 4

1 small ripe papaya

200g/7oz/scant 1 cup full-fat (whole) natural (plain) yogurt

45ml/3 tbsp sugar

250ml/8fl oz/1 cup water

15ml/1 tbsp rose water

COOK'S TIP

To make an even thicker and cooler drink, add a few ice cubes to the blender in step 3.

1 Cut the papaya in half lengthways, and remove the seeds and the white pith with a teaspoon.

2 Chop the papaya flesh roughly into small pieces, reserve a few pieces for a garnish and place the rest in a blender or large bowl.

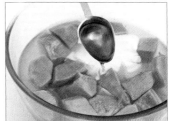

3 Add the remaining ingredients and process in the blender, or with a stick blender, until smooth. Top with the reserved papaya chunks and serve the drink chilled.

Per portion Energy 96kcal/409kJ; Protein 3g; Carbohydrate 19g, of which sugars 19g; Fat 2g, of which saturates 1g; Cholesterol 6mg; Calcium 109mg; Fibre 0.8g; Sodium 42mg.

Sweet yogurt drink

Lassi originated in the northern state of Punjab and became a favourite drink of the nation. The people of northern India favour savoury lassi, but those in central India are partial to all things sweet, and prefer this recipe, *Meethi Lassi*. Teetotallers enjoy it, others use it as a cure for hangovers, and vegetarians thrive on it!

SERVES 4

450g/1lb/2 cups full-fat (whole) natural
  (plain) yogurt
75g/3oz/⅔ cup caster (superfine) sugar
30ml/2 tbsp rose water
fresh rose petals, to garnish (optional)

1 Put the yogurt and sugar into a blender and add 600ml/1 pint/2½ cups water. Blend until smooth.

2 Taste and add more sugar if necessary. Pour the lassi into a jug (pitcher) and chill in the refrigerator for several hours.

VARIATION
You can vary this sweet lassi by using other flavourings, such as vanilla extract, orange blossom water or 15ml/1 tbsp mango purée, instead of rose water.

3 Shortly before you are ready to serve the drink, place some ice cubes in a clean dish towel and crush them by hitting them with a rolling pin.

4 Stir the rose water into the lassi, and serve immediately in tall glasses lined with the crushed ice. Garnish with fresh rose petals, if you like.

Per portion Energy 137kcal/581kJ; Protein 5.8g; Carbohydrate 28g, of which sugars 28g; Fat 1.1g, of which saturates 0.6g; Cholesterol 1mg; Calcium 224mg; Fibre 0g; Sodium 95mg.

Wheat pancakes with black peppercorns

Many varieties of *Malpuas* are made all over the sub-continent. This central Indian version, with sweetness from palm sugar (jaggery) and spiciness from crushed black pepper, offers a different taste sensation from other versions. Serve on their own with after-dinner coffee or as a dessert topped with cream and fruits.

MAKES 12

115g/4oz/⅔ cup semolina
115g/4oz/1 cup self-raising (self-rising) flour
5ml/1 tsp freshly ground black pepper
2.5ml/½ tsp ground cardamom
2.5ml/½ tsp freshly grated nutmeg
75g/3oz/⅓ cup full-fat (whole) natural
  (plain) yogurt
250ml/8fl oz/1 cup milk
110g/4oz palm sugar (jaggery) or soft
  dark brown sugar
75ml/2½fl oz/⅓ cup water
sunflower or light olive oil, for
  shallow-frying
whipped cream and seasonal fresh fruit,
  to serve

1 Dry-roast the semolina in a heavy pan for about 10 minutes, until it is golden brown, stirring constantly.

2 Transfer the semolina to a mixing bowl then add the flour, ground black pepper, cardamom and nutmeg. Mix well, then add the yogurt and stir to combine.

3 Put the milk in a non-stick pan and place over a medium heat. Cut the palm sugar into small pieces, add it or the brown sugar to the milk and stir until dissolved.

4 Add the sweetened milk to the semolina mixture, then add the water. Mix with a spoon until a smooth batter is formed.

5 In a frying pan, heat enough oil to cover the surface to a depth of about 2.5cm/1in over a medium heat.

6 Spread a generous tablespoon of the batter in a circular motion to form a pancake about 7.5cm/3in in diameter.

7 Fry the pancake until golden brown on both sides, then remove with a slotted spoon and drain on kitchen paper. Use the remaining batter to make more pancakes in the same way.

8 Serve warm, with whipped cream and fresh fruit.

Per portion Energy 155kcal/653kJ; Protein 3g; Carbohydrate 25g, of which sugars 10g; Fat 6g, of which saturates 1g; Cholesterol 4mg; Calcium 82mg; Fibre 0.9g; Sodium 57mg.

Baked cashew nut diamonds

An extremely popular sweet dish found all over India, these tasty cakes are made using cashew nuts and flavoured with delicate cardamom. *Kaju Burfi* is very simple to make: a soft dough is formed from a mixture of ground cashew nuts, sugar and ghee, then flattened and baked in the oven.

MAKES 16

225g/8oz raw unsalted cashew nuts
100g/3¾oz/½ cup caster (superfine) sugar
15ml/1 tbsp ghee or unsalted butter
2.5ml/½ tsp ground cardamom

COOK'S TIP
Ghee is the Indian version of clarified butter (i.e. butter that has had its moisture and milk solids removed, making it clear) and is traditionally made with buffalo rather than cow's milk. It has a nuttier flavour and darker colour than standard clarified butter and a higher burning point, which means it is good for frying. It is available in tins or jars and should be stored in the refrigerator, where it will keep for up to six months.

1 Put the cashew nuts in a small heatproof bowl and pour over enough boiling water to cover. Soak for 20 minutes, then drain them and place in a food processor or blender. Blend the nuts until a smooth paste forms, then transfer the paste to a large mixing bowl.

2 Add the remaining ingredients to the cashew nut paste in the bowl, and knead the mixture carefully, until it becomes smooth and buttery in texture.

3 Preheat the oven to 160°C/325°F/Gas 3. Line a baking sheet with a well-greased baking parchment and spread the mixture on it to form a 20cm/8in square. Bake in the centre of the oven for 35–40 minutes until lightly browned.

4 Remove the baking sheet from the oven and allow the mixture cool to 15 minutes. Remove from the baking sheet and cut into diamonds or squares. These are delicious served at tea time or after dinner with coffee or tea.

Per portion Energy 117kcal/490kJ; Protein 2.9g; Carbohydrate 9.2g, of which sugars 7.3g; Fat 7.9g, of which saturates 1.9g; Cholesterol 2mg; Calcium 8mg; Fibre 0.5g; Sodium 48mg.

Sweet samosas

These traditional Indian pastries, *Khusli*, are made during Diwali, the Hindu festival of lights. The small triangular filo parcels are usually deep-fried in oil, but here they are baked for a healthier treat. They have a wonderful fruit-and-nut filling, sweetened and moistened with evaporated milk and sugar. Try serving them with fresh fruit and thick yogurt or whipped cream for a special dessert, or with coffee.

MAKES 12

50g/2oz/½ cup desiccated (dry unsweetened shredded) coconut
25g/1oz/¼ cup ground almonds
25g/1oz/¼ cup raw unsalted cashew nuts, chopped
25g/1oz/⅛ cup seedless raisins
250ml/8fl oz/1 cup evaporated milk
50g/2oz/¼ cup light muscovado (brown) sugar
2.5ml/½ tsp freshly grated nutmeg
2.5ml/½ tsp ground cinnamon
12 sheets of filo pastry, 28cm x 18cm/ 11in x 7in
50g/2oz/¼ cup butter, melted, for brushing
icing (confectioners') sugar, for dusting

VARIATION

To deep-fry the samosas: Pour enough oil into a large, heavy pan suitable for deep-frying to come about 5cm/2in up the side of the pan. Heat the oil until it reaches 180°C/350°F on a thermometer, then carefully lower two or three samosas into the oil and fry for 2–3 minutes, until golden brown. Drain on kitchen paper. Repeat.

---

1 Put the desiccated coconut, almonds, cashew nuts, raisins, evaporated milk and sugar into a small, heavy pan and stir gently over a medium heat.

2 After about 5 minutes, when the sugar has dissolved and begins to bubble, reduce the heat to low and cook until all the milk has been absorbed, stirring frequently to prevent the mixture sticking and burning. This will take 8–10 minutes.

3 Remove the pan from the heat and stir in the nutmeg and cinnamon. Leave the mixture to cool completely, then divide into 12 equal-sized balls.

4 Preheat the oven to 180°C/350°F/Gas 4. Line a baking sheet with a piece of non-stick baking parchment.

5 Place a sheet of filo pastry on a flat surface and brush with some of the melted butter. Keep the rest of the pastry covered.

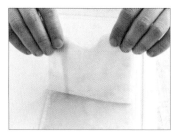

6 Fold the pastry in half lengthways, brush the surface with butter again, then fold it widthways to form a rough square.

7 Place a portion of the filling on to the filo, 5cm/2in from the edge.

8 Turn one corner of the pastry over to make a triangle. Fold the triangle over on itself to make a triangle half the size, fully enclosing the filling. You may need to squash down the filling a little. Seal the edges with melted butter, pressing down well to ensure a good seal.

9 Place the samosas on the prepared baking sheet and brush the outside with butter. Bake in the centre of the oven for 20–25 minutes or until the samosas are crisp and golden brown.

10 Lightly dust the baked samosas with icing sugar. Arrange on a serving dish and serve warm or cold.

Per portion Energy 147kcal/614kJ; Protein 3g; Carbohydrate 11g, of which sugars 8g; Fat 10g, of which saturates 6g; Cholesterol 16mg; Calcium 79mg; Fibre 1.0g; Sodium 67mg.

Coconut-stuffed parcels with cloves

The people of central India love desserts and sweetmeats. *Lavang Lata* is a pretty parcel of cardamom-scented coconut wrapped in a simple, home-made pastry with a whole clove to hold the parcel together. These delicious morsels are ideal with a cup of tea or after dinner with coffee instead of a dessert.

MAKES 12

For the pastry:
225g/8oz/2 cups plain (all-purpose) flour,
    plus extra for dusting
40g/1½oz/3 tbsp ghee or butter
125ml/4fl oz/½ cup cold water
12 whole cloves
sunflower oil, for deep-frying

For the filling:
50g/2oz/⅔ cup desiccated (dry
    unsweetened shredded) coconut
75ml/3fl oz/5 tbsp hot milk
50g/2oz seedless raisins
50g/2oz raw cashew nuts, chopped
5ml/1 tsp ground cardamom
2.5ml/½ tsp ground nutmeg

For the syrup:
175g/6oz/scant 1 cup granulated
    (white) sugar
5 cardamom pods, bruised
300ml/10fl oz/1¼ cups water

1 First make the pastry. Sift the flour into a mixing bowl and rub in the ghee or butter. Mix until the flour looks crumbly and has the texture of breadcrumbs.

> **COOK'S TIP**
> It is always very important to allow pastry to 'rest' for 30 minutes before rolling out and shaping, or it is likely to shrink during cooking.

2 Gradually add the water to the flour mixture and stir with a spoon until a soft dough is formed.

3 Transfer the dough to a flat surface and knead for about 1 minute, until it is smooth and pliable.

4 Cover with clear film (plastic wrap) and allow to rest for 30 minutes.

5 Meanwhile, mix all the ingredients for the filling together in a large bowl until thoroughly combined. Set aside.

6 Put all the syrup ingredients into a pan and place over a high heat. Bring to the boil, then reduce the heat to low. Simmer the mixture for 10–12 minutes, then switch off the heat.

7 Divide the dough into 12 equal parts and make a round cake out of each portion. Roll each one into a 7.5cm/3in circle.

8 Divide the filling into 12 equal parts and place one portion in the centre of each pastry circle. Enclose the filling by folding over the edges to form a square. Secure with a clove.

9 Heat the oil for deep-frying over a low/medium heat until it reaches 180°C/350°F. Fry the coconut parcels in a few batches, until they are crisp and golden brown.

10 Immerse the parcels immediately in the hot syrup (reheat the syrup gently if necessary). Spoon some of the syrup over the top and leave them immersed until you have finished frying the next batch.

11 Remove the first batch from the syrup and place them in a serving dish, then immerse the second batch in the syrup, spooning over some of the syrup as before.

12 When you have taken the last batch out of the syrup, boil the remaining syrup and reduce it by half. Spoon this syrup over the parcels and serve at room temperature.

Per portion Energy 267kcal/1118kJ; Protein 3.2g; Carbohydrate 34.1g, of which sugars 19.2g; Fat 14g, of which saturates 5g; Cholesterol 1mg; Calcium 46mg; Fibre 1.4g; Sodium 21mg.

Soft fudge with cardamom

Lentils provide protein for the vast majority of vegetarians in India. This fudge, *Mung Dhal Halva*, is an example of how many different ways lentils can be cooked. Here, yellow split lentils are cooked in milk and sugar until the mixture reaches a soft fudge consistency.

SERVES 4–6

250g/9oz yellow split lentils (moong or mung dhal)
115g/4oz/½ cup ghee or unsalted butter
600ml/1 pint/2½ cups full-fat (whole) milk
115g/4oz/generous ½ cup sugar
a good pinch of saffron threads, pounded
150ml/¼ pint/⅔ cup double (heavy) cream
5ml/1 tsp ground cardamom or other flavourings such as nutmeg or cinnamon
30ml/2 tbsp roasted unsalted pistachio nuts, crushed, to garnish

1 Wash the lentils in several changes of water, then soak in a bowl of cold water for 2–3 hours.

2 Drain well and grind to a fine paste in a food processor without adding any water.

3 In a large frying pan, melt the ghee or butter over a low heat and add the lentil paste. Stir and cook for 10–12 minutes, until the lentil paste is dry and crumbly.

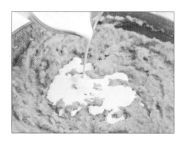

4 Add the milk, sugar and pounded saffron. Increase the heat slightly and let it come to the simmering point.

5 Reduce the heat to low and beat the mixture in order to break up any lumps.

6 Continue cooking, stirring regularly, for 10–12 minutes. Add the cream and continue to cook, stirring, for a further 8–10 minutes.

7 Add the cardamom or other flavourings and cook until the mixture stops sticking to the bottom and sides of the pan.

8 Remove from the heat and spread in a buttered 25 x 25cm/10 x 10in square tin (pan).

9 Smooth the top and sprinkle with the pistachio nuts. Press them down gently and leave the fudge to cool completely. Cut into squares and serve.

Per portion Energy 586kcal/2444kJ; Protein 13g; Carbohydrate 50g, of which sugars 26g; Fat 39g, of which saturates 24g; Cholesterol 102mg; Calcium 149mg; Fibre 4.5g; Sodium 76mg.

West India

Fertile land and plentiful supplies of vegetables, seafood and dairy produce have produced a delightful and varied cuisine in west India. A rich tapestry of cultures, the cooking has been influenced over the years by other nations, such as Portugal and Persia, resulting in a range of delectable and unique dishes, from Goan Prawn Curry and Crab in Roasted Coconut Sauce, to Sweet Peppers with Whole Cashew Nuts and Spicy Stuffed Bananas.

West India

Four states make up the region of west India: Goa, a tiny enclave perched on the west coast; Maharashtra, a large state stretching from the Arabian Sea across almost the whole width of India; Gujarat, another coastal state that proudly claims to be the birthplace of many of India's political leaders, including Gandhi; and Rajasthan, a vast landlocked desert region bordering Pakistan. The food in all of these is fragrant and flavoursome, packed with spices and influenced by the settlers and traders who visited the region.

GOA

The tiny state of Goa, popularly known as 'Golden Goa' and 'Pearl of the Orient', lies on the southern edge of west India. A rich tapestry of cultures, it was ruled, in turn, by Hindus, Muslims, Portuguese Christians and the British. The lure of Indian spices and silks brought the Portuguese explorer Vasco da Gama to this part of India, and the Portuguese established an eastern empire for themselves with Goa as the central state.

Although local ingredients such as fish and coconut predominate, Goa's cuisine also reflects the influence of European culture, with dishes such as Portuguese Pullao and the now ubiquitous *vindaloo*, a term for a spicy pork dish that originally derived from the Portuguese words for 'vinegar' and 'garlic'.

MAHARASHTRA

The food of the large state of Maharashtra is fiery, as both chillies and black pepper are used with great relish. Peanuts and cashew nuts are another distinctive feature of Maharashtrian cooking, and peanut oil forms the basis for many dishes. Pulses, sugarcane and wheat are also plentiful.

The people here have a sweet tooth, and use a lot of palm sugar (jaggery) and kokum, a purple berry-like fruit with a pleasant sweet-and-sour taste. Mumbai

Above *Central Gujarat produces many grain crops, such as wheat.*

(Bombay), the capital of Maharashtra, is a historic and cosmopolitan city, also known as the 'Gateway of India'. Here, all sorts of dishes have been created by the different communities that have made Mumbai their home – it is a real food-lover's paradise and is probably the only city in India where you can sample food from almost anywhere in the country, as well as recipes that owe much to foreign influences. The newest arrival in Mumbai is the Bollywood film industry, helping to maintain a high level of excitement and artistic passion in the city.

GUJARAT

Within the colourful diversity of Indian regional cuisine, Gujarat merits a special position of pride as the state that has perfected the true art of vegetarian cooking. This is mainly due to the influence of the Jain religion, which prescribes an attitude of non-violence to all things and therefore

Left *Coconuts grow in abundance in Goa, and their flesh and milk appear in most local dishes.*

Far left *The array of foods on offer in Gujarat will be transformed into vegetarian dishes.*
Left *Fresh produce, such as chillies, is dried in the sun in Rajasthan, to help preserve it.*

RAJASTHAN

This is the ancient land of Indian emperors and princes, where an elaborate cuisine was developed, often using the game caught during a day's hunting. Despite the royal culinary tradition, which is evident in the number of game dishes that are still enjoyed today, there are many vegetarians in this state, including most members of the Marwari community, the main controllers of business whose influence has spread throughout India.

This is, perhaps, surprising, given the desert climate, and the fact that only a small variety of vegetables can be grown in regions that are slightly less dry or where farmers can afford irrigation systems. The little produce harvested then tends to be sun-dried. Most dishes are cooked in ghee and flavoured with spices, yogurt and dried fruits, and curries tend to be based on pulses or gram flour (besan).

forbids the consumption of any food whose production may involve the harming of animals. This means that meat, fish, eggs and, for some, dairy products are not permitted. Despite these limitations, Gujarati cooks have created a dazzling array of delicious and nutritious dishes that have become famous across the whole of India.

In addition to the influences of Jainism on the dishes of the region, Persian cuisine has also played its part in shaping the local diet. Situated on the banks of the Arabian Sea, the region attracted and absorbed a variety of immigrants over the centuries, including Persians, and over time the native Parsis integrated the distinctive flavour of Persian food with their own traditional dishes, creating exotic and colourful treats, such as the world-famous *dhansak*.

The three main regions of Gujarat have distinct climatic differences, which has led to a very varied cuisine. Western Gujarat is an arid area where there is a scarcity of fresh vegetables, but it is rich in dairy produce, and there is a strong tradition of making delicious sweetmeats and desserts based on milk and yogurt. Central Gujarat is known as the 'granary of Gujarat' because of its abundance of grain crops. The south of the state, with a much wetter climate, is covered with lush green vegetation, and here a fantastic variety of fresh vegetables grow.

The concept of a *thali* (a meal served on a steel platter), which is popular in India as well as in the Indian restaurants in the West,

originated in Gujarat. *Roti*, an unleavened flat wheat bread, is a speciality not to be missed, as is cool, cumin flavoured *lassi*, a diluted natural (plain) yogurt drink for the long, hot summer. Gujaratis are also very partial to *farsan* (snacks) and an exotic variety is made and used to welcome guests, to pack in children's lunchboxes or just to enjoy with a cup of afternoon tea.

Right *Lentils, such as those sold at this market in Jaisalmer, are widely used in Rajasthani food.*

Spinach soup with potato purée

The influence of Portuguese rule in Goa is still evident in its cuisine. This hearty soup, *Caldo Verde*, originated in Portugal and over the years has been adapted to suit fresh local ingredients. Like many soups, its success lies in a well-flavoured, aromatic stock and fresh ingredients.

SERVES 4

For the spiced stock:
15ml/1 tbsp ghee or unsalted butter
15ml/1 tbsp sunflower oil or light olive oil
250g/9oz leeks, roughly chopped
2 carrots, peeled and thickly sliced
1 stick celery, roughly chopped
675g/1½lb raw beef and lamb bones
300g/11oz raw chicken wings, skinned,
  or 1 cooked chicken carcass
6 large garlic cloves, lightly crushed with
  the skin on
25g/1oz unpeeled fresh root ginger,
  sliced into rounds
5ml/1 tsp black peppercorns
2 x 2.5cm/1in pieces cinnamon stick
3 brown cardamom pods, bruised
2 bay leaves
4 cloves

For the soup:
15ml/1 tbsp ghee or unsalted butter
15ml/1 tbsp sunflower oil or light
  olive oil
1 onion, finely chopped
1 clove garlic, crushed, or 5ml/1 tsp
  garlic purée
250g/9oz potatoes, roughly chopped
150g/5oz fresh spinach leaves, chopped
750ml/1¼ pints/3 cups spiced stock
150ml/¼ pint/⅔ cup double (heavy) cream
salt and ground black pepper

1 To make the stock, heat the ghee or butter and oil in a large pan and cook the leeks, carrots and celery for 3–4 minutes over a medium-high heat. Add the remaining stock ingredients and 2.4 litres/4 pints/10 cups water. Bring to the boil, reduce the heat to low, cover and simmer for 1 hour.

2 Leave the stock to cool, then chill in the refrigerator until the fat that will float to the top has solidified.

3 Remove the fat with a slotted spoon, then strain the stock through a large sieve lined with muslin (cheesecloth) into a bowl positioned underneath.

4 For the soup, heat the ghee or butter and oil together over a medium heat. Add the onion and garlic and fry for 5 minutes, until they begin to brown.

5 Add the potatoes and fry for 3–4 minutes. Add the spinach and spiced stock and season to taste with salt and pepper. Stir to combine, then bring to the boil, cover the pan and simmer for 10–15 minutes, until the potatoes are tender.

6 Remove the soup from the heat, and purée in a food processor or blender.

7 Return the soup to the pan, stir in most of the cream and gently reheat until hot. Ladle into warmed soup bowls and serve with a swirl of the reserved cream.

Per portion Energy 358kcal/1478kJ; Protein 3g; Carbohydrate 15g, of which sugars 4g; Fat 32g, of which saturates 16g; Cholesterol 62mg; Calcium 96mg; Fibre 2.2g; Sodium 165mg.

Prawn soup

Sopa De Camrao is an example of the Portuguese influence on western Indian cuisine. It is easy to make once you have prepared the aromatic stock. You can either make your own, use bought fresh stock, or combine a good-quality fish stock cube (bouillon) with other flavouring ingredients, as suggested here.

SERVES 4

For the fish stock:
2 fish stock cubes (bouillon)
1 large unpeeled onion, quartered
7 large garlic cloves, lightly crushed with the skin on
2 bay leaves
2.5cm/1in piece cinnamon stick
5ml/1 tsp black peppercorns, lightly crushed
10ml/2 tsp fennel seeds

For the soup:
25g/1oz unsalted butter
15ml/1 tbsp sunflower oil or light olive oil
1 small onion, chopped
2 cloves garlic, crushed, or 10ml/2 tsp garlic purée
150g/5oz potatoes, finely chopped
750ml/1¼ pints/3 cups fish stock
200g/7oz cooked prawns (shrimp), defrosted and drained if frozen
120ml/4fl oz/½ cup double (heavy) cream
2.5ml/½ tsp salt, or to taste
ground black pepper
15ml/1 tbsp chopped fresh parsley, to garnish

2 Leave to cool slightly. Strain the stock through a large sieve lined with muslin (cheesecloth) into a bowl underneath.

3 For the soup, heat the butter and oil in a large pan over a low-medium heat and add the onion and garlic. Fry gently until the onion has softened, then add the potatoes and cook for 2–3 minutes, stirring.

4 Pour in the stock and bring to the boil, reduce the heat, cover and simmer for 10 minutes, or until the potatoes are tender.

5 Reserve a few prawns and add the remainder to the soup with the cream, salt and pepper. Simmer gently for 2 minutes.

1 Put all the ingredients for the stock in a large pan and add 2 litres/2½ pints/8 cups water. Bring to the boil, cover and simmer for 45 minutes.

6 Cool slightly, then purée the soup in batches in a blender or in the pan using a hand-held blender. Serve garnished with the parsley and the reserved prawns.

Per portion Energy 307kcal/1276kJ; Protein 11g; Carbohydrate 8g, of which sugars 1g; Fat 26g, of which saturates 14g; Cholesterol 153mg; Calcium 63mg; Fibre 0.6g; Sodium 939mg.

Chickpea flour squares with coconut and mustard

This is a new version of a delicious savoury snack, *Khandvi*, from the state of Gujarat, which uses yogurt in place of curds and incorporates chilli and desiccated (dry unsweetened shredded) coconut for added flavour. They are low in fat and packed with essential nutrients. Served with chutney, they make a perfect appetizer.

SERVES 4

275g/10oz/2½ cups gram flour (besan)
115g/4oz/½ cup full-fat (whole) natural (plain) yogurt
5ml/1 tsp salt, or to taste
2.5ml/½ tsp ground turmeric
2 fresh red chillies, finely chopped (deseeded if preferred)
30ml/2 tbsp sunflower oil or light olive oil, plus extra for brushing over
15ml/1 tbsp desiccated (dry unsweetened shredded) coconut
30ml/2 tbsp fresh coriander (cilantro) leaves, chopped
tangy chutney, to serve

For the tempering:

10ml/2 tsp sunflower oil or light olive oil
2.5ml/½ tsp black mustard seeds
1 dried red chilli, torn into pieces
6 fresh or 8 dried curry leaves
1.25ml/¼ tsp Asafoetida

1 Sift the gram flour into a large mixing bowl and make a well in the centre.

2 Blend the yogurt with 90ml/6 tbsp water in a separate bowl or jug, and add the mixture to the flour.

3 Add the salt, turmeric, chillies and oil. Mix everything thoroughly with a wooden spoon, making sure that all the ingredients are well blended together, to make a thick paste. Cover the bowl with a damp dish towel and set aside for 30 minutes.

4 Brush a little oil on a 30cm/12in heatproof plate and spread over half the gram flour mixture, like a thick pancake, covering the entire surface of the plate. It is easier to spread the mixture if you use lightly greased palms or a greased metal spoon.

5 Divide the coconut and coriander equally into two portions and sprinkle one portion on the surface of the mixture.

6 Place the plate on a steamer positioned over a pan of simmering water and steam the pancake for 8 minutes, or until the surface is set.

7 Remove the plate from the steamer and set aside for 5 minutes to cool slightly, then gently ease away the steamed pancake with a thin metal spatula or a fish slice.

8 Place the pancake on a cutting board and cut it into 2.5cm/1in squares. Cook the remaining mixture in the same way, and cut into squares.

9 In a non-stick wok or other pan, heat the remaining oil over a medium heat until it reaches smoking point, then switch off the heat source.

10 Add the mustard seeds and as soon as they start popping add the chillies, curry leaves and Asafoetida and let them sizzle for 15–20 seconds.

11 Add the pancake squares and mix gently, being careful not to break them up. Transfer to a serving dish and serve hot or cold with a tangy chutney.

VARIATION

You could also leave the pancakes whole, spread them with chutney and then roll them up.

Per portion Energy 353kcal/1482kJ; Protein 16g; Carbohydrate 37g, of which sugars 5g; Fat 17g, of which saturates 4g; Cholesterol 3mg; Calcium 191mg; Fibre 10.1g; Sodium 544mg.

Split chickpea squares with coconut

This simple, delicious and highly nutritious dish, *Amiri Khaman*, comes from the mainly vegetarian state of Gujarat, which is well known for its aromatic spiced snacks, known as *farsan*. Every Gujarati housewife has a supply of home-made *farsan* in the store cupboard, which helps them to follow the age-old Indian custom of looking after their guests, whether invited or unexpected. These wonderfully flavoursome squares make a fabulous appetizer when served with chutney, and are ideal for afternoon tea.

SERVES 4–5

350g/12oz/2 cups split Bengal gram
  (channa dhal or skinless split chickpeas)
45ml/3 tbsp sunflower oil or light olive oil
2.5ml/½ tsp black mustard seeds
1.25ml/¼ tsp Asafoetida
10ml/2 tsp ginger purée
10ml/2 tsp garlic purée
2–4 fresh green chillies, finely chopped
  (deseeded if preferred)
2.5ml/½ tsp ground turmeric
5ml/1 tsp salt, or to taste
5ml/1 tsp sugar
425ml/¾ pint/1¾ cups full-fat (whole) milk
30ml/2 tbsp lemon juice
15ml/1 tbsp fresh coriander (cilantro)
  leaves, finely chopped
15ml/1 tbsp desiccated (dry unsweetened
  shredded) coconut
chutney, to serve

VARIATION
You can vary the topping, adding very finely chopped fresh chilli if you like a fiery kick, or use other soft herbs, such as chopped mint or flat leaf parsley.

1 Wash the split Bengal gram in a sieve (strainer), then transfer to a bowl and soak in cold water for 5–6 hours or overnight.

2 Drain the split Bengal gram well, then process in a food processor or blender until a fine paste is formed.

3 In a wok or non-stick pan, heat the oil over a medium heat. When hot, but not smoking, add the mustard seeds and reduce the heat to low.

4 Add the Asafoetida, followed by the ginger, garlic, chillies and turmeric. Stir to combine well and fry them gently for about 1 minute.

5 Add the gram paste, salt and sugar, and cook over a medium/low heat, stirring constantly so it doesn't stick, for about 6 minutes, until the mixture is completely dry and looks crumbly.

6 Add one-third of the milk and continue to cook, stirring, for 3–4 minutes. Repeat the process with the remaining milk. Add the lemon juice and stir until well blended.

7 Spread the mixture on a lightly greased plate to a 30cm/12in rectangle and sprinkle over the coriander and coconut.

8 Press down the coconut and coriander so that they stick. Cut into squares or diamonds and serve hot or cold with chutney.

Per portion Energy 357kcal/1499kJ; Protein 18.5g; Carbohydrate 40.9g, of which sugars 5.9g; Fat 14.5g, of which saturates 3.3g; Cholesterol 12mg; Calcium 221mg; Fibre 7.5g; Sodium 76mg.

Vegetable samosas

The original recipe for *Samosas* is a vegetarian one. Potatoes and garden peas are the most common fillings, but other vegetables such as carrots and cauliflower are also used in some regions. Filo pastry is a quick and easy alternative to traditional Indian pastry, and makes a delicious samosa that is also lower in fat. These samosas have been baked in the oven, but they can also be deep-fried in a light cooking oil.

MAKES 12

60ml/4 tbsp sunflower oil or light olive oil
1.25ml/¼ tsp Asafoetida
2.5ml/½ tsp black mustard seeds
5ml/1 tsp cumin seeds
2.5ml/½ tsp nigella seeds
1 medium onion, finely chopped
2 fresh green chillies, finely chopped
    (deseeded if preferred)
2.5ml/½ tsp ground turmeric
5ml/1 tsp ground cumin
350g/12oz boiled potatoes, cut into
    bitesize pieces
110g/4oz/1 cup fresh peas, cooked or
    frozen peas, thawed
50g/2oz/½ cup carrots, coarsely grated
5ml/1 tsp salt, or to taste
2.5ml/½ tsp garam masala
30ml/2 tbsp fresh coriander (cilantro)
    leaves, chopped
12 sheets filo pastry, each about
    18 x 29cm/7 x 11in
75g/3oz/6 tbsp butter, melted

1 Heat the oil over a medium heat. When it is hot but not smoking, add the Asafoetida, mustard, cumin and nigella. Add the onion and chillies and fry until the onion is brown.

2 Add the turmeric and cumin, cook for about 1 minute, then add the potatoes, peas, carrots and salt. Stir them around until the vegetables are coated with the spices. Stir in the coriander and remove from the heat. Allow to cool completely.

3 Preheat the oven to 180°C/350°F/Gas 4. Line a baking sheet with baking parchment.

4 Remove the filo pastry from its packaging and cover with a moist cloth or clear film (plastic wrap). Place one sheet of filo pastry on a board and brush generously with melted butter.

5 Fold the pastry sheet in half lengthways, brush with some more butter and fold lengthways again to form a long strip.

6 Place about 15ml/1 tbsp of the vegetable filling on the bottom right-hand corner of the pastry sheet.

COOK'S TIP

It is important to work quickly when using filo pastry, and keep sheets that you are not using covered, as it dries out quickly.

7 Fold over the pastry and filling to form a triangle. Continue to fold to the top of the strip, maintaining the triangular shape. Moisten the ends and seal the edges.

8 Place on the prepared baking sheet and brush the outside with melted butter. Make the rest of the samosas in the same way. Bake just below the top of the oven for 20 minutes or until browned.

Per portion Energy 180kcal/752kJ; Protein 3.6g; Carbohydrate 19.6g, of which sugars 2.5g; Fat 10.4g, of which saturates 4.1g; Cholesterol 26mg; Calcium 38mg; Fibre 1.6g; Sodium 58mg.

Spiced gram flour dumplings

In this recipe for *Methi Na Muthia*, a golden gram flour (besan) mixture is combined with fenugreek and a range of spices, then formed into small dumplings and steamed. The cooked dumplings are then sliced into bitesize pieces and dressed with a spicy oil.

SERVES 4

For the dumplings:
300g/10½oz/2½ cups gram flour (besan)
30ml/2 tbsp dried fenugreek leaves
  (kasuri methi)
1.25ml/¼ tsp bicarbonate of soda
  (baking soda)
1.25ml/¼ tsp Asafoetida
2.5ml/½ tsp chilli powder
2.5ml/½ tsp ground turmeric
3.75ml/¾ tsp salt, or to taste
juice of 1 lime
30ml/2 tbsp sunflower oil or light
  olive oil, warmed

For the tempering:
30ml/2 tbsp sunflower oil or light
  olive oil
2.5ml/½ tsp black mustard seeds
2.5ml/½ tsp cumin seeds
1.25ml/¼ tsp Asafoetida
8–10 curry leaves
30ml/2 tbsp fresh coriander (cilantro)
  leaves, finely chopped

1 Sift the gram flour into a large mixing bowl and add all the remaining dumpling ingredients except the lime juice and oil. Mix thoroughly to combine.

2 Make a well in the centre, then add the lime juice and warmed oil, and mix again. Make another well in the centre, add 100ml/3½fl oz/⅓ cup cold water and mix until a dough is formed.

3 Divide the dough into four equal portions and roll each one into a cylinder shape 8cm/3¼in long.

4 Place the dumplings in an electric steamer or a metal steamer positioned over a pan of simmering water, and cook for 15–16 minutes.

5 Remove from the heat, transfer them to a cutting board and leave to cool a little.

6 Cut the cylinders into 1cm/½in-thick slices and put them on a serving dish.

7 Heat the oil for the tempering over a medium heat. When hot, add the mustard seeds. As soon as they pop, add the cumin seeds, Asafoetida and curry leaves.

8 Let them sizzle for 10–15 seconds, then pour the oil and spices over the dumplings. stir in the coriander and serve immediately.

Per portion Energy 285kcal/1201kJ; Protein 8.7g; Carbohydrate 40.8g, of which sugars 1.3g; Fat 11g, of which saturates 1.4g; Cholesterol 0mg; Calcium 35mg; Fibre 5.4g; Sodium 4mg.

Poached cabbage rolls

Kobi Na Moothia is a delicious and healthy snack from the state of Gujarat, the home of vegetarian cooking. They can be served hot or cold, so can easily be made in advance.

SERVES 4

225g/8oz/2 cups gram flour (besan), sifted

2.5ml/½ tsp bicarbonate of soda
  (baking soda)

5ml/1 tsp salt, or to taste

1.25ml/¼ tsp Asafoetida

5ml/1 tsp dried red chilli flakes

10ml/2 tsp ginger purée

5ml/1 tsp ground turmeric

1 small green cabbage, about 200g/7oz,
  finely shredded

For the tempering:

10ml/2 tbsp sunflower oil or light olive oil

2.5ml/½ tsp black or brown
  mustard seeds

8–10 curry leaves

3–4 whole dried red chillies

1.25ml/¼ tsp Asafoetida

15ml/1 tbsp desiccated (dry unsweetened)
  shredded), coconut, to garnish

1 In a large bowl, mix the gram flour with all the remaining ingredients, except the shredded cabbage.

2 Add the cabbage and 75ml/5 tbsp cold water. Mix together with your hands until a stiff dough is formed.

3 Turn out the dough on to a lightly floured surface and knead for a couple of minutes.

4 Divide the mixture into three equal portions and form each into 5cm/2in-long cylindrical shapes.

5 Wrap the cylinders individually in clear film (plastic wrap), securing the edges so that no water can get inside, then wrap again with foil, securing the edges well to form a tight seal.

6 Bring a large pan of water to the boil and add the rolls. Cook for 25 minutes.

7 Remove from the pan with a slotted spoon and leave to cool. Remove the foil and clear film, then cut them into 1cm/½in thick slices.

8 Heat the oil for tempering over a medium heat in a non-stick pan, until almost smoking. Switch off the heat source and add the mustard seeds, followed by the curry leaves, dried red chillies and Asafoetida. Allow the chillies to blacken.

9 Switch the heat back on and add the cabbage roll slices to the pan. Cook gently on both sides until heated through, transfer to a serving dish and garnish with the coconut and chopped coriander.

Per portion Energy 238kcal/1002kJ; Protein 13g; Carbohydrate 31g, of which sugars 4g; Fat 8g, of which saturates 3g; Cholesterol 0mg; Calcium 140mg; Fibre 0.9g; Sodium 379mg.

Spicy scrambled eggs

If you want a breakfast that really wakes you up in the morning, these spicy scrambled eggs, *Akoori*, are ideal. Served with Indian bread or toast with lashings of butter, they are delicious. They can also be served as a topping for canapés at drinks parties, where they go well with chilled white or rosé wine. This recipe comes from a group of people in western India, known as the Parsis, whose name reflects their Persian origins.

SERVES 4

45ml/3 tbsp sunflower oil or olive oil
1 large onion, finely chopped
1–2 fresh green chillies, finely chopped
  (deseeded if preferred)
5ml/1 tsp grated fresh root ginger
  (optional)
2.5ml/½ tsp ground turmeric
2 salad tomatoes, finely chopped
15ml/1 tbsp chopped fresh coriander
  (cilantro) leaves
2.5ml/½ tsp salt, or to taste
4 large (US extra large) eggs, whisked
warm Indian bread or toast spread with
  butter, to serve

1 Heat the oil in a frying pan over a medium heat and add the onion, green chillies and ginger, if using. Stir-fry for 5–6 minutes, until the onion is soft.

2 Add the turmeric and chopped tomatoes to the pan and cook for 1 minute, then add the coriander and salt.

3 Add the eggs to the pan and whisk until they reach the desired consistency.

4 Transfer to plates and serve with warm Indian bread, or alternatively, try crunchy toast spread with butter.

VARIATIONS

• Indian scrambled eggs are usually made slightly drier than the Western version, but if you prefer creamier eggs, add 15ml/1 tbsp full-fat (whole) milk to the whisked eggs before cooking.
• For a really substantial dish, add cubes of boiled potato to the pan with the onion, chillies and ginger, browning them well.

Per portion Energy 203kcal/843kJ; Protein 8.4g; Carbohydrate 10.8g, of which sugars 7.2g; Fat 14.6g, of which saturates 2.7g; Cholesterol 190mg; Calcium 64mg; Fibre 1.9g; Sodium 79mg.

Prawn rissoles

Rissóis De Camrao is a Portuguese-influenced dish from Goa, where a huge range of spectacular seafood is caught and cooked on a daily basis. However, since seafood can be expensive elsewhere, small frozen prawns (shrimp) can be used instead of fresh ones for this recipe, since they will be chopped and blended with a selection of pungent spices and you won't be able to taste much of a difference.

MAKES 12

2 slices of white bread, a day or two old
400g/14oz cooked peeled prawns (shrimp),
 defrosted and drained if frozen
45ml/3 tbsp sunflower oil or olive oil
5ml/1 tsp fennel seeds
1 large onion, finely chopped
2 fresh green chillies, finely chopped
10ml/2 tsp ginger purée
2.5ml/½ tsp garam masala
30ml/2 tbsp chopped fresh coriander
 (cilantro) leaves
salt, to taste
25g/1oz/¼ cup plain (all-purpose) flour
1 egg, beaten
75g/3oz/1½ cups golden breadcrumbs
sunflower oil, for deep-frying
cucumber, tomatoes and lemon wedges,
 to serve

1 Soak the bread in cold water and drain. Place it in a food processor and blend until it is smooth. Add the prawns and, using the pulse action, chop them coarsely. Transfer the mixture to a mixing bowl.

2 Heat the oil in a small pan over a medium heat and add the fennel seeds. Stir-fry for 30 seconds. Add the onion, chilli and ginger. Continue stir-frying until the mixture begins to brown, then add the garam masala.

3 Add the onion mixture to the chopped prawns with the coriander and salt to taste. Mix, cover and chill for 30–40 minutes.

4 Divide the chilled prawn mixture into 12 equal portions and form each of these into rissoles by flattening them slightly with your fingers. Dip each rissole first in the flour, then in the beaten egg, and then roll in the golden breadcrumbs.

5 Heat the oil in a wok and deep-fry the rissoles over a medium to high heat in small batches, until they are crisp and golden brown. Drain well on kitchen paper and serve with a salad of cucumber and tomatoes, and wedges of lemon.

Per portion Energy 165kcal/688kJ; Protein 8.1g; Carbohydrate 11.2g, of which sugars 2.2g; Fat 10.1g, of which saturates 1.2g; Cholesterol 81mg; Calcium 53mg; Fibre 0.7g; Sodium 139mg.

Aubergine in peanut sauce

The state of Maharashtra is well known for its vegetarian dishes, which combine simple cooking methods and complex flavours. Both peanuts and sesame seeds add an opulent taste to this dish, *Baingan Ki Subzi*, and it more than merits its place as a main course.

SERVES 4

50g/2oz sesame seeds
25g/1oz desiccated (dry unsweetened shredded) coconut
25g/1oz dry-roasted peanuts
2 aubergines (eggplants), about 500g/1¼lb
45ml/3 tbsp sunflower oil or light olive oil
1 large onion, finely chopped
3 cloves garlic, crushed
2.5ml/½ tsp ground turmeric
5ml/1 tsp chilli powder, or to taste
5ml/1 tsp ground cumin
5ml/1 tsp salt, or to taste
2.5ml/½ tsp garam masala
15ml/1 tbsp tamarind or lime juice
15ml/1 tbsp fresh coriander (cilantro) leaves, chopped
rice or bread, to serve

1 In a heavy pan, dry-roast the sesame seeds over a medium heat for 1 minute, until they are just a shade darker. Remove from the heat and leave to cool.

2 In the same pan, dry-roast the coconut for 1–2 minutes, until it turns a pale creamy colour. Leave to cool, then mix with the sesame seeds. Grind the mixture in batches in a coffee grinder and set aside.

3 Crush the roasted peanuts to a coarse texture and set aside.

4 Cut the aubergine into 5cm/2in cubes and soak them in a bowl of cold water.

5 Heat the oil over a medium heat and fry the onion for 5 minutes, until soft but not brown. Add the garlic and cook for 1 minute, then add the turmeric, chilli powder and cumin. Cook for about 2 minutes.

6 Drain the aubergine and add to the pan. Add the salt and pour in 500ml/17fl oz/ generous 2 cups warm water.

7 Bring to the boil, reduce the heat to low, and cook for 10 minutes.

8 Add the sesame seeds and coconut and cook for 2–3 minutes, or until the aubergine is tender. Add the garam masala, tamarind or lime juice and the coriander, stir and remove from the heat. Sprinkle over the peanuts and serve with rice or bread.

Per portion Energy 306kcal/1268kJ; Protein 7g; Carbohydrate 12g, of which sugars 9g; Fat 26g, of which saturates 6g; Cholesterol 0mg; Calcium 135mg; Fibre 05.6g; Sodium 558mg.

Parsee spiced omelette

This recipe, *Parsee Poro*, comes from the colourful collection of Parsee cuisine that is prevalent in west India. It is often served at breakfast, but can also be enjoyed as a first course, with naan bread, and drizzled with a tomato relish.

SERVES 4

4 eggs, separated
salt, to taste
4 spring onions (scallions), very
  finely chopped
2 fresh red chillies, finely chopped
  (deseeded if preferred)
30ml/2 tbsp fresh coriander (cilantro)
  leaves, finely chopped
60ml/4 tbsp sunflower oil or light olive oil
strips of naan and tomato relish, to serve

4 Add a quarter of the beaten egg mixture. Tilt the pan so the egg covers the base. Reduce the heat slightly and allow the omelette to brown on the underside.

1 Separate the eggs and beat the whites until soft peaks form. Add the yolks and salt and blend well.

2 Divide the spring onions, red chillies and chopped coriander into four equal portions.

5 Lift up an edge to check whether it is brown, then flip the omelette over and brown on the other side.

6 Remove from the pan and keep warm while you make the remaining omelettes in the same way. Serve warm or at room temperature with naan and tomato relish.

3 Heat 15ml/1 tbsp of the oil in an ovenproof frying pan over a medium heat and add one portion of each of the spring onion, chilli and coriander. Stir-fry for 1 minute.

Per portion Energy 230kcal/950kJ; Protein 8g; Carbohydrate 1g, of which sugars 1g; Fat 22g, of which saturates 4g; Cholesterol 232mg; Calcium 52mg; Fibre 0.3g; Sodium 186mg.

Eggs on spiced potatoes

The inspiration for this recipe, *Sali Pur Eeda*, comes from the wonderful culinary repertoire of the Parsis, a people who migrated to India centuries ago from their homeland in Persia. This is a healthier version of the original recipe as the potatoes are shallow-fried rather than deep-fried.

SERVES 4

700g/1½lb potatoes
60ml/4 tbsp sunflower oil or light olive oil
1 medium onion, finely chopped
1–2 fresh green chillies, finely chopped
 (deseeded if preferred)
5ml/1 tsp salt, or to taste
15g/½oz fresh coriander (cilantro) leaves
 and stalks, finely chopped
4 large (US extra large) eggs
1.25ml/¼ tsp chilli powder or paprika
1.25ml/¼ tsp ground cumin
chapatis or pooris, to serve

VARIATION
For a really luxurious treat, use duck eggs instead of hen's eggs.

1 Peel the potatoes and slice them thinly. Cut the slices into strips about the size of thin French fries. Rinse, then dry with a cloth.

2 In a non-stick pan with a lid, heat the oil over a medium heat and fry the onion and chillies for 5–7 minutes, until the onions begin to brown.

3 Add the potatoes and salt to the onion mixture. Stir and mix well.

4 Cover and cook for 10–12 minutes. Stir occasionally and reduce the heat for the last 2–3 minutes. The potatoes should brown slightly.

5 Stir in the chopped coriander. Spread out the mixture and smooth the surface by gently pressing down with a spoon.

6 Break the eggs on top of the potatoes, spacing them out evenly.

7 Reduce the heat to low, cover the pan and cook for 6–7 minutes or until the eggs are set. Remove the pan from the heat and sprinkle the chilli powder or paprika and cumin over the surface.

8 Serve with a wide spatula or fish slice so that you can pick up a portion of potato and one egg together. Serve with chapatis or pooris.

Per portion Energy 303kcal/1270kJ; Protein 9.6g; Carbohydrate 29.7g, of which sugars 3.2g; Fat 17.2g, of which saturates 3.1g; Cholesterol 190mg; Calcium 52mg; Fibre 2.2g; Sodium 91mg.

Vegetables and split chickpeas in spinach sauce

Sai Bhaji is the national dish of Sindh, in the Indus Valley, the site of the world's most ancient civilization. A selection of vegetables mixed with split Bengal gram (channa dhal or skinless split chickpeas) are cooked together until they reach a soft, pulpy texture.

SERVES 4

125g/4½oz/¾ cup split Bengal gram
  (channa dhal or skinless split chickpeas)
225g/8oz potatoes, peeled and cut into
  2.5cm/1in cubes
125g/4½oz carrots, scraped and cut into
  2.5cm/1in chunks
1 large aubergine (eggplant), cut into
  2.5cm/1in chunks
30ml/2 tbsp dill leaves, roughly chopped
250g/9oz fresh spinach, roughly chopped
5ml/1 tsp salt, or to taste
225g/8oz canned chopped tomatoes with
  their juice
60ml/4 tbsp sunflower oil or light olive oil
1 medium onion, finely chopped
10ml/2 tsp ginger purée
10ml/2 tsp garlic purée
2 fresh green chillies, finely chopped
  (deseeded if preferred)
2.5ml/½ tsp ground turmeric
1 small tomato, cut into julienne strips,
  to garnish
Plain Boiled Rice and Indian bread, to serve

1 Wash the split Bengal gram, transfer to a large bowl and soak in cold water for 30–60 minutes. Drain well, then put them into a pan with the potatoes, carrots, aubergine and dill.

2 Pour in 425ml/15fl oz/1¾ cups water and bring it to the boil. Reduce the heat to low, cover and simmer for 15 minutes.

3 Add the spinach and salt to the pan and stir for 1–2 minutes, until the spinach has wilted. Cover the pan and cook for 10–15 minutes, then remove from the heat.

4 Mash the vegetables lightly, making sure that the potatoes are mashed well in order to thicken the sauce. Add the chopped tomatoes and return the pan to the heat. Cook for 2–3 minutes, then set aside.

5 In a separate pan, heat the oil over a medium heat and fry the onion, ginger, garlic and green chillies, stirring regularly, until the mixture begins to brown. Stir in the turmeric and add this spice mixture to the vegetables. Stir to mix thoroughly.

6 Transfer to a serving dish. Garnish with the julienne strips of tomato and serve with Plain Boiled Rice or any Indian bread.

Per portion Energy 336kcal/1406kJ; Protein 12.2g; Carbohydrate 42.7g, of which sugars 16g; Fat 14.1g, of which saturates 1.7g; Cholesterol 0mg; Calcium 214mg; Fibre 9.6g; Sodium 124mg.

Spicy stuffed bananas

This unusual vegetarian recipe from Gujarat, *Kela Na Sambhariya*, is easy to prepare and requires very little time to cook – perfect for unexpected guests. It makes a substantial and healthy main course when teamed with a lentil dish or a vegetable curry and accompanied by basmati rice.

4 Preheat the oven to 180°C/350°F/Gas 4. Pull the slit banana apart very gently and fill the cavity with a portion of the gram flour mixture, packing the filling in very tightly. Fill the remaining bananas in the same way.

5 Heat the oil in a shallow, ovenproof pan over a medium heat. Place the bananas in the hot oil, stuffed-side up, reduce the heat to low, cover and cook for 2 minutes.

SERVES 4

4 ripe, firm bananas
50g/2oz/½ cup gram flour (besan), sifted
2.5ml/½ tsp ground cumin
5ml/1 tsp ground coriander
1 fresh green chilli, finely chopped,
 (deseeded if preferred)
1 fresh red chilli, finely chopped,
 (deseeded if preferred)
15ml/1 tbsp chopped fresh coriander
 (cilantro) leaves
2.5ml/½ tsp salt, or to taste
60ml/4 tbsp sunflower oil or olive oil
Plain Boiled Rice, to serve

1 Wash the bananas, then trim the ends. Slit each banana lengthways halfway through its diameter, leaving 2.5mm/⅛in uncut at each end. Slit to half its diameter and set aside.

2 In a small, heavy pan, dry-roast the gram flour for 1 minute, stirring constantly, then add the cumin, coriander and green and red chillies. Stir over a medium heat for 1 minute, then remove and leave to cool.

3 Add the chopped coriander and salt and mix well. Divide into four portions.

6 Spoon some hot oil on the stuffing, pressing it down gently. Transfer the pan to the oven. Bake for 12–15 minutes, basting with the oil once or twice. Serve with Plain Boiled Rice.

COOK'S TIP
These bananas look great when served on a banana leaf and garnished with strips of fresh red chillies. Banana leaves can be bought from all good Asian shops.

Per portion Energy 268kcal/1122kJ; Protein 3.1g; Carbohydrate 39.6g, of which sugars 26.3g; Fat 11.9g, of which saturates 1.5g; Cholesterol 0mg; Calcium 30mg; Fibre 1.8g; Sodium 3mg.

Sweet peppers with whole cashew nuts

In this recipe, *Kairas*, sweet (bell) peppers in red, emerald and golden colours are enrobed in a thick, rich sauce with the nutty taste of sesame and poppy seeds, the earthy taste of channa dhal and the fragrance of intense yellow turmeric. Whole cashew nuts add a crunchy bite as well as substance.

SERVES 8

1 each sweet red, yellow and green (bell)
   pepper, about 150g/5oz each
200g/7oz potatoes, cut into
   2.5 cm/1in cubes
15ml/1 tbsp each sesame and white
   poppy seeds
10ml/2 tsp split Bengal gram (channa dhal)
10 black peppercorns
1 dried red chilli, torn into pieces
45ml/3 tbsp sunflower oil or olive oil
2.5ml/½ tsp black mustard
2.5ml/½ tsp cumin seeds
2.5ml/½ tsp ground turmeric
50g/2oz raw whole unsalted cashew nuts
5ml/1 tsp salt, or to taste
7.5ml/1½ tbsp lemon juice
15ml/1 tbsp soft light brown sugar
Plain Boiled Rice, to serve

5 Heat the sunflower or olive oil in a pan over a medium heat, then add the mustard seeds, followed by the cumin. Add the ground ingredients, turmeric and cashew nuts. Stir-fry for 30–40 seconds, then add the peppers and salt.

6 Add the potatoes and the reserved cooking liquid, plus another 150ml/5fl oz/ ⅔ cup warm water. Cook for 3–4 minutes and add the lemon juice and sugar. Cook for a further 2–3 minutes until the sugar has dissolved. Serve with Plain Boiled Rice.

1 Cut the peppers in half, remove and discard the cores, then cut the flesh into 2.5cm/1in cubes.

2 In a medium-sized pan, bring 300ml/ 10fl oz/1¼ cups water to the boil and add the potatoes. Bring back to the boil, cover and cook for 5–6 minutes, until tender.

3 Remove the potatoes and spread them on a large plate to prevent further cooking. Reserve the cooking liquid.

4 Grind the sesame seeds, poppy seeds, lentils, peppercorns and chilli in a coffee grinder until they are finely ground.

Per portion Energy 146kcal/607kJ; Protein 3.45g; Carbohydrate 9.5g, of which sugars 4g; Fat 10.8g, of which saturates 1.6g; Cholesterol 0mg; Calcium 45mg; Fibre 1.8g; Sodium 24.8mg.

Mixed vegetable stew

This dish, *Laganshala*, would traditionally form part of a Parsi wedding feast, which is famous for its elaborate and extensive range of dishes – in fact it is so lavish that the invitees often fast before attending so they can eat more! The recipe has a complex yet subtle flavour with a sweet-and-sour undertone that reflects the influence of Gujarati cooking on the region.

4 Add 425ml/15fl oz water and bring it to the boil. Reduce the heat to medium, cover and cook for 15 minutes.

1 Heat the oil over a medium heat and add the onion. Fry for about 5 minutes, until the onion is soft.

SERVES 4

45ml/3 tbsp sunflower oil or light olive oil
1 large onion, finely chopped
10ml/2 tsp ginger purée
10ml/2 tsp garlic purée
5ml/1 tsp chilli powder, or to taste
5ml/1 tsp ground turmeric
5ml/1 tsp ground cumin
5ml/1 tsp ground coriander
225g/8oz potatoes, peeled and cut into
    2.5cm/1in cubes
225g/8oz sweet potatoes, peeled and cut
    into 2.5cm/1in cubes
225g/8oz carrots, scraped and cut into
    thick rounds
150g/5oz green beans
2 ripe tomatoes, chopped
15ml/1 tbsp Worcestershire sauce
15ml/1 tbsp vinegar
5ml/1 tsp salt, or to taste
5ml/1 tsp sugar
30ml/2 tbsp fresh coriander (cilantro)
    leaves, chopped
Indian bread or Plain Boiled Rice,
    to serve

2 Add the ginger and garlic and stir. Cook for 2 minutes, then add the chilli powder, turmeric, cumin and coriander. Cook for 1 minute, then add 15ml/1 tbsp water. Continue to cook for 2 minutes, then add a further 15ml/1 tbsp water.

5 Add the beans and tomatoes, Worcestershire sauce, vinegar, salt and sugar. Cook, uncovered, for 5–6 minutes or until the sauce has thickened.

6 Stir in the chopped coriander and remove from the heat. Serve with any bread or Plain Boiled Rice.

VARIATION
Use 45ml/3 tbsp canned chopped tomatoes in place of fresh ones.

3 Add all the vegetables, except the green beans and tomatoes.

COOK'S TIP
This dish can easily be made in advance and chilled in the refrigerator for a couple of days. To reheat, either transfer the stew to a pan and heat until simmering, or place it in the microwave and cook for about 3 minutes, or until piping hot.

Per portion Energy 260kcal/1088kJ; Protein 4g; Carbohydrate 36g, of which sugars 15g; Fat 12g, of which saturates 2g; Cholesterol 0mg; Calcium 78mg; Fibre 6.2g; Sodium 584mg.

Vegetables with gram flour dumplings

Gram flour is made from ground chickpeas and is a staple ingredient in both Gujarat and Rajasthan. High in protein and gluten-free, it can be used for both sweet and savoury dishes. For this recipe, *Oondhiu*, it is turned into little dumplings as a topping for a spicy mixture of vegetables cooked in a coconut sauce.

SERVES 4–6

For the dumplings:
185g/6½oz/1⅔ cups gram flour (besan)
pinch of bicarbonate of soda (baking soda)
2.5ml/½ tsp ground aniseed
2.5ml/½ tsp ground turmeric
5ml/1 tsp ginger purée
10ml/2 tsp dried fenugreek leaves
   (kasuri methi)
1–2 fresh red chillies, finely chopped
   (deseeded if preferred)
30ml/2 tbsp chopped fresh coriander
   (cilantro)
2.5ml/½ tsp salt, or to taste
60ml/4 tbsp sunflower oil

For the vegetable mixture:
30ml/2 tbsp sunflower or light olive oil
1 garlic clove, crushed, or 5ml/1 tsp
   garlic purée
5ml/1 tsp ginger purée
1–2 fresh red chillies, finely chopped
   (deseeded if preferred)
2.5ml/½ tsp ground turmeric
200g/7oz carrots, thickly sliced
200g/7oz green beans, cut into
   2.5cm/1in lengths
200g/7oz sweet potatoes, peeled and cut
   into 2.5cm/1in chunks
1 small or ½ large aubergine (eggplant),
   about 200g/7oz, cut into 2.5cm/1in chunks
400g/14oz can coconut milk
2.5ml/½ tsp salt, or to taste
200g/7oz boiled potatoes, cut into
   2.5cm/1in cubes
30ml/2 tbsp tamarind juice or lemon juice
Plain Boiled Rice or warm Indian bread,
   to serve

COOK'S TIP
Ensure that the pan is large enough to hold everything. If not, transfer the fried garlic and spice mixture to a larger pan before adding the vegetables in Step 4.

1 For the dumplings, sift the gram flour and bicarbonate of soda into a bowl. Add the aniseed, turmeric, ginger, fenugreek, chillies, coriander and salt. Stir together.

2 Heat 30ml/2 tbsp of the oil in a large, deep frying pan. Add 75ml/5 tbsp cold water to the dry ingredients and stir. When the mixture comes together, add the oil and, using dampened hands, mix to a soft dough.

3 Shape into about 24 cherry-sized balls and loosely cover with clear film (plastic wrap) to prevent them drying out.

4 Blanch the carrots and green beans in a pan of lightly salted boiling water for 5 minutes, then drain immediately and plunge them into iced water.

5 Heat the remaining 30ml/2 tbsp oil in the pan over a medium heat. Fry the dumplings in batches until browned, turning them frequently to ensure they cook evenly. Lift out of the pan and drain on kitchen paper.

6 For the vegetable mixture, heat the oil in the same pan you used for frying the dumplings, if possible. Add the garlic and ginger and fry over a low heat for 1 minute, then add the chillies and turmeric. Cook for about 30 seconds, then add the chunks of sweet potato and aubergine.

7 Pour in 300ml/10fl oz lukewarm water and bring it to the boil. Cover the pan and cook over a medium heat for 5 minutes.

8 Add the coconut milk, fried dumplings, boiled potatoes, and blanched carrots and green beans, and stir in the salt. Bring to a slow simmer, cover the pan and cook gently for 6–8 minutes or until the vegetables are tender but still firm.

9 Stir in the tamarind or lemon juice and remove the pan from the heat.

10 Serve immediately with Plain Boiled Rice or warm Indian bread such as chapatis or naan.

Per portion Energy 328kcal/1375kJ; Protein 9g; Carbohydrate 37g, of which sugars 10g; Fat 17g, of which saturates 2g; Cholesterol 0mg; Calcium 101mg; Fibre 6.8g; Sodium 431mg.

Vegetable curry with dumplings

Oondhiu is a fabulous mixture of fresh vegetables such as potatoes, green beans, aubergines (eggplants), sweet potatoes and bananas, cooked with spicy gram flour (besan) dumplings and enhanced by dried fenugreek leaves (kasuri methi). This recipe provides a healthy and substantial vegetarian main course.

SERVES 4

For the dumplings:

125g/4½oz/generous 1 cup gram flour (besan)
1.25ml/¼ tsp salt
a pinch of bicarbonate of soda (baking soda)
2.5ml/½ tsp aniseed
30ml/2 tbsp dried fenugreek leaves
1 fresh green chilli, finely chopped
  (deseeded if preferred)
15ml/1 tbsp fresh coriander (cilantro)
  leaves, finely chopped
15ml/1 tbsp hot sunflower oil
15ml/1 tbsp lime juice
15ml/1 tbsp water
sunflower oil, for deep-frying

For the vegetable curry:

50g/2oz desiccated (dry unsweetened
  shredded) coconut
10ml/2 tsp ground coriander
20ml/4 tsp garlic purée
20ml/4 tsp ginger purée
20ml/4 tsp chilli powder, or to taste
5ml/1 tsp ground turmeric
30ml/2 tbsp sunflower oil or light olive oil
1.25ml/¼ tsp Asafoetida
200g/7oz potatoes, cut into 2.5cm/1in cubes
200g/7oz aubergine (eggplant), cut into
  2.5cm/1in chunks
150g/5oz sweet potato, cut into
  2.5cm/1in cubes
125g/4½oz green beans, cut into
  2.5cm/1in lengths
2 unripe bananas, thickly sliced
Indian bread, to serve

1 For the dumplings: put the gram flour into a mixing bowl and add the remaining dumpling ingredients, up to and including the chopped coriander.

2 Mix thoroughly and add the hot oil, lime juice and water. Mix until a stiff dough is formed and knead it for about 1 minute. Divide the dough into 10 equal balls.

3 Heat the oil in a wok or other suitable pan for deep-frying over a medium heat. Fry the dumplings until they are crisp and golden brown. Drain on kitchen paper and set aside.

4 For the vegetable curry: grind the coconut in a coffee grinder and mix in a bowl with the coriander, 10ml/2 tsp of the garlic, 10ml/2 tsp of the ginger, the chilli powder and turmeric. Add 150ml/4fl oz/½ cup water and stir until it forms a paste. Alternatively, put the coconut in 150ml/4fl oz/½ cup water, bring to the boil and allow to cool, then purée in a blender along with the spices. Set the purée aside.

5 Heat the oil over a medium heat and add the Asafoetida and the remaining garlic and ginger, and cook until they begin to brown.

6 Add the coconut spice paste to the pan, increase the heat slightly, and cook for 3–4 minutes, stirring.

7 Add the potatoes to the pan and pour in 450ml/16fl oz/1¾ cups warm water. Bring the mixture to the boil, reduce the heat to low, cover the pan and cook for 7–8 minutes.

8 Add the aubergine and sweet potato, bring back to the boil, reduce the heat to medium, cover and cook for 5–6 minutes.

9 Add the green beans and the banana slices, cover and cook for 4–5 minutes. Add the dumplings to the pan and cook for 3–4 minutes longer.

10 Remove from the heat and serve with any Indian bread.

Per portion Energy 523kcal/2182kJ; Protein 7.8g; Carbohydrate 47.6g, of which sugars 5.8g; Fat 35.1g, of which saturates 9.8g; Cholesterol 0mg; Calcium 98mg; Fibre 5.8g; Sodium 30mg.

Spicy lentils with wholewheat rolls

From the desert region of Rajasthan, this recipe, D*hal Baatis*, uses ghee and yogurt instead of water to make the rolls. These are then served with spiced lentils and generous amounts of ghee, which is the best choice for a traditional flavour, although sunflower oil or light olive oil can be used instead.

SERVES 4

For the baatis*:*

300g/10½oz/2½ cups wholemeal
  (whole-wheat) flour
50g/2oz/⅓ cup semolina
2.5ml/½ tsp baking powder
2.5ml/½ tsp salt
50g/2oz/4 tbsp ghee or unsalted
  butter, melted
75g/3oz/⅓ cup full-fat (whole) natural
  (plain) yogurt
sunflower oil, for roasting

For the dhal:

150g/5oz/scant 1 cup whole mung beans
  (sabut mung dhal)
75g/3oz/½ cup split Bengal gram (channa
  dhal or skinless split chickpeas)
5ml/1 tsp salt, or to taste
25g/1oz/2 tbsp ghee or unsalted butter
1 medium onion, finely chopped
10ml/2 tsp ginger purée
10ml/2 tsp garlic purée
2.5ml/½ tsp ground turmeric
2.5–5ml/½–1 tsp chilli powder
5ml/1 tsp ground coriander
5ml/1 tsp ground cumin
2.5ml/½ tsp garam masala
juice of 1 lime
30ml/2 tbsp fresh coriander (cilantro)
  leaves, chopped

1 To make the dhal: wash the mung beans and the split Bengal gram and soak them separately for 4–5 hours. Drain well.

2 To make the *baatis*: put the flour, semolina, baking powder and salt in a large mixing bowl and stir to mix. Beat the melted ghee or butter and the yogurt together and add to the flour.

3 Mix with your fingertips and gradually add 150ml/5fl oz/½ cup water. Mix until a dough is formed.

4 Transfer the dough to a flat surface and knead until it has absorbed all the moisture – it will be quite sticky at first.

5 Cover the dough with a damp dish towel and leave for 30 minutes. Preheat the oven to 190°C/375°F/Gas 5.

6 Shape the dough into marble-sized balls. Pour enough oil into a roasting pan to cover the base to about 5mm/¼in depth, heat it over a medium heat and add the dough balls in a single layer, spacing them apart slightly. Shake the pan so that all the balls are coated with the fat.

7 Roast in the centre of the oven for about 20 minutes, until crisp and well-browned, turning them often so they brown evenly.

8 Place the mung beans in a large pan with 1.2 litres/2 pints/5 cups water. Bring to the boil, reduce the heat to medium and partially cover the pan.

9 Cook for 10–12 minutes, then add the gram. Bring back to the boil, cover and simmer for 20–25 minutes longer. Add the salt, mash some of the beans and peas with the back of a spoon and mix well. Switch off the heat.

10 Melt the ghee or butter over a low heat and fry the onion, stirring, for 4–5 minutes until softened. Add the ginger and garlic and cook for 1 minute. Add the turmeric, chilli powder, coriander and cumin, stir-fry for about a minute and add to the cooked dhal with the garam masala, lime juice and chopped coriander. Stir to mix well and serve with the *baati*.

Per portion Energy 820kcal/3439kJ; Protein 27.6g; Carbohydrate 101.3g, of which sugars 10g; Fat 36.8g, of which saturates 11.1g; Cholesterol 2mg; Calcium 136mg; Fibre 11.2g; Sodium 300mg.

Spiced split chickpeas with fried bread

This recipe, *Dal Pakwan*, is from Sindh, across the north-western border, a former part of India which is now in Pakistan. Comprising spiced split Bengal gram (channa dhal or skinless split chickpeas), accompanied by deep-fried bread with cumin and nigella seeds, this vegetarian meal can easily match any meat dish.

SERVES 4

For the spiced chickpeas:

250g/9oz split Bengal gram (channa dhal or skinless split chickpeas)

30ml/2 tbsp sunflower oil or light olive oil

5ml/1 tsp cumin seeds

2–3 fresh green chilies, chopped (deseeded if preferred)

5ml/1 tsp ground turmeric

2.5ml/½ tsp chilli powder

5ml/1 tsp salt, or to taste

2.5ml/½ tsp garam masala

30ml/2 tbsp fresh coriander (cilantro) leaves, chopped

For the bread:

275g/10oz/2½ cups plain (all-purpose) flour, plus extra for dusting

2.5ml/½ tsp salt

2.5ml/½ tsp sugar

2.5ml/½ tsp cumin seeds

2.5ml/½ tsp nigella seeds

30ml/2 tbsp sunflower oil or light olive oil

150ml/¼ pint/⅔ cup lukewarm water

sunflower oil, for deep-frying

1 Wash the split Bengal gram thoroughly in a sieve (strainer) under cold running water, then soak in a bowl of water for 2–3 hours. Drain well.

2 Heat the oil over a medium heat and add the cumin, chilli, turmeric and chilli powder, followed by the drained Bengal gram. Stir-fry for 2–3 minutes, then pour in 750ml/1¼ pints/3 cups warm water.

3 Bring it to the boil, cover the pan and reduce the heat to low. Simmer for 35–40 minutes or until the peas are tender.

4 Add the salt, garam masala and chopped coriander, stir to combine, then remove from the heat.

5 To make the bread: mix the flour, salt, sugar, cumin and nigella seeds in a large mixing bowl. Rub in the oil and gradually add the water, then mix until a dough is formed. You may need a little less or more water as the absorbency level of flour can differ.

6 Transfer the dough to a lightly floured surface and knead for 3–4 minutes, then cover with a damp dish towel and set aside for 30 minutes.

7 Divide the dough into 16 equal portions and shape them into balls, then flatten them into cakes by pressing them between your palms.

8 Heat the oil in a wok or other suitable pan for deep-frying over a medium heat. Check that the temperature is right by dropping a little of the dough into the oil. If it floats to the surface immediately without turning brown, then the temperature is just right. Alternatively, check the temperature on a thermometer; it should be at least 180°C/350°F.

9 Dust each flattened cake lightly in the flour and roll out to about a 7.5cm/3in disc. Using a fork, pierce the surface all over so that it does not puff during frying.

10 Carefully lower one bread into the hot oil using a slotted spoon and fry for about 2 minutes, until it is well browned.

11 Lift out and drain on kitchen paper. Keep warm by covering with foil while you repeat with the remaining breads.

12 Serve the breads immediately with the spiced chickpeas.

Per portion Energy 647kcal/2725kJ; Protein 21g; Carbohydrate 91g, of which sugars 25g; Fat 3g, of which saturates 25g; Cholesterol 0mg; Calcium 135mg; Fibre 9.2g; Sodium 769mg.

Black-eyed beans in coconut and tamarind sauce

This recipe, *Feijoada*, originates from the Christian community of Goa. The black-eyed beans (peas) are packed with protein and other nutrients that provide a well-balanced vegetarian diet. Ginger, garlic, chilli and onions make up the flavours of the sauce, which is enriched with coconut milk and the tart taste of tamarind.

2 Blend the gram flour with 10ml/2 tsp water, making sure there are no lumps, and add it to the beans. Stir over a low heat and let it simmer for 5–6 minutes.

3 Meanwhile, heat the oil in a small pan over a medium heat and add the onion. Fry, stirring often, for 5–7 minutes, until the onion begins to brown.

4 Add the ginger and garlic and continue to cook for a further 2–3 minutes, stirring frequently. Add the coriander, turmeric and chilli powder and cook for 1 minute longer.

5 Add the onion and spice mixture to the beans. If you are using lemon juice instead of tamarind concentrate, add it at this stage. Stir well to combine everything thoroughly.

6 Remove the pan from the heat and transfer the mixture to a serving dish. Garnish with the toasted flaked coconut and serve with Plain Boiled Rice.

SERVES 4

700g/1¼lb/4½ cups canned black-eyed
  beans (peas), rinsed and drained
400ml/14fl oz/1½ cups coconut milk
5ml/1 tsp salt, or to taste
5ml/1 tsp tamarind concentrate or
  22.5ml/1½ tbsp lemon juice
5ml/1 tsp gram flour (besan)
60ml/4 tbsp sunflower oil or light olive oil
1 large onion, finely chopped
10ml/2 tsp ginger purée
10ml/2 tsp garlic purée
10ml/2 tsp ground coriander
5ml/1 tsp ground turmeric
5–7.5ml/1–1½ tsp chilli powder
toasted flaked coconut, to garnish
Plain Boiled Rice, to serve

1 Put the rinsed, drained black-eyed beans in a large pan and pour in the coconut milk, salt and tamarind concentrate, if using. If you are using lemon juice instead of tamarind concentrate, do not add it yet. Stir to combine.

Per portion Energy 354kcal/1487kJ; Protein 14.3g; Carbohydrate 48.9g, of which sugars 19.6g; Fat 12.7g, of which saturates 1.7g; Cholesterol 0mg; Calcium 193mg; Fibre 13g; Sodium 797mg.

Konkan coast fish curry

Konkan cuisine is often hot and fiery, and coconut – whether as fresh grated, dried, coconut paste or made into coconut milk – is used liberally as it contrasts with and cools the heat of chillies. Salmon is a robust fish, which keeps its texture and works well with the spices in this dish, *Machli Ghashi*.

SERVES 4

675g/1½lb salmon fillets, skinned

5ml/1 tsp salt, or to taste

juice of 1 lime

45ml/3 tbsp sunflower oil or light olive oil

3 garlic cloves, crushed, or 15ml/1 tbsp
   garlic purée

15ml/1 tbsp ground coriander

5–7.5ml/1–1½ tsp chilli powder

2.5ml/½ tsp ground turmeric

400g/14oz can coconut milk

sprigs of fresh coriander (cilantro),
   to garnish

Plain Boiled Rice, to serve

1 Cut the salmon into 5cm/2in chunks and gently rub in half the salt and all the lime juice. Set aside for 10–15 minutes.

2 Heat the oil in a large, heavy frying pan over a low heat and add the garlic. Fry until the garlic begins to brown, then stir in the coriander, chilli powder and turmeric.

3 Cook for about 1 minute, then stir in the coconut milk and remaining salt. Simmer gently for 5–6 minutes.

4 Add the fish along with any juices left in the dish. Simmer gently, uncovered, for 8–10 minutes or until the fish is opaque. Serve garnished with the sprigs of fresh coriander and with some Plain Boiled Rice.

Per portion Energy 429kcal/1787kJ; Protein 35g; Carbohydrate 5g, of which sugars 5g; Fat 31g, of which saturates 84g; Cholesterol 84mg; Calcium 78mg; Fibre 0.1g; Sodium 686mg.

Crab in roasted coconut sauce

For this recipe, *Crab Xec Xec*, fresh crabs, cut into pieces, are simmered gently in a spice-laced roasted coconut sauce, and then served with plain boiled rice. For those who don't fancy preparing live crabs, frozen crab claws may be used, or alternatively, pre-prepared crabs, along with all the juices. This is a hot curry, but you can adjust the level of pungency to taste by reducing the amount of green chillies.

SERVES 4

2 large fresh uncooked crabs, about
   400g/14oz each
75g/3oz/1 cup desiccated (dry
   unsweetened shredded) coconut
3 cloves
10 black peppercorns
5–6 dried red chillies
15ml/1 tbsp coriander seeds
5ml/1 tsp cumin seeds
45ml/3 tbsp sunflower oil or olive oil
1 large onion, finely chopped
5ml/1 tsp ginger purée
5ml/1 tsp garlic purée
1–2 fresh green chillies, finely chopped
   (deseeded if preferred)
2.5ml/½ tsp ground turmeric
3.75ml/¾ tsp salt, or to taste
22.5ml/1½ tbsp tamarind juice or
   lime juice
Plain Boiled Rice, to serve

COOK'S TIP
Fresh crabs are available all year round, but check which months they are at their best where you live and try to buy them then.

1 To prepare a fresh uncooked crab: lay the crab on its back and remove the claws and legs with a twisting action, then remove the feathery toes. Pull the centre portion from the main shell and remove the stomach sac, gills and lungs. Extract the meat, wash the shell and reserve. This will add flavour to the sauce. Some people discard the toes, but these will add extra flavour to the dish and they do have a little meat inside the shell. Finally, wash the claws, legs and toes and reserve.

2 In a small, heavy pan or frying pan, dry-roast the coconut over a low heat, stirring constantly until the coconut is lightly browned. Do not allow it to darken too much. Remove the coconut to a large plate and wipe the pan clean.

3 In the same pan, dry-roast the cloves, peppercorns, dried chillies, coriander and cumin seeds for 1 minute, until they release their aroma. Remove and allow to cool.

4 Grind the cooled dry-roasted coconut and spices in a coffee grinder or blender, in small batches if necessary, until fine, and set aside.

5 Heat the oil over a medium heat and fry the onion, ginger, garlic and green chillies for 8–10 minutes, or until the mixture is just beginning to brown.

6 Stir in the turmeric, crab pieces (including the reserved shell but not the extracted meat) and the salt.

7 Pour in 350ml/12fl oz/1½ cups warm water and add the spices. Stir to combine well and cook gently for 3–4 minutes, then add the reserved crab meat.

8 Cook for a further 2–3 minutes, then add the tamarind or lime juice. Stir gently and cook for about 1 minute, then remove from the heat. Serve immediately with Plain Boiled Rice.

Goan prawn curry

Perhaps it is no surprise that an exquisite seafood cuisine has developed in Goa – an area of India resplendent with flourishing rice fields, coconut palms, cashew trees, and a vast coastline that yields a steady harvest of top-quality fish and shellfish. Goan dishes such as this, *Camrao De Caldeen*, use generous amounts of chilli.

SERVES 4

500g/1¼lb peeled king or tiger prawns (jumbo shrimp), deveined
2.5ml/½ tsp salt, plus extra to taste
30ml/2 tbsp palm or cider vinegar
60ml/4 tbsp sunflower oil or olive oil
1 large onion, finely chopped
10ml/2 tsp ginger purée
10ml/2 tsp garlic purée
2.5ml/½ tsp ground cumin
5ml/1 tsp ground coriander
2.5ml/½ tsp ground turmeric
2.5ml/½ tsp chilli powder
2.5ml/½ tsp ground black pepper
75g/3oz/1 cup creamed coconut, cut into pieces, or 250ml/8fl oz/1 cup coconut cream
4 whole fresh green chillies
30ml/2 tbsp chopped fresh coriander (cilantro) leaves
Plain Boiled Rice, to serve

1 Put the prawns in a non-metallic bowl and add the salt and palm or cider vinegar. Mix together well, cover with clear film (plastic wrap) and set aside for about 10–15 minutes.

2 Heat the sunflower or olive oil in a medium pan and add the onion. Fry over a medium heat for about 5 minutes, until the onion is soft and translucent.

3 Add the ginger and garlic to the pan and continue to fry for about 2 minutes over a low heat, being careful to lightly brown, but not burn, the ingredients.

4 Mix the cumin, coriander, turmeric, chilli powder and black pepper in a bowl and add 30ml/2 tbsp water to make a mixture with a good pouring consistency.

5 Add the spice mixture to the onion and cook, stirring, for 4–5 minutes until the mixture is dry and the oil has separated from the spice mix.

6 Pour in 200ml/7fl oz/¾ cup warm water and the creamed coconut, or just the coconut cream without the water. Add salt to taste. Stir over a medium heat for 3–4 minutes until the creamed coconut, if using, has completely dissolved.

7 Add the prawns to the pan, along with all the juices in the bowl, and stir gently to combine everything. Bring the pan to the boil, reduce the heat to low and cook, uncovered, for 5–7 minutes more. When the prawns are opaque, they are cooked.

8 Add the whole chillies and simmer for an additional 2–3 minutes. Stir in the chopped coriander, remove from the heat and serve immediately with Plain Boiled Rice.

Per portion Energy 171kcal/723kJ; Protein 21.9g; Carbohydrate 10g, of which sugars 7.4g; Fat 5.3g, of which saturates 2.5g; Cholesterol 227mg; Calcium 136mg; Fibre 1g; Sodium 344mg.

Prawns in tamarind sauce

The combination of sightly tart, tangy tamarind and sweet palm sugar, or jaggery, give this Parsi dish, *Kolmino Patio*, a distinctive and delicious sweet and sour flavour. This, combined with pungent fresh chilli and aromatic ground cumin, makes a delectable base for large prawns (shrimp).

SERVES 4
60ml/4 tbsp sunflower oil or light olive oil
1 large onion, finely sliced
1 fresh green chilli, finely chopped
  (deseeded if preferred)
2 cloves garlic, crushed, or 10ml/2 tsp
  garlic purée
5ml/1 tsp ground turmeric
2.5–5ml/½–1 tsp chilli powder
5ml/1 tsp ground cumin
15ml/1 tbsp grated palm sugar (jaggery)
  or light muscovado sugar
45ml/3 tbsp tamarind juice
5ml/1 tsp salt, or to taste
500g/1¼lb peeled raw tiger prawns (jumbo
  shrimp), tails on, deveined
30ml/2 tbsp chopped fresh coriander (cilantro)
Plain Boiled Rice or a lentil dhal dish,
  to serve

2 Add the garlic and continue to cook until the onion begins to brown. Add the turmeric, chilli powder and cumin. Cook for about a minute, then stir in 50ml/2fl oz lukewarm water.

3 Stir in the palm sugar or sugar, tamarind juice and salt.Increase the heat slightly and stir until the palm sugar has dissolved.

COOK'S TIP
Leaving the tails on prawns (shrimp) helps them retain their shape when cooking, and makes the finished dish look more attractive. It also makes it easier to eat them with your fingers!

4 Add the prawns to the pan and cook gently for 6–8 minutes or until they are completely pink and just cooked. Stir in the fresh coriander.

5 Serve immediately with Plain Boiled Rice or a lentil dhal.

1 Heat the oil in a large, heavy frying pan over a medium heat and fry the onion and chilli until the onion is soft, but not brown.

Per portion Energy 298kcal/1245kJ; Protein 24g; Carbohydrate 16g, of which sugars 14g; Fat 016g, of which saturates 2g; Cholesterol 244mg; Calcium 141mg; Fibre 0.9g; Sodium 742mg.

Portuguese pullao

This delicious Portuguese favourite, *Arroz Refogado*, is packed with colourful ingredients. *Refogado* refers to the technique of sautéing onions and spices, which brings out their flavour.

SERVES 4

275g/10oz/1¼ cups basmati rice
3 spicy sausages, sliced diagonally
50g/2oz/¼ cup ghee or unsalted butter
2.5cm/1in piece cinnamon stick
6 green cardamom pods
4 cloves
10 black peppercorns
1 bay leaves
1 large onion, finely sliced
2 fresh green chillies, finely chopped
   (deseeded if preferred)
2.5cm/1in fresh root ginger, grated, or
   10ml/2 tsp ginger purée
2 garlic cloves, crushed, or 10ml/2 tsp
   garlic purée
2.5ml/½ tsp ground turmeric
75g/3oz cooked chicken, sliced
2.5ml/½ tsp salt, or to taste
600ml/1 pint/2½ cups boiling chicken
   or vegetable stock
2 hard-boiled eggs, sliced
sprigs of fresh coriander (cilantro),
   to garnish

1 Wash the rice in a sieve under cold running water until the water runs clear. Transfer to a bowl, cover with cold water and leave to soak 20–25 minutes. Drain well and set aside.

2 Meanwhile, heat a heavy pan, preferably non-stick, and fry the sausages in their own fat until they are just beginning to brown. Remove with a slotted spoon, leaving the fat behind, and set aside.

3 Melt the ghee or butter in the pan, then add the cinnamon, cardamom, cloves, peppercorns and bay leaf. Let them sizzle gently for 20–25 seconds, then add the onion and green chillies.

4 Fry until the onion is just beginning to brown, stirring frequently, then add the ginger and garlic and continue to fry until the onion is well browned.

5 Stir in the turmeric and add the cooked chicken, salt, drained rice, fried sausages and stock. Bring to the boil, and simmer, uncovered, for 2–3 minutes.

6 Reduce the heat to low and cover the pan tightly. Cook for 9–10 minutes, then turn off the heat and leave the pan to stand undisturbed for 10–15 minutes.

7 Fluff up the rice with a fork and transfer half to a serving dish. Arrange the eggs on top, reserving a few slices for garnishing and cover with the remaining rice.

8 Garnish with the remaining eggs and sprigs of fresh coriander before serving.

> ## VARIATION
> If you are unable to find Indian- or Portuguese-style spiced sausages, Spanish chorizo will also work well in this recipe.

Per portion Energy 580kcal/2435kJ; Protein 22g; Carbohydrate 66g, of which sugars 5g; Fat 28g, of which saturates 13g; Cholesterol 147mg; Calcium 81mg; Fibre 1.2g; Sodium 798mg.

Hot chicken curry from Kolhapur

This very hot curry, *Murgh Kolhapuri*, comes from the small town of Kolhapur, in the state of Maharashtra. Large amounts of chillies as well as hot spices such as cloves and peppercorns are used, but the final taste is balanced by the sweetness of a generous amount of onion, yogurt and coconut. For a milder taste, reduce the amount of chillies, peppercorns and cloves or add extra coconut and yogurt.

SERVES 4

1.1kg/2⅓lb chicken joints
115g/4oz/½ cup natural (plain) yogurt
10ml/2 tsp gram flour (besan)
5ml/1 tsp ground turmeric
5ml/1 tsp salt, or to taste
25g/1oz/⅓ cup desiccated (dry
  unsweetened shredded) coconut
1 large onion, roughly chopped
2.5cm/1in piece of fresh root ginger,
  chopped
5 large garlic cloves, roughly chopped
60ml/4 tbsp sunflower oil or olive oil
5cm/2in piece of cinnamon stick, halved
6 green cardamom pods, bruised
6 cloves
5–10ml/1–2 tsp chilli powder
2.5ml/½ tsp ground black pepper
115g/4oz canned chopped tomatoes,
  with their juice
2.5ml/½ tsp garam masala
15ml/1 tbsp chopped fresh coriander
  (cilantro) leaves
1 small tomato, deseeded and cut into
  julienne strips, to garnish
1–2 fresh green chillies, deseeded and
  cut into julienne strips, to garnish
Plain Boiled Rice, to serve

1 Skin the chicken joints and cut each of them into two pieces by separating the leg from the thigh and cutting each breast joint in half.

2 In a large mixing bowl, whisk the yogurt with the gram flour, then add the turmeric and salt. Add the chicken pieces and mix thoroughly. Cover with clear film (plastic wrap) and set aside for 1 hour.

3 In a heavy pan, dry-roast the coconut over a medium to low heat until it is lightly browned. Do not allow it to darken or it will taste bitter. Remove from the pan, cool and grind in a coffee grinder until fine.

4 Purée the onion, ginger and garlic in a food processor or blender until smooth.

5 Heat the oil over a low heat and add the cinnamon, cardamom and cloves. Stir-fry these for 1–2 minutes, until the cardamom pods have puffed up.

6 Add the puréed onion, ginger and garlic mixture gradually. Increase the heat slightly and cook until the mixture is beginning to brown, stirring regularly and being careful not to let it burn.

7 Add the chilli powder and black pepper, and continue to cook for an additional 2–3 minutes, adding about 15ml/1 tbsp water if the mixture sticks to the pan.

8 Add the chicken pieces and stir over a high heat until it changes colour. Add the canned chopped tomatoes and pour in 200ml/7fl oz/¾ cup warm water. Bring to the boil, reduce the heat to low, cover the pan and cook until the chicken is tender when pierced with a fork.

9 Stir in the roasted coconut and cook for 4–5 minutes. Stir in garam masala and coriander. Remove from the heat. Transfer to a dish, garnish with the tomato and chilli strips, and serve with Plain Boiled Rice.

Per portion Energy 605kcal/2508kJ; Protein 37.8g; Carbohydrate 13.8g, of which sugars 8.9g; Fat 44.7g, of which saturates 13.2g; Cholesterol 176.2mg; Calcium 107.8mg; Fibre 2.5g; Sodium 170mg.

Tandoori-style whole guinea fowl

The word *mussallam* means 'whole', and fabulous dishes using whole game birds regularly graced the dinner tables at royal households in Rajasthan. Most of these dishes were very extravagant and took many hours to prepare. *Jungli Murgh Mussallam* is a somewhat simplified version of a regal dish, which is cooked tandoori-style in a hot oven. Guinea fowl has a subtle gamey flavour and delicious tender meat.

SERVES 4

1 guinea fowl, about 1.3 kg/3lb
juice of 1 lemon
5ml/1 tsp salt, or to taste
2.5cm/1in fresh root ginger, grated, or
    10ml/2 tsp ginger purée
2 cloves garlic, crushed, or 10ml/2 tsp
    garlic purée
45ml/3 tbsp Greek (US strained plain)
    yogurt
10ml/2 tsp gram flour (besan)
30ml/2 tbsp double (heavy) cream
5ml/1 tsp ground coriander
5ml/1 tsp ground cumin
2.5ml/½ tsp ground turmeric
5–10ml/1–2 tsp chilli powder
5ml/1 tsp garam masala
45ml/3 tbsp sunflower oil or light olive oil
wedges of lemon, onion rings and
    cucumber slices, to garnish
Indian bread or Pilau Rice with Raisins,
    to serve

For the stuffing:

30ml/2 tbsp sunflower oil or light olive oil
175g/6oz minced (ground) turkey
1 small onion, finely chopped
5ml/1 tsp ginger purée
1 clove garlic, crushed, or 5ml/1 tsp
    garlic purée
1.25ml/¼ tsp ground turmeric
2.5ml/½ tsp salt
30ml/2 tbsp chopped fresh coriander
    (cilantro)
1 small (US medium) egg, beaten
50g/2oz/¼ cup butter, melted

VARIATIONS

• Minced (ground) chicken makes a good alternative to the minced turkey used in the stuffing mixture.
• You could use a chicken instead of a guinea fowl if you prefer – they are easier to find and cheaper.

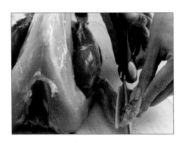

1 Skin the guinea fowl and carefully remove the tips of the wings and legs using sharp kitchen scissors. You could ask a butcher to do this for you. Lightly score the breast, legs and thighs with a sharp knife.

2 Mix the lemon juice, salt, ginger and garlic together and rub this mixture all over the guinea fowl. Cover the bird with clear film (plastic wrap) and set aside for 30 minutes to marinate.

3 Whisk the yogurt and gram flour together in a bowl until smooth, then stir in the cream, coriander, cumin, turmeric, chilli powder, garam masala and oil.

4 Place the guinea fowl in a glass dish or bowl, pour over the marinade and rub well into the meat, including all the slashes made earlier. Cover with clear film and refrigerate for 4–6 hours or overnight, if possible. Bring the guinea fowl to room temperature before cooking.

5 For the stuffing, heat the oil over a medium-high heat and add the turkey. Stir-fry for 4–5 minutes, until the meat begins to brown, then add the chopped onion, the ginger and the garlic. Stir-fry for 3–4 minutes, then add the turmeric and salt. Continue to stir-fry for a further 3–4 minutes, then stir in the coriander.

6 Transfer the mixture to a large mixing bowl and leave to cool, then add the beaten egg and mix well. Preheat the oven to 200°C/400°F/Gas 6.

7 Fill the guinea fowl with the stuffing mixture and tie it up with fine string or secure with trussing needles. Put it on a roasting pan and spread any remaining marinade over the breast and legs.

8 Roast for 20 minutes, then reduce the temperature to 180°C/350°F/Gas 4. Cook for a further 45 minutes, basting every 15 minutes with the melted butter as well as the pan juices.

9 Remove the guinea fowl from the oven, loosely cover with foil to keep it warm and let it rest for 10–15 minutes before carving. Strain the pan juices and serve separately.

10 Serve, garnished with wedges of lemon, onion rings and cucumber slices, accompanied by any Indian bread or Pilau Rice with Raisins.

Per portion Energy 296kcal/1237kJ; Protein 30g; Carbohydrate 3g, of which sugars 1g; Fat 19g, of which saturates 5g; Cholestero124mg; Calcium 58mg; Fibre 0.3g; Sodium 614mg.

Stuffed quails

The Mughal emperors of Rajasthan were passionate about hunting, so their chefs created a range of game dishes. This one, *Batair Mussallam*, follows the dictums of traditional Mughal cooking: the birds are stuffed with grated Indian cheese, dried apricots, chillies and spices, then gently braised in an aromatic sauce.

SERVES 4

4 quails
naan or Griddle-cooked Flaky Bread,
  to serve

For the stuffing:
50g/2oz/½ cup grated paneer (Indian cheese)
15g/½oz seedless raisins
2 dried, ready-to-eat apricots, finely
  chopped
10ml/1 tsp ginger purée
1–2 fresh green chillies, finely chopped
15ml/1 tbsp coriander (cilantro) leaves,
  chopped
1.25ml/¼ tsp salt
15ml/1 tbsp double (heavy) cream

For the sauce:
15ml/1 tbsp coriander seeds
2–3 dried red chillies, chopped
30ml/2 tbsp white poppy seeds
15ml/1 tbsp sesame seeds
½ mace blade
1.25ml/¼ tsp ground turmeric
45ml/3 tbsp sunflower oil or olive oil
4 green cardamom pods, bruised
2.5cm/1in piece of cinnamon stick
1 medium onion, finely chopped
10ml/2 tsp ginger purée
10ml/2 tsp garlic purée
115g/4oz/½ cup natural (plain) yogurt
10ml/2 tsp gram flour (besan)

1 Clean the quails and wipe them inside and out. Score the skin, making a few incisions in the flesh at the same time.

2 Thoroughly combine all the stuffing ingredients in a large bowl, then divide into four equal portions.

3 Fill the stomach cavity of each quail with the stuffing mixture, pushing it up as far as possible. Truss the birds with toothpicks (cocktail sticks), so that the legs are pinned to the sides of the body.

4 To make the sauce, process the coriander, dried red chillies, poppy and sesame seeds, and the mace in a coffee grinder until finely ground. Place in a bowl and mix in the turmeric, then set aside.

5 In a large heavy pan, heat the oil over a low heat and add the cardamom and cinnamon. Stir-fry for 1–2 minutes, until the cardamom pods have puffed up.

6 Add the onion, ginger and garlic to the pan and fry for about 5–6 minutes, until the onion is soft, stirring frequently. Add the ground ingredients and cook for 1 minute.

7 Whisk the yogurt and gram flour together in a small bowl and then add the mixture to the pan. Cook for 2–3 minutes. Pour in 120ml/4fl oz/½ cup warm water and stir well to combine.

8 Add the stuffed quails and turn them around in the pan until they are completely coated with the spices. Put the birds close together in the pan, breast side down. Turn the heat to very low.

9 Soak a piece of baking parchment and squeeze out the excess water. Place the paper in the pan, making sure it is not touching the birds. Cover the pan tightly and cook for 20 minutes.

10 Remove the lid, turn the birds on their backs and re-cover as before with the baking parchment. Cook for 20 minutes. Prick the thighs with a fork to see if the juices are running clear; if not, cook for a few minutes longer. Serve with naan or Griddle-cooked Flaky Bread.

Per portion Energy 378kcal/1581kJ; Protein 25g; Carbohydrate 18.8g, of which sugars 9.1g; Fat 23.6g, of which saturates 6.4g; Cholesterol 97mg; Calcium 194mg; Fibre 1.9g; Sodium 144mg.

Pork in garlic and vinegar

Vindaloo is Goa's signature dish, first introduced by Portuguese traders who took pork preserved in vinegar (vin) and garlic (alhoo) with them on their long voyages to India. More than just the fiery-hot taste its reputation suggests, Vindaloo presents a well-rounded, spicy and enjoyable dish.

SERVES 4

2–6 dried red chillies
25g/1oz fresh root ginger, roughly chopped
25g/1oz garlic, chopped
120ml/4fl oz/½ cup cider vinegar
15ml/1 tbsp tamarind juice or lime juice
5ml/1 tsp cumin seeds
5ml/1 tsp coriander seeds
6 cloves
5cm/2in piece of cinnamon stick, broken up
8–10 black peppercorns
1 blade of mace
seeds of 2 black cardamom pods
1.25ml/¼ tsp fenugreek seeds
675g/1½lb pork leg steaks, cut into
 2.5cm/1 in cubes
60ml/4 tbsp sunflower oil
2 large onions, finely chopped
5ml/1 tsp salt, or to taste
5ml/1 tsp soft dark brown sugar
Plain Boiled Rice or Indian bread, to serve

For the flavoured oil:
10ml/2 tsp sunflower or vegetable oil
8–10 curry leaves

COOK'S TIP
You can make the spice mix, up to the end of Step 3, in advance, and store in the refrigerator.

1 Soak the chillies in hot water for about 10–15 minutes, until softened. Put them into a blender or food processor along with the ginger, garlic, vinegar and tamarind or lime juice. Blend the ingredients until they make up a smooth purée.

2 Grind the cumin, coriander, cloves, cinnamon, peppercorns, mace, cardamom pods and fenugreek seeds together in a coffee grinder or blender until you have a fine powder.

3 Add the spice mixture to the puréed ingredients and make a paste.

4 Rub about a quarter of the spice paste into the pork leg steaks, then transfer to a bowl, cover with clear film (plastic wrap) and set aside to marinate for 30 minutes.

5 Heat the oil in a heavy pan over a medium heat and fry the finely chopped onions for about 5 minutes, until they are lightly browned, stirring frequently.

6 Add the reserved spice paste and fry for 5–6 minutes, stirring. Sprinkle in a little water to prevent the spices from sticking.

7 Add the pork and sauté for 5–6 minutes. Add the salt and sugar and pour in 250ml/8fl oz/1 cup warm water. Bring to the boil, then reduce the heat to low and simmer for 30 minutes, until the meat is tender.

8 For the flavoured oil, heat the oil until it is hot. Switch off the heat and add the curry leaves. Pour this over the curry and serve with Plain Boiled Rice or Indian bread.

Per portion Energy 419kcal/1728kJ; Protein 41.5g; Carbohydrate 19.4g, of which sugars 11g; Fat 19.7g, of which saturates 3.8g; Cholesterol 110.3mg; Calcium 76mg; Fibre 2.7g; Sodium 132mg.

Lamb cooked with lentils and vegetables

This deliciously piquant dish, *Dhansak*, originated in the state of Gujarat, where the ancient Persians first landed after fleeing from their own country (now known as Iran). Here, cubed lamb is browned and simmered with a mouthwatering medley of pungent, freshly ground spices, then brought together with separately prepared lentils and vegetables, before being served alongside basmati rice.

SERVES 4

45ml/3 tbsp sunflower oil or olive oil
1 large onion, finely chopped
10ml/2 tsp ginger purée
10ml/2 tsp garlic purée
5ml/1 tsp coriander seeds
2.5ml/½ tsp cumin seeds
4 green cardamom pods
2.5cm/1in piece of cinnamon stick, broken
10–12 black peppercorns
2 bay leaves
5–6 fenugreek seeds
2.5ml/½ tsp black mustard seeds
5ml/1 tsp chilli powder, or to taste
675g/1½lb boned leg of lamb, cut into
  2.5cm/2in cubes
150g/5oz canned chopped tomatoes
5ml/1 tsp salt, or to taste

For the lentil and vegetable mixture:
75g/3oz/⅓ cup yellow split gram
  (channa dhal)
75g/3oz/⅓ cup red split lentils (masoor dhal)
30ml/2 tbsp sunflower oil or olive oil
1 medium onion, finely chopped
2 fresh green chillies, chopped
5ml/1 tsp ground turmeric
1 small aubergine (eggplant), cut into
  5cm/2in pieces
5ml/1 tsp salt, or to taste
30ml/2 tbsp tamarind juice or lime juice
15ml/1 tbsp chopped coriander (cilantro)
  leaves, plus extra sprigs, to garnish
Plain Boiled Rice, to serve

1 Heat the oil in a heavy pan over a medium heat and add the onion. Stir-fry for 5 minutes, until the onion is soft but not brown, then add the ginger and garlic and continue to stir-fry for 3–4 minutes, until the mixture begins to brown.

2 Grind the coriander, cumin, cardamom, cinnamon stick, peppercorns, bay leaves, fenugreek and black mustard seeds in a coffee grinder or blender, until fine.

3 Add the chilli powder and ground spices to the onion mixture and cook for 2 minutes, then add the meat. Stir-fry over a high heat for 5 minutes, until the meat changes colour.

4 Add the tomatoes and salt, then pour in 120ml/4fl oz/½ cup warm water. Bring the pan to the boil, cover and simmer for 35–40 minutes, stirring occasionally.

5 Meanwhile, for the lentil and vegetable mixture, wash both types of lentils and drain.

6 Heat the oil in a medium pan and fry the onion and green chillies for 8–9 minutes over a medium heat, until the onion is browned. Stir in the turmeric, followed by the drained lentils and aubergine pieces. Reduce the heat to low and stir-fry the mixture for 1–2 minutes.

7 Pour in 600ml/1 pint/2½ cups warm water, bring to the boil, reduce the heat to low and simmer for 20–25 minutes, stirring. Stir in the salt, remove the pan from the heat and cool slightly, then push the lentils through a sieve. Discard any coarse mixture that is left in the sieve.

8 Add the tamarind or lime juice to the lentils. Pour the mixture over the lamb and simmer for 15–20 minutes longer, stirring to ensure the lentils do not stick to the pan.

9 Stir in the coriander and remove from the heat. Garnish with the sprigs of coriander, and serve with Plain Boiled Rice.

Per portion Energy 470kcal/1970kJ; Protein 32.7g; Carbohydrate 36.5g, of which sugars 9g; Fat 22.7g, of which saturates 7.1g; Cholesterol 85.5mg; Calcium 106mg; Fibre 4.8g; Sodium 133mg.

Yellow rice

Tinged with turmeric, this golden rice, *Peela Bhat*, is delicately spiced with a small quantity of cinnamon and cloves. The earthy taste and musky aroma of turmeric, combined with its health benefits, make this rice a wonderful, nutritious change from boiled rice, and it is the perfect accompaniment to any dish.

SERVES 4

225g/8oz/generous 1 cup basmati rice
15ml/1 tbsp ghee or 10ml/2 tsp butter and
  10ml/2 tsp light olive oil
2.5cm/1in piece of cinnamon stick
5 cloves
2.5ml/½ tsp ground turmeric
2.5ml/½ tsp salt, or to taste

4 Reduce the heat to low, cover and cook for 8 minutes. Switch off the heat and let it stand undisturbed for 20–25 minutes. Fluff up the rice with a fork and serve.

COOK'S TIP
Be careful when using turmeric, as it can easily stain clothing.

1 Wash the rice until the water runs clear. Put it in a large bowl, cover with cold water and leave to soak for 20 minutes, then drain.

2 Heat the ghee or butter and oil over a low heat and add the cinnamon and cloves. Sizzle for 25–30 seconds, then stir in the turmeric and rice. Stir-fry for 2 minutes.

3 Pour 450ml/16fl oz/1¾ cups warm water into the pan and add the salt. Bring it to the boil and allow to boil steadily for about 2 minutes.

Per portion Energy 239kcal/995kJ; Protein 4.3g; Carbohydrate 45.2g, of which sugars 0g; Fat 4.2g, of which saturates 1.8g; Cholesterol 0mg; Calcium 13mg; Fibre 0g; Sodium 1mg.

Rice with caramelized sugar

This rice dish, *Peela Bhat*, is the traditional accompaniment for *Dhansak*. To make it, the uncooked rice is briefly tossed in caramelized sugar before being cooked with fragrant cumin seeds and cardamom pods.

SERVES 4–5

275g/10oz/1⅓ cups basmati rice
60ml/4 tbsp sunflower oil or olive oil
60ml/4 tsp granulated (white) sugar
5ml/1 tsp cumin seeds
2.5cm/1in piece of cinnamon stick
4 cardamom pods, bruised
6 cloves
10 black peppercorns
5ml/1 tsp salt, or to taste

1 Wash the rice two or three times in cold water or until the water runs clear, then soak it for about 20 minutes. Leave the rice to drain in a sieve.

2 In a heavy pan, heat the oil over a medium heat and add the sugar. The sugar will begin to turn brown in a few seconds.

3 As soon as the sugar has browned, add the cumin seeds, cinnamon stick, bruised cardamom pods, cloves and black peppercorns, but do not stir. Let these sizzle for 15–20 seconds.

4 Add the rice and salt to the pan. Stir-fry for 2–3 minutes, then pour in 600ml/1 pint/2½ cups warm water. Stir to combine, then bring the pan to the boil and let it boil steadily for 1 minute.

5 Cover the pan tightly with a lid, or a layer of foil and then a lid if the lid isn't tight enough, and reduce the heat to low. Cook for 10 minutes without lifting the lid.

6 Remove the pan from the heat and leave it to stand, undisturbed, for 10 minutes.

7 Fluff up the rice with a fork and serve as an accompaniment to any type of meat or vegetable curry.

> **COOK'S TIPS**
> • Take care not to overcook the sugar or it will burn and taste bitter.

Per portion Energy 324kcal/1353kJ; Protein 4.1g; Carbohydrate 56.4g, of which sugars 12.5g; Fat 9.1g, of which saturates 1.1g; Cholesterol 0mg; Calcium 17mg; Fibre 0g; Sodium 1mg.

Wholemeal flat bread with fenugreek leaves

Methi Na Thepla is a delicious spiced chapati from Gujarat, where they serve it with meals, and also as a snack (*farsan*). In a Gujarati home, fresh fenugreek leaves are the obvious choice, but dried ones (kasuri methi) are more easily available elsewhere and make a lovely aromatic alternative.

3 Cover with a damp dish towel and let it rest for 30 minutes.

4 Divide the dough into two equal parts and cut four equal portions from each.

5 Form into balls and flatten each one to form a neat cake. Dust each cake lightly with flour and roll out to a 15cm/6in circle.

6 Preheat a cast iron griddle over a medium heat and place a flat bread on it. Cook for 30–35 seconds, then turn it over. Spread about 10ml/2 tsp oil over the surface of the cooked side and turn it over again. Let it cook for about 1 minute or until brown patches have appeared.

MAKES 8

450g/1lb chapati flour (atta) or fine
  wholemeal (whole-wheat) flour
5ml/1 tsp salt, or to taste
30ml/2 tbsp dried fenugreek leaves
  (kasuri methi)
2.5–5ml/½–1 tsp chilli powder
2.5ml/½ tsp ground turmeric
2.5ml/½ tsp ground cumin
45ml/3 tbsp sunflower oil or light olive oil
250–300ml/9–10fl oz/generous 1 cup
  warm water
sunflower oil, for shallow-frying

1 Sift the flour into a large mixing bowl and mix in the salt, fenugreek leaves, chilli powder, turmeric and cumin.

2 Rub in the oil with your fingertips, then gradually add the water while continuing to mix. When a dough has formed, transfer it to a lightly floured surface and knead until soft and pliable. Alternatively, make the dough in a food processor.

7 Spread the second side with the same amount of oil, turn it over and cook as before, until brown patches appear.

8 Transfer to a plate lined with kitchen paper. Cook all the bread in the same way. Serve on its own or with any vegetable curry.

Per portion Energy 279kcal/1171kJ; Protein 7.4g; Carbohydrate 36.6g, of which sugars 1.2g; Fat 12.5g, of which saturates 1.4g; Cholesterol 0mg; Calcium 25mg; Fibre 5.1g; Sodium 248mg.

Goan puffed bread

Many different types of Indian bread, usually made without yeast, are cooked throughout the country. They are often served instead of, and occasionally as well as, rice. Many are cooked on a griddle pan, others are oven-baked, but some like these *Vodde* are deep-fried in oil.

MAKES 24

250g/9oz/2½ cups chapati flour or fine
   wholemeal (whole-wheat) flour
50g/2oz/½ cup semolina
2.5ml/½ tsp salt
2.5ml/½ tsp sugar
25g/1oz butter, chilled
150ml/¼ pint/⅔ cup warm water
sunflower oil, for deep-frying

1 Sift the flour into a large mixing bowl and stir in the semolina, salt and sugar. Cut the butter into small cubes and rub in with your fingers and thumbs until the mixture resembles fine breadcrumbs.

2 Sprinkle over most of the water, then stir with a fork to make a soft dough, adding a little more of the water if needed, to form a soft dough.

3 Knead the dough on a lightly floured surface for about 10 minutes, until smooth and elastic. Alternatively, knead for 5 minutes with a dough hook in an electric mixer.

4 Divide the dough in half and form two flattened rounds. Cover one with clear film (plastic wrap), then roll out the other to a circle about 25cm/10in in diameter.

5 Using a 7.5cm/3in cutter, stamp out about 12 small circles. Repeat with the second piece of dough.

6 In a wok or other suitable pan for deep-frying, heat the oil over a medium-high heat. If you have a thermometer, check that the oil is at 180°C/350°F, otherwise, drop a small amount of the dough into the hot oil. If it floats immediately without browning then the oil is at the right temperature.

7 Carefully lower one of the dough circles into the hot oil using a slotted spoon. Gently press it down into the oil for just a second or two, then let it float to the surface. When the bread puffs up, let it brown on the underside then turn it over and brown the other side.

8 Remove from the oil and drain on kitchen paper. Cook the other breads in the same way. Serve immediately.

Per portion Energy 93kcal/387kJ; Protein 2g; Carbohydrate 8g, of which sugars 0g; Fat 6g, of which saturates 1g; Cholesterol 2mg; Calcium 5mg; Fibre 1.0g; Sodium 48mg.

Leeks with garlic, chilli and gram flour

Traditionally, in this recipe, *Jhunko*, a large amount of sliced onion is sautéed with garlic and chillies, and gram flour (besan) is added at the end to soak up all the juices. The mixture is then stir-fried until the gram flour releases its nutty, toasted aroma. This version uses leeks instead of onions for a more subtle flavour.

SERVES 4

60ml/4 tbsp sunflower oil or light
  olive oil
2.5ml/½ tsp black mustard seeds
5ml/1 tsp cumin seeds
450g/1lb young leeks, finely sliced
1 small red (bell) pepper, cut into
  2.5cm/1in strips
2.5ml/½ tsp ground turmeric
2.5ml/½ tsp chilli powder
2.5ml/½ tsp salt, or to taste
50g/2oz/½ cup gram flour
  (besan), sifted
any light curry, to serve

1 Heat the oil in a non-stick pan over a medium heat. When it is hot but not smoking, add the mustard and cumin seeds.

2 Add the leeks, red pepper, turmeric, chilli powder and salt. Increase the heat slightly and stir-fry the vegetables for 4–5 minutes.

3 Sprinkle the gram flour into the pan and stir-fry for 1 minute. Remove from the heat and serve with any light curry.

Per portion Energy 177kcal/738kJ; Protein 3.5g; Carbohydrate 14.3g, of which sugars 2.7g; Fat 12.2g, of which saturates 1.5g; Cholesterol 0mg; Calcium 51mg; Fibre 2.9g; Sodium 4mg.

Potatoes in chilli-tamarind sauce

In this dish, *Batata Saung*, boiled and cubed potatoes are tossed in a chilli-hot tamarind sauce that is flavoured with onion and a generous amount of crushed garlic. It makes a delicious accompaniment to any meal. It is essential to boil the potatoes in their skin in order to preserve the starch content.

SERVES 4

450g/1lb potatoes
60ml/4 tbsp sunflower oil or light
   olive oil
2.5ml/½ tsp black mustard seeds
1 large onion, finely chopped
4–5 large garlic cloves, crushed
2.5–5ml/½–1 tsp chilli powder
5ml/1 tsp salt, or to taste
22.5ml/1½ tbsp tamarind juice or
   lime juice

1 Boil the potatoes in their skins in a large pan of lightly salted boiling water for about 10 minutes, until tender. Drain, leave to cool completely, then remove the skins and cut into 2.5cm/1in cubes.

2 Heat the oil over a medium heat and add the mustard seeds. As soon as they pop, add the onion and fry, stirring regularly, until the onion is golden brown.

5 Add 150ml/5fl oz/⅔ cup warm water and cook over a medium heat for 3–4 minutes, stirring often. Stir in the tamarind juice or lime juice and remove the pan from the heat. Serve immediately.

COOK'S TIP

The potatoes can be boiled, cooled and refrigerated in advance. They are much easier to cut into neat pieces once chilled.

3 Add the garlic and cook for 2 minutes, stirring frequently.

4 Add the cooked potatoes, chilli powder and salt. Stir to mix thoroughly.

Per portion Energy 135kcal/568kJ; Protein 4g; Carbohydrate 29.3g, of which sugars 8.5g; Fat 1.1g, of which saturates 0.2g; Cholesterol 0mg; Calcium 45mg; Fibre 2.9g; Sodium 18mg.

Split mung bean kedgeree

Different variations of this dish are cooked all over India, and in the 15th century one of them became the inspiration for the British dish kedgeree, which includes hard-boiled eggs and smoked fish. This recipe, *Ghau Na Phada Ni Khichdi*, is delicious as well as nutritious.

SERVES 4

175g/6oz skinless split mung beans
  (mung dhal)
175g/6oz cracked wheat (dalia)
50g/2oz ghee, plus 15ml/1 tbsp for tempering
5cm/2in piece of cinnamon stick, halved
5 cloves
2.5ml/½ tsp black peppercorns, crushed
1 large onion, finely sliced
10ml/2 tsp ginger purée
2–3 fresh green chillies, sliced at an angle
  (deseeded if preferred)
5ml/1 tsp ground turmeric
5ml/1 tsp chilli powder, or to taste
5ml/1 tsp salt, or to taste
200g/7oz carrots, scraped and cut like
  French Fries
150g/5oz green beans, cut into
  2.5cm/1in lengths
250g/9oz cauliflower, cut into florets
  1cm/½in in diameter
5ml/1 tsp black mustard seeds
5ml/1 tsp cumin seeds
2.5ml/½ tsp Asafoetida
Thickened and Seasoned Yogurt, to serve

3 Let them sizzle for 15–20 seconds, then add the onion. Fry for about 5 minutes, until the onion is soft, but not brown.

4 Add the ginger and chillies and fry for a further 4–5 minutes, until the onion is brown.

5 Drain the mung beans and the cracked wheat and add them to the pan. Add the turmeric, chilli powder and salt and cook, stirring, for 2–3 minutes.

6 Add the vegetables and pour in 900ml/1½ pints/3¾ cups hot water. Bring to the boil, reduce the heat to low, cover and cook for 20 minutes. Switch off the heat and set aside.

1 Wash the mung beans in a sieve (strainer), then transfer to a large bowl and stir in the cracked wheat. Cover with cold water and leave to soak for 30–40 minutes.

2 In a heavy pan, heat the ghee over a medium heat and add the cinnamon stick, cloves and black peppercorns.

7 Heat the ghee for tempering over a medium-high heat. When almost smoking, add the mustard seeds, switch off the heat and add the cumin and Asafoetida. Pour over the *khichdi* and mix it gently. Serve with Thickened and Seasoned Yogurt.

Per portion Energy 330kcal/1371kJ; Protein 9g; Carbohydrate 42g, of which sugars 7g; Fat 15g, of which saturates 9g; Cholesterol 35mg; Calcium 90mg; Fibre 06.1g; Sodium 523mg.

Banana in spiced yogurt dressing

Banana is an unusual fruit to use in a raita, but *Paka Kela Nu Raitu* is very popular in Gujarat. Here, ripe bananas are steeped in yogurt that has a faint tinge of turmeric and the pungency of mustard powder, and the sweetness of the fruit complements both the spices in the dish and the food it accompanies.

SERVES 4

225g/8oz/1 cup full-fat (whole) natural (plain) yogurt
1.25ml/¼ tsp salt
10ml/2 tsp caster (superfine) sugar
5ml/1 tsp mustard powder
2 large ripe, firm bananas with a hint of green on their skins
15ml/1 tbsp lemon juice
1.25ml/¼ tsp chilli powder, to garnish
1.25ml/¼ tsp ground cumin, to garnish

1 Beat the yogurt until smooth. Add the salt, sugar and mustard and mix well.

2 Peel the bananas and quarter them lengthways. Chop each of these into bitesize pieces and sprinkle over the lemon juice, to prevent them discolouring.

3 Mix well, then gently fold into the yogurt mixture. Cover and chill for 1 hour.

4 Transfer the raita to a serving dish and sprinkle the chilli and cumin on top.

Per portion Energy 283kcal/1192kJ; Protein 3g; Carbohydrate 44g, of which sugars 16g; Fat 2g, of which saturates 2g; Cholesterol 0mg; Calcium 73mg; Fibre 3.7g; Sodium 620mg.

Aubergine pickle

In this tangy pickle recipe, B*rinjal Achar*, the most important step is preparing the aubergine (eggplant) carefully, as described below, since the moisture from the vegetable must be extracted completely. This pickle is delicious served with a range of snacks, and as a condiment to accompany many different curries.

MAKES 350–400g/12–14oz

1 large aubergine (eggplant), about
   400g/14oz, peeled
15ml/1 tbsp salt
5ml/1 tsp mustard seeds
5ml/1 tsp fenugreek seeds
7.5ml/1½ tsp cumin seeds
120ml/4fl oz/½ cup vegetable oil
2.5ml/½ tsp ground asafoetida
10 garlic cloves, crushed
5cm/2in piece of fresh root ginger, grated
25g/1oz/2 tbsp granulated (white) sugar
20g/¾oz/2 scant tbsp salt
175ml/6fl oz/¾ cup white wine vinegar

COOK'S TIP

There are several ways to sterilize jars. Washed, dried jars can be placed in the oven, which is then switched on and set to 120°C/ 250°F/Gas ½. Leave the jars for 10 minutes, then remove and fill when cool. Alternatively, place the jars on the top rack of a dishwasher and wash on a normal cycle. The heat used to dry the dishes will sterilize the jars. You can also carefully fill the jars with boiling water, leave them for 10 minutes, then discard the water.

1 Cut the aubergine into 2.5cm/1in chunks. Place in a bowl and sprinkle with the salt.

2 Put the aubergine in muslin (cheesecloth), tie it up, and place in a colander positioned over a bowl. Put a clean weight on top and leave for 7 hours to drain off all the water.

3 Grind the mustard, fenugreek and cumin seeds finely in a coffee grinder or blender. Heat the oil in a large pan, then add the ground spices and fry for 2–3 minutes, until they release their aroma.

4 Add the asafoetida, crushed garlic, ginger, sugar, salt, vinegar and aubergine chunks. Stir to combine, then simmer, stirring occasionally, for 20–25 minutes or until the aubergine is tender.

5 Cool completely and store in a sterilized jar (*see* Cook's Tip). Allow 12–14 days for the pickle to mature, then serve as a condiment with any snack or curry.

Per portion Energy 870kcal/3609kJ; Protein 9.1g; Carbohydrate 46.7g, of which sugars 34.8g; Fat 73.7g, of which saturates 8g; Cholesterol 0mg; Calcium 89mg; Fibre 9.6g; Sodium 3946mg.

Thickened and seasoned yogurt

Kadhi is the traditional partner for *khichdi* and there are many types of both dishes around India. This version, *Meethi Kadhi*, with a slightly sweet and sour taste, is the most popular. Traditionally, palm sugar (jaggery) is used, but soft dark brown sugar is substituted in this recipe.

SERVES 4

500g/1¼lb/2¼ cups full-fat (whole) natural (plain) yogurt
25g/1oz/¼ cup gram flour (besan)
40g/1½oz/3 tbsp soft dark brown sugar
7.5ml/1½ tsp salt, or to taste
10ml/2 tsp finely grated fresh root ginger
15ml/1 tbsp sunflower oil or light olive oil
2.5ml/½ tsp cumin seeds
2.5cm/1in piece cinnamon stick
4 cloves
6–8 curry leaves
1.25ml/¼ tsp Asafoetida
15ml/1 tbsp fresh coriander (cilantro) leaves, chopped, plus extra, to garnish

1 Mix the yogurt and gram flour together in a bowl until smooth and creamy.

2 Add 300ml/½ pint/1¼ cups water and whisk until well blended. Add the sugar, salt and ginger and mix well.

3 Pour the mixture into a heavy pan and place over a medium-high heat.

4 Bring the mixture to the boil, reduce the heat slightly and cook, stirring, until it has thickened to the consistency of a pancake batter. Remove the pan from the heat and set aside.

5 In a small pan, heat the oil and add the cumin seeds, cinnamon, cloves, curry leaves and Asafoetida. Add to the yogurt mixture and stir in the coriander.

Per portion Energy 189kcal/797kJ; Protein 9g; Carbohydrate 23g, of which sugars 20g; Fat 8g, of which saturates 3g; Cholesterol 14mg; Calcium 279mg; Fibre 0.8g; Sodium 844mg.

Rice pancakes with coconut

These Portuguese-influenced pancakes from Goa, *Apa De Arroz*, can be eaten on their own, or served with lentils and vegetable curries. They are also a delicious way of serving kebabs, rolling the meat up inside.

MAKES 8

150g/5oz/1¼ cups rice flour
75g/3oz/3/4 cup plain (all-purpose) flour
40g/1½oz/scant ½ cup desiccated (dry unsweetened shredded) coconut, ground in a coffee grinder until as fine as flour, or coconut powder
2.5ml/½ tsp chilli powder
2.5ml/½ tsp ground cumin
30ml/2 tbsp chopped fresh coriander (cilantro)
2.5ml/½ tsp salt, or to taste
30ml/2 tbsp sunflower or light olive oil, plus extra for shallow frying

> **COOK'S TIP**
> The pancake batter should be of a spreadable consistency. Sift and stir in an extra spoonful of flour, or add a little more water if necessary, to achieve this.

1 Put the rice, plain flours and ground coconut in a bowl. Add the chilli, cumin, coriander and salt. Stir together.

2 Drizzle the oil over the dry ingredients, then rub in with your fingertips and thumbs.

3 Make a hollow in the middle of the dry ingredients, then pour in 300ml/½ pint/1¼ cups cold water. Using a wooden spoon, gradually mix in the flour from the sides to make a thick batter.

4 Heat a cast iron griddle or other heavy pan over a medium heat. Add 5ml/1 tsp of the oil and swirl it over the base of the pan. Spoon 30ml/2 tbsp of the batter onto the hot griddle and spread it out to a circle about 15cm/6in in diameter.

5 Cook for 3–4 minutes, until the top is well set and the underside has brown patches.

6 Brush a little oil on the top and turn it over carefully. Cook for a further 2–3 minutes until the other side is browned.

7 Line a large tray with kitchen paper and arrange the cooked breads in a single layer on it. Do not stack them up, or they will become soggy. Keep warm in a low oven while you make the rest of the breads. Serve warm, as they do not keep very well.

Per portion Energy 210kcal/871kJ; Protein 2g; Carbohydrate 23g, of which sugars 0g; Fat 12g, of which saturates 4g; Cholesterol 0mg; Calcium 22mg; Fibre 1.4g; Sodium 128mg.

Sweet tamarind chutney

This sweet and tart chutney, *Amli Ni Chutney*, enlivens all kinds of fried and grilled (broiled) snacks. Use it as dip and serve with kebabs, pakoras and bhajiyas. In India, tamarind pods are soaked in water, then the seeds are removed and the flesh is pushed through a sieve (strainer) to prepare the chutney.

SERVES 6–8

150g/5oz dried stoned dates
5ml/1 tsp cumin seeds
5ml/1 tsp coriander seeds
5–7.5ml/1–1½ tsp chilli powder
10ml/2 tsp concentrated tamarind paste
150ml/¼ pint/⅔ cup cold water
10ml/2 tsp soft light brown sugar
5ml/1 tsp salt

> ### COOK'S TIP
> The chutney will keep in a covered dish in the refrigerator for 1 week.

1 Put the dates in a heatproof bowl and cover with boiling water. Leave to soak for 20 minutes to rehydrate them, then drain in a colander or sieve (strainer).

2 Dry-roast the cumin and coriander seeds in a small, heavy pan for about 1 minute, until they release their aroma.

3 Remove the seeds from the pan, leave to cool, then crush with a mortar and pestle.

4 Place the dates in a blender and add the spices and the remaining ingredients. Blend until smooth, then serve at once or store in a sterilized jar.

Per portion Energy 59kcal/250kJ; Protein 1g; Carbohydrate 15g, of which sugars 15g; Fat 0g, of which saturates 0g; Cholesterol 0mg; Calcium 16mg; Fibre 1.5g; Sodium 253mg.

Sweetcorn in coconut and green chilli sauce

In this popular Maharashtrian side dish, *Makki Usli*, golden corn kernels are bathed in a thick coconut sauce enhanced by the nutty taste of mustard seeds and aromatic fresh chillies. It tastes wonderful served on its own with bread, or with any simple vegetable curry.

SERVES 4
45ml/3 tbsp sunflower oil or light olive oil
2.5ml/½ tsp black or brown mustard seeds
2.5ml/½ tsp cumin seeds
1 medium onion, finely chopped
2.5ml/½ tsp ground turmeric
450g/1lb frozen sweetcorn, thawed and drained, or canned sweetcorn, drained and rinsed
5ml/1 tsp salt, or to taste
25g/1oz desiccated (dry unsweetened shredded) coconut
2 fresh green chillies, chopped
julienne strips of fresh red chilli, to garnish
Indian bread or vegetable curry, to serve

1 Heat the oil in a frying pan over a medium heat, and add the mustard seeds followed by the cumin. Stir briefly, then add the onion and fry for 6–8 minutes, until soft.

2 Stir in the turmeric, then add the corn and the salt. Pour in 250ml/8fl oz/1 cup warm water, bring to the boil, and simmer over a medium heat for 6–8 minutes.

3 Meanwhile, grind the coconut and green chillies in a coffee grinder until smooth, then add to the pan. Stir and simmer for 2–3 minutes, until the sauce has thickened. Serve garnished with the chilli strips.

Per portion Energy 258kcal/1077kJ; Protein 5g; Carbohydrate 23g, of which sugars 5g; Fat 17g, of which saturates 5g; Cholesterol 0mg; Calcium 22mg; Fibre 5.6g; Sodium 496mg.

Saffron-scented strained yogurt

Shrikand is Maharashtra's famous signature dish. You will need a large quantity of yogurt, as it has to be strained to remove nearly all the liquid. Traditionally, *Shrikand* is served with puris, deep-fried puffed breads, but it is also good with fresh seasonal fruits as a refreshing dessert.

SERVES 4–5

3 x 425g/15oz cartons of full-fat (whole)
  natural (plain) yogurt
a pinch of saffron threads, pounded
15ml/1 tbsp hot milk
75g/3oz/⅓ cup caster (superfine) sugar
2.5ml/½ tsp ground cardamom
fresh fruits such as mango, strawberries
  or pomegranate seeds, to serve

VARIATION

This dessert can be transformed into a form of cheesecake by layering the yogurt and fruit on a base made from crushed cookies mixed with melted butter.

1 Pour the yogurt on to a large, clean muslin cloth (cheesecloth). Bring together the four corners of the cloth and tie up into a knot. Hang the muslin over the sink or in a sieve (strainer) over a bowl until all the liquid has been removed. This takes up to 6 hours, so you can leave it overnight.

2 When the yogurt is nearly ready, soak the saffron in the hot milk for 10 minutes.

3 Empty the strained yogurt solids into a mixing bowl, then beat until smooth.

4 Add the sugar, cardamom and saffron along with the soaking milk. Mix well, then chill for at least 2 hours.

5 Serve in stemmed glasses, either in alternate layers of yogurt and fruit, or topped with the fruit of your choice.

Per portion Energy 260kcal/1101kJ; Protein 14.6g; Carbohydrate 35.5g, of which sugars 35.5g; Fat 7.6g, of which saturates 4.3g; Cholesterol 28mg; Calcium 518mg; Fibre 0g; Sodium 205mg.

Milky orange dessert

Basundi is a sweet, milky dessert that works well with most fruits, and especially tropical ones such as oranges, pineapples or mangoes. The traditional cooking method is rather time-consuming, but this quicker version uses evaporated and condensed milk as well as ground rice to speed up the thickening process.

3 Blend the ground rice with just enough water to make a paste with a pouring consistency, then add it to the milk in the pan when it comes to boiling point.

4 Cook very gently, stirring constantly, for 10–12 minutes, until the mixture has thickened to a creamy consistency.

5 Remove from the heat, cool, then chill in the refrigerator for 4–5 hours.

6 Squeeze the oranges, then stir the juice into the milk mixture with the cardamom and nutmeg. Stir in half the mandarin segments.

7 Transfer the mixture to stemmed glasses and garnish with the remaining mandarin segments and the mint sprigs.

SERVES 4–6

sunflower oil, for brushing
400g/14oz canned evaporated milk
400g/14oz canned sweetened
  condensed milk
15ml/1 tbsp ground rice
2–3 large oranges
5ml/1 tsp ground cardamom
1.25ml/¼ tsp freshly grated nutmeg
300g/10½oz canned mandarin
  segments, drained
3–4 fresh mint sprigs, to decorate

1 Grease the base of a heavy pan and pour both types of milk into it.

2 Mix the two types of milk with a whisk to combine, then place the pan over medium heat. Stir the liquid regularly as it comes to a slow simmer.

COOK'S TIP
Prepared up to the end of step 4, the dessert will keep, chilled, for 2 days.

Per portion Energy 482kcal/2032kJ; Protein 17.1g; Carbohydrate 75.8g, of which sugars 73.8g; Fat 14.2g, of which saturates 8.8g; Cholesterol 53mg; Calcium 566mg; Fibre 0.3g; Sodium 262mg.

Milky almond dessert

Doodh Pak is a luxurious dessert made from almond purée that is cooked in milk flavoured with golden saffron and fragrant cardamom. A favourite in Gujarati homes, it is eaten on its own, but is also excellent when served topped with a combination of tropical fruits such as papayas, mangoes or kiwis.

SERVES 4

150g/5oz blanched almonds
900ml/1½ pints full-fat (whole) milk
a large pinch of saffron threads, pounded
15ml/1 tbsp hot milk, for soaking
sunflower oil, for brushing
25g/1oz raw pistachio nuts, lightly crushed
75g/3oz/scant ½ cup sugar
5ml/1 tsp ground cardamom
fresh fruit and/or toasted flaked (sliced)
  almonds, to serve

1 Put the almonds in a heatproof bowl, cover with boiling water and soak for 20 minutes. Drain, then place in a blender.

2 Add 175ml/6fl oz/¾ cup of the milk to the almonds. Blend until it forms a fine purée.

3 Put the saffron in a small bowl with the hot milk and set aside.

4 Brush a non-stick pan with a little oil. Put the remaining milk in the pan and bring it to simmering point over a low heat.

5 Add the puréed almonds and cook until the mixture begins to bubble, stirring often. Add the saffron, pistachio nuts and sugar.

6 Continue to cook, stirring regularly to prevent sticking, for 20–25 minutes, until the mixture thickens.

7 Stir in the cardamom, remove from the heat and leave to cool.

8 Pour into the serving dishes and chill the dessert for at least 2 hours. Top with fruits and/or garnish with toasted flaked almonds, then serve.

Per portion Energy 521kcal/2168kJ; Protein 17g; Carbohydrate 33g, of which sugars 32g; Fat 36g, of which saturates 8g; Cholesterol 32mg; Calcium 371mg; Fibre 4.8g; Sodium 141mg.

Sago with raspberry coulis

Sabu Dane Che Alone is a traditional recipe from western India, served with a modern twist by adding a puréed raspberry sauce. Here, sago is cooked in creamed coconut and milk and flavoured with spices such as cardamom, cinnamon and nutmeg.

SERVES 4–5

115g/4oz/⅔ cup sago
25g/1oz ghee or unsalted butter
5 green cardamom pods, bruised
2.5cm/1in piece cinnamon stick
25g/1oz/¼ cup cashews
25g/1oz raisins
300ml/½ pint/1¼ cups full-fat (whole) milk
150ml/¼ pint/⅔ cup hot water
90g/3½oz creamed coconut, chopped,
  or 150ml/¼ pint/⅔ cup coconut cream
115g/4oz/½ cup caster (superfine) sugar, or
  to taste
1.25ml/½ tsp freshly grated nutmeg

For the sauce:
450g/1lb fresh or frozen raspberries
115g/4oz/½ cup caster (superfine) sugar
2 star anise

1 Rinse the sago in a sieve, then pour it into a large bowl, cover with cold water and leave to soak for 10 minutes, then drain.

2 Meanwhile, melt the ghee or butter in a non-stick pan over a low heat. Add the cardamom, cinnamon, cashews and raisins, and fry gently for 2–3 minutes, until the cashews begin to brown.

3 Pour in the milk and the water, if using creamed coconut; do not add water if using coconut cream. Add the creamed coconut and stir over a medium heat until dissolved, or add the coconut cream. Add the sago.

4 Add the sugar and cook for 10–12 minutes, until the mixture thickens. Stir constantly towards the end of the cooking time to ensure that the mixture does not stick to the bottom of the pan.

5 When the mixture is thick enough to stop sticking to the sides of the pan, the sago is cooked. Stir in the nutmeg and remove from the heat.

6 Spoon the mixture into individual ramekins or one large decorative mould. Leave at room temperature for at least 1 hour to set.

7 For the sauce, put the raspberries, sugar and star anise in a pan and place over high heat. Add 150ml/¼ pint/⅔ cup water and stir until the sugar has dissolved. Cook for 4–5 minutes, then remove from the heat.

8 Leave the sauce to cool, remove the star anise, and purée the mixture in a blender. Push the mixture through a sieve and discard the seeds.

9 Turn out the sago desserts and serve drizzled with a few spoonfuls of the sauce. Serve the extra sauce separately.

Per portion Energy 475kcal/2005kJ; Protein 5g; Carbohydrate 82g, of which sugars 60g; Fat 16g, of which saturates 11g; Cholesterol 22mg; Calcium 111mg; Fibre 2.6g; Sodium 36mg.

Goan banana fritters

Banana fritters, *Filoss*, can be served as a scrumptious dessert with a generous dollop of fresh whipped cream, or eaten as a snack on their own. Delicately spiced with nutmeg and cinnamon, every mouthful of these fritters will delight the palate with its wonderful mixture of varied textures. Their sweetness and smooth finish provide the perfect finale for a meal that has featured a spicy hot main dish.

3 Chop the bananas into medium-sized chunks. put them in a small bowl and mix in the lemon juice.

4 Place the flour in a large mixing bowl with the ground spices, sugar and salt. Mix all of the ingredients until well combined, then add the bananas.

5 Beat the eggs and gradually add the milk while still beating. Add the egg and milk mixture to the bananas, stirring carefully until the bananas are fully coated.

6 Heat the oil in a wok or other pan suitable for deep-frying over a medium heat, and put in as many large spoonfuls of the fritter mixture as the pan will hold in a single layer. Fry for 2–3 minutes, then carefully turn over and fry the other side for a further 2–3 minutes, until the fritters are brown all over. Lift out with a slotted spoon and drain on kitchen paper. Repeat with all the mixture.

7 Transfer the fritters to a serving plate and brush them evenly with the apricot glaze.

8 If using apricot jam instead, heat the jam gently in a ladle or small pan until it just begins to bubble, then push it through a sieve (strainer) into a small bowl positioned underneath. Brush over the fritters.

9 Serve the fritters hot, with a dollop of whipped cream and top with a few toasted almonds. Alternatively, vanilla ice cream can be served with the dish for a cooling summer treat.

SERVES 4

15ml/1 tbsp flaked (sliced) almonds
4 large bananas
15ml/1 tbsp lemon juice
150g/5oz/1¼ cups plain (all-purpose) flour
1.25ml/¼ tsp ground nutmeg
2.5ml/½ tsp ground cardamom
2.5ml/½ tsp ground cinnamon
30–45ml/2–3 tbsp soft light brown sugar
2.5ml/½ tsp salt
2 medium eggs
120ml/4fl oz/½ cup milk
oil, for deep-frying
15ml/1 tbsp brandy (optional)
25g/1oz apricot glaze or apricot jam
whipped cream or vanilla ice cream,
  to serve

1 Toast the sliced almonds by placing them in a pre-heated shallow frying pan, then dry-roast by holding the pan above a medium heat for 10–15 seconds and shaking it to prevent the almonds burning. The almonds should just begin to turn a slightly brown colour.

2 Remove them from the pan immediately and transfer to a large dish to cool. Set aside while preparing the bananas.

Per portion Energy 522kcal/2199kJ; Protein 9.6g; Carbohydrate 72.3g, of which sugars 40g; Fat 23.7g, of which saturates 3.3g; Cholesterol 97mg; Calcium 122mg; Fibre 2.6g; Sodium 56mg.

Index